TERRIBLE BEAUTY

Also by Diana Norman

Non-fiction
The Stately Ghosts of England
Road From Singapore

Fiction
Fitzempress' Law
King of the Last Days
The Morning Gift

TERRIBLE BEAUTY

A Life of Constance Markievicz
1868–1927

Diana Norman

Hodder & Stoughton

LONDON SYDNEY AUCKLAND TORONTO

The poems of W. B. Yeats are quoted from *The Collected Poems of W. B. Yeats* by permission of A. P. Watt Ltd on behalf of Michael B. Yeats and Macmillan, London; James Stephens' poem 'The Red-Haired Man's Wife' is quoted by permission of the Society of Authors on behalf of the copyright owner, Mrs Iris Wise; Cecil Day Lewis's poem 'Remembering Con Markievicz', from *The Whispering Roots*, is quoted by permission of Jonathan Cape and the Executors of the Estate of C. Day Lewis.

British Library Cataloguing in Publication Data

Norman, Diana
  Terrible beauty: a life of Constance
  Markievicz, 1868–1927.
  1. Markievicz, Constance Markievicz,
  Countess   2. Revolutionists – Ireland –
  Biography   3. Politicians – Ireland –
  Biography
  941.5081'092'4   DA965.M35
  ISBN 0-340-39525-7

To Emma Norman

With all my love.

Acknowledgments

If I had not had the great good luck to meet Christine Sheridan of Blackrock, County Dublin, I doubt if I could have coped. She helped with the research and arranged interviews with two remarkable people, Mrs Louie O'Brien and Mr Sean MacBride, who, in their youth, knew Constance Markievicz; she showed me Dublin and Sligo and introduced me to her family to whose unfailing encouragement and lavish hospitality I am greatly indebted. Her father, Mr Martin Sheridan, has translated pieces of interest from Irish into English, has illuminated for me the history he knows so well and, with great patience, corrected the manuscript of its many mistakes. If there are any left in it, that is not his fault. To say that I am grateful to Christine and Martin is to understate the case.

Mrs Louie O'Brien's generosity included introducing me to the family of her son and daughter-in-law, Mr and Mrs Conal O'Brien, who so kindly showed me round the Arts Club in Dublin which Constance helped to found.

Thank you, too, to Mr Breandán MacGiolla Choille, retired Keeper of State Papers, who gave me the clue to the maze of State Papers; the staffs of the National Library of Ireland; the State Paper Office at Dublin Castle; the Shelbourne Hotel, especially Christy Singleton; Tim Pat Coogan; Sgt Gregory Allen at the Garda Museum, Phoenix Park; Bill Rolston of the Department of Sociology and Social Anthropology at the University of Ulster; and Ann Hope of the Workers' Educational Association, Belfast; Edward Kruger; Mrs Máire Gannon; William Mullen and his father; Eilís Dillon and her mother, Geraldine Plunkett Dillon; John Boland; Marlene Lyng and Dave Cullen.

In England I owe a great deal to Isobel Stockton and Dr J. B. Poole of the House of Commons Library; Mary Poole, as always; Rt Hon Shirley Williams; Frank Delaney; John Lawton of Curtis Brown, agent, adviser, book-lender and first-class critic; Sue Freathy of Curtis Brown; my editor at Hodder and Stoughton, Margaret Body; Carol Tilley and Edgar Tilley, without whom the manuscript wouldn't have been on time; to the staff of the British Library, the London Library and, especially, my local Stevenage Central Library; my family, who have put up with a great deal, my mother, Mrs Aeron Narracott, my husband, Barry, and daughters, Samantha and Emma Norman. Thank you very much.

D.N.

Remembering Con Markievicz

Child running wild in woods of Lissadell:
Young lady from the Big House, seen
In a flowered dress gathering wild flowers: Ascendancy queen
Of hunts, house-parties, practical jokes – who could foretell
(Oh fiery shade, impetuous bone)
Where all was regular, self-sufficient, gay
Their lovely hoyden lost in a nation's heroine?
Laughterless now the sweet demesne,
And the gaunt house looks blank on Sligo Bay
A nest decayed, an eagle flown.

The Paris studio, your playboy Count
Were not enough, nor Castle splendour
And fame of horsemanship. You were the tinder
Waiting a match, a runner tuned for the pistol's sound,
Impatient shade, long-suffering bone.
In a Ballaly cottage you found a store
Of Sinn Féin papers. You read (maybe the old sheets can while
The time). The flash lights up a whole
Ireland which you have never known before,
A nest betrayed, its eagles gone.

The road to Connolly and Stephen's Green
Showed clear. The great heart which defied
Irish prejudice, English snipers, died
A little not to have shared a grave with the fourteen.
Oh fiery shade, intransigent bone!
And when the Treaty emptied the British jails,
A haggard woman returned and Dublin went wild to greet her.
But still it was not enough: an iota
Of compromise, she cried, and the Cause fails
Nest disarrayed, eagles undone.

Fanatic, bad actress, figure of fun –
She was called each. Ever she dreamed,
Fought, suffered for a losing side, it seemed
(The side which always at last is seen to have won),
Oh fiery shade and unvexed bone.
Remember a heart impulsive, gay and tender,
Still to an ideal Ireland and its real, poor alive.
When she died in a pauper bed, in love
All the poor of Dublin rose to lament her.
A nest is made, an eagle flown.

CECIL DAY LEWIS

PREFACE

Constance Markievicz,[1] the first woman in any country to be appointed a Minister of Labour, was born in England, a member of the Protestant Ascendancy which ruled British Ireland. From the age of forty until her death at fifty-nine in 1927 she fought as hard as she could and gave everything she had to rid Ireland of that rule and her own class.

In 1937 Sean O'Faolain went into the poor areas of Dublin to find people who remembered her. He discovered men and women for whom the Countess Markievicz had carried coal up tenement steps, paid the rent and cooked the dinner. While he was writing his book on the Irish Troubles, Ulick O'Connor was in a pub when he saw an old lady in her seventies get up and do a shuffling jig. 'She was barely able to lift her feet and . . . told us why she got up to dance. "I was taught by the Countess." For a second a presence lit the room.'

Now that presence is fading and something else is taking its place. 'Don't you know,' asked two men of letters on two separate occasions in Dublin recently, 'that Markievicz shot a policeman in cold blood during the Easter Rising?' No, I don't and neither does anybody else, but intelligent men and women all over Ireland have grown up accepting the story as true. It is an extreme example of a process by which women are denigrated until they disappear from history.

To be honest, there was a time when I might have thought this theory was paranoid nonsense. But then I wrote a magazine series on women who changed society or, at least, society's perceptions. It proved so popular that it was extended, and I began putting down boreholes of research throughout the centuries. Welling to the surface came the records of astounding women; philosophers, soldiers, the first computer programmer, scientists, pirates, educationalists, reformers, writers and administrators; some were vaguely remembered names but most I had never heard of.

Their common denominator was that they had challenged the accepted idea of their time as to what women could and should do.

---

[1] There are various spellings of the name, but Constance herself always used 'Markievicz'.

Throughout history it has been the male establishment which has set the standard of what is normal and good. By refusing to stick to the rules these women proved themselves abnormal, i.e. bad. Subsequent critics, sometimes even their biographers, reflect unease at their abnormality. Women reformers were 'obsessive', where, you feel, their male equivalent would have been wholehearted. Thinkers were 'derivative', suffragettes 'neurotic'. Their sex life or lack of it was always an issue; Aphra Behn, the seventeenth-century playwright, was 'promiscuous' (or, as one male writer insisted, did not exist at all) and Harriet Martineau was 'frigid'.

The result, because we all to some extent accept the judgment of male history, has been to make people uncomfortable in the company of these women and so gradually they have disappeared. One by one I discovered women who played their part and were then steamrollered flat into the surface of a history on which the monuments are to great men.

Of all the women I studied, the one who intrigued me most, the one who still leaves me amazed and yet I feel I understand best, the one I have come to admire and love very much, was Constance Markievicz. It illustrates my point, I think, that I read her name for the first time in my life in a book called *Women on the Warpath*. Nobody can dispute the author's right to include her under such a heading – Constance did her fair share of fighting – but as he also mentioned that she was the first woman elected to the British Parliament and the world's first woman Minister of Labour, I felt I should have come across her before and elsewhere.

Perhaps my schooling had been at fault; I enquired of her among better-educated friends. Nearly all responded with 'Who?' but one said: 'She never took her seat at Westminster, and, let's face it, she did fight for the *Irish*.' That would explain it; Irish history isn't taught in English schools any more than English history, except where it so forcibly impinged upon it, is taught to Ireland. It was in turning to Ireland for information that I found the process of denigration and disappearance of this, one of its greatest daughters, already far advanced.

Nearly all Constance's contemporaries loved her; they thought she was witty, compassionate and brave. Sean O'Casey was about the only one who hated her, but Sean O'Casey hated practically everybody at one time or another. Even O'Casey said she was clothed with physical courage 'as with a garment'. Also they regarded her as a force to be reckoned with in the Nationalist movement – and in the Labour and Women's movements, come to that. They recognised too that she was the prime mover in forming the Fianna Éireann, the highly-individual boy scout movement that also made an important contribution to nationalism. Certainly the British thought so and sentenced her to death for her part in the Easter Rising, the only woman to be so sentenced. Fifteen of her fellow revolutionaries were shot and Constance was recommended for mercy – penal servitude for life – 'solely and only on account of her sex'.

Yet in modern histories of the formative years of Irish freedom, Constance Markievicz gets the barest mention if she is mentioned at all. Gill's *Irish Lives* has not included any women in its series and does not intend to. Its life of Eamon de Valera contains no reference to Constance and the last full biographies of her were written in the 1960s. Her contribution to the Fianna has been downgraded by Robert Kee to having 'helped' Bulmer Hobson in its formation. Elsewhere Kee says 'her intellect was not great' and that it was a 'lonely wildness' which she carried into Irish nationalist politics. 'Wild' is the favourite adjective for Constance nowadays.

Her political achievements in the 1918 General Election, when she won the first woman's seat at Westminster, and again in 1919 when de Valera selected her for his Cabinet, are taken for granted. They need putting into a wider context than the Irish situation to see just what great achievements they were.

Sean O'Faolain in his affectionate but patronising biography described her thought processes as 'intuitive' and this assessment has been quite mindlessly accepted ever since. As Dale Spender points out: 'The realm of the intellectual is still retained by men. Even when we display our power to think in terms men have validated ... we will rarely receive credit for it ... For the consensus will invariably be that it was not *reason* that we used to arrive at our conclusions, but a much inferior, capricious and lucky process ... *intuition.*'

That she was a woman with a foreign title, an English-born, Protestant-born Irish Catholic socialist revolutionary seems a more bothersome combination today than it was to her fellow leaders in rebellion, who were a pretty mixed bunch themselves. It is easier to accept a received caricature of a bloodthirsty Lady Bountiful than to search for the true character behind accounts in which she never walked out but 'strode', never uttered a word without saying it 'proudly' and never held a piece of paper unless she 'brandished' it.

Countess Markievicz is disappearing like the Cheshire Cat in *Alice* and what remains is not a grin, but a swagger.

Yet the real Constance is too good to lose. We should not deprive ourselves of the example of this courageous, funny, honest human being who, because she was human, certainly blundered many times but also achieved more politically than any woman of her generation and could still pause in the middle of it to teach a small girl in a slum to dance.

Irish feminists are determined not to be cut off from the inspiration of the tradition of their own sex as other generations of women have been. They are doing their best to reinstate Constance along with all the other women who played such a crucial, and forgotten, role in freeing their country of British rule.

I hope they will accept this book as a small contribution to their cause from an Englishwoman to whom their history, and they themselves, have been a revelation.

CHAPTER ONE

It was typical of the old Liberty Hall in Dublin that even on the evening of Saturday, March 22, 1916, when orders for the mobilisation of the rising against the British were being issued from it, a woman visitor could wander in to look round. Liberty Hall never turned anyone away, except the police.

Inside was controlled pandemonium as large numbers of men and women went in and out, boy scouts of the Fianna Éireann squirmed through the crowd with messages and the printing press clacked away in the basement where members of the Irish Citizen Army were also stacking grenades and ammunition. A misplaced match could have sent the whole place up like a firework factory.

Blessedly unaware and curious, the visitor stopped the Countess Markievicz, who was passing, to ask: 'Rehearsing, I presume?' (The Liberty Hall Players' dramatic productions in the theatre every Sunday night were well known.)

'Yes,' said Madame.

'Is it for children?'

'No,' said Madame, 'this is for grown-ups.'

Two days later, on Easter Monday, the men and women loaded their ammunition on to trucks and marched away to begin the Rising.

The old Liberty Hall – it has since been pulled down in favour of a new one, a high office block – stood in Beresford Place facing the River Liffey. It was a stone, gracefully-fronted building which in the 1830s had been a coffee shop and then a hotel until Jim Larkin, building up the Irish Transport and General Workers' Union in the first decade of this century, took it over as its headquarters and re-named it, presumably from the line in Goldsmith's *She Stoops to Conquer*: 'Gentlemen, this is Liberty Hall.' The christening was more apt than even he knew: the Hall was to represent liberty for many and varied people.

Draughty it may have been, and the complexity of its corridors took some mastering – James Connolly's daughter, Nora, said she always kept finding new ones – but to its members it was the working-class version of a gentleman's club, where they could escape for a while from some of the worst living conditions in Europe to meet, smoke and debate or enjoy the luxury of a theatre and a billiard room.

In 1913 the Hall's kitchens and storerooms gave the locked-out workers and their families the liberty to stay alive by providing free meals and clothing on a vast scale. In 1914 it showed its freedom from the war that had broken out in Europe by hanging out a linen banner declaring: 'We serve neither King nor Kaiser – but Ireland.' (The authorities kept tearing it down and Liberty Hall kept putting it up again.) In 1916 the seditious press in its basement printed the Proclamation of Ireland's Freedom from British Rule which Patrick Pearse read from the portico of the General Post Office on Easter Monday.

Above all it was one of the few places in Dublin, or for that matter in Europe, where, thanks to its socialist principles and James Connolly's strong feminism, women were regarded as equals. The Irish Women's Workers Union with its links to the women's franchise movement had its headquarters there, and when the Citizen Army marched off on Easter Monday, among its ranks were women, not just as nurses, doctors and messengers, but as combatants.

Suffragettes, actresses, trade unionists – a few, like Helena Moloney, were all three – found their spiritual home at Liberty Hall. A branch of the Countess's Fianna had a room there. Poets, playwrights and double-barrelled names rubbed shoulders with tram drivers and dockers.

It was the meeting place for those who believed that nationalism, republicanism, socialism and women's rights had to be one, indissoluble goal.

Of all the backgrounds of the people who met at the Hall none was more inimical to it than that of Constance Markievicz, née Gore-Booth, who was brought up in a society where the air she breathed was pro-British, anti-socialist, anti-Roman Catholic and anti-suffrage. She has been criticised for not joining the cause before she did; the marvel is that for forty-odd years she could remain so unaffected by her upbringing that when at last she did discover Liberty Hall and the *idea* that was Liberty Hall she knew at once that her square peg of a soul had found the space it had been waiting to fit.

Constance Georgina Gore-Booth was born in Buckingham Gate in London on February 4, 1868, and the amount of Gaelic blood in her veins was probably minimal. Her family was of the ruling class in Ireland, the Protestant Ascendancy, which was made up of English and Scottish invaders and settlers, whose menfolk looked for a wife among English heiresses, daughters of families like their own. In the days when marriage was meant to advantage one's estates rather than one's emotional life there was no point in a legal alliance with a native.

And, to the Victorian empire-builders with whom the Anglo-Irish identified themselves, the indigenous Irish were just as native as the peoples of colonial India or Africa except that they had managed to retain the same skin colour as their overlords.

As far as England was concerned, Ireland had always been too geographically close for comfort. While the Normans had invaded it in the even-handed way they invaded anywhere which offered land and wealth and saw no shame in marrying Gaels nor, eventually, in integrating themselves to become 'more Irish than the Irish', to later monarchs Ireland was a postern through which a foreign enemy could approach the English fortress. The fear intensified when, after the English Reformation, the Irish persisted in keeping to their old faith and the threat of an invasion by Catholic France, or Spain, became a real possibility.

Elizabeth I, therefore, decided that the Irish rebel must finally be brought to heel 'so low that he shall have no heart nor ability to endure his wretchedness . . . so pluck him on his knees that he will never be able to stand up again'. The soldiers and freebooters entrusted with this task carried it out as capably as they could; in Munster more than 30,000 Irish were recorded as having starved to death and 'a most populous and plentiful country made void of men and beasts'.

The Elizabethans' passage was made smoother by the fact that the Irish did not see themselves as a homogenous people; one clan could regard another with as much enmity as it did the English and could be exploited into doing the invaders' work for them. A certain Sir Paul Gore, a captain of horse, typified these methods when, in 1608, he took Tory Island in County Donegal with a comparatively small force by encouraging the island's larger Irish contingent to fight among themselves and then massacring the victors.

He had already been granted Irish lands by Elizabeth, now he was rewarded with more by James I as well as a baronetcy and the hand in marriage of a niece of the Earl of Strafford.

The clans may have lacked a sense of nationhood but they possessed innate brilliance at guerrilla warfare, using the quagmires, mountains and forests of their country for ambush and escape. So an English Parliament sanctioned what it considered would be a more lasting method of subjugation, the 'planting' on lands taken away from the Irish, especially in Ulster, of approved settlers, mostly Scots Presbyterians and Episcopalians, with results that are still being harvested in Northern Ireland.

But it would be a mistake to think of the whole history of Ireland as a struggle along the battle lines which have now been drawn up in the North. Catholics could and did regard themselves as loyal subjects of the English throne, whereas a man like Wolfe Tone in the eighteenth century could plan revolution against it while being middle-class, Irish and a Protestant. Nevertheless, dissension and repression revolved around religion and as successive laws deprived Catholic Irish of their land, their right to worship and even their language, they clung more desperately to their belief in a Roman Catholic heaven and the memory of their wrongs.

To flourish under such disparate governments as Cromwell, the Restoration, and William and Mary cannot have been easy, nor strictly honourable, but the descendants of Sir Paul Gore managed it; those of his first son became the Earls of Ross, those of his second the Earls of Arran. The descendants of the fourth son, Constance's direct ancestor, did not fly quite so high but they managed to acquire land of their own, a double-barrelled surname (the addition of Booth celebrated the marriage of Nathaniel Gore to a high-spirited, well-endowed Letitia of that name), a baronetcy and a motto which covered all bets: 'We hope for what we shall be.'

In 1800, by the Act of Union, Ireland lost its own Parliament of three hundred members and was brought under the rule of Westminster where it was represented in the House of Commons by just thirty-two, most of them with loyalty only to the Protestant, land-owning Anglo-Irish. For many years in the middle of the nineteenth century one of these MPs was Constance's grandfather, Sir Robert Gore-Booth, though he was an infrequent attender, being more concerned with London social life and his estates in County Sligo.

It was Sir Robert who, between 1837 and 1839, built the limestone mansion of Lissadell in which Constance grew up. Its site was, and is, lovely; on the north shore of Sligo Bay protected from the Atlantic by Ben Bulben; to the east is Loch Gill and Yeats' Isle of Innisfree – 'lake water lapping with low sounds by the shore' – and to the west, the hill of Knocknarea, according to legend, the burial place of the warrior queen, Maeve.

Constance was later to call Lissadell a barracks, but, though the house now looks forbidding, she was referring as much to its political situation as to its architecture. Not for nothing were families like Sir Robert's called the garrison class. Between them and their tenants existed none of the sense of community that could be found on the better English manors where squire and villagers at least met on the cricket field and crammed into the same church for Harvest Festival.

The Ascendancy's position was nearer that of early American pioneers among the Red Indians, never sure that there wouldn't be a rising. There was a military garrison of British Army regiments in

Dublin to protect the Castle, where Ireland's administration was centred. There were fortified posts in every major town; even the villages had a barracks of armed Irish Constables whose priority was to watch out for signs of disaffection. It was a source of shame for Ireland's Nationalists that this force was constituted entirely of Irishmen.

The more the Irish were reduced the greater the contempt their reducers felt. The age-old tradition of the Irish joke, which has been traced back to Giraldus Cambrensis in the twelfth century, reinforced a divide that had become racial.

As late as 1886 Lord Salisbury opposed Home Rule for Ireland with: 'You would not confide free representative institutions to the Hottentots, for instance.' In 1832 an English Poor Law Commissioner protested at the recommendation to institute workhouses in Ireland by pointing out, with immutable logic, that the system was meant to discourage laziness by its severity 'and what sort of habitation can you put him [the Irish peasant] in that will not be infinitely superior to his damp, dark cabin, which admits the rain and wind? . . . And how is he to be fed in a Workhouse in a manner inferior to his ordinary mode of subsistence?'

The menace to the Ascendancy grew with the Irish population which, by 1845, had increased to 8.3 million. But a large proportion of that population depended for its food on the potato, and in that same year the crop failed. In the following four years of famine more than 700,000 people died of hunger and disease while 800,000 had to emigrate. In the words of A. J. P. Taylor, 'All Ireland was a Belsen.'

Under Sir Robert Peel the government really did try to help; it contributed the then huge sum of eight million pounds, set up relief organisations and undertook public works on a scale never attempted before, but after Peel's resignation official aid came under the aegis of men such as Sir Charles Trevelyan, an adherent of the laissez-faire school of economics, who, believing that the waste of public money was a sin, imposed so many qualifications on the relief that it was almost impossible to administer. The fact that in the Famine years he never went nearer to the hunger than Dublin – and that only once – blinkered his view of Ireland to a logistical problem rather than a human disaster.

Individuals and some religious organisations such as the Quakers showed compassion, administrators drove themselves to death and often provided food out of their own pockets, doctors treating the fever victims died of it themselves. But as blight and famine returned year after year and the Victorians became baffled by their inability to cope with the scale of the suffering, the public conscience eased itself

19

by beginning to blame the Irish for their wilful persistence in dying. The exasperation extended to the Anglo-Irish landlords who were told to relieve their starving tenants out of their rents, which would have been a brighter idea if all tenants had been able to pay rent, and if some of the absentee landlords had cared whether their people starved or not.

Before the Famine Sir Robert Gore-Booth had blackened himself in his tenants' eyes by evictions which were to become commonplace throughout Ireland and helped to reduce the population to 4.4 million by the end of the century. In 1834 he had added 800 acres of pasture to his estates by evicting the tenants of Ballygilgan, known locally as the Seven Cartrons, and replacing them with the beef which sold well in England. The Irish were offered land elsewhere but it was of such poor quality that they all took up the alternative offer of £2.00 passage money and £4.00 compensation (generous for the time) and sailed for America. Local legend persists that the boat Sir Robert hired for them was a typical 'coffin' ship, which sank outside Sligo Bay with the loss of all lives, though perhaps not surprisingly, no evidence for this survives in the family papers.

But if Sir Robert was not a good landlord, neither was he a bad man; during the Famine he spent something like £40,000 on relief for the victims and stayed on the spot to help, unlike most of his contemporaries. There is a pathetic address of thanks hanging on a wall in Lissadell which expresses the gratitude of the tenants for Gore-Booth generosity in keeping them alive.

His elder son drowned in a boating accident, and so it was the younger, Henry, who became the 5th baronet. He married Georgina Hill, a granddaughter of the Earl of Scarborough, in 1867 and their first child, Constance, was born the next year. Then came the first son, Josslyn, and in 1870, Eva; another son, Mordaunt, was born when Constance was ten years old and a final daughter, Mabel, two years after that.

Though Sir Henry received death threats in the land agitation which bedevilled the last half of the nineteenth century in Ireland, he was a conscientious landlord for his time, reducing rents, allowing tenants in distress to dig turf free and, when famine looked like returning when the potato crop failed again in 1879, he and his wife distributed food with their own hands. He probably never really trusted his tenants though, being unable to forget that people like them had risen against people like him time after time, and they in their turn would never forget what had happened to people like them when they did. Sir Henry and Lady Gore-Booth knew their tenants' names, took soup to the sick and enquired after the children. Then they returned to their drawing room at Lissadell and the tenant would retire to his one-roomed house which he shared with wife, children, cow and donkey and each resumed existences as different as if they circled separate suns.

Constance was a shock. She had all the looks and brains Sir Henry could have wanted for his daughter, perhaps too much. It was not that from the first she challenged the society into which she had been born – secure child of loving parents that she was, it seemed to her as ancient and as rigidly ordained as Ben Bulben. But she was a misfit in it. She had no reserve, no detachment, no idea of the boundaries to be kept. She always went too far. She talked to peasant children as if they were equals and brought their bare-footed persons home for tea, and could never understand what the ensuing fuss was about.

Unaware that the general suffering could ever be altered, she was made instantly miserable by individual misery and had to do something about it, then and there. Where her mother offered soup and sympathy, Constance rolled up her sleeves. The son of Lissadell's stud groom remembered the time when his mother, near a confinement, was washing clothes: 'Miss Con came in and she just put her away from the tub and washed out the clothes herself.' On another occasion his father caught pneumonia and nearly died, 'and would have died if Miss Con hadn't sat up with him night after night and nursed him through it'.

She was always 'Miss Con' just as later in the slums of Dublin she was always 'Madame'; there was no attempt to soften her clear, Victorian, upper-class English accent into a brogue. She was the equal of anybody and anybody was the equal of her, take it or leave it. She was incapable of pretending to be other than she was, which may explain why, though she adored dressing up and appearing in plays, she was a rotten actress.

Once, walking along a Dublin street, a drunk kept pestering her for pennies until finally she turned and gave him a slam which bowled him into the gutter. But then again, as a debutante in London, she stopped her carriage while returning from a bridge party to nip out and press her winnings into the hands of tramps trying to keep warm on the benches along Hyde Park. In Constance's code of honour the distinction between the two events was perfectly clear.

It was equally comprehensible to the ordinary Irish, and so was Con herself. 'Whoever misunderstood Madame,' Eamon de Valera was to say of her, 'the poor did not.' Across the chasm of incomprehension which existed between conqueror and conquered the Irish recognised something pleasant and familiar in Constance.

In a country where racing results may still take precedence over every other sporting news, it helped, of course, that she was a superb horsewoman. Love of horses was bred nearly as deep into the bones of the upper-class English as it was into the Irish and was the one factor that drew them on to common ground. Sir Robert Gore-Booth had kept a pack of hounds and a riding school at Lissadell, and had been delighted before he died to find that his granddaughter took after him. Her parents were less entranced; they detailed a groom to try to stop her breaking her neck, but even on her pony she outdistanced him. An old hunting gentleman, Mr E. Rowlette of Cash, County Sligo who'd seen her hunt when she wasn't yet in her teens, wrote:

> her hair flowing about her shoulders, mounted on a small pony ... I remember some of the fences they jumped. I have sometimes seen them jumped since but never without considerable self-congratulation by the few who got over safely. I remember the groom who was out to take care of the child, looking far from happy as he tried rather hopelessly to keep close to his charge. And I remember the delighted exclamations of some of the country people on foot – 'My God! Look at little Miss Gore. Isn't she great!' ... It is my considered opinion that I have never known any woman whose skill in riding to hounds equalled that of Miss Gore-Booth. I am doubtful whether I ever knew any man who was an all round better rider.

W. B. Yeats visited Lissadell during Constance's childhood and wrote of her:

> When long ago I saw her ride
> Under Ben Bulben to the meet
> The beauty of her countryside
> With all youth's lonely wildness stirred . . .

Tempted perhaps by those lines some subsequent historians, Robert Kee among them, have fallen into the easy trap of drawing an analogy between her career and the hunting field, as if Constance suddenly saw the fence that was Irish nationalism, shouted 'Tally Ho', and jumped it. Certainly she always gave the impression that she acted on impulse, but there was a lot of spadework behind her apparently quick decisions. If an analogy is to be made, let's do it thoroughly. While saying that she was 'absolutely without fear' Mr Rowlette took pains to point out that, for all her speed, she was a careful rider:

> In point-to-point races she always took far more than the usual amount of care to familiarise herself thoroughly with the course beforehand ... And I have never known her to deviate by a yard from the course selected by her ... The great difference between her and other good riders was that she could always be

depended upon to remember and to put into practice the tactics she had decided upon at the right time, while so many good riders remember just a little too late.

It is significant too that when Mr Rowlette visited Constance's hunter, Max, during his leisurely old age at Lissadell,

he had neither scratch nor scar nor blemish on any leg. Indeed, I do not remember that during his whole career he ever once cut himself. He was a wonderful hunter, but much of the credit for his prowess was undoubtedly due to the way he was trained, cared for and ridden by his owner. I have heard her express a hope that when she went to Heaven, Max would be there to carry her.

The picture her mother commissioned Sarah Purser, the Dublin artist, to paint of Constance and Eva shows what Lady Gore-Booth expected of her daughters; two nice, grave little girls – they are in a woodland setting and Con is holding flowers – predestined, it would seem, to adorn upper-class society and marry well. Sarah Purser liked Eva the better of the two, Constance fidgeted too much and insisted on recounting details of her governess's love life: she was always the scourge of her governesses. The fact that both, in their varied ways, grew up to help destroy that society bewildered their mother all her days but to her credit she kept in touch with Constance, though secretly, when the rest of the family did not.

The two sisters were very different: Eva was quiet, reflective and poetic. Several books of her poetry were published and one poem, 'The Little Waves of Breffny', was well-known in its day. Eva was a pacifist almost from the first, who might have been expected to be horrified by the sister who not only loved hunting but was a crack shot. In fact they adored each other. One of Eva's early poems dedicated to 'Con' depicts someone almost superhuman:

> Some fair Goddess white and tall,
> Shadowy-limbed majestical.

They spent most of their adult lives apart. Eva never married but went to live with her friend and colleague, Esther Roper, in England where they worked together for the Labour movement and some of the most unpopular women's causes. But the two sisters frequently holidayed together and during Con's imprisonments kept in continual touch by letter and a telepathic rapport which eventually included Esther Roper as well.

Fewer legends are told about Eva in County Sligo than about Constance. She was the less vivid character and she chose to work for the poor of England, not Ireland, but to Constance her sister was always a massive influence. After Eva's death Con wrote to Esther Roper: 'Her gentleness prevented me getting very brutal and one does get very callous in a War. I once held out and stopped a man being shot because of her.'[1] She only survived Eva by one year.

Esther Roper eventually compiled a book of the letters Constance wrote during her five imprisonments to Eva[2] and, apart from a youthful diary and her political writings – which were almost entirely propaganda – they are very nearly all the evidence of Constance on herself. Even so they had to pass the censorship of her prison Governor which allowed no politics, no slang or 'improper expressions'. In return Constance imposed her own censorship so that nothing deeply intimate to her would come under the hated censor's gaze. Although prison brought her a lot of suffering and, in her friend Hanna Sheehy Skeffington's view, shortened her life by many years, all the letters are unremittingly cheerful: she was not going to have Eva worrying about her. Nevertheless, her friends have testified that to read the enthusiasm in the letters was to have her 'brilliantly alive again', so we can take it that the character of the letters rang true to the Constance people knew.

Despite everything she went through, she was like Dr Johnson's friend, who said that he, too, in his time had tried to be a philosopher 'but, I don't know how, cheerfulness was always breaking in'. Constance's memory has suffered because philosophy and cheerfulness are held to be mutually exclusive. Enthusiasm is a drawback in somebody who should be taken seriously; it makes them vulnerable and slightly comic, as if gloom and cynicism are the only proper qualities for the truly mature. But Constance couldn't help it. She had what one friend described as a 'nakedness of soul' which made her incapable of bolstering her own ego by running down everything around her.

Although she was born at the end of the Dickensian era, she inherited what G. K. Chesterton calls its Great Gusto, its almost vulgar vitality, its love of the sentimental and melodramatic, its belief that if men would only behave decently the world would be decent. But she would have horrified Dickens whose heroines, apart from Bella Wilfer, are always victims. With Constance it was more often the men who were victims. Male guests at Lissadell found themselves

---

[1] Constance saved a man's life more than once during and after the Rising, so we can't be sure to which incident she is referring.

[2] *Prison letters of Countess Markiewicz*, Longman, Green, 1934. Eva's letters to Constance, which had been carefully preserved by the elder sister, were accidentally destroyed during Constance's last days in hospital.

risking their necks as, with Constance at the helm, they scudded across Sligo Bay in her cockleshell boat, or pitched along sandbanks at high speed in the tandem of her own contrivance harnessed to two ponies. When one young man had the bad manners to be rude to peasant girls, she taught him a lesson by dressing up as a beggar, accosting him on the road and soliciting alms. As expected, he was abusive and Constance let him give tongue for a while until shaming him by revealing her identity.

She was not acquainted with the term 'sexual harassment' but she knew how to cope with its reality. Once, at a formal dinner party at Lissadell, she felt her thigh being fumbled by the man next to her. A Dickens heroine would have fainted or run from the room. Constance gripped the offending hand, waved it in the air, and announced: 'Just look what I've found in my lap.'

She wore a pet snake in her hair for parties in the hope that it would bite her dancing partners. A young officer of the Royal Dublin Fusiliers, who was in love with her 'like all Ireland to a man', was made to throw his cap into the air so that she could shoot at it.

Her governesses did not find her a restful companion either. It was a disadvantage to her all her life that she received no schooling in any sense of the word; instead, like most girls of her class, she received tuition with her sisters from a succession of gently-reared, impoverished ladies who, because of their inferior position and Con's overriding personality, could never discipline her into doing anything she did not want to do. Her spelling was shaky to the end of her days. There was no science, of course, and no attempt to help the young ladies of the schoolroom understand economics or politics. Such history as Constance could be bothered to learn was always English history.

She was good at languages, taking trouble to learn French, German and, later, Italian so that she could read their literature in the original. She could memorise poetry at length and her stepson has described her when she was older taking off her spectacles and reciting her favourite lines from Schiller, Heine and Goethe. (Eva was the classicist who learned Latin and Greek.) She was also clever with her hands and had a great interest in gardening. When, much later, she was working in the slums she would frequently nip through an archway into the yard at the back of a tenement and plant flowers. It is said that to this day Dublin is scattered with plants which came from Madame's original cuttings.

Most of all she applied herself to art for which she had a facility. She sketched everything, landscapes, horses, the tenants and drew recognisable caricatures of her family, and her reward when she was eighteen was to be sent on the artistic Grand Tour of Europe with Miss Noel, known as 'Squidge', the last and best-loved of her governesses – though even Squidge retired to a convent once she had discharged her duty to Constance Gore-Booth.

A diary Constance kept a little later shows that despite the perpetual activity, behind all the dressing up, and the awful practical jokes, the girl felt the lack of something deeper. 'What do I want? I don't know.' On another day: 'I feel the want. Women are made to adore and sacrifice themselves and I as a woman demand as a right that Nature should provide me with something to live for, something to die for.'

She had not been taught to analyse anything, including herself, and at that time she thought, as society had taught her to think, that 'the want' was love for and from a man. (She had just read *Anna Karenina*). But viewing her life as a whole it becomes apparent that the real want was not so much romance as Romance in its medieval sense. The need to do great deeds, to gain honour, to fight evil, was as much in her blood as in any of Malory's knights or the swashbucklers of Louis XIII. It was this, and not just desire for attention, that motivated her derring-do on the hunting field, her play-acting and her chivalry; they were the only outlets for the grand gesture which Victorian society allowed her.

When, some ten years before Constance was born, Sam Beeton, the husband of Mrs Beeton of cookery-book fame, brought out the first adventure magazine for boys, the *Boy's Own Paper*, it did not occur to him, although he was a radical man, to produce an equivalent for girls. The popular feminine outlook was catered for in his *English-woman's Domestic Magazine* with its fashion plates, agony column and cookery hints. Nineteenth-century society, like most societies before it, tried to mould the spirit of its women into a predetermined shape as tightly as its fashion squeezed their bodies into corsets and wasp waists. The list of women reformers and explorers it produced shows in how many cases it failed.

It nearly succeeded with Constance who was dependent on her parents for money and, in any case, had heard no vocation, and was therefore forced to assume that she was merely what everyone assured her she was, a tomboy, and would grow out of it. In the year 1887 it looked as if she *was* growing out of it – the year of Queen Victoria's Golden Jubilee and Constance's debut into London society. For weeks at Lissadell her mother had been making her practise the tricky manoeuvre to be accomplished in the royal presence of curtseying and then walking off backwards without tripping over one's regulation three yards of train.

Con positively hated curtseying. She submitted, however, and Lady Gore-Booth must have drawn a sigh of relief as her daughter set off to London while she herself stayed behind to preside over the ladies of Sligo as they busied themselves about raising money for a gift to Queen Victoria on her Jubilee. Sligo was one of the most 'planted' towns in Ireland and its strong pro-English element wanted to dissociate itself from Gladstone's move the year before when he had joined with Parnell to urge Irish Home Rule. 'When one old woman complained that she needed her penny for bread,' says Jacqueline Van Voris, 'she was curtly told to enforce her pledge of love and allegiance with a coin.'

On March 17, 1887 Constance, looking beautiful in white satin, was presented to the Queen by the Countess of Erroll, a lady-in-waiting to Her Majesty and a cousin of Lady Gore-Booth, curtseyed nicely and went on to make a success of that and following seasons. But after that first one, which she enjoyed, discontent began to creep in. Sean O'Faolain suggests that this may have been because she did not feel herself completely accepted, that the Anglo-Irish were provincial fish who belonged neither in Ireland nor in England but somewhere in the middle of the Irish Sea. Whether this is true or not, it did not apply to the Gore-Booths who were related in one way or another to a large section of the English aristocracy, who were well off and who entertained, and were entertained by, the 'best families'. It has been said that if Con had been shot after the Rising half of *Debrett* would have had to go into mourning. The young Lady Fingall chaperoned Constance for much of her London season and later wrote: 'All the young men wanted to dance with her . . . she was the life and soul of any party. She was much loved as well as admired.'

Constance did the rounds of Ascot, fancy dress balls and walked in the Park after church on Sundays with the rest of the aristocracy, but as one season gave way to another her diary shows herself distancing herself from them. One entry reads: 'What vulgar people the Royalties must be. This is the conclusion I have come to after being to the Victorian Exhibition. No taste in anything and every family event, birth and marriage being celebrated by an awful daub by an incompetent painter.' Another entry refers to one young man without enthusiasm as 'typically English'.

Occasionally the old Constance burst through the debutante. Going to the theatre one night in a friend's carriage she saw two drunks fighting, leapt out, pushed herself between them and made passers-by help her stop the brawl. And on another occasion during the Dublin season when she and Elizabeth Fingall were coming back from a Viceregal ball, they found a drunken soldier clinging to a post in the garden of the house in Harcourt Terrace where they were staying. Lady Fingall wrote:

> Constance said: 'You must not make that noise. You will wake my mother' . . . She took him by the arm, down to the gate, put him outside and shut it. She had sympathy with him even then and wanted him to get back to his barracks without trouble . . . We had just got into our dressing-gowns when the peace of the quiet terrace was disturbed by drunken singing. Our friend had returned.

Flinging on coats they went out again and led the soldier to the canal and set him on his way.

> Only when, upstairs again, we saw ourselves in a mirror did the full humour of our appearance reach us. I was still wearing my tiara and with it my dressing-gown and slippers. Constance seized pencil and paper at once to make a sketch of me in this strange attire.

She was getting on badly with her family – except Eva, of course. 'Eva seems heaps better which had an elating effect. I am proud of that girl,' she wrote. (Eva's health was never good.) Probably Sir Henry and Lady Gore-Booth were disappointed that all the money spent on the dresses and the socialising had not yet produced a husband for Constance; this was, after all, the raison d'être of the debutante season. But Constance had not been sufficiently impressed by what English or Anglo-Irish manhood had to offer and turned her suitors down. She was beginning to work seriously at her painting under the tuition of Anna Nordgren, and had decided that perhaps Art was her destiny.

> If I could only cut the family tie and have a life and interest of my own I should want no other heaven and I see an opening daylight and freedom if I can only persevere and drudge and get my parsimonious family to pay. All the season I have worked my four hours daily with Miss Nordgren . . . and have got beyond my wildest dreams and am encouraged to see success at the end if only if if . . . Success and Art walled round with Family Pride, stinginess and conventionality. What is one to do? How am I to coerce them? How to break away? If I was sure of myself and knew I could succeed for sure and make a name or, more to the point, money, I would bolt, live on a crust and do. But to do all that with the chance of having to return and throw oneself on the charity of one's family a miserable failure is more than I can screw up my courage to face. So many people begin with great promise and greater hope and end up in nothing but failure and the poor house or improper.

It might seem unfair for Constance, with her horses and ball gowns, to accuse her family of 'stinginess' but her allowance was not hers by right: it could be withheld. The hand that held the purse-strings also held the whip over Victorian girls to see that they did not deviate from the path their parents wanted them to pursue. Only a generation before the Nightingale family had imprisoned their daughter, Florence, in affectionate luxury; and she was thirty-four years old before they gave in to her pleading and allowed her to begin nursing.

Times were changing, though slowly; the Gore-Booths were less tyrannous and Constance was a more forceful nuisance. In 1893, at the age of twenty-five, she was allowed to enrol at the Slade School of Art in London.

By this time her contemporary and, later, good friend, Maud Gonne, was up to her neck in the fight for justice in Ireland, resisting evictions and putting a roof over the heads of the evicted. The inevitable comparison of the two women leaves Constance looking a late starter who couldn't see what was crying out to be seen.

But once it has been said that both women were Anglo-Irish, Protestant and beautiful, the comparison ends. Con was brought up in rock-solid, blinkered security: Maud's mother died in Ireland when her child was four and from then on Maud and her younger sister travelled with their father, a colonel in the Lancers, in the care of governesses, the most influential of whom was French. While Constance imbibed the acceptable version of English history, Maud was hearing a different case on the other side of the Channel, receiving anti-English prejudices which were reinforced when, after her father's early death, the girls were put in the care of an English uncle who was prepared to swindle them out of their inheritance. He was partly foiled, but not before Maud Gonne had been forced to try to earn her own living as an actress and decided that all Englishmen were as perfidious as her governess had told her they were. Even more influential on her was her attachment to Lucien Millevoye, a French politician, journalist and hater of England who first encouraged her to work for Irish freedom as he was fighting to free Alsace-Lorraine from Germany.

For all her nonconformity to the ideal of Victorian girlhood, Constance was deep down conventional – even the wild Irish girl from the Big House was a convention in its way. She might disconcert, but she would not scandalise in the one area where society would not forgive scandal, that is, sexually. Though the man she eventually chose was not at all what her parents would have wanted for her, they must have been relieved that she was respectable enough to marry him, and it is doubtful if Constance could have considered a relationship which was not going to lead to wedlock. Her diary shows her dislike of becoming 'improper'.

Millevoye was married, though unhappily, when he and Maud Gonne fell in love but she was sufficiently free-thinking to allow an affaire anyway and, while Constance was studying her Art, Maud was giving birth to two illegitimate children. The first, a boy, died in infancy, but the second, a daughter, Iseult, survived and Maud managed to bring her up on her own, even after the quarrel which separated her from Millevoye.

Even a Maud Gonne, however, could not have been taken as a public figure into society by puritan Ireland, or England at that stage, if she had acknowledged Iseult as her daughter so the child was always introduced as 'my niece' or, later, 'my kinswoman'. The pretence was never quite believed. The legend that Maud Gonne was 'free with her favours' is current to this day. She was not in the least free with her favours, but people found the idea intriguing while at the same time accepting the subterfuge.

The point is that Maud Gonne was financially and in every other way independent long before Constance. She was indomitable enough to survive her early tragedies, insecurities and entanglements and they cut her free from the preconceived notions of her class so that she was able to hear the call of her chosen country and follow it while still a young woman. She was quite astoundingly beautiful, nearly six foot with a mass of auburn hair and strange, golden eyes. Men floundered when she came into a room. Her photographs don't do her justice, partly because they are in black and white and partly because they don't capture that 'star' quality, that consciousness of beauty which put her in the same legendary category as a Garbo or a Monroe and drew, as they did, the admiration of other women. 'She dressed beautifully . . . When one met her walking in a Dublin street one felt as if a goddess had come to earth.'

She knew her power and used it almost entirely in the cause of Ireland, inspiring the floundering men to do what she wanted. W. B. Yeats was spellbound by her, although he later distorted her image because, like Constance, she refused to stay on the pedestal he made for her and got down into the mud of real-life politics, using her exquisite actress's voice to preach causes for which he had no sympathy. Then again, she did not love him back. Elizabeth Coxhead points out: 'Yeats is a figure of such towering importance, and Maud Gonne was for so long the centre of his life, that none of his numerous biographers seem to have realised how far away he was from the centre of hers.'

Constance did not care to use her beauty as a weapon and was anyway prepared to laugh at it. When she was being fitted into a green creation with a high ruff at the back of the neck by Worth, the most prized dressmaker of the day, she peered in the mirror and said: 'I look like a rabbit sitting in a cabbage.' After she left society she hardly bothered with what she wore and did not give a damn whether her voice screeched so long as it reached the back of a crowd. What was to rejoice her was that tension of equality with the men and women of all walks of life who were going her way, being one among the other questers for the Grail in that strange, close companionship which comes to soldiers in wartime and to women sharing hardship. Between her and some men that partnership may have teetered on the edge of romance but it never went over. To Constance the circumstance of the companionship was romance enough.

Considering her background the wonder is not that she came late to political involvement but that she came to it at all. As she wrote later:

> No one was interested in politics in our house. It was rare that anyone mentioned them. Everyone accepted the status quo, almost as if it had been the will of God. It was there, just as the mountains and the sea were, and it was absurd to try and alter it, for that led nowhere and only made trouble. It was unlucky that landlords had been so bad, for if they had only done what they ought everything would have been all right now. Anyhow you could not go back and everything will soon be all right. Irish history was also taboo, for 'what is the good of brooding over past grievances?'

At this last stage of her long childhood she did question the will of God once. In 1896 she and Eva and Mabel became suffragettes. Con's friend, Hanna Sheehy Skeffington, was to say of her: 'She was not a feminist ever and only a mild suffragist.' That seemed true only because her fight for women became part and parcel of her nationalism, and few feminists would now agree with Hanna. Con's first political act was to help form a County Sligo branch of the Irish Women's Suffrage and Local Government Association at a time when its membership was only forty-three and one of her last questions in the Dáil Éireann was a demand for women to hold land.

The public meeting the Gore-Booth sisters organised at Drumcliffe just before Christmas was an attempt to increase awareness of the legal and social inequalities affecting women and to agitate for at least a vote in local government with a view to full suffrage eventually. The hall was crowded, two thirds of the audience being men who had gone along for fun. Constance was elected president and her address was typical of her later style:

> Now in order to attain to any Political Reform, you all know that the first step is to form societies to agitate and force the government to realise that a very large

class have a grievance and will never stop making themselves disagreeable till it is righted. John Stuart Mill said thirty years ago that the only forcible argument against giving women the suffrage was 'that they did not demand it with sufficient force and noise'. Silence is an evil easily remedied and the sooner we begin to make a row the better.

A heckler who said that if his wife went to vote she might never come back was squashed with: 'She must think very little about you then.'

Obviously the men were won over because the resolution demanding the franchise for women was passed on a show of hands. Despite its good start, however, the Sligo IWSLGA had an unspectacular career, mainly because in the next year Constance finally won her parents' consent to go to Paris and study art.

After her departure from it in 1897 Lissadell and what it stood for was never to be her real home again. Much of the happiness Yeats ascribes to the house in his poem about Constance and Eva, written long after their deaths, went with her.

Yeats had spent some of the 1894–5 winter with the Gore-Booths in Sligo while he was lecturing and researching Irish fairy lore. He liked the family: 'These people are much better educated than our own people and have a better instinct for excellence.' He was dismissive of Josslyn's plans for agrarian reform, 'The eldest son is "theoretically" a Home Ruler and practically some kind of humanitarian, much troubled by the responsibility of his wealth and almost painfully conscientious.' In the poem are his other prejudices, terror of growing old – something that never bothered Con – his revulsion at the real world and that beautiful women should mix with it. It says more about Yeats than about Con and Eva, but the images are imperishable:

> In Memory of Eva Gore-Booth and Con Markievicz
>
> The light of evening, Lissadell,
> Great windows open to the south,
> Two girls in silk kimonos, both
> Beautiful, one a gazelle.
> But a raving autumn shears
> Blossom from the summer's wreath;
> The older is condemned to death,
> Pardoned, drags out lonely years
> Conspiring among the ignorant.
> I know not what the younger dreams –
> Some vague Utopia – and she seems,
> When withered old and skeleton-gaunt,

An image of such politics.
Many a time I think to seek
One or the other out and speak
Of that old Georgian mansion, mix
Pictures of the mind, recall
That table and the talk of youth,
Two girls in silk kimonos, both
Beautiful, one a gazelle.
Dear shadows, now you know it all,
All the folly of a fight
With a common wrong or right.
The innocent and the beautiful
Have no enemy but time;
Arise and bid me strike a match
And strike another till time catch;
Should the conflagration climb,
Run till all the sages know.
We the great gazebo built,
They convicted us of guilt;
Bid me strike a match and blow.

CHAPTER TWO

The Polish Count Casimir Dunin-Markievicz was once described by
Padraic Colum, the poet, as 'the only stage Irishman I ever met'. He
was over six-foot-four tall with a personality that made him seem
bigger. (In the 1912 cartoon of its members in the Dublin Arts Club,
which he and Constance helped to found, he is depicted twice as large
as anybody else.)

He did everything well and nothing seriously. He had studied and
practised law, was a champion fencer, possessed a fine, trained singing
voice, had exhibited and won prizes for his painting, wrote plays,
flirted with journalism, fought duels, got drunk, loved women, told a
great tale, adored dressing up and was amusing about, and amused
by, all around him. It seems inevitable, even if Constance had not
brought him to it, that he should have gravitated to Dublin during its
literary and artistic revival, not because he was a stage Irishman –
though one can see what Padraic Colum meant – but because he was
a Renaissance man. During those first twelve or so years of the new
century Ireland fitted him more cosily than his native Poland and even
Paris, where he and Constance met.

That it did not fit him later was because he owed it no allegiance
and because, unlike Con, he did not pursue anything to its
depth.

When he and Constance met they were sufficiently alike to feel at
ease together, with enough points of difference to find each other
exotic. They were both vigorous and cultured. Both were practical
jokers. Both lived on an allowance and neither was the heir to the
estate they came from – Casi was a second son and the 'Count' was
a courtesy title inherited from a twelfth-century ancestor, Peter Dunin,
'the Dane'. Whereas Constance's family held their lands from an
original conquest, Casi's held theirs under conquerors in the
Russian-occupied part of the Ukraine. Like many other Poles, among
them Marie Curie, he had left his native land for Paris to study – in
his case, art. While there he had married a childhood sweetheart,
Jadwiga Neyman, but the marriage had not been a success and early
in 1899 she died, after giving birth to their second son who only

34

survived her by a few months. Their first child, Stanislas, was back home in the Ukraine with his grandparents. During that same year Casi met Constance.

For eighteen months she had been having a whale of a time, studying by day in the women's studio of Julian's art school in the Rue Vivienne and spending her evenings with the other students in the boulevard café world of Puccini and Toulouse-Lautrec. At first, because of her English accent and because she had more money to live on than most of the others, she came in for some heavy teasing, but her way of dealing with it had won respect – she had marched the chief offender to the nearest tap and held her head under it – and she became an accepted part of the art world's peculiar democracy. In 1899, the year after her arrival in Paris, the Boer War broke out and Constance disowned the British action: '*Je suis Irlandaise.*' She wore a ring to show that she was wedded to Art but it is possible, even before Casi came on the scene with another ring, that she had realised the marriage wouldn't work because she would never be a first-class painter. If the knowledge caused her pain she hid it, as she hid all pain, and continued to paint as a happy amateur for the rest of her life.

The man who introduced them was the Polish writer, Stefan Krzywoszewski, who has left an account of it in his autobiography, *A Long Life*. It was at a students' ball:

> . . . a bizarre gathering, every class and nationality was represented and the clothes echoed the diversity.
>
> Near me stopped two Englishwomen. The older was of the type that you could meet ten or twenty times and yet not be able to recognise her five minutes later. The other one [Constance], who appeared to be about twenty years of age[1] was conspicuous for her proud bearing. She was a living Rossetti or Burne-Jones. Her profile was delicately drawn, her eyes grey-blue. Her ball dress, an over-stylish one and not too fresh, barely covered the skinny shoulder-blades and the smooth planes where men gladly look for convexities.

He invited her to dance.

> We squeezed into the dense crowd of waltzers. In spite of her easy, woman-of-the-world manners, typical of the Parisian art student world, this was an intelligent Miss with a background of good society . . . Markievicz was passing at this moment. I stopped him. 'Do dance with this lady. You will be well matched in height and bearing.' Markievicz immediately seized her and started to talk animatedly in his

[1] In fact she was thirty-one, but she always looked ten years younger than she actually was.

broken English. They looked well together – outstanding in the lively, dancing crowd.

A few days later he saw them again from the terrace of the Café Flore. They were both on bicycles, obviously on the best of terms, chattering in French, tutoying, teasing and quarrelling like old friends, absorbed in each other.

Sean O'Faolain, who met some of their later acquaintances, suggests that Constance married Casi rather than the other way round, that there was another girl, Alice, for whom Casimir had tender feelings but did not declare himself because she was a friend of Constance's. Alice died and, it is said, Con's and Casi's daughter was given the second name of Alys in her memory. If this is true, Casi wouldn't have been the first man – or woman – to carry around the image of a conveniently-unobtainable someone who would have provided the perfect relationship if only . . .

Most people, however, thought they made a perfect couple and at that stage of Constance's development they did. Casi might later have liked to fancy that he could have been better suited, just as there came a time when a different sort of man would have been more help to Constance, but in those early years he was attached to her as she to him and during their long engagement he never tried to disentangle himself from it. Even when the physical love went out of their marriage they remained friends. After Constance's death he denounced the rumours that they had quarrelled, telling Esther Roper that there had never been an unkind word between them. She believed him and so do I.

The truth is they mistook each other. Casi thought he had landed a beautiful, entertaining, intelligent, fun-loving woman of his own class but without that class's idiotic pretensions. He couldn't see, because at that stage she hardly knew it herself, that her lack of pretension was not just an endearing negative, as it was with him, but a positive force. Casi took a hail-fellow-well-met pleasure in any company as long as it was congenial and went on doing so: Constance became one of those uncomfortable people who not only hailed a fellow but fought for his rights as well. Casi perceived her as uncomplicated and for that he can be forgiven; Constance thought herself uncomplicated and unconsciously tricked everybody, then and since, into taking her at her own valuation.

But her 'intuition', the nine-tenths of her mental process which absorbed and appraised knowledge without her being overtly aware of it, was already grappling with the fact that sooner or later she would have to do something about the world's irritating inequalities, and it saw in Casi a possible leadership towards it. Significantly, she wrote to Eva: 'He fills me with the desire to do things. I feel with the combination I may get something done too.' And for that she may be forgiven as well. Casi was unique in her experience at that point and his egalitarianism was exciting after the rigid class-consciousness of the Englishmen who had courted her. So were his ideas. Casi always had ideas. And potential. He just did not fulfil them. There is no reason why he had to, but at the age of twenty-five, when they met – he was six years younger than Constance – it looked as if he were heading for great things. She never complained when it turned out that he would not follow her in that direction and, without admitting it to herself, just accepted him for what he was – a huge, lovely, oddly weightless man.

In the meantime he was extremely attractive, and so was she. To celebrate their engagement towards the end of 1899 Casi painted a large oil of his fiancée, 'Constance in White', which was exhibited in the Grand Palais for the Paris Great Exhibition in 1900 and was eventually presented to the Polish Embassy in London. His fellow Pole, the artist Szankowski, also painted her, this time in black, in a picture her stepson later gave to the National Gallery in Dublin.

The two went everywhere together. Cycling was a rage at this time and when Casi entered for the Paris to St Malo bicycle race, Constance was there to see him cross the finishing line. (He nearly won, but his chain broke at the last minute.) They were at a masked ball – Constance in Empire dress with an eyeglass, Casi as Marshal Ney – when a roisterer flicked away Con's monocle, saying: 'Why veil that glance with this cold glass, *ma petite*?' Casi knocked him down, a challenge was issued and duel fought, ending with Casi wounding his opponent in the thigh. For a later ball he was asked by a shipping line magnate what costume he would wear and said: 'I will paint my bottom red and come as a liner.'

The only cloud in the sky was the failing health of Constance's father. He and Lady Gore-Booth went to Europe for a cure and Con spent Christmas with them both at St Moritz, but Sir Henry contracted influenza and died there on January 13, 1900. Constance took her mother and the coffin back to Lissadell and stayed on there to give comfort. In May Casi joined her and was introduced to those members of the family he had not previously met in Paris.

A somewhat impoverished, eccentric Polish widower cannot have been the Gore-Booths' ideal son-in-law, especially as Constance could have taken her pick among the more conventional sprigs of British nobility; however, knowing Constance as they did, they were probably relieved it was no worse, and received him kindly. Like everyone else, they proved vulnerable to his charm. The five looming male Edwardian figures they allowed him to paint on the columns of the dining room at Lissadell, portraits of himself, his future brother-in-law Mordaunt, the gamekeeper, the butler and the forester, are the most humorous things in the place.

In July he went back to the Ukraine to see his mother and young son, returning for the wedding in September. Constance suddenly realised how poor his English was – they had mostly conversed in French – and rehearsed him in his responses, 'Wilt thou have this Woman to thy wedded wife?' while they travelled on top of a bus, to the interest of the other passengers. She also told him that the words 'Hell' and 'damn' were de rigueur in society conversation.

They were actually married three times, once at the Russian Legation, again at a London registry office and, although Casimir was a Catholic, for the religious ceremony at St Mary's parish church, Marylebone, on September 29, 1900. Because they were still in official mourning for Sir Henry it was a quiet wedding by society standards – Eva, Mabel and two friends were the only bridesmaids – and a conventional one, except that Con had the word 'obey' omitted. Bride and groom looked spectacular, Constance in white satin, Casimir in Russian court uniform, and behaved with decorum through the reception and send-off later at Victoria Station. At the next stop, though, they got off the train and nipped back into town to let their hair down at a party with their racier friends.

They returned to France, first holidaying in Normandy on their beloved bicycles and then setting up in Paris in a small studio flat in Montparnasse. They had a maid, presumably paid for out of Constance's money, although Casimir's success at the Paris Exhibition had brought in some large portrait commissions.

Con became pregnant in the spring and wanted the baby born at Lissadell so they returned to Ireland and their daughter Maeve was born on November 13, 1901. It was a difficult birth and Constance nearly died.

Whether that made a difference to her feeling for the child we don't know; perhaps not. But the charge most frequently laid against Constance by her enemies and even a few saddened friends was: 'She was a bad mother' – the most terrible thing you can say about a woman in Ireland. They meant 'bad' in the sense of 'absent'. Constance returned to Paris with Casimir in 1902 leaving Maeve in the care of Lady Gore-Booth. She took her back to live with them when they settled in Dublin the following year, having paid visits to her in the meantime, but in 1908, when Constance's political life began, Maeve was left with her grandmother more or less permanently. Maeve's governess, a Miss Clayton, remembers the Markieviczes descending on Lissadell for the summer holidays and the Countess romping with her daughter like an elder sister, then departing as suddenly as she had come, 'leaving the child to mutter rather bitterly: "Well, that's over, she won't think of me for another year."' Children want love in the particular not the general and it would not have comforted Maeve that her mother was beginning to work for all the youth of Ireland. Later, of course, after the Rising, Constance was either in prison or a marked woman and by the time the Civil War was over Maeve had grown up. They were friends but it was too late for deep attachment because by then Maeve had absorbed the standards of Lissadell. Louie O'Brien recalls Maeve visiting Constance in her last years, which she spent at Louie's family home, Frankfort House in Rathgar, and says: 'It is not true that Maeve was deserted. She was a different type from her mother; she ran true to the Gore-Booths. We felt when she came to visit her mother in our best parlour that she was saying, "Mother dear, what are you doing in a place like this?"'

It is doubtful if Con was seen as a bad mother in Ascendancy circles; just odd. To them it was normal for a baby to be placed in the everyday care of servants from the moment it was weaned, and sometimes before – wet nurses were still in occasional use – to be brought down to the parental presence in the evening by Nanny. You have only to read English children's literature – E. Nesbit, for example – to see that upper-class parents were frequent absentees.

Men are never bad fathers unless they actually maltreat their children, so Casimir is left out of the condemnation, but Maeve was as much his daughter as Constance's and he definitely preferred his life untrammelled by children. His attitude may have forced Constance to make a choice though, being the loyal soul she was, she would never have admitted as much. When his first wife and second son died he did not, for instance, rush to the side of his other, bereaved child – it was about the time he first met Constance – and much of the affection in young Stanislas' life for which he was ever grateful came from Con herself.

This is always presented, incidentally, as confirmation that Constance liked boys better than girls but, again, that is not strictly true. She got on very well with girls who were on her wavelength – James Connolly's daughter, Nora, for instance – but few girls at that time *were* on her wavelength, conforming as most of them had been taught to do with the pink-and-white, sugar-and-spice stereotype of Edwardian femininity. She generally found boys more fun, not because they were boys but because they responded to her love of adventure.

Maud Gonne was one of the few people who really knew Constance

39

and in a letter to Stanislas in 1931 she defended the friend who, by
that time, had been dead for four years:

> Constance loved children and it was a great sacrifice when she sent Maeve to be
> brought up by her mother because life's evolution had made things too strenuous
> for the child at home. I have heard people criticise Con for this and speak of her
> as a neglectful mother. Nothing could be falser than that, but she was so unselfish
> she sacrificed everything for Ireland, and in this case did what she thought best
> for the child. Only people who knew her very closely and intimately knew how
> deeply she felt, for with all her open and exuberant manner and frank way of
> speaking, she was very reserved about her personal feelings and kept things hidden
> deep in her heart.

In May 1902 Casi and Con went to visit his home in the Ukraine
and young Stanislas met his stepmother for the first time. He remembered her as 'tall, slim and exquisite' and 'as kind as she was beautiful',
wafting in with her a smell compounded of cigarettes, delicate perfume
and paint. She was an equal hit with the Markievicz family who bred
thoroughbreds and were entranced by her horsemanship and the fact
that she bought herself a peasant's festival dress, linen embroidered
blouse, full skirt, beribboned headdress and high, red boots. (She
kept those boots and wore them much later when she was alone, poor
and needing to keep warm.)

It was a peculiar situation to find herself in, related to people who
led a life similar to Lissadell's and yet, through Russian persecution,
akin to the Old Irish in having to defend their customs, language and
religion. What concerned her most was the feudal condition of the
peasants, some of whom were still expected to sleep across their
master's door. It was in the Ukraine that she painted one of her most
effective pictures. Entitled 'The Conscript', it shows a peasant boy
and his family on the eve of his call-up to the Russian Army and
catches the misery of parting. The subject was actually killed two
years later in Manchuria during the Russo–Japanese War. Con was
powerless to help him, but on their second visit to the Ukraine the
following year she managed to smuggle out with her a Polish Jew, son
of a Markievicz tenant, who was also threatened with conscription. In
1913 he turned up at her home and gave her money towards her
collection for the strikers as a thank-you for her kindness to him.

From that second visit she and Casi also brought back with them
a delighted Stanislas. The Markieviczes had decided on a more
regular family life and were going to settle in Dublin.

CHAPTER THREE

The story goes that some four or five years after her return to Ireland Constance came upon some back numbers of *Sinn Féin* and found in them an article about the United Irishman, Robert Emmet, which quoted his speech from the dock before he was hanged in 1803 for his revolt – 'When my country takes her place among the nations of the earth, then and not till then, let my epitaph be written' – and was instantly converted to Irish nationalism.

It is nonsense. Moreover it is nonsense which Con, with one of those simplifications about herself which make you want to slap her, helped to spread in an article she later wrote for *Éire* in 1923. There is no doubt she did read the Emmet article and that it did have a deep effect on her and when she wrote the *Éire* piece she was, as usual, in a hurry and remembered it and, in order to get her point across, scribbled the story down with, again as usual, no care for how naïve and impulsive it might make her look.

The process which actually made Constance Markievicz an Irish nationalist was the same one which made her a socialist – she always saw the two causes as indivisible – and both went deeper and had begun much earlier than she made out. Her brief foray as a suffragette before she left for Paris and her careful distancing of herself from British action in the Boer War show her attitude to what was going on. Even on the occasion of her wedding, R. D. Blomenfeld of the *Daily Express* had noted that she was a clever but rather erratic girl 'who prefers to talk Irish politics'. Her help to the Jewish refugee and her dislike of the feudalism in her husband's country show the way she was heading, but her marriage arrested the progression for a while. By the time she and Casi settled in Dublin she had undoubtedly made up her mind to become the conventional upper-class wife and mother. She would carry on with her painting but she would socialise with the Ascendancy, partly because her family expected her to and partly because it would help to put Casi in the way of fat portrait commissions. She was thirty-five years old; it was time she settled down.

Whether she was aware of it or not, she was already a political animal and by returning to Ireland at that point she had about as much chance of settling down as a river of avoiding the sea. But she did try.

Like the Athens of Plato, or the London of Wilkes and Johnson, Dublin between the 1890s and the 1920s was one of those cities at one of those times when the arts really mattered.

Nobody has ever properly explained it, but it was as if some literary seed pod in Ireland had burst to throw out dramatists and writers such as Oscar Wilde, George Bernard Shaw, George Moore, James Stephens, J. M. Synge, Sean O'Casey, William Butler Yeats and James Joyce. Yeats and Shaw were awarded the Nobel Prize within two years of each other. Most of them were Anglo-Irish and some, like Wilde, Shaw, Moore and Joyce, found Irish soil infertile and took their genius abroad, to be followed later by O'Casey and Samuel Beckett. But others, notably Yeats, stayed to bring about what is variously described as the 'Irish Revival' or 'Celtic Twilight'.

This rebirth had begun, oddly enough, with sport when, in 1884, an Irish-speaker, Michael Cusack, had founded the Gaelic Athletic Association to foster the playing of traditional native games. Its aim seemed innocent enough but it was to come under almost constant police scrutiny because of its fearsomely nationalistic policy – it prohibited its members from playing any English games. Despite this restriction, or because of it, branches of the Gaelic Athletic Association spread throughout the country, promoting Gaelic football, hurling and patriotism.

Then in 1892 two young Protestants, Yeats and Douglas Hyde, who was to become President of the Republic of Ireland in 1938, began the Irish National Literary Society to encourage work which, while written in English, would be inspired by things Irish, especially the past. But Douglas Hyde was a Gaelic speaker. He had learned it first from the country people round his home in Roscommon and continued his study of it while an undergraduate at Trinity College, Dublin. (When a don had asked whether he knew Irish, he said: 'I dream in Irish.')

Soon after its founding he delivered to his new society a lecture which was to have far-reaching results, on 'The Necessity for the de-Anglicising of Ireland'. In it he urged the recovery of the Irish language, customs, games, place names and surnames. 'It has always been very curious to me,' he said, 'how Irish sentiment . . . continues to apparently hate the English, and at the same time continues to imitate them; how it clamours for recognition as a distinct nationality and at the same time throws away with both hands what would make it so.' He warned that if Ireland did not stop reading English 'garbage' it would become 'what, I fear, we are largely at present, a nation of imitators'.

The drawback was that 'garbage' was all there was to read, just as English melodrama and music-hall was about all there was to go and see. Those who, like Hyde, had access to Gaelic classics were by now a tiny minority. So when Eoin MacNeill, a young Catholic clerk with a passion for Irish history and literature, decided there should be a society which would give Gaelic back to its people, Hyde joined him and the Gaelic League was founded in 1893. By 1908 it had some 600 branches and had achieved one of its aims, the introduction of Irish lessons into the national primary schools. Long before then it had helped to push back the curtain which had obscured Irish archaeology, legend, bardic verse and love songs for so long. The effect was dynamic. The poet, George Russell, who wrote under the psuedonym AE, said: 'I felt exalted as one who learns he is among the children of kings.' It inspired in him and others a new form of poetry and drama and moved Yeats and Lady Gregory to scour the Irish countryside for its fairy tales and folklore before they disappeared.

There was a great deal of misty mysticism, while the back-to-the-earth glorification of simple country life tended to devalue the urban and industrial, just as the English movement inspired by William Morris – a man much admired by the young Yeats – was tending to do on the other side of the Irish Sea. Joyce dismissed the whole thing as 'Cultic Twalette'. Nevertheless, they were all, even Joyce, helping a resurgence which freed poetry, drama, the novel, music, architecture, stained glass and painting from what Eoin MacNeill called 'the second-hand hand-me-down life of somebody else' to make a distinctive Irish culture.

The Ascendancy, of course, and much of the middle class remained unmoved and continued to ape the manners of England, but among the new intelligentsia it was no longer a sign of low status to speak Gaelic if you could learn it – and it was very hard – while Patricks became 'Pádraic' and Marys 'Máire' overnight.

One of the many lovely things about the Revival was that most of its protagonists saw it as a concept to take in all the origins, classes and creeds of Ireland. There was no sectarianism. If it was identified at all by a religion, that religion was the esoteric, spiritualistic Theosophic Movement. And nearly all of them felt an aesthetic revulsion for outright political action.

It is true that Yeats was getting dragged into nationalism by the magnet of Maud Gonne and the production of his play *Kathleen Ni Houlihan* in 1902, with Maud herself as the eponymous figure of Ireland calling her sons to herself, brought its audience to their feet in a fever-pitch of patriotism. But the following year, when Maud Gonne became Mrs John MacBride[1] in what proved to be a disastrous marriage, Yeats suffered disenchantment with the cause. In his old age he was to ask:

> Did that play of mine send out
> Certain men the English shot?

It is a question of such egocentric remorse that one longs to answer 'No', except that it would not be quite true. At least one member of its audience went home wondering whether such plays should be produced 'unless one was prepared for people to go out to shoot and be shot'. And at the turn of the century William Rooney, a progenitor of Sinn Féin, had pointed out that the logical progression for any organisation taking on the job of promoting Irish nationality was agitation '. . . and agitation means politics, more or less, and the movement has got to face it, if it is not to come to a standstill'.

The fact was that the disgrace and death of Parnell in 1891 had left his heirs in the constitutional Home Rule party in disarray and although they later re-formed effectively, there was for a time a vacuum in Irish politics and the Renaissance, knowingly or not, was helping to fill it.

Somebody else, a friend of William Rooney's, was abhorring the vacuum, a small, aloof, brilliant journalist called Arthur Griffith. He was a conservative, non-violent separatist. To Arthur Griffith the example of Hungary under the Austrian Empire was what Old Ireland was to the Revival.

In the middle of the nineteenth century the Hungarian representatives had refused to attend the Austrian Diet in Vienna and had instead re-established their own Parliament in Budapest. Their action had eventually forced Austria to recognise Hungary as a separate nation under the Emperor. That, said Arthur Griffith, was what Ireland should do: unlink itself from England, establish its own government and became constitutionally and economically independent, owing allegiance only to the King.

It seemed a far-fetched idea then, and Griffith and his supporters gave it a comic tinge by their personal embargo on English goods, smoking only Gallaher tobacco and drinking only Irish liquor – not one of life's hardships – though even that was discouraged because 'it ruined the character'. But Griffith, despite many faults – one of

---

[1] John MacBride was a nationalist who had helped command an Irish brigade fighting against the British during the Boer War.

them was anti-feminism – foresaw that the continual emphasis on the Irish land question demoted the importance of Irish industry. He didn't want Ireland to be 'just the fruitful mother of flocks and herds'. The original society he formed, Cumann na nGaedheal, was a loosely federal body through which other nationalist movements could keep in touch. But out of it came a much more forceful policy to which one of his women supporters, Máire Butler, gave the name 'We Ourselves' which, in its original Gaelic, was 'Sinn Féin'.

All this activity was only a small part of the diverse goings-on in this city of less than 400,000 souls. Padraic Colum wrote of that time:

> Irishmen were ceasing to be men and becoming movements. It was impossible to be intellectually active without being drawn into one of them. Poets wrote treatises on wireless telegraphy and wireless telegraphists produced drama. Every organisation produced plays; some produced propaganda plays, others produced non-propaganda plays that they might raise funds to carry on their propaganda. It was rather like taking in each other's washing. Those who were not interested in any particular propaganda produced plays to revenge themselves on the propagandists.

Into this cultural, political, social cauldron of rebirth in the autumn of 1903 moved the Count and Countess Markievicz and their children. Lady Gore-Booth had leased and furnished for them No. 1, Frankfort Avenue in the upper-class suburb of Rathgar and had also provided a cook-general, Ellen Banks, and two dailies so that Constance should be free to take her place in Dublin society – Lady Gore-Booth would have meant Castle society – as befitted a daughter of Lissadell.

The Conservative Government's policy of killing Home Rule by kindness had by this time introduced measures such as the Local Government Act of 1898, which for the first time gave the Irish people a direct share in their own administration, and, in 1903, a Land Purchase Act which allowed large-scale transfers of land ownership from landlord to tenant. The peasantry were also being helped by Sir Horace Plunkett and AE through their Irish Agricultural Organisation Society which established co-operatives. Constance's brother, Sir Josslyn, was an enthusiastic supporter of this. Furthermore, the installation of Lord and Lady Aberdeen as Viceroy and Vicereine presented the more acceptable face of British imperialism since both were convinced Home Rulers and humanitarian. Though the Dubliners came to dislike them as 'bourgeois' and 'parsimonious', Lady Aberdeen's charity work gave her social events a glow of philanthropy.

It was possible therefore to have an easy conscience and join in the activities of what Griffith contemptuously called 'the West Britons'; Constance and Casi re-dressed in Empire costumes for a State Ball and were photographed in them, they were seen at horse shows, at the Viceroy's drawing rooms, the Under-Secretary of State's dances, at musical evenings, horticultural fêtes and Lady Aberdeen's anti-tuberculosis charities. There are indications that Con's conscience was less quiet than Casi's. While painting a portrait of the Lord Chief Justice, known as 'Peter the Packer' for his tendency to pack juries, she was heard to chant: 'Peter Packer packed a pack of perjured jurors, so if Peter Packer packed a pack of perjured jurors, how many packs of perjured jurors did Peter Packer pack.' On another occasion, when asked if she was going to the next function at the Castle, she was heard to mutter: 'No, I want to blow it up.'

However, Casi was getting his commissions. In 1905 he painted an outsize picture of the investiture of Lord Mayo as Knight of St Patrick with Constance shown sitting next to the future Queen Mary.

The unease cannot have been all one way either. Constance tended to scandalise her set – and her own housekeeper – by allowing Stanislas and his friends to play naked in the garden during a heatwave. Nor was it in accord with the status of a Countess to be seen, as she frequently was, with her children and painting things loaded on to bicycles and pedalling off for a day in the country to the half-cottage she had rented near the village of Balally. Casi, too, raised some eyebrows by his custom of keeping a bottle of what he called 'Whiskey-balls' – his version of *usquebaugh* – in the back pocket of his tail-coat; he found teetotal events intolerable: 'Constance, tell them I *drink*.'

It is significant that even then Con's unorthodoxy aided people to believe that she could commit graver sins. While gathering recollections of their early Dublin days, Sean O'Faolain was assailed by stories of 'the famous Markievicz scandal' when Con and Casi had shocked everybody by attending a ball with Casi dressed as Christ and Con on his arm as Mary Magdalene. It was out of character and he tracked the story down to find that it was not them at all and that the actual culprit was a young lieutenant named Lewis and his lady and that the papers, especially the *Daily Sinn Féin*, had made such a to-do about it that the lieutenant had been forced by an angry populace to flee by night to England.

The Ascendancy had a wide tolerance of eccentrics among its own ranks, Con *was* a Gore-Booth and Casi *was* titled; what must have bothered it more was the Markieviczes' enthusiasm for the Revival which it regarded, with some justice, as subversive. But the couple's connection with it was inevitable and early.

Even before their arrival in Ireland, AE, in a letter to Sarah Purser announcing that he had discovered Padraic Colum, 'a new Irish genius ... only twenty, born an agricultural labourer's son', had written: 'The Gore-Booth girl, who married the Polish count with the unspell-

46

able name, is going to settle in Dublin . . . as they are both clever it will help create an art atmosphere. We might get the materials for a revolt, a new Irish Art Club.' And AE lived just round the corner from Frankfort Avenue. Of all the many diverse and frequently quarrelsome personalities which made up the Irish Renaissance, he was the most beloved. Anybody who was anybody in it, artistic or political, met at his house on Sunday nights to be wrapped round by his welcome and immediate, brilliant conversation. James Stephens, author of *The Crock of Gold*, who first met Constance at AE's and became her devoted admirer, wrote that while Yeats would go about Dublin 'like something that has just been dreamed into existence by himself and for which he has not yet found the precisely fantastic adjective', AE would jog along 'confiding either a joke or a poem into his own beard, the sole person in the street who is not aware that he is famous'.

Within a few weeks of settling into Frankfort Avenue the Markieviczes had joined forces with AE to put on a combined exhibition of their paintings, 'Pictures of Two Countries', which proved such a success that they continued the venture for some years. In 1905 the three of them, together with Yeats and others, founded the Arts Club. Its painting members held life classes every week. Page Dickinson, the artist and architect, remembers the Markieviczes as the best draughtsmen there, while 'Madame' was the soul of good nature in helping others with her knowledge. 'They were both painters of considerable merit,' he wrote, 'and could both have been really first-class if they had worked. They never did, however, their energies were too diffuse to concentrate on painting.'

A combination of AE and their mutual love of dressing-up took the Markieviczes into the world of the theatre. Like everyone else Casi began to write plays. They were full of action and heroics and extremely creditable, especially from a man whose first language was Polish and who still conversed with his wife in French more often than not. One or two proved very popular, partly due to Casi's insistence on realism and, one fears, the hilarity which could arise from it. In *Eleanor's Enterprise*, for instance, he hired a live donkey which one night refused to be led off by the hero. The hero pulled, the donkey resisted and the reins gave, tumbling the actor into the stalls. 'Dam' good actor, donkey,' Casi hissed from the wings. 'Only one ass on stage now!'

Constance, billed as 'Miss Gore of the Theatre of Ireland', appeared in most of them, looking magnificent though her voice was agonising. Casi told her frankly she was terrible. Sean O'Faolain says: 'Though she did not resent it she would expostulate and he would insist: "No,

47

Con, you were rotten in that part." She would laugh an appeal to the company and go her way unbelieving . . . the only art she excelled in was the art of living, splendidly and with grace.'

When drama took over from art as their main interest, their home became the theatrical wardrobe of Dublin. Visitors found themselves passing ladies of barbaric splendour on the stairs and looking for the furniture under piles of wigs, swords and top boots. One of their most regular visitors, Padraic Colum, however, noticed that Constance was beginning to move on. 'Constructive work was the prevalent disease in Dublin to which the Countess fell an easy victim. She began to move from one group to another asking: "What can I do for Ireland?" with the earnestness of a new convert.'

There was no lack of people to tell her, but it was herself she was really asking because when she finally chose her course it was one that nobody else had thought of undertaking. Neither was the conversion a new one; exposure to the Revival merely confirmed the trend of her thinking. That she was still being seen at Castle functions as late as 1908 must have been through her loyalty to Casi – certainly he went on attending them some time after she gave up.

The final severance of her allegiance to the Castle arose out of a small, but to Constance momentous, incident which she never forgot. She was being driven home from a Castle function one night when a small girl jumped up and clung on to her carriage to beg. The sight of Constance, beautiful in her satin and diamonds, made the child forget her formula and she just stared. When she jumped off Con peered back after her and saw the child being slapped across the face by her mother, furious that she'd missed an opportunity. She wrote later that Castle life was exposed as hollow. It was as if she had had a direct appeal from the poor.

About the same time she read the Emmet article. At AE's next At Home she went straight up to Arthur Griffith. 'I told Mr Griffith quite frankly that I only just realised that there were men in Ireland whose principles did not allow them to take an oath of allegiance to the foreign King, whose power they were pledged to break and overthrow.' She asked to join them.

Mr Griffith did not trust women, especially he did not trust society women – he had been very rude in print about Lady Aberdeen's attempts to understand nationalism – and he told Constance, the woman who was to help him realise his dream, to go away and join the Gaelic League. Much later she discovered that he thought she was a Castle spy. They were always closed books to each other; Griffith could never believe what he read in Constance's and she was incapable of understanding a man whom St John Ervine once described as incorruptible but 'juiceless'. Typically, she didn't hold the snub against him and when he next spoke at the Rotunda she was in the audience to hear him.

It was Helena Moloney, Secretary of Inghínidhe na hÉireann (Daughters of Ireland), founded in 1900, who gave Constance the opportunity to join up. Women were Constance's first political friends as they were her last. They were the force that first galvanised her and they provided the support she needed to keep her going. They were the ones who hid her when she was on the run and theirs were the houses which gave her shelter after she became homeless; when she was dying it was the women who gathered at the hospital to pray for her. Best of all, they understood her; many bitter things have been written about Constance Markievicz, but not by women.

But the women who emerged during those years did not do so in order to be just a support group for Constance, or even Ireland. They are often represented as such in charming, if brief, what-would-we-have-done-without-them pats on the back; to give their contribution more weight would be to acknowledge a debt that has never been paid. Women, or at least, the women with whom Con was about to come into contact, had their sights not just on a Celtic Revival but a Woman's Dawn. They found it incredible that an Ireland always represented as feminine from '*Shan Van Voght*' (Poor Old Woman) to Kathleen Ni Houlihan could gain its liberty without granting equality to women.

> Peter: Did you see an old woman going down the road?
> Patrick: I did not: but I saw a young girl and she had the walk of a queen.

The irony, which may have been lost on the audiences cheering those last lines of Yeats' *Kathleen Ni Houlihan* implicit with the demand for a new status for Ireland, was that Maud Gonne herself, who created the role, had originally been refused membership of practically every nationalist society at the turn of the century because she was a woman. 'Surely,' she'd said, 'Ireland needs all her children.' She went on to found the Inghínidhe na hÉireann, for 'girls who, like myself, resented being excluded as women from National Organisations. Our object was to work for the complete independence of Ireland.' The women who joined it, however, including Constance, began to think of themselves not only as daughters but as sisters of that half of the population which needed help as much as Ireland herself.

In 1903 a priest, bewailing the fact that so many girls who emigrated to England or America were forced into prostitution, wrote:

49

How blessed would have been the lot of an Irish girl, the poor betrayed victim of hellish agencies of vice, had she remained at home and passed her days in the poverty, aye and the wretchedness, of a mud wall cabin – a wife and mother, mayhap – her path in life smoothened by the blessed influence of religion and domestic peace until it ended at a green old age.

He was rather missing the point that they emigrated in most cases because they had no hope of becoming wife or mother, or of finding employment other than unpaid labourer.

Until the Famine the children of Irish peasant farmers had, by and large, married as they pleased; obligingly and traditionally the father had subdivided his land between his sons as and when they did so. But the desperate suffering of the 1840s and the Land War which followed had brought home the unviability of small units and put iron into the soul of the survivors. After that the father held on to his land as long as he could, chose one son to inherit it and discouraged both him and any other of his offspring from marrying early. Frequently he and his wife had to endure the subsequent emigration of their children, but they did so with resignation, seeing no help for it.

The Irish marriage rate became the lowest in the world. The annual average number of marriages per 1,000 of the population fell to 24.1 in the 1890s. When country people did marry, they did so late and a situation was eventually reached whereby ninety-seven per cent of men and eighty-one per cent of women between the ages of twenty to twenty-four were unmarried, and between the ages of thirty and thirty-four the percentage of single men and women was sixty-eight per cent and thirty-six per cent respectively.

The job market for women was small and unattractive. The only large-scale industry was in Ulster where the manufacture of linen provided the biggest employment for women and children, who could earn twelve shillings a week, which was half what a man could earn. Otherwise, there was domestic service in big houses and in the towns but, despite Jacobs thriving biscuit makers in Dublin, unemployment, especially among women, was high. Religious orders proliferated in the nineteenth century, but so did Red Light districts, especially the area round Dublin's Talbot Street where Mr Leopold Bloom encountered vice on his eventless, immortal odyssey round Dublin in James Joyce's *Ulysses*. Or there was emigration.

The agrarian population fell from almost seven million in 1841 to three million in 1911, and by 1925 the number of men and women who had gone to the United States was 3,750,000 with another million lost to Canada and Australia, besides the numbers who made their homes in England.

Would a large proportion of girls who had a chance to make Irish marriages have gone anyway? The almost continuous childbearing and drudgery of their mothers, the high infant mortality rate – it was ninety-nine out of every 1,000 in the last decade of the nineteenth century – must have seemed less than compelling compared with a new life in a new world. Yet any attempt to indicate the reality behind the sentimentalised view of life in the mud wall cabin, 'smoothened by the blessed influence of religion and domestic peace', was shouted down. Arthur Griffith was furious when, in 1903, Synge's play, *In the Shadow of the Glen*, depicted a young woman depressed and frustrated by her marriage to an older man and by the monotony of peasant life, and ended with her decamping with a travelling man. 'All of us know,' said Griffith, 'that Irish women are the most virtuous in the world' and 'in no country are women so faithful to the marriage bond as in Ireland'.

For the more resourced middle-class women, however, things were slowly improving. Higher education was becoming available as Irish universities opened their doors to women and new colleges sprang up for them. In the Catholic colleges especially, education was more tuned to turning out young ladies than academics, but they were valuable in teaching Gaelic which gave their students a head start in the Gaelic League. The League itself had set a revolutionary trend by holding co-educational classes and even céilís where the sexes could socialise together. The Catholic Church saw this as a dangerous precedent and withdrew its church halls from the League's use; even Arthur Griffith condemned the Church for that.

In 1870 married women were granted rights over their own property and, in 1873, over their own children. By 1896 propertied Irishwomen could serve as Poor Law guardians and in 1898, again as long as they had certain property qualifications, were given the local government vote.

The poor battered bill to give women the parliamentary vote which had been drafted by Dr Pankhurst (husband of Emmeline) was being defeated again and again in the House of Commons and the attitude of the Establishment towards women generally, summed up by the then Attorney General during its 1883 defeat still pertained. He had told the House that while the opinion of men was valuable in politics because they could contribute knowledge on law, trade, commerce, armies and war: 'To any of these subjects can woman contribute any experience? (Cries of "No"). She can tell us no doubt of her great experience of domestic life, but unhappily for us that is not a subject with which we have to deal here.'

The peculiar situation of Ireland, however, had catapulted many of its women out of domestic life and into politics. If, as has always been said, England's difficulty was Ireland's opportunity, the same proved true for the two sexes. Men's incarceration ensured women's participation. On January 31, 1881, a unique event had taken place; Parnell, the Home Ruler, who had combined with some more extreme Fenians to form the Land League and campaign for peasant proprietorship, had reluctantly asked women to control the movement if and when they (the men) went to prison for their activities, as they eventually did. So it came about that, for the first time in Irish history, women were given the opportunity to participate in a political movement and show what they could do.

Parnell and the others had only tried this 'dangerous experiment' because they thought it would keep the League ticking over during their enforced absence. But under the leadership of Parnell's brilliant and uncompromising sister, Anna, the Ladies' Land League gave new, fiercer determination and help to tenants who could not pay their rent. The agitation they caused and the publicity they received forced Gladstone to come to an agreement with the imprisoned Parnell, who had himself become alarmed that the ladies were using the League, 'not for purposes he approved of, but for a real revolutionary end and aim'. He was released and the Ladies' League was repressed by the very men who had brought it into existence. Anna Parnell never forgave her brother.

When Maud Gonne later enquired what had happened to the Ladies' Land League, John O'Leary, the Fenian, told her that they were really suppressed because they were 'honester and more sincere than the men'. But it went deeper than that. They had unleashed the masculine fear of unbridled women. They had shown a disturbing ability and independence, formed branches of their own, distributed the League's paper even though it was proscribed, raised funds, received and allocated financial support from America and England, built huts for the evicted and addressed mass meetings at which, reported the *Belfast Newsletter* in horror, the ordinary woman no longer viewed the proceedings at a respectful distance, but thronged around the platform 'as if she had a right to be there'.

In the next decade the Ladies' mantle fell on the shoulders of Maud Gonne and her helpers, female and male; perhaps because she was so beautiful Maud never quite inspired in men the fear that other, less 'feminine', women revolutionaries did, though she could be as extreme as any. She opposed evictions, stopped a potential famine in County Mayo by forcing the authorities to bring in food supplies, and secured the release of the Treason Felony bombers in prison under bad conditions in England. When Dublin proposed to celebrate Queen

Victoria's Jubilee, Maud protested against honouring 'the Famine Queen' and countered the celebrations by holding a highly successful children's party of her own, which was attended by 15,000 in defiance of the monarch. It was Maud Gonne, too, who founded the Inghínidhe na hÉireann.

Early in 1908 the Inghínidhe gained a new recruit. Helena Moloney, their secretary, had heard Constance's: 'What can I do for Ireland?' and had invited her to come along to one of their meetings. The night Constance chose was rainy and dark and the meeting had already convened in its uninviting committee room – they used places like St Teresa's Total Abstinence Hall, which sounds as dour as it undoubtedly was. The door flung open and the recruit came in; Constance had been attending some function at the Castle and was still in evening dress, complete with short train, velvet cloak and diamonds in her hair. The Inghínidhe, who tended to dress soberly and patriotically in Donegal tweeds, were horrified; like Arthur Griffith, they suspected her of being a Castle spy.

Helena Moloney introduced her, Con sat down to listen, first taking off her shoes and putting them by the fire to dry. Also attending for the first time was Sidney Gifford who later became a journalist under the name 'John Brennan' because she thought, despite her already male name, that she'd be listened to with more respect if she sounded like a Wexford farmer. She was fascinated when, during the debate on the possibility of bringing out their own newspaper, Con immediately offered to sell a diamond ornament she was wearing to raise funds. The offer was refused so coolly it was almost a snub; the Inghínidhe na hÉireann did not accept gifts from the Ascendancy. Constance was delighted with them. She told Helena Moloney later that she liked them from the first because they did not 'kowtow' to her. Soon they were to like her back. 'She was like a twelve-year-old boy, boisterous and noisy, coming bouncing in with her dogs,' Helena Moloney recalled later with affection.

After the meeting Sidney Gifford and Constance walked to the tram together, Con with her train dragging in the puddles. Sidney pointed it out and Constance gathered it up carelessly and said she wouldn't have much time in the future for wearing fashionable clothes. The Castle had seen her for the last time.

CHAPTER FOUR

The Inghínidhe na hÉireann saw themselves as much a part of the revival of old, great Ireland as the literary renaissance. They could, and did, refer to Celtic mythology in which the action turned on female personalities, especially women warriors, more than in almost any other. They could claim with justice that the early Brehon laws had given Irish clanswomen an equality with men until the common law of England took it away from them.

But, rebirth or not, the Inghínidhe and the other women's organisations in Ireland at this time were part of the labour pains convulsing most of the Western Hemisphere as the new, voting woman struggled to be born.

The women's vote had been seen as desirable among the enlightened for over a century; by 1900 the delay in giving it to them had turned into a glaring wrong. Like the cry of 'Rescue the Holy Places' seven hundred years before, 'Votes For Women' had the beautiful simplicity which promised that lives which had become over-complicated, over-stressful, boring, or too spiritually or financially impoverished could be miraculously transformed by the victory of this particular crusade. Women responded according to their temperament and means: some marched and threw stones to court arrest, others addressed envelopes in a more constitutional plea, others merely lobbied their MPs or their husbands. The suffragist, Dr Mary Gordon, wrote: 'We do not know how it sprang into life, no one explanation is entirely satisfactory, certainly not the theory that it was the work of "leaders". It began all over the country, even in silent lonely places. It was a spiritual movement and had a fire.'

A form of inflammatory lend-lease pertained as women crossed boundaries and seas to carry the message or to help their sisters in other countries. The elderly Charlotte Despard, for instance, campaigned on both sides of the Irish Sea, opposing her brother who became Lord Lieutenant of Ireland in 1918. Members of the Women's Social and Political Union went to Dublin to help the militant tactics of Irish suffragettes.

Considering that they saw themselves as democracies, it is interesting how long countries such as the United Kingdom and the United States withstood this appeal to enfranchise the other half of their adult population. (France did not give its women the vote until after the Second World War.) Asquith, who became British Prime Minister in 1908, blamed democracy itself which, he said repeatedly, had no quarrel with the divisions ordained by Nature. The underlying reason for the refusal, of course, was the fear that if women gained a voting place in society they would change society itself. Yet, oddly enough, the women who were to terrify the Establishment most posed the least threat to it; Emmeline and Christabel Pankhurst's militant Women's Social and Political Union saw the vote as an end in itself and left the field once it was won in 1928, though, to be fair, it had kept the cause under the public's nose right up to the First World War and Emmeline died, exhausted, in that same year of 1928.

The real revolutionaries, whose story has only comparatively recently been researched, were the radical suffragists who combined to campaign constitutionally for much more than the vote in working areas such as Manchester and Belfast and who for the first time mooted subjects such as child care and allowances, women's right to work, and equal pay. Because they were radical yet non-militant, they attracted little popularity and success in their own lifetime, but they have been vindicated since because the issues they raised then were the very issues fought for by the new wave of feminism which came after them.

In the thick of this particular battle was another daughter of Lissadell, County Sligo – Eva Gore-Booth. In the same year that Constance left home to study art in Paris, Eva went to Italy to recuperate from illness. In fact, she was convinced she was dying of TB. There she met Esther Roper who was taking a holiday from her job as secretary to the Manchester National Society for Women's Suffrage, an organisation which had been in the doldrums until Esther took it over and galvanised it into embracing the cause of working women, taking it to the factory gates of the mill towns and bringing cotton workers themselves into the campaign.

The two young women found each other irresistible. 'We spent the days walking and talking on the hillside by the sea,' wrote Esther. 'Each was attracted to the work and thoughts of the other and we became friends and companions for life.' Eva decided to devote what time she had left to her new friend and her new friend's causes in the North of England; as it turned out she had thirty years left and the use she made of them has earned her a place in the history of working women in England.

Both the elder Gore-Booth girls had an endearing, almost absent-minded, inability to classify people. It was as if their chronic short-sightedness – one of the reasons Con gave up painting was her myopia – blurred the distinctions which others of their background instinctively made when evaluating people. Con was to be as much at ease among Dublin dockers as she was among the Castle set, possibly more, and addressed both in the way she expected to be treated, as an equal. Eva was the same woman among the Lancashire millgirls as she was in her poetry circle back home. One of the things she did, apart from helping to fight their political battles, was to start up dramatic classes in the Manchester slums where, considering the privations suffered by the girls who lived there, Shakespeare might not have seemed a priority, but Eva considered they had as much right to him as anyone else, and was loved for it. A machinist who joined her class, and her fight for the suffrage, said: 'We were *rough* . . . But I don't think I exaggerate when I say we worshipped her, but she never knew it she was so selfless.'

Sylvia Pankhurst said it was Eva who drew Christabel Pankhurst into the suffrage movement:

Tall and excessively slender, intensely short-sighted, with a mass of golden hair worn like a great ball at the nape of her long neck, bespectacled, bending forward, short of breath with high-pitched voice and gasping speech, she was nevertheless a personality of great charm. Christabel adored her and when Eva suffered from neuralgia, as often happened, she would sit with her for hours, massaging her head. To all of us at home this seemed remarkable indeed, for Christabel had never been willing to act the nurse for any other human being . . . Yet through this friendship Christabel was finding the serious interest she had hitherto lacked.

Thanks to Eva and Esther Roper, Christabel became an active member of the North of England Women's Suffrage Society executive and of the Women's Trade Union Council in 1901.

There was bad unemployment in the mill towns, as there was everywhere, and its effect (now familiar) was to give priority of jobs to men. Even a Labour MP whose election had been secured by the campaigning of the radical suffragists, refused to support their right to work, saying that a man was the important breadwinner for his family, even though – as his female constituents pointed out – he had been supported through a period of unemployment by his wife's wage packet.

One of the Liberal Government's proposals in 1908 to relieve the situation was to prohibit women from working after 8 p.m. This would not only have severely restricted women's overtime but also, at a stroke, put barmaids out of work. In the spring of 1908 Winston Churchill, then a member of the Liberal Party, was contesting the

North-West Manchester seat in a by-election. Eva and Esther took a deputation of women to ask him to support women's suffrage and oppose the barmaid legislation. He refused. The suffragists decided to make an example of him and use the by-election for their own publicity. Usually their un-militant methods were kept out of the limelight by the activities of their more bellicose sisters in the Women's Social and Political Union, but this time their efforts were given 'untypical panache' because Eva had written to Ireland and recruited her newly-awakened sister to come and give a helping hand.

The *Manchester Guardian* of April 22, 1908 reported:

A coach of olden times was driven about Manchester yesterday to advertise the political agitation on behalf of barmaids. It was drawn by four white horses and the 'whip' was the Countess Markievicz, sister of Eva Gore-Booth. In all parts of the city the coach and its passengers excited general interest and in the North-West division especially, the cause of the barmaids was made known not only by demonstration but by speeches and personal interviews.

The 'general interest' included the sort of heckling suffragettes were getting used to. One man shouted: 'Can you cook a dinner?' 'Yes,' shouted back Con. 'Can you drive a coach and four?'

Winston Churchill was defeated, and Con went back to Ireland with a new awareness of the power of publicity and her own flair for it. Behind her, however, there was division between Eva's side of the movement and the strong temperance faction, which wanted to see the abolition of pubs, never mind barmaids. Christabel Pankhurst and the WSPU had already broken away from the Gore-Booth/Roper type of suffrage agitation because it would not follow them down the militant path. Eva said: 'I am one of those quite hopeless people who refuse to fight for any cause.' The WSPU also broke with the Independent Labour Party because it would not give them unconditional support.

Ultra-respectable suffragists had already gone their own way because they did not like the connection with Labour that Eva and Esther maintained. Yet the Labour Party, with the honourable exceptions of men such as Keir Hardie, was giving poor support to the radical suffragist for fear that their demands would adversely affect men's jobs.

Similar complications awaited Constance in Ireland, but there they were compounded to labyrinthine proportions by British rule. The figure which blocked the light of the vote to Englishwomen had the two heads of male prejudice and political expediency and was, shamefully, of their own nationality. To Irishwomen the monster had a third, a *foreign* head and many of them preferred, like Con and the

Inghínidhe na hÉireann to think that if this head was cut off the rest of the creature must surely die. If they fought as equals under the nationalist banner then, of necessity, it would follow that equality could not be refused them when independence was achieved.

It was not an unreasonable expectation. Feminism was still so new a factor in politics that there was no historical precedent on which they could have based their course. The young radical women in Tsarist Russia were in a similar situation and had come to the same conclusion: that if they did not help to bring about the revolution they could not demand benefits from it.

Some Irishwomen, however, were putting the female cause first and the most outstanding of these was Hanna Sheehy Skeffington. Born Hanna Sheehy – her sister became the mother of the Irish politician and writer, Conor Cruise O'Brien – she married the delightful Francis Skeffington, whom James Joyce had described as the second cleverest man at the Royal University (the first, of course, being Joyce himself), and each had tagged the other's surname onto their own. 'Skeffy' was a strong feminist and in 1904 had resigned as University Registrar over women students' rights. He was an equally strong pacifist. Conor Cruise O'Brien quotes the story of an argument between his grandfather and Frank Skeffington which grew so heated that Skeffy was thrown out of the house and down the steps. 'Frank simply got up, knocked on the door, said "Force solves nothing, Dick" and resumed his argument with grandfather.'

In the same year that Constance joined the Inghínidhe, Hanna founded the Irish Women's Franchise League, which was modelled on the lines of the Pankhursts' WSPU and which, being prepared to accept suffrage from whatever source, began lobbying the Irish Parliamentary Party to include a Votes for Women clause in the next Home Rule Bill, to the chagrin of the Inghínidhe, who regarded the Irish Party as English lackeys and therefore untouchable.

Hanna was as keen on her country's freedom as anyone else but she also had a healthy and, as it turned out, far-sighted distrust of revolutionary parties to which, she later wrote, 'women have always been welcomed, partly by reason of their inherent taste for martyrdom, a crown never denied their womanhood once it enters the lists. It is when parties grow circumspect through partial success and line up after the fight . . . that woman falls naturally out of step and is duly left behind.'

Lobbying the Irish MPs in the House of Commons turned out to be a lost cause for Hanna; in 1912 they refused to vote for a suffrage bill for women. They had been persuaded by Asquith that to do so would prejudice any forthcoming Home Rule Bill for Ireland – not that John Redmond, the parliamentary leader, or his successor, John Dillon, needed much persuading. They opposed votes for women out of conviction. Dillon told one of Hanna's deputations: 'Women's suffrage will, I believe, be the ruin of our Western civilisation. It will destroy the home, challenging the headship of men laid down by God. It may come in your time – I hope not in mine.'

Like so many other women Hanna Sheehy Skeffington changed to the nationalist view after 1916 when Skeffy was shot and killed by an English officer in cold blood during the Rising, although the only part he had played in it was to try to prevent looting.

Though the Inghínidhe na hÉireann believed that every good thing would come about with Ireland's freedom from British rule, they did not take the advent of women's rights for granted. Their paper, *Bean na hÉireann* (Woman of Ireland), the first woman's paper to be produced in Ireland, advocated militancy, separatism *and* feminism with a good sprinkling of the growing socialism of its editor, Helena Moloney. It hit out at fellow nationalists like Griffith for not propounding republicanism at the same time as it criticised those suffragettes who demanded the vote without insisting on Irish independence. Its banner was 'Freedom for our Nation and the complete removal of all disabilities to our sex'.

The first issue came out in November 1908 with a title page designed by Constance Markievicz, who also had considerable fun as its gardening correspondent:

> It is a very unpleasant work killing slugs and snails but let us not be daunted. A good Nationalist should look upon slugs in the garden in much the same way as she looks on the English in Ireland and only regret that she cannot crush the Nation's enemies with the same ease that she can the garden's, with just one tread of her fairy foot.

About the same time she gave a lecture to the Students' National Literary Society:

> I would ask every Nationalist woman to pause before she joined a Suffrage Society or Franchise League that did not include in its programme the Freedom of the Nation. 'A Free Ireland with no Sex Disabilities in her Constitution' should be the motto of all Nationalist women. And a grand motto it is.

The lecture closely followed *Bean na hÉireann*'s line, and the Inghínidhe published it, reprinting in 1918, complete with its plethora of capital letters. Constance spoke to the public in capital letters. Her style was grandiloquently patriotic and called on the children of Ireland to fight England in the same *Boy's Own Paper* phrases with which England recruited her sons to fight Boers, Fuzzy Wuzzies and, later, Germans. She digested complex notions and regurgitated them with an almost crude simplicity that a child could understand. But she was effective. She was always in demand as a speaker because she could rouse uneducated or apathetic audiences in a way more sophisticated orators could not. The Irish may have winced at her voice and her English slang, they may not have believed everything she told them, but they always believed that she believed it.

Her thinking, however, was subtler than her words. True to the Inghínidhe line she refused to have any truck with the Irish Parliamentary Party, but she tried hard to heal divisions between other nationalist and feminist groups, frequently giving speeches at Irish Women's Franchise League meetings and even, on occasion, turning out to demonstrate with them. Though she was a strong republican by this time, she rejected the purist attitude of those republican women, such as Helena Moloney and Mary MacSwiney, who would have nothing to do with Griffith and Sinn Féin because they could not accept the idea of a King of Ireland.

Con had refused to be rebuffed by Arthur Griffith and had joined Sinn Féin, despite his hostility, because she saw that it needed to be drawn away from Griffith's conception of a dual Irish–English kingdom towards republicanism. In this she was eventually successful. More than any other person in public life during those years, Con Markievicz crossed boundaries, trying to hold together differing groups whose aims she saw as an integer. She managed to keep the respect of almost all of them – Hanna Sheehy Skeffington kept Constance's portrait on her wall all her life – and when the divisions became irreparable she died.

1908 had been a busy year for her. By the end of it she had formulated nearly all her political ideas, was contributing regularly to *Bean na hÉireann*, attending meetings of the Inghínidhe and Sinn Féin and speaking at most of them, learning the necessary minutiae of activist politics, the putting out of chairs, the committee work, taking copy to the printers. Like Eva in Manchester, she started organising drama classes, mainly for children through whom she began to discover the poverty that lay around her.

Inevitably, that was the year when normal family life at the Markievicz home ended. Maeve went to her grandmother's and stayed there. Stanislas went to boarding school. They all spent Christmas at Lissadell together and took part in a Christmas Carnival in Sligo but, although Con continued her acting career in Casi's plays for some years to come, it was no longer a preoccupation; Casi, however, between increasingly frequent trips to Poland, was to make dramatic writing and production a full-time business – or as full-time as Casi could ever make anything – devoting his days to the theatre and his nights to drinking with his friends Martin Murphy, the Dublin Gaiety's stage manager and carpenter, and Dubronsky, a Polish tailor; the three of them became familiar characters around Dublin and contributed to its folklore.

Sean O'Faolain hints that Casi had other women, and, since the physical relationship between him and Con seems to have ended by this time, perhaps he did[1]; the respect and affection between husband and wife, however, was too great for him to flaunt them publicly or for Con to break openly with him because of them.

Whether it was Casi's fault, or Con's, or nobody's fault at all but just circumstance, the Markieviczes' as a conventional marriage was over; from here on Con swam her political sea without a family lifeline. Then and after, of course, people had to search for some psychological explanation for her actions, as they have for any woman who ventures away from the norm, some neurosis, sexual frigidity or other inadequacy of womanhood. Those who believed that Con took up politics because her marriage failed were as numerous as those who believed her marriage failed because she took up politics. It was not enough to accept that she adopted her causes because she could not bear not to, although that it is a large part of the truth; she was landed with a deep sense of responsibility for life's inequalities.

Nevertheless, it is impossible to miss the sense of relief with which she threw off family life, as if she had escaped from complications and intimacies with which she could not cope. Her ceaseless political activity from this point could be regarded as a frenetic cover-up for failure as wife and mother, but it is probably more accurate to see it as the enlargement of somebody who had found a lifestyle which suited her better. Now she had the opportunity to fight injustices which had worried her badly and now she could spread her affection more widely, and necessarily more thinly, over a huge nationwide family, rather than concentrating it on a few individuals and having their affection concentrated on her. Con undoubtedly had an aversion to being probed to her emotional depths; and, like the Victorian she was, she never exposed her inner self. Those who had the opportunity to get behind her outer defences respected the privacy of what they found there. Maud Gonne hinted at what might be there when she said that for Con to give up Maeve was a sacrifice and that she kept

[1] The writer, Eilís Dillon, kindly passed on to me the memories of her mother, Geraldine Plunkett Dillon, aged ninety-eight, who knew the Markieviczes and says Casi was 'a blackguard' whose activities forced Con to send Maeve away from home. But she refused to go into detail.

things hidden in her heart, but she does not say what those 'things' were, nor why her friend went to such lengths to protect them.

In the absence of evidence we must accept that Con's deepest love was reserved for causes – Ireland, women's rights, the poor – and that she had an infinite capacity for giving less passionate, though no less sincere, affection to people. She emerged from marriage with her husband as her friend because friendship was what she was best at. There is no lack of fulfilment, no sign of inner sexual turmoil, nor that her life from 1908 onwards was a flight from some demon. On the contrary, it left her serene; in the *Prison Letters* she mentioned her dreams more than once and always they were 'beautiful'. If all this is aberration, then perhaps Ireland and women everywhere for whom she pushed back the frontiers should be grateful for her abnormality.

She had spent 1908 absorbing ideas and learning the political alphabet. She was forty years old and she had limbered up. By 1909 she was ready to take the initiative.

In England Robert Baden-Powell had founded his Boy Scout movement and by 1909 his idea had spread to Dublin where the citizens were treated to the spectacle of their youth parading before the Viceroy under the Union Jack. There was much gnashing of teeth from watching nationalists but it was only Con who said: 'Why can't we do that?' If Casi, who was now calling his wife 'my floating landmine', gave a groan at this point nobody can blame him, but, considering the effect her answer to her own question was to have on the morale of its next generation, Ireland could have raised a cheer.

CHAPTER FIVE

'The Baden-Powell Scouts never attained a vigorous life in Dublin,' wrote Padraic Colum. 'Parents who'd watched their sons go forth radiant in battle array saw them return later minus hats and poles and plus black eyes.'

The takers of the hats and poles and givers of the black eyes were the members of Na Fianna Éireann, 'Madame's Fianna' as they became known in Dublin by those who favoured them and 'those little Fianna sods' by those who didn't.

Fighting other small boys for their uniform might not seem to accord with Baden-Powell's tenet of a good deed a day, but Con did not found the Fianna to perform good deeds for British organisations or the Irish who joined them. Nevertheless there were parallels between the Boy Scouts and the Fianna; both disciplined boys as future soldiers and encouraged patriotism. It was just that Con's Fianna, like Con herself, was more overtly militaristic. From the first she saw it as a project to 'weld the youth of Ireland together to work and fight for Ireland', the beginnings of an army.

Her republican friends were sympathetic but unhelpful, while Arthur Griffith was positively hostile to the idea; Con was infiltrating Sinn Féin too deeply for his liking and he was, then, opposed to all idea of physical force. Con complained of him later:

> He always came to meetings with his mind made up, only being concerned with forcing his own point of view on his colleagues. He did not want anyone to begin to talk of fighting for Ireland's freedom. In fact, the only difference between himself and the 'Party' [the Irish Parliamentary Party] was his disapproval of men going 'hat in hand to Westminster' . . . the Sinn Féin programme contained no provision for organising an army.

When Con asked for it to at least include provision for rebel boy scouts she was 'gently but firmly turned down'.

To be fair to Griffith, it may be that he felt a natural revulsion at teaching children to fight, but such revulsion is a luxury which only the people of an unoccupied country can afford. Nearly every resistance force before and since has used its youth against the enemy;

in fact, the Fianna Éireann was later studied as a model by the Zionist, Vladimir Jabotinsky, when he was working out a method of training young men and boys in Palestine in the 1930s.

And to be equally fair to Con, not only did she regard Ireland as occupied territory, but she recognised the Boy Scout movement in Ireland as a form of indoctrination which would eventually be turned against the Irish themselves. If they didn't train their youth, the British would. 'In ten years these boys would be men. I could see these children growing to manhood and gaily enlisting in the British Army or Police forces and being used to batten [sic] their own class into submission.' If any precedent were needed she had one in the Royal Irish Constabulary which was recruited entirely from Irishmen.

Padraic Colum reinforces the point:

> Irishmen opposed to furnishing any recruits for the English Army or Navy, saw in the attempt to enlist Irish boys into the Baden-Powell scouts a new and subtle method of recruitment for the English forces. They were to be drilled by officers of the English Army and inspected by high government and army officials.
>
> Baden-Powell wrote to Pádraic Pearse [then a schoolmaster at St Enda's] to write a book suitable for use by an Irish branch of English boy scouts. Pearse refused and many national voices were raised against it, but none of them thought of the possibility of forming an Irish national boys' organisation as a counter-blow to the English one. Madame mooted the idea at several meetings without much encouragement . . . the idea of training and arming boys of twelve to thirteen seemed useless labour.

Con didn't give up. She put the idea in *Bean na hÉireann*, having enlisted Helena Moloney to her way of thinking; she raised the subject at every Sinn Féin meeting. Somehow she managed to persuade the headmaster of a National School in Brunswick Street to find eight young volunteers from among his pupils for her first troop, giving them the name 'the Red Branch Knights'. With the help of Helena Moloney and two Sinn Féiners, Dr Patrick McCartan and Seán McGarry, and with Casi guffawing from the window, she taught them signalling, drill and tracking on her front lawn. (Where she learned these skills from nobody knows; it would be like her to have cribbed them from Baden-Powell's own *Scouting for Boys*.)

She and Helena took six of them camping in the Dublin hills and, from her own account much later, in the 1914 Christmas issue of *Fianna*, everything possible went wrong. They had a job getting the pony and cart up the track to the site, had endless trouble pitching the tents, found they had left candles behind and were flooded out by a storm. The Knights used the only towel to black their boots with ('After long experience I have come to the conclusion that the only thing you can be quite sure that every boy will bring to camp is boot polish') and, when it was time to go home, couldn't catch the pony because, wrote Con, 'he had found camp life just as much to his taste as we did'. She had actually enjoyed herself and, what's more, so had the boys.

The next phase was her alliance with a Sinn Féiner who had already befriended her, Bulmer Hobson, son of Ulster Quakers, a Republican and the man who, according to Robert Kee in *The Green Flag*, founded the Fianna 'helped by Constance Markievicz'. Bulmer Hobson himself made no such claim, even though the events of 1916 were to put him and Con into different camps. What Hobson had done in 1901 in Belfast was to form classes of boys and girls for the study of Irish history and language and the playing of Gaelic games, promoting a junior hurling league – a very different business from the eventual Fianna. Because of their later division we only get a curt account from Hobson about the beginnings of the new Fianna, although he is fair. 'I told Constance, Countess Markievicz, then a very new recruit into the Sinn Féin movement, about my venture in Belfast. *She suggested* [my italics] we should start again in Dublin.' Anyway, Hobson was to leave Dublin towards the end of 1909 to look for a job in Belfast where he stayed during 1910, the year when the Fianna spread nationally and was licked into shape.

Con adopted for the scouts Hobson's original name for his Belfast group, Na Fianna Éireann, after the young warrior bands of ancient Ireland, but the impudence, the sheer *joie de vivre* which was the hallmark of the new Fianna and which was to attract boys in their thousands all over Ireland could never have come from the rather earnest Hobson and was entirely due to the inspiration of Constance Markievicz.

Bulmer Hobson had no money, so it was Con who became the tenant of 'Fianna Hall' at 34, Lower Camden Street, once the rehearsal rooms of the Irish National Theatre Society (later the Abbey Theatre) at ten shillings a week, a rent she paid out of her own pocket for many years.

Monday, August 16, was fixed for the first meeting and notices went out to nationalist publications requesting the attendance of boys 'willing to work for the Independence of Ireland'. One hundred boys of assorted ages turned up, and the tenets read out:

Object: To establish the Independence of Ireland.
Means: The training of the youth of Ireland mentally and physically by scouting and military exercises, Irish history and language.
Declaration: 'I promise to work for the Independence of Ireland, never to join England's armed forces, and to obey my superior officers.'

65

Hobson took the chair and was elected president, but when it came to the nominations of Con as joint secretary and Helena Moloney as committee member, there was a hitch. One of the elder boys got up and said: 'This is a physical force organisation, and there are two women in the room. This is no place for them, they must be put out.' Hobson pointed out that Con was paying for the hall and 'that we could not accept her financial help and refuse her membership'. Con and Helena were elected but rumblings about women officers in a boys' organisation went on for some years, though not among those who got to know them.

Con Colbert, executed by the British in 1916 for his part in the Rising along with another Fianna boy, Seán Heuston, was at the first meeting and on the next day took the recruits for drill of his own devising which used commands in Gaelic.

Sinn Féin disclaimed any connection with the scouts and put a notice saying so in its paper on August 21. The one organisation which gave complete support to the Fianna during its formative years was, ironically in view of the boys' original attitude to women, the Inghínidhe who gave their activities full coverage in *Bean na hÉireann*. Con backed up this lesson in feminism by including in the lectures to the boys a talk on the heroism of the women in the United Irish Rebellion of 1798.

Being not only the best shot in the Fianna, but one of the best in Dublin, she also taught them how to shoot. She had discovered a loophole in the law against firearms which permitted their use in a householder's 'own compound'. Accordingly, she took relays of Fianna boys out to her cottage for training. She did it well and strictly. She began with Winchester rifles, then moved to service rifle and revolvers. The boys were taught how to carry, handle and clean guns. If she caught a Fianna boy pointing a gun at another, even in fun, she so clouted his ears that he never did it again.

Like nearly all countrybred women, Con had deep faith in the therapeutic effect of the countryside on children, especially poor, city-born urchins as so many of her Fianna were. She hauled them off to camp and to her cottage as often as possible, but the idea of how nice it would be for them to live permanently beside fields and fresh air became an obsession. She had read about the experimental commune established some seventy-five years earlier at Ralahine, County Clare, where the Anglo–Irish landlord, Arthur Vandeleur, had turned his estate into an agricultural co-operative for the mutual benefit of himself and his tenants. The whole thing had ended in disaster when, having gambled away his money, Vandeleur decamped, but that had not been the fault of the commune which, until then, had flourished.

'Why can't we do that?' asked Con. If she found a country house and started a co-operative market garden with friends and the Fianna, it would not only give the boys healthy living and future employment, but would solve some of the organisation's financial problems by providing an HQ, free food, camping site and shooting range. Bulmer Hobson and, after some thought, Helena Moloney agreed to go in with her. Before anybody had time to think, the lovely house in Frankfort Avenue with its studio built for art had been let for £90 a year and Belcamp Park at Raheny had been taken on a three-year lease at £100 a year. (Casi was away in Poland and does not appear to have been consulted.) Raheny, then a village, is on the road to Malahide, within easy reach of Dublin. It was an Ascendancy area, full of Georgian mansions and rolling, English-type parkland of lime, beech and chestnut. Belcamp Park had twelve bedrooms, outhouses, stable yard and a seven-acre garden which had been neglected for years. The commune took up residence late in the summer of 1909; Con, Helena, Bulmer Hobson, Donald Hannigan – a graduate of Glasnevin Agricultural College who was to be the gardening expert – and an indeterminate number of Fianna boys.

As Sean O'Faolain reported: 'Dublin watched with interest, a grin hovering about its lips.'

Dublin was not disappointed. The Raheny co-operative was a farce enjoyed by everybody except its commune. The house was damp and too big to be heated or lit properly and there was no electricity. Helena and Con had to cycle to Dublin every day to work for the Inghínidhe. In addition, Con had been elected to the executive of Sinn Féin, much to the chagrin of Arthur Griffith. They came back at nights to work their fingers to the bone.

Tradesmen didn't call, the garden produced nothing but weeds; in fact the only proliferation was in Fianna boys who arrived, it seemed to the commune, in their millions and promptly began raiding their neighbours' land for milk and hens 'because', Con ruefully excused them, 'they thought everything in the countryside grew wild'.

Stanislas returned for the summer holidays to find he had a new home, but the burning question in Dublin was: 'What will Casi say?' What Casi said on his return from Poland towards the end of 1909 was retailed to his Arts Club friends:

I have great trouble to find this house but at last I find it and I send away the cabbie. I find the house at the end of the avenue, all dark and silent. I knock and

I knock but not a sound. I go around the back and I call out 'Constance!' After a while a window goes up and a dirty little ragamuffin puts out his head and say: 'Who da?' . . . I say 'I am Count Markievicz and I want to see Countess Markievicz.' I hear much scuffling and running and at last the door open. It is all dark but I see Constance. 'It's very dark, Constance,' I say; 'We have only one lamp,' she says, 'and the gardener is reading with that.' We go into the drawing room and there I find the gardener with his legs on the mantelpiece and he is smoking a dirty, filthy shag tobacco. He does not stand up when I go in. I say, 'I am hungry. Cannot I have some food?' and they scuffle and whisper again while I talk to the gardener. At last they bring me cold meat and bread and butter. That is how I return to my home.

Con had painted herself into a corner, and for once Casi roused himself to get her – and himself – out of it. He went and discussed the matter with AE, an authority on communes, and returned with such searching questions on profit, loss and viability that the gardener, Donald Hannigan, panicked, cut down a mature holly tree, sold it in Dublin for thirty shillings and left. Con later had to pay the landlord £5.00 compensation for it.

At this point Bulmer Hobson left for Belfast where he spent the next year. Helena Moloney also eventually moved out, but Con and Casi stayed on until they could dispose of the lease, which they did in 1911 with a net loss of £220. Staying on with them was an ever-changing tenancy of Fianna boys who had taken up semi-permanent residence with Con and never left her, not even when she and Casi moved out of Raheny and into Surrey House, Leinster Road, in the suburb of Rathmines, which was to be her last home.

Casi called them 'sprouts' because they sprouted under his bed, beneath his chairs, out of cupboards '. . . and the little devil sprouts drink whiskey, even locked whiskey'.

Raheny left Constance's image almost irredeemably comic, that of an erratic, impulsive begetter of daft ideas, easy to love but difficult to take seriously, which was a pity because she learned a great deal from it and never again started something she couldn't finish. Dubliners, however, were not the people to let fairness get in the way of a good joke; she had to take a lot of ribbing, most of it from Casi, but she continued undaunted to mould the Fianna.

In the absence of Bulmer Hobson she became its President and Chief Scout appointing a general staff from the boys themselves. One of the things Raheny had taught her was that countryside and city boys like hers did not mix, so while other *sluaite* (troops) practised their tracking and woodcraft along with first aid, drill and signalling, the Fianna Hall boys were encouraged in what they were good at; to use their knowledge of the streets and back alleys to carry messages, dodge police, listen and report and, when necessary, disrupt. It was the basic training for urban guerrilla warfare. The first victims of it were the unfortunate, respectable Baden-Powell scouts.

Con had devised a Fianna uniform, a saffron kilt and sash over a dark green jacket and topped by a bush hat; few of her boys could afford such splendour and turned up in the nearest travesty of it. The point of honour, however, was to get a hat and the cheapest source for that was to knock it off the head of an 'English' scout. 'Incredible quantities of Baden-Powell trophies were won in honourable combat on the streets of Dublin,' said Padraic Colum. Sceptics questioned how 'honourable' these tactics were and even some nationalists thought Madame was allowing her Fianna to get out of hand; she refused to punish any of them for these raids. She knew exactly what she was doing.

> She knew [says Colum], they were the sons of men who'd had the superiority of Englishmen preached to them from their earliest days, men who had behind them failure and defeat, who'd been taught to believe that the Irish went forth to battle but they always fell. Those victories counted much in the training of the boys . . . above all, they learned their own strength. They were veterans when the men were raw recruits in the Irish Volunteer Movement.

The speeches Con made about this time are full of nationalist hyperbole and the need for self-sacrifice, reiterated in what she wrote for the *Fianna Handbook*:

> We have heard the imperious demand of Kathleen Ni Houlihan, her call to those who would serve her, to give her all, to give her themselves. It will take the best and noblest of Ireland's children to win freedom, for the price of freedom is suffering and pain. It is to the young that a nation must look for help; for life itself. Ireland is calling you to join Fianna na hÉireann, the young army of Ireland and help to place the crown of freedom on Her head.

In practice she gave them confidence that this time they would actually make it.

Perhaps the strangest thing of all about the young Fianna boys is that, though their parents often found Con comic, they never did. Boys are self-conscious animals and to have as their chief this beanpole with the jarring English voice, and a woman at that, laid them open to ridicule, especially from their peers. They must have looked, as they marched along the streets with her, like a flotilla of coracles around a high-masted clipper, but they followed her everywhere just the same. Dr Brighid Lyons Thornton was impressed by the scouts' adoration for her but remembered being shocked by her first sight of Madame at a Fianna gathering.

> I expected her to come in with a tiara and a few ermine robes. And this withered hag came in ... that's not unkind, I don't mean to be, but she was sallow, you know, and anything but what my idea of a countess was like. But they [the boys] rallied round her and the emotion and enthusiasm for her made a greater impression once I'd got over the first.

Margaret Skinnider wrote:

> Madame never went anywhere that they did not follow as a bodyguard. If her work had been either a pose or mere hysterical enthusiasm as some English 'friends' in Dublin have sought to make the world believe, they wouldn't have. They loved her and trusted her, a high compliment as I have always found boys are keen judges of sincerity.

Margaret Skinnider, a Glaswegian of Irish parents, who was badly injured during the 1916 Rising, went to the United States after she had recovered and wrote her book to raise support for the Irish cause. A large part of it is devoted to Constance, by then in prison, and the time Margaret spent with the Fianna during the first two years of the First World War. By then they had become the scourge of the Royal Irish Constabulary and English soldiery. 'Whenever we passed a British soldier we made him take to the gutter, telling him the streets of Dublin were no place for the likes of him.' The boys whistled rebel tunes at police constables and disrupted the booths where NCOs were recruiting for the British Army, 'singing Madame's anti-recruiting song: "The recruiters are raidin' old Dublin, boys. It's them we'll have to be troublin', boys."' They heckled, they dived under the platforms, upset them and made their escape through the crowd. 'This sounds like rowdyism,' Margaret Skinnider commented, 'but it is only by such tests of courage that the youth of a dominated race can acquire self-confidence for the real struggle.' Afterwards they took her to a shooting gallery where, a girl after Constance's heart, Margaret Skinnider hit the bull's eye time and again. Her companions were unsurprised 'for Madame had accustomed them to expect good marksmanship in a woman'.

There is no doubt Con was as willing to have these boys sacrifice themselves for the cause as she was to sacrifice herself. 'Giving one's life for Ireland' was a phrase that fell easily from her lips; she could not think of a nobler end for herself or anybody else. But to Con that was not the end; her faith in eternity was quite literal. If she and her Fianna were killed they would be translated in some mystical but

70

perfectly solid form to a Heaven where they could resume life in a gleeful, endless jamboree.

In the meantime the poorer boys found a haven in her home such as few of them could have known elsewhere. Surrey House was full of books, according to Margaret Skinnider, and as equally full of boys from ten years old upwards

either studying hard or sliding down the banisters . . . She took a real interest in the personal problems of the boys. I was staying with her at Christmas (1915) when she was teaching a boy to sing. He was slowly going blind and nothing could save his sight but she was determined he should have a livelihood. If any of the boys were sick she brought them over to Surrey House to nurse them herself.

Con admitted to Desmond Fitzgerald, afterwards Minister of External Affairs in the Free State Cabinet, that there were times when organising the Fianna was such hard work that she was almost hopeless.

A branch would start up spontaneously, crowded with enthusiastic kids, all wanting to start fighting at once, and then they would gradually disappear one by one when they found they were not to go out fighting the English the next week. But out of each branch started, a couple of really sincere, clever boys would come to the surface and these boys formed the nucleus of the real Fianna.

By their first anniversary conference – and somehow Con got the Mayor of Dublin's permission to hold it at the Mansion House – the secretary, Pádraic Ó Riain, was able to report that besides five *sluaite* in Dublin there was one in Waterford and one in Glasgow. Sir Roger Casement, then in the British diplomatic corps, sent £10 to buy 'kilts for the boys'.

The advent of one young man, Liam Mellowes, helped to make the Fianna the nationwide organisation it eventually became. He turned up on Con's doorstep one day, prepared to give up his job in Dublin and set out on his bicycle to start up *sluaite* all over Ireland if she would give him thirty shillings to begin with and guarantee him ten shillings a week in case he needed to buy food and sleeping accommodation which he did not think he would because sympathisers would provide board and lodging. It says much for his powers of persuasion and her judgement of character that she agreed, although it was a lot to find from her over-stretched purse. He became one of her ablest lieutenants, later helping organise the Irish Volunteers. In 1916 he was put in charge of the Rising in the West, became a representative of Meath in the Dáil Éireann and a Director of Purchases for the Republican Army. He was executed by the Free State Government in 1922.

Bulmer Hobson suspected Mellowes of being a member of the Irish Republican Brotherhood and that his journeyings for the Fianna cloaked a recruitment drive for the IRB. Liam Mellowes was certainly in the Brotherhood later and Bulmer Hobson was in it long before he met Con, but each might have been unaware of the other's membership because the IRB was a very secret organisation indeed. Had an ordinary Irishman been questioned about it, he would have said that the IRB had been brought into existence in the 1850s to establish an independent democratic republic in Ireland by armed revolt but that it had died with the Fenians and was now defunct.

He would have been nearly right. By 1907 the Brotherhood had degenerated in the main into a collection of elderly men doing little for the movement. Their function had been more or less usurped by Sinn Féin. However, a group of young men in Ulster, among them Bulmer Hobson, had been reviving the IRB. And, after a long period of imprisonment for his part in the dynamiting campaign in the 1880s, followed by a stay in America, an old IRB man had returned to Dublin who looked not back but forwards; Tom Clarke, who was to be the first signatory on the proclamation of the Irish Republic in 1916. The tobacconist's shop he took over in North Great Britain Street became a nationalist reading room and meeting place to which Con was a frequent visitor. She liked his eyes: 'You noticed how kindly they were.' They may have looked kindly on Constance, of whom they approved, but they gazed on British rule with hatred and impatience.

In 1909 Arthur Griffith began to hold his political fire since it seemed that at last Redmond and the Irish Parliamentary Party were making headway in getting a Home Rule Bill passed and Griffith did not want to jeopardise their chances. Those like Con and Tom Clarke, to whom Home Rule was a contemptuous crumb from the rich man's table, fumed at the new Sinn Féin policy and there were inflamed exchanges at meetings. Dr Patrick McCartan wrote to John Devoy, an old Fenian who ran the extreme Irish republican organisation, Clan na Gael, in the States, in March 1910: 'Things here are in a queer mess ... McCullough, Countess Markievicz talk of the advisability of all clearing out of it and leaving them to go their own way ... So you see there is not much hope.'

The problem was there seemed no other clearly defined way to go. However, the younger men of the Irish Republican Brotherhood like Bulmer Hobson, now back in Dublin, Denis McCullough and Maud Gonne's husband, Major John MacBride, backed by Tom Clarke, made a concentrated bid to take over the control of the IRB's Supreme

Council, which consisted of seven representatives from Ireland, England and Scotland and four others chosen by, and known only to, the seven. By 1910 they had made sufficient headway to get the Supreme Council to finance a paper, *Irish Freedom*, mainly written by Bulmer Hobson and the journalist, P. S. O'Hegarty, to advocate 'the independence of Ireland by every practicable means, including the use of physical force'. (The paper was banned by the British Government in 1914 but by then circumstances had brought the Irish Volunteers into existence and things were on the move.)

Also by this time, and now that Con had done the groundwork and shown the potential of young Ireland, the Irish Republican Brotherhood began to pay attention to the Fianna.

'The IRB took no part in its [the Fianna's] promotion,' wrote Bulmer Hobson, 'and was not consulted regarding it. It was, nevertheless, my aim to recruit suitable members of the New Fianna into the IRB.' In 1911 Hobson formed a separate branch of the IRB known as the John Mitchel Circle for members of the Fianna who were over the age of seventeen and whom he considered good material. Since the young men retained their original membership it meant that the Fianna, like every other nationalist organisation, was infiltrated, and had its policy partly shaped, by the IRB.

Con was aware of the situation and disliked it. Clandestine organisations were not at all in her line, especially those which cloaked their activities from their own side. It was galling to have done the spadework on her idea and see it taken up and manipulated by men who now saw what a good idea it was. Then again, the IRB was anti-feminist. Bulmer Hobson said that Maud Gonne was the only woman permitted to join the Brotherhood, although Diarmuid Lynch, another member of the pre-1916 Supreme Council, indicated that there were some women members outside Dublin – which shows the confusion caused by the IRB's extreme secrecy. At the Fianna Convention of 1912 Con and two of James Connolly's daughters, Nora and Ina, demanded the admittance of girls into the Fianna. The IRB influence was evident in the fierce opposition to the motion which was eventually carried, though only by one vote. But the same influence seems to have prevented the girls' Fianna, the Clan Maeve, ever flourishing, except in Glasgow and, especially, in Belfast which at that time was the Connollys' home territory.

To the younger boys, who knew nothing of a secret caucus, and to the rest of Ireland, however, it was always Madame's Fianna, and they were right; the spirit of disciplined enthusiasm which motivated the Fianna came from her.

Assessing the contribution to a nation's war effort by the financial,

73

auxiliary, nursing, secretarial, morale-giving support of women's and youth groups is difficult, mainly because they have never had to be assessed; they have always been able to be taken for granted. To say, as many did at the time, that without the Fianna there would have been no Volunteers and therefore no Easter 1916, is probably not true and anyway cannot be quantified. But what distinguished 1916 from other Irish rebellions was that, despite the hundreds of things that went wrong, it was not a farce. The British had been forced to take it seriously, had brought in artillery, and diverted a large body of troops needed in the war against Germany to quell it. Had it gone according to plan, it would have been a near thing; the army knew it and was scared into taking reprisals which turned against the authorities a population which had been comparatively neutral. And much of the professionalism of the Irish fighters *can* be credited to the Fianna; when untrained men enlisted in the Volunteers they found waiting for them Fianna-trained drillmasters and disciplined handlers of guns who could teach them to shoot straight. They also found a morale that raised their own and others; a farmer told Margaret Skinnider that he'd had no faith in a Rising until he came across a uniformed Countess and the Fianna on manoeuvres.

There was a story current after the Rising told by Margaret Skinnider and others – and if it is apocryphal it still shows the status the Fianna had acquired in folklore – that for three days after everybody else had surrendered or been rounded up, accurate sniper fire from a Dublin rooftop continued to hold off a British troop. Eventually reinforcements were brought up and the snipers' position stormed. They were discovered to be three boys, all under sixteen years old.

'Who taught you to shoot like that?' asked the British captain.

'Countess Markievicz.'

'I wish she'd taught my men,' said the captain.

74

Chapter Six

The Countess Markievicz's public appearances in Ascendancy circles were now confined to occasions on which she could literally flaunt her new colours – in 1911, during the mourning period for the death of King Edward VII, she turned up among the totally black-clad audience at a theatre wearing a bright red velvet dress – and it was obviously only a matter of time before she proved her betrayal to her class by being arrested.

Desmond Ryan recorded an image of Con at a meeting of Sinn Féin's Drumcondra Branch during this period:

> Madame de Markievicz sat in the middle of the room, pensive and beautiful with a costly lace collar draping her shoulders, ready to explode into the most unconvincingly bloodthirsty sentiments . . . but speaking with a gentle charm to any one who approached her in private. She was, although her fury expressed in such polite accents had a comic aspect, a very courageous woman for she had broken with all her friends and immediate circle to champion an obscure movement.

Her fury was caused by Arthur Griffith's policy of sitting back at this time to allow John Redmond and his Parliamentary Party to pursue Home Rule. Redmond's demand, which he had put before the electorate during the General Election of 1910, had become modest: 'A policy which, while explicitly safeguarding the supremacy and indefeasible authority of the Imperial Parliament, will set up in Ireland a system of full self-government in regard to purely Irish affairs.' It was a platform calculated to allay the fears of Unionists but did nothing for the fears of nationalist separatists, a body he regarded as insignificant. As Dorothy Macardle, whose *The Irish Republic* (1937) became the standard history of the establishing of the Irish State, wrote: 'He knew Ireland too little and the English House of Commons too well.' He seemed vindicated, however, by the results of what he called 'the Great Home Rule Election' because they gave his party control of the balance of power; the passing of the Home Rule seemed inevitable. An Irish Parliament must surely sit in Dublin before the end of 1913.

To militants like Con it was obvious that they were being ignored because of their low profile. They should be seen to be protesting, and the occasion which presented itself as likely to get maximum publicity was the State visit to be made to Dublin in July 1911 by the new King George V and Queen Mary.

Sinn Féin was divided on what its response to the visit should be. Like nearly every other influential nationalist organisation at that time, it had been infiltrated by members of the Irish Republican Brotherhood, and the Brotherhood, for reasons which are still not clear, had decided that the royal visit should not be opposed, just ignored. During a Sinn Féin meeting called to discuss the subject, Tom Clarke tipped off Dr Patrick McCartan that the Brotherhood element was playing political games and did not want protests along the route when the King and Queen passed by. McCartan, sitting next to Con, immediately scribbled a resolution demanding that Sinn Féin *should* protest. He showed it to Con, who said: 'For God's sake do, and I'll second it.' Knowing her unpopularity with the older, more conservative, members of the Brotherhood, McCartan advised her not to. He jumped up and proposed the motion, Tom Clarke quickly seconded and it was passed 'with a whoop'.

A committee was formed to co-ordinate opposition to the visit, which Arthur Griffith agreed to head, though he wanted none of the vulgarity that Con was advocating, such as soap box orators along the processional route. Con remembered him turning to Michael O'Rahilly, descendant of the head of his clan and therefore known as The O'Rahilly, and saying: 'Surely, O'Rahilly, we must stand on our dignity,' and O'Rahilly smiling and saying: 'Well, if we go on standing on our dignity much longer, we soon won't have anything else left to stand on.' Griffith, said Con, was 'always in great dread of a riot'. The O'Rahilly was not; with Con he spent hours on his knees stencilling out a gigantic banner which read: 'Thou are not conquered yet, dear land' and was eventually strung on poles at the foot of Grafton Street. The Fianna's antiquated printing press churned out handbills which the Inghínidhe were to distribute along the route. They reek of Con's style:

Today another English Monarch visits Ireland. When will Ireland regain the Legislature which is by everyone granted to be her mere right? Never! as long as Irish men and women stand in the streets of Dublin to cheer the King of England and crawl to those who oppress and rob her. God Save Ireland.

On the day of the actual Coronation in London the committee organised an enormous nationalist meeting in Beresford Place which was attended by a crowd estimated at 30,000 and at which the speakers

76

included Con, the O'Rahilly, John MacBride, Patrick McCartan, Arthur Griffith, Cathal Brugha and James Connolly. In the crowd that day was a certain Eamon de Valera, who later told McCartan it was the first time he had heard an Irish Republic advocated, and that he went home thinking it was a fine ideal, but not likely to be attained.

With Griffith the IRB had organised a large expedition to Wolfe Tone's grave at Bodenstown for the day of the State visit thus keeping, first, their dignity, and, second, out of the way 'all the turbulent young men who might possibly make a disturbance'. Bulmer Hobson, newly returned from Belfast, joined 'the Bodenstown crowd' to Con's disgust: 'He was one of those who preferred the limelight and laurels to be won by a fierce speech at a rebel's graveside to the possibility of getting a hammering from the police or being arrested.'

Because of IRB secrecy it is still difficult to know if there was some devious plan behind *not* disrupting the visit, whether they were even then planning the Rising and did not want to attract attention or, like Griffith, afraid of making fools of themselves. So, not being in their confidence, it was the turbulent young women and the Fianna who stayed in Dublin on July 8 to protest. Con later wrote:

> Most of the crowd had Union Jacks and were very loyal. We had a black flag, and as soon as the procession was audible . . . we produced it and began to hand out our bills. We timed it well, for just as the first carriage came along the row started. It was a very tame one. An irate old 'gentleman' started whacking me with the stick on which his flag was mounted, but my back is pretty stiff and the stick broke almost at once. However, it created a disturbance and the same sort of little disturbances occurred all down the line of the route so we congratulated ourselves . . . The Unionists were quite tolerant and amused at our audacity. Everything had been so tame for so many years that they had come to believe that they had succeeded in pacifying Ireland. They never dreamed that there was anything more in it than a little spark from the ashes of a dead idea.

To Helena Moloney went the distinction of being the first nationalist woman of her generation to be arrested for the cause. She had spotted an irresistible target in an oculist's window where the lenses of an enormous pair of spectacles displayed pictures of King George and Queen Mary, and had chucked stones at them. She was imprisoned for a month when she refused to pay her fine.

Her release was celebrated in August by a demonstration in Beresford Place. The Socialist Party of Ireland, to which Helena now belonged, provided a lorry as the platform. Francis Sheehy Skeffington made a speech of welcome, peaceably, and Con made another, much less so. Con said that everything was orderly at first.

Miss Moloney was speaking when the police took exception to something she said and charged the platform. [What Helena had said was that George V was the worst scoundrel in Europe.] . . . I stood up from where I was sitting at the table scribbling notes and a policeman . . . made a grab at my ankles . . . another seized me from behind. He picked me up and literally threw me into the arms of a policeman standing on the ground, who luckily caught me, so I was not hurt. I was never so taken by surprise in my life.

She was dragged through the stampeding crowd to Store Street police station with a small Fianna boy following all the way kicking at the legs of her captors and shouting: 'Ah, you devils, ah you brutes.'

Con was not displeased by her arrest, although she was cross that the charge of throwing dust and pebbles at the police was not true. The only other person charged, Helena, was accused of 'degrading the king in speeches'. They were kept in the police station all day while a crowd cheered them from outside. Arthur Griffith supported them on the principle that free speech was being threatened and brought in lawyers for their defence, though Con wanted to conduct her own. They were found guilty but released without a fine. Obviously the authorities wanted no sympathy extended to nationalist harpies, but they could do nothing about the publicity over the arrest of a countess. The papers had a field day. As far as most nationalists were concerned Con had won her spurs: to everyone else she had become notorious. The *Sligo Champion* reported in full this beginning of what was to be a long police record, to the distress of her family at Lissadell who, presumably, brought pressure to bear on their local paper since it carried no further mention of her activities – apart from an almost passing reference in 1916 – until 1917, when public opinion changed and Con became Sligo's famed daughter. (Con and Casi were at Lissadell for Christmas in that year of 1911, but as far as the Gore-Booths were concerned goodwill was being strained to the limit.)

The royals had either ignored or been unaware of the disturbances caused by their visit, for their telegram of thanks to Lord Aberdeen said that 'the hearty cheers of the Irish people' were still ringing in their ears.

Con summed up the visit with one of her better pieces of writing:

So the king passed. Red streamers floated from pole to pole and red paper flowers danced in the wind, red flags, red carpets everywhere. But he passed, too, through sad, grey slums where . . . a dispossessed people huddled together in misery . . . looked at all the splendour and saw nothing but red. Red through a grey mist.

She herself had begun to see everything from behind that same mist of the slums; it was as if she had wandered through the political

78

labyrinth after the little girl who had exposed the hollowness of her life by jumping up on her carriage to beg, and now, while keeping tight hold of the threads to other parts of the maze, had finally discovered the child's world and, from here on, her own baseline.

It was a terrible place. The poet, Gerard Manley Hopkins, had been disturbed by conditions in the slums when he was Professor of Classics in Dublin in the 1880s and, if anything, they were worse now. In the north of the city with its rampant tuberculosis, the death rate of 27.6 per cent compared unfavourably with Calcutta's, infested by cholera. It could make the dreary claim of having the worst housing conditions in Europe; the number of families who lived in only one room was 20,000 while of 5,000 two-roomed tenements 1,500 were condemned. (In 1913 two four-storey tenements collapsed, killing seven of their occupants and injuring others.) Many of the buildings had been beautiful homes for the gentry before they retired to residences south of the Liffey, an irony not lost on Margaret Skinnider when Con, now a familiar visitor to such places, was showing her round.

> 'What I really want to see,' I told her, 'is the poorest part of Dublin, the *poorest* part.' She took me to Ash Street. I do not believe there is a worse place in the world than Ash Street ... in a hollow full of sewage and refuse, not paved, and as full of holes as if it had been under shellfire. Some houses had fallen down, others were shored up at the side with beams. I found the poor among the ruins of grandeur. In one erstwhile drawing room four families lived, one to each corner without even sometimes a curtain for partition, under a ceiling of wonderfully modelled and painted figures. There was a pure white marble mantel over a fireplace, blocked up except for a small opening in which a few coals might be burning. Doors are often of solid mahogany, fifteen feet high. No sanitary arrangements, water from a single tap in the backyard or a dark, unventilated basement for the use of everybody. Starvation always hovering.

The Gas Company refused to fit pipes above the second floor so in the higher storeys meat was boiled because the fireplaces were too primitive for roasting and baking. That is, if meat was obtainable, which Margaret Skinnider said was only once a week. For the rest of the time it was 'Bread and tea for breakfast, potatoes sometimes with cabbage for lunch, bread and tea for supper.'

It was possible to live in Dublin and ignore its misery; it was even possible to be a nationalist and ignore it. James Connolly attacked those who did when he wrote:

> The man who is bubbling over with love and affection for 'Ireland' and can pass unmoved through our streets and witness all the sorrow and suffering ... without

burning to end it, is a fraud and a liar in his heart, no matter how much he loves that combination of chemical elements he is pleased to call 'Ireland'.

But not if you were someone like Constance Markievicz and certainly not if you were chief to whole gangs of undersized, underfed little boys who lived in such rat holes. This was not the poverty that had existed in the countryside and had seemed to the Gore-Booths as immutable as Ben Bulben. This crowded, urban poverty smacked of manufacture and was especially unbearable to Con, staring at her, as it did, through the skeletons of houses such as she had stayed in during her debutante days. She could not miss the symbolism of their elegant frontages screening the horror of what lay behind.

The effect on her was devastating. These people had been the responsibility of her class and had been abandoned. Behind her continued charity from then until the end of her life is not just the kindness of a human being to another in need, but a form of atonement. When she took her comforts into the slums, cooked dinners, paid rents, planted flowers, she was no Lady Bountiful: she was trying to right a wrong. Her new home, Surrey House, became a refuge not only for the Fianna but Jacobs Biscuit Factory girls who had been made redundant and anybody else who wanted help. She became poorer by the minute, had her shoes mended over and over again rather than buying new ones, took trams rather than cabs. At one point she literally gave away the shirt off her back; she was seen one hot day with her tweed jacket pulled together by a safety pin, having taken off her blouse to give to a woman who needed it more.

Hefty political action was the only way to cure the slums; Con knew it and took it, but the small, personal acts went on in her individual war to make things better.

The first political move against poverty Con helped to co-ordinate was over the matter of school meals. By this time the Inghínidhe na hÉireann had begun to break up as its more powerful members became absorbed into either Sinn Féin or the Labour movement – or, like Con, into both – and was only convened for specific activities such as opposition to the royal visit. Maud Gonne was badly missed; she was now apprehensive about leaving her home in France for Ireland in case John MacBride should manage to get custody of their son, Seán. The marriage had been dissolved in 1905, the year after the child was born, with publicity that had harmed the nationalist cause in which MacBride was an admired figure. She was forced to reveal that he got drunk and had knocked her about, and was herself hissed at an Abbey first night on her next visit. However, she continued to write for *Bean na hÉireann*, 'the ladies' paper that all young men read'.

The young men must have found it an education. Militancy, 'Learn to discipline and be disciplined, learn to shoot, learn to march, learn to scout, learn to give up all for Ireland' – this *must* have been Con – was interspersed with more subtle nationalism in feminist form, as in James Stephens' poem 'The Red-Haired Man's Wife' with its lovely last verse:

> I am separate still,
> I am I and not you;
> And my mind and my will,
> As in secret they grew
> Still are secret, unreached and untouched
> and not subject to you.

That the authorities did not ban it as they banned other nationalist papers advocating physical force is probably because they could not believe the threat of a publication where an article on street-fighting advising: 'The first thing is to break all the street lamps, leaving the district in total darkness. Then ropes and wires are stretched across the street . . .,' was printed side by side with another beginning: 'How perfectly lovely are the hats this season . . .'

The Inghínidhe kept their exiled founder in touch with what was going on in her home country and in 1910 Maud's article had dealt with the undernourishment of its working-class children. Local authorities in England had been enabled to provide meals for school-children by an act of 1906, but such enablement had not been extended to Ireland, and no council could legally go ahead with such a scheme until it was. *Bean na hÉireann* announced the Inghínidhe's intention of shaming the authorities into taking responsibility for children's care by setting up school meals canteens in the poorer areas themselves. The Irish Women's Franchise League immediately offered its help. No male-run nationalist organisation seems to have come forward – child starvation was obviously a woman's concern.

It must have been gall and wormwood for the Inghínidhe on the combined committee that resulted, because they had to abandon nationalist principle and help to lobby every Irish MP for an enabling bill for Ireland. They need not have bothered: they got the usual answer – 'Wait for Home Rule.'

Helena Moloney took a socialist stance in her column 'A Worker' and pointed out that such charity let the government off the hook, but it did not stop her, or Con, working in the canteens of those National Schools that permitted their help, alongside Maud – she had risked a visit to Ireland for the project – Hanna Sheehy Skeffington, the Gifford sisters and Kathleen Clarke, whose husband was Tom Clarke.

Some church-run schools, however, refused their aid because it came from such notorious women.

It must have been a busy time for Hanna Sheehy Skeffington, whose Irish Women's Franchise League was taking part in the renewed suffragette militancy in England, and thirteen of whose members were imprisoned with hard labour in London between November 1910 and March 1912. Hanna herself demonstrated for the vote at a large meeting in Belfast where Winston Churchill was speaking. A male member of the audience, enraged at her audacity, manhandled her to the top of the stairs and threatened to throw her down. She took hold of his lapels: 'You come too,' she said.

It was a bill drafted by Hanna and presented to Parliament by Stephen Gwynn, MP, which eventually enabled councils to give school meals to children – but not until 1914. The women's exercise had been good for co-operation between the Irish Women's Franchise League and the Inghínidhe, very good for the children it fed and was soon to be especially valuable in keeping thousands of Dubliners, children and adults, alive by having taught Countess Markievicz the rudiments of food distribution on a mass scale, but it had not, as Con realised, reached the essential problem of low wages and unemployment.

In England, during the first dozen years of the decade, working-class conditions were gradually improving; the Liberal Government, which looked so oppressive from the other side of the Irish Sea, was achieving a remarkable series of reforms at home; school meals in 1906, school medical service in 1907, an eight-hour day for miners, a system of old-age pensions in 1908. In 1909 Winston Churchill initiated labour exchanges and tackled the horror of the sweated workshops. In 1911 Lloyd George sponsored the National Insurance Act.

Social welfare might have come on a wider scale if it had not been at the mercy of the Conservative-controlled House of Lords' veto, an axe that hung over Irish Home Rule if the Commons had dared to present it. Ironically, when the Liberals destroyed the Lords' veto in 1911, progressive legislation as good as stopped.

At the other end of the scale the working class was organising. Twenty-nine Labour MPs had been elected and trade union membership had doubled. So had strikes – with varying success. Government intervention in major disputes was even occasionally on the side of the workers, though Winston Churchill's propensity for using troops as he did against miners and dockers was such that 'it proved wiser to shift his abilities and imagination to the Admiralty'. Lloyd George, however, intervened during the national railway strike and forced the railway companies to use negotiating machinery for the first time; it may be that the threat of war, now hovering in Europe, was concentrating the government's mind on the need for industrial co-operation.

The Labour movement in Ireland, however, commanded less attention. It was the runt of the British Isles' litter, emerging later and remaining weaker than the others. Lack of industry, employment and the general poverty enfeebled it; situations in which a day labourer worked a seventy-hour week for fourteen shillings, knowing that if he didn't another would do it for a shilling less, and many a woman worked a ninety-hour week for five shillings for the same reason, were not favourable to concerted action. Then again, as always happened in Ireland, the nationalist issue obscured the path forward.

In the main the Irish parliamentary members represented the land-owning class, though there were three or four artisans among them. Until 1894 Irish trade unions had sheltered under the umbrella of the British TUC but in that year, believing that English unions could not understand the peculiar situation in Ireland and anyway had troubles of their own, a Trades Union Congress in Ireland was established, but still roughly half of its fifty biggest unions remained affiliated to their English counterparts, feeling that in collective bargaining they could only profit from alliance with a more powerful neighbour.

There were, however, pluses on the Irish side and one of them was James Connolly who in 1911 took over as Belfast organiser of the Irish Transport and General Workers' Union which had been founded three years earlier by Jim Larkin, who was the other plus for Irish labour or, perhaps, more of its exclamation mark. In Belfast, Larkin, then in his thirties, had galvanised dockers, carters, coalmen and even the Royal Irish Constabulary into pressing for better conditions – troops had been brought in to suppress a police mutiny – to such effect that Belfast employers were relieved when, in 1908, he had turned his attention to Cork and then Dublin, though they weren't made any happier by his successor, Connolly.

Con had heard about Larkin while she was still living at Belcamp Park and cycled into Dublin to hear him speak at a mass meeting in Beresford Place. She realised at once she was in the presence

of something I had never come across before, some great primaeval force rather than a man. It seemed as if his personality caught up, assimilated and threw back to the vast crowd that surrounded him every emotion that swayed them, every pain and joy that they had ever felt made articulate and sanctified.

She saw him through her artist's eye: 'Taller than most men, every line of him was in harmony with his personality . . . A Titan who might have been moulded by Michaelangelo or Rodin.'

She recognised a liberator

who changed the whole life of the workers in Dublin and the whole outlook of trade unionism in Ireland. He forced his own self-reliance and self-respect on them; forced them to be sober and made them class conscious and conscious of their nationality. From that day I looked upon Larkin as a friend and was out to do any little thing that I could to help him in his work, but it was only much later that I got a chance to do so.

The feeling was mutual. When Larkin took over Liberty Hall for the ITGWU he gave Con a permanent home in it for the Fianna. In 1911, with his sister, Delia, he founded the Irish Women Workers' Union which also had its headquarters at Liberty Hall. Con spoke at one of its earliest meetings, calling on the women members to become an army of fighters for Ireland as well as for better wages and the vote.

To Dublin Castle and the Ascendancy it seemed as if Larkin was something elemental and that he brought with him into Ireland from his native Liverpool a new and dangerous force that whipped skittishly along the streets of its cities sending its people mad. Gradually violence began re-establishing itself in Dublin after the stolid hiatus of the Edwardian period, ringing strange and vicious changes; during a workers' demonstration there was confrontation between police versus workers and crowd, when suffragettes demonstrated at Home Rule rallies it was crowd versus women, police and workers; members of the ITGWU frequently protected suffragettes at meetings.

The blooding of the women came first. By 1912 it had become obvious that the Irish Parliamentary Party was not just fobbing off suffrage for women with 'Wait for Home Rule' but actively intended 'Home Rule for Men'. A huge meeting was held in Dublin in June 1912 attended by suffragists, militant and non-militant, nationalists and trade union women from all over Ireland. Con was on the platform with Delia Larkin and messages of support were received from Francis Sheehy Skeffington, James Connolly, Maud Gonne and AE. Its unanimous resolution called on the government 'to amend the Home Rule Bill by adopting the Local Government Register [which included women] as the basis for the new Parliament'. Copies were sent to each Cabinet member and to all Irish MPs, and were ignored by all. The Irish Women's Franchise League declared war.

So far Ireland had been left out of the militancy which had become common in England, but on June 13, 1912 eight suffragettes, including

Hanna Sheehy Skeffington, were arrested for breaking windows in the GPO, the Custom House and Dublin Castle. They were tried, fined, refused the fine, and imprisoned.

With Prime Minister Asquith due to visit Dublin on July 18, the Establishment became alarmed. Respectable newspapers published editorials warning suffragettes not to interfere with the visit, as well as letters putting the Home Rule supporters' view that harsh measures should be used if they did, such as 'whips on the shoulders of those unsexed viragoes . . . slender, springy, stinging riding whips'.

Unknown to the IWFL – and to its subsequent indignation – three militant suffragettes from England had travelled to Dublin to disrupt the Asquith visit. As the Prime Minister and John Redmond went past in a carriage one of them threw a hatchet which missed Asquith but grazed Redmond's ear. Another of their number attempted arson at the empty Theatre Royal where Asquith was due to speak. The Englishwomen were arrested and were found to have explosives in their possession.

'Reign of Terror,' cried the newspapers, and 'Dastardly Outrage'. Though the IWFL denied any knowledge of the incidents, suffragettes became overnight marked as man-hating, home-wrecking, Home-Rule-undermining hags with (this was one Catholic view) a desire for 'easily obtained divorce'. At a meeting the IWFL had organised in the open air at Beresford Place to coincide with the Asquith visit, a mob collected. Police had to escort the women through it with drawn batons. One suffragette was nearly thrown into the Liffey. By this time the crowd had decided that every respectably-dressed woman was a suffragette and, according to Katharine Tynan, the poet and novelist, 'the women were hunted like rats in the city'. Con was one of a group of women attacked at Eden Quay and she was badly mauled before she could reach at last the shelter of Liberty Hall.

Two of the three English suffragettes – Mary Leigh and Gladys Evans – were sentenced to five years' penal servitude and the third, Lizzie Baker, to seven months' hard labour. They all promptly went on hunger strike, to be followed in sympathy by the Irish imprisoned suffragettes, the first women to use that particular weapon in Ireland. Lizzie Baker was released on health grounds, but the other two Englishwomen were forcibly fed for forty-six days and fifty-eight days respectively. The authorities, however, did not make the same mistake with Hanna and the other Irish prisoners, refusing to duplicate the horror and martyrdom which was obtained by its use in England. The outcry against the forcible feeding of Mary Leigh and Gladys Evans showed them they were right in not using it and it was dropped as an option for the rest of the suffragette campaign, though sixty-two Irish

MPs endorsed its use in a vote of confidence in the government's forcible feeding policy.

Failed by their constitutional representatives, as Con had told them they would be, the suffragettes found Labour to have been their most consistent support – though in the following black year of 1913, it was Labour that needed theirs.

Larkin had been able to use the strike weapon to get effective wage increases for his dockers. He brought agricultural workers into his union and at harvest time they were able to force the farmers into paying them 'the princely sum of 17s for a 66-hour week'. The membership of the ITGWU rose from 4,000 in 1911 to 8,000 in 1912 and 10,000 in 1913. Larkin turned his attention to what seemed a natural recruiting ground, the Dublin United Tramways Co. But now the irresistible force met the immovable object; the tramways were owned by William Martin Murphy, a former MP, one of those who had turned on Parnell for his involvement in the O'Shea divorce. He was probably the richest man in Ireland, had pioneered tramways and electric railways in different countries, owned hotels and stores and the Irish Independent newspaper group – and was the stiffening in the backbone of the Dublin Employers' Federation. It was not that he was a low payer by the standards of the time, but his employment methods were harsh; he had two categories for his workers, permanent and casual. If a permanent man was late, or absent for any reason, or broke any other Murphy rule, his place was immediately taken by a man at the top of the casual list while he himself went to its bottom. To such a man, Larkinism was anathema; and he was determined to destroy it. Employees who belonged to the ITGWU were dismissed and replaced by non-union men. He prevailed on his fellow employers to follow suit and even to ask their workers to sign a declaration of loyalty. The Master Builders' Association was among those who dismissed anybody who would not sign an undertaking never to join the ITGWU. One of those who refused was a labourer, who later turned to writing plays, called Sean O'Casey.

At 9.40 a.m. on Tuesday, August 26, 1913, when Dublin was crammed with visitors for the Horse Show Week, the trams stopped wherever they happened to be. Conductors and drivers put on their Red Hand of Ulster badges (the ITGWU symbol) and walked away from vehicles and baffled passengers.

Immediately Murphy got on to his Federation, urging its members to lock out their employees. By September 22 some 25,000 Dublin men and women were locked out of work, regardless of which union they belonged to. The employers were out to break not only the ITGWU but the right of workers to organise; they were to be starved into submission, as Keir Hardie told a meeting of workers in Dublin, adding: 'Most of you have served too long an apprenticeship to starvation to be much afraid of that.'

Larkin and four colleagues were arrested and charged with seditious libel and conspiracy but were allowed out on bail. At the next night's meeting outside Liberty Hall Larkin set fire to the proclamation which banned the mass rally of workers which had been set for the following Sunday, August 31, in O'Connell Street, promising that he would be there whatever happened. 'I recognise no law but the people's law. We are going to raise a new standard of discontent and a new battle-cry in Ireland.' Immediately a second warrant for his arrest was issued, but Jim Larkin had gone underground.

His hiding place was Surrey House, Leinster Road. It no longer seemed odd to anybody that a wanted Marxist should choose to lie low at the suburban home of a count and countess, not even to the police; by this time detectives had it under surveillance. Obviously they had not sufficient evidence that Larkin was inside to get a warrant for entry: presumably they were watching the houses of all known subversives. Con regarded it as an honour.

Casi, who had been on his annual visit to the Ukraine, was due back, so Con held a welcome home party for him. The watching detectives were confused by the suspect house being brilliantly lit and filled with what Padraic Colum called 'a carefree Bohemian gathering'. Luckily the situation of having a hunted man in his house was right up Casi's theatrical street and he threw himself into the plan of smuggling Larkin out to the promised Sunday meeting. In those days of amateur dramatics and charades, dressing-up came as second nature. The year before, to get into an Asquith meeting and heckle for Votes for Women, Francis Sheehy Skeffington had dressed up as a clergyman. Perhaps Con recalled the incident now; anyway, a room was booked for Sunday at the Imperial Hotel in the name of the Reverend Donnelly and his niece.

They would probably have picked the Imperial Hotel anyway, for the second-floor balcony overlooking O'Connell Street was ideal for their purpose, but the fact that it belonged to Mr William Martin Murphy made it irresistible.

Sean O'Casey, who was there, described O'Connell Street that Sunday morning as being black with people swaying back and forth as they waited for Larkin to materialise somewhere in it.

There's a funeral to come along, said a voice at Sean's elbow, an' when th' hearse gets to the middle of th' crowd, Jim'll pop up outa th' coffin and say his say. – No, no, another voice replied: as a matter of fact, he's stealin' up th' river in a boat. –

87

Couldn't be that way, answered still a third, for the quays are crawlin' with polis. Scan shivered, for he was not a hero, and he felt it was unwise to have come here.

A taxi drew up at the Imperial Hotel entrance and an elderly, bowed and bearded clergyman dressed in frock coat and striped trousers which actually belonged to a Polish count – one of the few people with clothes to fit Larkin – debouched attended by a solicitous young woman. This was Nellie Gifford, sister of Sidney Gifford, still writing as John Brennan; her presence was necessary to forestall any question which might be addressed to her 'uncle' – Larkin had Irish parents but had been brought up in Liverpool and had a marked Scouse accent.

O'Casey goes on:

> There he is! suddenly shouted a dozen voices near Sean. Goin' to speak from the window of the very hotel owned by Martin Murphy himself! and there right enough, framed in an upper window, was a tall man in clerical garb, and when he swept the beard from his chin, the crowd saw their own beloved leader, Jim Larkin.

Unnoticed, or unmentioned, by O'Casey, Con had arrived in a car with Casi, Sidney Gifford and Helena Moloney. Somebody in the crowd recognised her and called on her to give a speech as well. Up above them Larkin had only managed to get out a few words before being jumped by police and taken off the balcony. Con managed to call out, 'Three cheers for Jim Larkin' and then the baton charge by the police, which was to put August 31, 1913 down in Dublin history as Bloody Sunday, began.

Con always maintained afterwards that the police were drunk and that they attacked not to disperse but to kill. 'They assemble on four sides and, on a given signal, rush towards the centre . . . use their batons like shillelaghs, swinging them around and around before bringing them down on the heads of people.' Other witnesses, O'Casey among them, also maintained the police were drunk and didn't care whether or not their batons crushed bone. 'Although the police were instructed to hit the shoulders of the people, they always struck at the top or the base of the skull,' he wrote and went on to give an account of that day's panic and brutality which still makes the hands sweat to read.

Other writers give other views. In a book called *Disturbed Dublin*, written in 1914, a Mr Arnold Wright said that later on the police themselves were attacked: 'Women with dishevelled hair and looking like maniacs were even more persistent than the men and youths in belabouring the police.'

No doubt old scores were settled – this was not the first baton charge since the trouble began – but while forty-five police were injured, 433 civilians were treated in hospital and two of them died.

Con only had time to wish Larkin luck as he was escorted out of the Imperial Hotel entrance:

> As I turned to pass down O'Connell Street the inspector on Larkin's right hit me on the nose and mouth with his clenched fist. I reeled against another policeman, who pulled me about, tearing all the buttons off my blouse, and tearing it out all round my waist. He then threw me back into the middle of the street, where all the police had begun to run, several of them kicking and hitting at me as they passed ... I could not get out of the crowd of police and at last one hit me a back-hand blow across the left side of my face with his baton. I fell back against the corner of a shop, when another policeman started to seize me by the throat, but I was pulled out of the crowd by some men, who took me down Sackville Place and into a house to stop the blood flowing from my nose and mouth, and to try and tidy my blouse.

Casi was outraged not only by the attack on his wife but by the general unprovoked savagery of the police whom he saw 'batoning the terror-struck passers-by who had taken refuge in the doorways'. Being who he was, he went straight to the Under-Secretary in Dublin Castle to complain and also informed the foreign press.

Lenin, who was a close watcher of the Irish scene at this time, denounced the police action and added: 'People are thrown into prison for making the most peaceful speeches.' Nobody but Lenin could have called Jim Larkin's speeches peaceful, but James Connolly, who had come down from Belfast, had been arrested merely, it seems, for being James Connolly and being present in Beresford Place when Jim Larkin was burning the proclamation. He went on hunger strike and, like Larkin, was released fairly quickly and recuperated in Surrey House. He stayed on in Dublin to help organise the lock-out relief work, and insisted on paying the Markieviczes ten shillings a week for his keep.

In London, the *Daily Herald* newspaper organised a huge meeting in Larkin's support at the Albert Hall. One of those who spoke at it was George Bernard Shaw: 'If you put a policeman on the footing of a mad dog, it can only end in one way, and that is that all respectable men will have to arm themselves. I suggest that you should arm yourselves with something which should put a decisive stop to the proceedings of the police.' It was not the first time that the idea of an Irish Citizen Army had been suggested, but Bloody Sunday was perhaps the greatest factor in bringing it about.

In the meantime something had to be done to stop 25,000 workers and their families from starving to death. Several organisations did relief work in Dublin that autumn and winter, but the greatest of all took place at Liberty Hall and the most lovingly remembered of all those in charge of it was the Countess Markievicz.

Money and food came in from well-wishers all over Great Britain; on September 26, SS *Hare* sailed in from Manchester with £5,000 worth of bread, potatoes, butter, sugar, tea, etc., bought by British Unions through the Co-operative Wholesale Society. It was unloaded by cheering dockers and distributed in parcels at Liberty Hall as workers turned up for their strike pay. But it became apparent that individual families would not be able to afford the fuel for hot meals and that catering could be better done large scale. Teams of locked-out girls from Jacobs Biscuit Factory peeled vegetables while locked-out men fetched water and stoked boilers for the gallons of soup based on the bacon bones Con begged from the Co-op.

Upstairs corridors and rooms became stacked with donated clothing and out-of-work seamstresses worked in shifts to do the necessary alterations. Literally hundreds of people helped the Liberty Hall welfare programme but almost all contemporary accounts put Con as the leading spirit; she was by now a first-class organiser with a network of contacts to rival Maud Gonne's and she was tireless. Milk depots, clothing distribution centres and soup kitchens were set up all over the city. She brought in Hanna Sheehy Skeffington and her suffragettes as helpers and the sight of their orange and green sashes advanced the cause of women's suffrage. She recruited bands of workers to go to the homes of those asking for help to see what was necessary. When it became apparent that mothers were giving their soup and food parcels to their children and leaving none for themselves, she set aside a dining room where they had meals under supervision to make sure they ate. Padraic Colum says she left home every morning for months at eight a.m. not returning until eight p.m. – and frequently she went on to a meeting after that. 'Many of the men working under her broke down with the strain but she continued until the struggle was over.'

She was in her element, she arranged treats for the children, she sang rebel songs, she was happy in actively doing something about the general misery in a greater endeavour which might one day abolish it altogether. A trade union leader, Harry Gosling, remembered her working all day long, her sleeves rolled up, smoking, never failing in energy, spirits and resource. She had found contentment; being Con, she showed it, and perhaps the only man in Ireland who begrudged it to her was Sean O'Casey.

O'Casey was a dramatic genius, although at that point he had not begun writing plays, and a difficult man. He managed to find reasons for disliking Con and was to leave the Citizen Army in a sulk because men whom he admired, Connolly, Larkin, and Captain Jack White, refused to expel her from it; just as later he abandoned Ireland because Dublin audiences, somewhat short-sightedly, did not like his plays. But he would have resented her anyway; when he looked at Con, he saw Lissadell and refused to believe his eyes if they saw anything else.

In 1945, when Con had been dead eighteen years, he published the third of his autobiographies, *Drums Under the Window*, and in it exploded 'the myth' of Countess Markievicz in one of the most extraordinary attacks ever made on a woman who had been on the same side as the attacker.

In all the time he had pushed a way through a crowd of ragged women, and ragged children, . . . he had never seen the Countess doing anything anyone could call a spot of work . . . Whenever a reporter from an English or an Irish journal strayed into the Hall and cocked an eye over the scene, there was the Countess in spotless bib and tucker, standing in the steam, a gigantic ladle in her hand . . . She usually whirled into a meeting, and whirled out again, a spluttering Catherine-wheel of irresponsibility . . . No part of her melted into the cause of Ireland, nor did she ever set a foot on the threshold of Socialism. She looked at the names over the doors, and then thought she was one of the family. But the movements were no more to her than the hedges over which her horses jumped . . . Then she pounced on Connolly and dazzled his eyes with her flashy enthusiasm . . . yet she never reached the rank of failure, for she hadn't the constitution to keep long enough at anything in which, at the end, she could see a success or a failure facing her. One thing she had in abundance – physical courage: with that she was clothed as with a garment. She wasn't to be blamed, for she was born that way, and her upbringing in which she received the ready Ay, ay, madame, you're right of the Sligo peasants, stiffened her belief that things just touched were things well done. So she whirled about in her scintillating harlequin suit . . . bounding in through windows and dancing out through doors, striking, as she went by, her cardboard lath of thought against things to make them change, verily believing that they did, but never waiting to see whether they did or not. Well, well, may she rest in peace at last.

It is a clever caricature in that, like all clever caricatures, it distorts the original; this is Con's outline without the depth, Con without her kindness, without the bruise on her face from the policeman's baton, without the steadfastness which made men like Connolly and Larkin and Tom Clarke prefer her help to O'Casey's.

The tribute to her courage is a graceful one from a man who elsewhere in his autobiographies ruthlessly exposes himself as a physical coward, which makes it even odder that the faults he ascribes to Constance were not hers, but his. Con embraced many causes and stuck with them all: the one without 'the constitution to keep long enough at anything', was Sean O'Casey. In his study of the playwright's life and works, James Simmons said: 'O'Casey seemed to stumble

91

into movements, get enthused and then disillusioned and move on.'

As for hogging the limelight, Con certainly attracted much-needed publicity to Liberty Hall – reporters dubbed her 'The Red Countess' – and if O'Casey thought that as many pictures of the soup kitchen would have got on to front pages with an unknown ladling out the food rather than a renegade member of the aristocracy, then he did not understand the newspaper business.

Much may be forgiven Sean O'Casey; if you can trace it among the jungle of words in his autobiographies, there's a picture of the meanness, humour, squalor and endurance of Dublin's poor that has never been surpassed. But it is not for a man who, by 1945, had long settled down to a comfortable old age in one of England's more genteel seaside towns – he died at eighty-four in Torquay, Devon – to damn for inconstancy a woman who stayed on in Ireland to die a great deal tireder, very much younger and considerably poorer than he did.

As the winter came in and the lock-out went on, the sheep separated from the goats as far as the unemployed were concerned. They found some surprising friends and even more surprising enemies. Many of the Celtic Dawn intellectuals came out in favour of their resistance, Patrick Pearse, Yeats, James Stephens, Padraic Colum, Joseph Plunkett, Thomas MacDonagh, Susan Mitchell and AE. When Murphy and the other employers backed out of an enquiry set up by the Board of Trade, AE wrote an open letter to the *Irish Times* addressed to 'The Masters of Dublin', perhaps the most withering letter written since Dr Johnson put down the Earl of Chesterfield.

> Your insolence and ignorance of the rights conceded to workers universally in the modern world were incredible, and as great as your inhumanity. If you had between you, collectively, a portion of human soul as large as a threepenny bit, you would have sat night and day with the representatives of labour, trying this or that solution of the trouble, mindful of the women and children, who at least were innocent of wrong against you.
>
> But no! You reminded labour you could always have three square meals a day, while it went hungry. You went into conference with representatives of the State . . . you withdrew and will not agree to accept their solution, and fall back again on your devilish policy of starvation. Cry aloud to Heaven for new souls!

'Extraordinary Outburst by AE,' said the Redmondite *Freeman's Journal*, which was by now siding with the employers. So was Arthur Griffith who, in Sinn Féin, attacked the workers for following Larkin whom he regarded as an English troublemaker, injuring the industrial revival.

The Catholic Church joined the ranks of the goats, when it stepped in to halt a scheme to send some of the neediest Dublin children to stay for a while in English homes, where they could be fed and kept warm. Dr Walsh, Archbishop of Dublin, wrote to the *Freeman's Journal* wondering that Catholic mothers should 'so forget their duty as to send away their children to be cared for in a strange land without security of any kind that those to whom the poor children are to be handed over are Catholics, or, indeed, are persons of any faith at all.' Priests picketed ships to stop the children boarding and they were sent back to the slums of sanctity.

At the sharp end of the dispute there were vicious clashes between scab workers and their protective escorts of police and the lock-outs; inevitably the bitterness spread to the children. But here Con put her foot down. Hanna Sheehy Skeffington was helping in the soup kitchens when

> One day a youngster came along, a boy of about ten, with his little soup-can, only to be recognised and pushed aside scornfully by the others with a taunt, 'Go away, your father is a scab.' Madame, seeing the hurt look in the child's face and the quick withdrawal, called him back. 'No child is going to be called a scab. He can't help his father. When he grows up he'll be all right himself, won't you, sonny? And now have some soup.'

The strain of leading so vulnerable an army against the big battalions told on James Larkin. In order to win he needed reinforcements that only the British unions could provide. He went to England and demanded of the TUC that it call for sympathy strikes. Congress had given almost £100,000 of the £150,000 which British sympathisers had sent to the Irish workers, but it refused strike action. Larkin lost his temper and alienated what was left of their desire to support him.

What made the British workers pause in their support for their Irish brothers was the older bugbear of nationalism – in this case, fear of nationalism – which had arisen in Ulster. Perhaps the English unions would not have gone out on a limb for their Irish comrades anyway – they had only just emerged from some horrific strikes of their own – but when, from their perspective, the Irish class struggle looked likely to escalate into North versus South, Orange versus Green, Catholic versus Protestant, they drew back from becoming involved in the 'Irish problem'. By the New Year of 1914 their supplies of food and money had dried up. Beaten men shambled back to places of employment to sign undertakings that they would not 'remain or become in the future a member of the Irish Transport Workers' Union . . . take no part in or support any form of sympathetic strikes'.

James Connolly wrote:

93

And so we Irish workers must again go down into Hell, bow our backs to the last of the slave drivers, let our hearts be seared by the iron of his hatred and instead of the sacramental wafer of brotherhood and sacrifice, eat the dust of defeat and betrayal. Dublin is isolated.

If gaining the bitterness of an entire class is victory, then Murphy and his fellow employers had won. But many of his workers secretly retained their membership of the ITGWU and its flag still hung over Liberty Hall.

Larkin's prestige remained untarnished but emotionally he had been defeated. He became increasingly quarrelsome and difficult, even with his own union, and in October 1914 he left for a lecture tour of the United States where his Labour activities got him a prison sentence in Sing Sing. He did not return to Ireland until 1923.

James Connolly took his place as Labour's hope at Liberty Hall; he, too, had become embittered by the failure of union action but it became transmuted into determination that the next move must be by political force.

Constance Markievicz acknowledged no defeat; the fact that she agreed with James Connolly on the next stage was entirely consistent. She had maintained, all along, that neither women nor Labour could achieve their rights while Ireland was tied to Britain. The country must be free and it must be socialist. True to the code that had been imposed by her upbringing and character, she showed no crack in her relentlessly vigorous optimism. It was no pose but her own peculiar form of chivalry; she could no more have appeared without it in public than she could have appeared unclothed.

If she could have seemed gloomier she would have been given more credit for sensitivity, but she could not, and so went down in the books of those who like stereotypes as being incapable of thought or sorrow. We only know now that she was capable of crying because, much later, when she was completely defeated, somebody barged into the room where she was alone to find her in tears, and was so appalled by the fact that they recorded it. Neither Sean O'Casey, nor her first biographer, Sean O'Faolain, looked beyond the outward appearance. Men think; women have instinct. O'Casey said of the woman who read Schiller in the original for her own pleasure, that 'he had never seen her fondling a book, and he thought that odd'. He would have thought it odder if she *had* been fondling one, since he only saw her in the Liberty Hall soup kitchens and at committee meetings. O'Casey has her 'dazzling' Connolly: O'Faolain has Connolly 'hypnotising' her. It seems to have occurred to neither that the flamboyant countess and the slow-speaking socialist were both going in the same direction and doing so arm-in-arm.

She may not have paraded them, but Con, too, had sustained losses during 1913–14. She had worked like a dog for eight months and, while she had at least kept people alive, all the suffering that had filed past her in the soup queues had been for nothing.

She had seriously impoverished herself by over-borrowing and the gas was frequently being cut off at Surrey House because she could not pay the bill. The story goes that a man had been on permanent stand-by at Liberty Hall ready to dash off to Con's solicitors at Ormond Quay with a note to draw another loan on her dwindling securities so that she could buy more food for the kitchens. She herself had been cut off by nearly all her former friends who considered that she had finally gone native. There had been ridiculous, but hurtful slights; the Dublin Repertory Theatre, which she and Casi had helped to found and for which she still occasionally appeared, had decided that she must pollute its boards no longer. 'Owing to the high feeling which prevails in the city at the present moment, and owing to the prominent part which the Countess has taken in the labour disputes . . . her appearance on the stage would not be good for business.' Casi had resigned his position as co-director in protest.

And now Casi had gone. Hostilities had broken out in the Balkans and he went off to cover them as a war correspondent. He never lived in Dublin again. The only creature who completely belonged to her now was a black Irish spaniel called Poppet who, like the Fianna, followed her everywhere.

On the other hand she had been received into the citizenship of Liberty Hall. She was made an honorary member of the ITGWU and the following year was given an Illuminated Address from its grateful members.

At a time when all the forces of Capitalism had combined to crush the Workers, when the forces of the British Crown were exhibiting all their traditional brutality and hatred of the people, in ferocious batonings and murders; when the prisons were full of innocent men, women and girls, and all looked black before us, you came to our aid to organise relief, and for months worked amongst us, and served the cause of labour by such untiring toil, far-seeing vigilance and sympathetic insight as cheered and encouraged all who were privileged to witness it . . .

One form of love had been replaced by another. If she was lonely, that was a personal matter and never to be exposed.

CHAPTER SEVEN

When James Larkin had been organising in the Belfast docks back in 1907 he had achieved a remarkable thing in combining for a short while Catholic and Protestant workers against the employers. For a few heady weeks, Larkin, a Catholic, had spoken on the same platform and to the same end as members of the Orange Order.

Yet, however exploited, however poor the Protestant worker was – in fact, the *more* exploited and poor he was – he clung to the belief that he was apart from, and better than, his Catholic fellow. The observation made about his kind by the historian Lecky two centuries before, that 'even if he had nothing else to boast of, he at least found it pleasing to think that he was a member of a dominant race', still held true. Generally he voted Tory, not because he was a Tory, but because, since 1886, the Conservative Party was also the Unionist Party, and it was vital to his moral superiority that the Union between Great Britain and Ireland remain in being.

Larkin cut horizontally through this vertical and sectarian grouping of Protestant worker with Protestant employer. His handbills read: 'Not as Catholics or Protestants, as Nationalists or Unionists, but as Belfast men and workers, stand together.' But even a James Larkin could not dissolve the formation of centuries; after the brief blending of Orange and Green on a Labour canvas 'the pigment proved soluble in the religious wash' as Unionists, rich and poor, reverted to type with the third reading in the House of Commons of the bill which would give Ireland Home Rule. Or, as the Orangemen and women of Ulster saw it, 'Rome Rule'.

By granting a minimum of Home Rule, Asquith was hoping for acquiescence, if not enthusiasm, from both Orange and Green. As it turned out, he was asking one section of Irish to surrender too much and another to accept too much.

The Irish Party under Redmond was prepared to compromise, but it made clear that it was a sacrifice. As the MP, William O'Brien, put it, the bill meant 'the renunciation by Irish nationalists of the old school, of dreams, perhaps only dreams, but dreams that came in the youth of some of us as blood in our veins', unaware obviously that it was

96

a renunciation that the new school of dreamers, Connolly, Countess Markievicz, Patrick Pearse, were not prepared to make.

But to Ulster Protestants, the bill, watered down as it was, presaged a nightmare which had disturbed their sleep since they had first planted North-East Ireland. They knew the force of nationalist temper if the government did not; a completely independent Ireland would isolate them on an island among a people with whom there had been bloodbaths in the past.

And it brought hotfoot from England a former Solicitor General in Balfour's Conservative Government to lead them, Sir Edward Carson. If ever a man embodied personal and political contradictions, it was Carson. A hypochondriac who lived to the age of eighty-two, a Southern Irish Protestant with a Dublin accent who had supported the establishment of a Catholic University, a Loyalist who was prepared to fight England in order to stay loyal, he was the man, who, as much as any individual, brought about the partition of Ireland which – next to severance from Great Britain – was the last thing he wanted. Eventually he was to see himself as a pawn used by Bonar Law and the Conservative Party to gain power. 'What a fool I was, and so was Ulster, and so was Ireland,' he was to say long afterwards, in his first speech to the House of Lords.

At the time it looked as if partition was exactly what he was threatening, and by force. At the first of a series of enormous Unionist rallies, he promised not only to resist Home Rule but was prepared, in the event of it being passed, to 'use such measures as will carry on for ourselves the government of those districts of which we have control. We must be prepared ... to become responsible for the government of the Protestant province of Ulster.'

It was a combination of bluff and blackmail against the Liberal Government; Carson firmly believed that an Ireland without Ulster would be so unviable that the entire Home Rule scheme would collapse.

If Carson was bluffing, he was certainly prepared to be called, and his adoring Unionists were not bluffing at all. As soon as the removal of the House of Lords' veto in 1911 had signalled that the next step would be an introduction of Home Rule, Unionist Clubs and members of the Orange Order had started secretly drilling. By 1912 they were drilling openly. On September 28, Belfast work places closed and after a church service with the hymn 'O God Our Help in Ages Past', Carson and William of Orange's banner led a procession to Belfast Town Hall where Carson was the first to sign the Solemn League and Covenant pledging that Ulster's loyal subjects of King George V would use all necessary means to defeat the 'conspiracy' of King George's Government to set up Home Rule in Ireland. 'And in the event of such a Parliament being forced upon us we further solemnly and mutually pledge ourselves to refuse to recognise its authority.' That day and for some days afterwards people queued to sign it, sometimes in their own blood. There were nearly 220,000 male signatories. Women signed a supportive counterpart, not the Covenant itself, but their signatures outnumbered the men's.

It was a demonstration to put fear into any government and it was followed in 1913 by an even more menacing development – the raising of an Ulster Volunteer Force of 100,000 men and the purchase from Germany of 20,000 guns and three million rounds of ammunition.

In October 1913 Redmond found himself having to state the obvious: 'Ireland is a unit . . . The two nations theory is to us an abomination and a blasphemy.' But by March 1914 the position had deteriorated to the point where he agreed that any Ulster county which wished to do so could opt out of Home Rule for six years, afterwards coming under an Irish Parliament. It was a disastrous admission because it recognised that Ireland was *not* a unit. Home Rule had become of such paramount importance to him that he was desperate to get it on almost any terms and he saw the chance of it disappearing as the government wavered. It was thought that even the King, faced with a constitutional crisis and sympathising with his Protestant subjects, might step in and dissolve Parliament.

The concession did nothing to placate Carson, who said it was 'a sentence of death with a stay of execution for six years', and returned to Belfast where, people believed, he was about to set up an Ulster provisional government. In an incident that became known as the Curragh Mutiny, British Army officers indicated that, even if ordered to do so, they would refuse to fight Carson.

Asquith was helpless. Whatever else it did, the outbreak of war with Germany on August 4, 1914, at least gave him the opportunity to shelve the problem. The Home Rule Bill was passed but with the provisos that it would not come into operation until the war was ended and that Parliament should be given the opportunity to make special provision for Ulster. Britain marched off to war not realising that it would last for four dreadful years and that by the time it was over the Home Rule Bill, Redmond and Asquith would be redundant.

The way nationalists in the South reacted to what Carson was doing in the North was unexpected. Instead of bitterness and resentment they were full of admiration.[1] Here was a son of their own soil refusing

[1] Such admiration still exists. In an article to mark the fiftieth anniversary of Carson's death, Dr A. T. Q. Stewart wrote in the *Irish Times* on October 19, 1985: 'If there is no place for him in the ranks of Irish patriots, he was nonetheless a man who deeply loved his country.'

to be pushed around by England and, what's more, raising an army to resist her machinations. The Countess Markievicz wasn't the only one to ask: 'Why can't we do that?'

The Gaelic League magazine *An Claidheamh Soluis* published an article called 'The North Began' by Professor Eoin MacNeill, praising Carson's actions as 'a decisive move towards Irish autonomy' and suggesting that a similar opportunity be taken in the South. 'There is nothing to prevent the other twenty-six counties from calling into existence citizen forces to hold Ireland for the Empire.'

The idea of raising a nationalist volunteer force had been given respectability and the Irish Republican Brotherhood moved in with speed to ensure that it was they who controlled it. Under MacNeill's chairmanship, a provisional committee was set up which seemed to represent all parties, bar the extremists'. (Arthur Griffith was left out, for instance: so was Tom Clarke.) In fact, half of the thirty members secretly belonged to the IRB.

The force that began as the 'Irish Volunteers' was inaugurated on November 25, 1913 at Dublin's Rotunda. Its manifesto detailing its duties as purely 'defensive and protective' was read to a huge audience. Eoin MacNeill's address was almost cosy:

> We do not contemplate any hostility to the Volunteer movement that has already been initiated in Ulster . . . The more genuine and successful the local Volunteer movement in Ulster becomes, the more completely does it establish the principle that Irishmen have the right to decide and govern their national affairs. We have nothing to fear from the existing Volunteers in Ulster, nor they from us.

He didn't actually call for three cheers for Sir Edward Carson, though he did later at a similar meeting in Cork to discover from the booing that not everyone was as sanguine about Carson's intentions as he was.

Men surged forward to sign up. At first the response was mainly in the cities but it spread to the entire country, accelerating with Britain's declaration of war on Germany as the streets began to echo to the sound of marching troops and songs bidding Goodbye to Dolly Grey and regretting the distance to Tipperary. Recruiting posters attempting to get Irishmen to enlist in the British Army showed a wistful, be-shawled colleen and asked: 'Have you any women-folk worth defending?' Signing on for the Volunteers was a way of entering into the prevailing martial spirit by drilling and marching yet remaining patriotic to Ireland. (Eamon de Valera was one of those who joined on inauguration night.) Very few joined for an insurrection. By July

1914 the Volunteers had 160,000 members. Kathleen Ni Houlihan was alive and well and had donned a grey-green uniform.

But there was another Kathleen already in existence, a poor, bedraggled but brave young thing: the Irish Citizen Army.

It had come into being during the lock-out, when Jim Larkin, speaking to a mass rally from a window at Liberty Hall, called for a workers' force that could defend them from police charges 'and evolve a system of unified action, self-control and ordered discipline that Labour in Ireland might march at the forefront of all movements for the betterment of the whole people of Ireland'.

His place was then taken at the window by a recruit new to the workers' cause and one very nearly as unlikely as the Countess working down in Liberty Hall's kitchens, Captain Jack White, DSO, a young but retired British army officer, whose father, Field Marshal Sir George White, had led the relief column to Ladysmith during the Boer War. An admirer of Tolstoy's philosophy, his sympathy for workers had made him something of a misfit among his fellow officers. On coming to live in Dublin – he was actually an Ulsterman – he had been appalled by the lock-out and the actions of the police and had joined forces with Jim Larkin and James Connolly. He had the backing of Sir Roger Casement, who had sent a telegram: 'I understand you begin to drill and discipline Dublin Workers. That is a good and healthy movement, I wish to support it and I hope it may begin a widespread national movement . . .'

It didn't. The Citizen Army's influence always far outweighed its size. During the lock-out it attracted thousands of men who had nothing else to do but drill and march out to camp in Croydon Park, the house and three-acre estate in Clontarf which Larkin had bought for his members and other unionists, so that they should have a bit of countryside of their own. At that stage the Citizen Army lacked organisation because its leaders, Larkin, Constance – who joined on the spot – and Connolly were too busy at Liberty Hall or, in Larkin's case, too often in prison, so responsibility fell almost entirely on Captain White. With the ending of the lock-out, men dribbled back to work. Those who didn't sink into the apathy of defeat and still wanted to march were attracted by the beat of the Volunteers' drum and joined them instead – to the fury of Sean O'Casey, who became the Citizen Army's secretary.

O'Casey's first professional writing – for which he received fifteen guineas – was *The Story of the Irish Citizen Army*, published in 1919 under the Gaelic version of his name, S. Ó Cathasaigh, which he assumed in those days. It is undeniably the work of an amateur, falling into heroic purple passages which would have made even Constance

Markievicz blush, but it is, for O'Casey, a more or less objective piece of work, and his summing up of why the working class responded more to the Volunteers than to the Citizen Army is significant. Pointing out that among the Volunteers were some of the employers who had followed Murphy in locking out their union men, he said: 'Looking back on this surprising anomaly, it becomes obvious that because of the undeveloped comprehension by the workers of the deeper meaning of the Labour movement, the call of the National Tribe appealed to them more strongly than the call of the Tribe of Labour.'

To counter the appeal of the Volunteers, O'Casey and Captain White decided to turn what men they had into a systematic unit. At a general meeting of Dublin workers in the Concert Room of Liberty Hall on March 22, 1914, Captain White became President, O'Casey the honorary secretary, and Countess Markievicz and Richard Brannigan joint treasurers.

A new constitution for the Irish Citizen Army was read out. It held that the first and last principle of the Army was the avowal of the ownership of Ireland, moral and material, being vested in the right of the people of Ireland. Con proposed an additional clause that every applicant must, if eligible, be a member of a Trades Union, 'such union to be recognised by the Irish Trades Union Council'. She, of course, was by now an honorary member of the ITGWU and wore the Red Hand badge to prove it.

From the first there was hostility between many of the executives of the two forces, though the lower ranks seem to have fraternised fairly well. Labour was the only organisation which had not been invited to attend the Volunteers' inauguration at the Rotunda. Accordingly, the Citizen Army's first handbill detailed reasons why Irish workers should not join the Volunteers: 'Because many members of the Executive are hostile to the workers . . . Because they refuse to definitely declare that they stand for the Democratic principle of Wolfe Tone . . .' etc. As winter drew in and it became impossible for the Citizen Army to continue drilling on the ITGWU's estate at Croydon Park, they looked for rooms in which to carry on. They needed several – the Citizen Army Dublin regiment had three battalions. Con, who was still paying for Fianna Hall, put it at their disposal, but they had difficulty in finding others to accept them. It may be, of course, that the honorary secretary deliberately applied to halls used by the Volunteers, or sympathetic to the Volunteers, like the Gaelic League's, for the perverse satisfaction of being turned down; nevertheless, turned down he was and read into the refusals snobbery on the part of the Volunteers' founder, Eoin MacNeill. (In *The Story of the Irish Citizen Army* Sean O'Casey constantly refers to him as 'John' MacNeill, implicitly taking away his right to use, as O'Casey did himself, the Gaelic version of his name.)

Maddened, O'Casey demanded that the Volunteers confess to being supporters of John Redmond and the 'imperial Parliament', that they bring out into the open their antagonism to the claims of Labour, that they hold a public debate with the Irish Citizen Army on these matters, that they put into their constitution a clause to show they stood for the Rights of Man as well as the Rights of Ireland.

Eoin MacNeill replied in a rather dignified letter that O'Casey seemed to think his executive drew a distinction between the noble and the obscure, the rich and the poor: 'I am ignorant of the existence of such a distinction.'

It didn't mollify O'Casey whose aggression towards the Volunteers grew with every slight, real – and there were some real ones – or imagined. He transferred some of it to Constance who 'frequently opposed the antagonism toward the Volunteers'. So did Captain White, but O'Casey didn't blame him so much.

O'Casey bends over backwards to be fair to Con in *The Story of the Irish Citizen Army*; since he was writing it in 1919 when she had achieved glory to rival Joan of Arc, he would probably have been lynched if he hadn't. He mentions that at an Irish Citizen Army festival in Croydon Park, which was attended by so many thousands it was very nearly a fiasco, 'the gallant Countess Markievicz tried to be in ten places at once', that when they were out recruiting, the crowds seemed to prefer her 'passionate and nervous eloquence' to his. And, although O'Casey doesn't mention her part in it, there is no doubt that an incident which occurred about this time convinced him of her physical courage. She and Captain White had been leading a march of unemployed men from Beresford Place outside Liberty Hall to the Mansion House to protest about their joblessness. Up to this point the Citizen Army had been keeping out of the Dublin Metropolitan Police's way by marching in Croydon Park, a ploy the police found infuriating; now they saw their chance. They baton-charged the marchers just as they reached Butt Bridge. Captain White was badly hit round the head and was dragged off to the police station. He told Sean O'Faolain:

But she [Constance] followed me all the way hammering the police on their back with her little fists, or dodging between their legs in the vain effort to release me. In the end they got me inside and slammed the door on her. Did she go? She remained there hammering on the panels and they could not get her to go away until she was permitted to come into my cell and dress and wash my wounds with some disinfectant lent her from the kitchen.

Since his head was 'a bloody pulp' and Con also insisted the police send for a doctor, Captain White believed she saved his life.

Nevertheless O'Casey's resentment of Con increased and in *The Story of the Irish Citizen Army* he gives the impression that she belonged to the Volunteers as well as the Citizen Army, which wasn't true, although she had joined its female support group, Cumann na mBan.

What Con was doing was, as usual, acting as sheepdog; desperately trying to keep the flock together so that it arrived in the same place undiminished. She refused to cut off contact with any organisation which stood for Irish freedom, but if nationalism had been her only consideration she would not have been spending her time, money and energy on the Irish Citizen Army, and if O'Casey had not been blinded with class hatred he would have seen as much. The two had already clashed over the matter of uniforms; Con and Captain White wanted the Citizen Army to be uniformed – for a long time the men were only able to wear blue brassards, the St Patrick blue which Con pointed out was the ancient colour of Ireland. Uniforms, they felt, would give their soldiers a sense of pride and *esprit de corps*, match the smartness of the Volunteers, and, perhaps, protect their wearers if they were captured in action by giving them prisoner-of-war status and prevent them being shot. O'Casey pointed out that the Volunteers could afford uniforms: the Citizen Army could not. He added, that if it came to fighting, their soldiers would do better to use guerrilla, strike-and-dodge tactics and blend back into the crowd to make their escape. Both sides had a point, but it was White and Con who won; uniforms were ordered and the men paid for them in instalments, appearing on parade in dark green, with matching slouch hats pinned up on one side by a Red Hand badge.

They wore them in June on the annual pilgrimage to Wolfe Tone's grave at Bodenstown, although when O'Casey informed the Wolfe Tone Committee that the Citizen Army wanted to attend, they were afraid of fighting between them and the Volunteers, and were going to ban the Citizen Army. The Committee chairman, however, was Con's old friend and respected member of the Irish Republican Brotherhood, Tom Clarke. He stepped in and insisted not only that the Citizen Army be allowed to attend but that, as the first armed force in nationalist Ireland – not that either force was armed at that point – they should lead the procession. The occasion went off well, with the Fianna forming an inner ring round the graveside and the grey-green of the Volunteers and the dark green of the Citizen Army alternating in the outer ring, so that even O'Casey had to admit that his men had received 'equal honour'.

Soon after the amicability at Bodenstown, however, O'Casey became aware of moves within the Volunteer Executive which made it impossible for him to stand in alliance next to any of its members or – and this meant Con – supporters.

What had happened was that Redmond and his Irish Parliamentary Party had suddenly become aware of the importance of the Volunteers. Why Redmond hadn't raised such a force himself the moment Carson began puffing and blowing in the North is still incomprehensible. Not only didn't he think of it but when it was formed he distrusted it. 'Redmond does not like this thing,' an Irish MP wrote to a party member in Cork, '. . . It could not be controlled, and if the army met some day and demanded an Irish Republic where would our Home Rule leaders be?' But as the thing's membership went up to six figures, Redmond and his deputy, John Dillon, saw that they must take the reins or let Ireland gallop off without them. They demanded that Eoin MacNeill give them a majority on the Volunteers' Provisional Committee, expecting that a man who had consistently declared his support for them and Home Rule would acquiesce at once. But MacNeill had shifted his position somewhat during his chairmanship or, at least, had become aware of the strength of nationalist feeling. He hesitated. Redmond delivered a public ultimatum: twenty-five people nominated by the Irish Parliamentary Party must be added to the Volunteers' Committee.

The man who did most to influence the Committee into giving way to Redmond's demand – as it did – was Bulmer Hobson. He did it, he wrote later, to prevent 'a disastrous and, indeed, a fatal split', through the entire movement, but it finished him with his fellows on the Irish Republican Brotherhood's Supreme Council, from which he was forced to resign. Tom Clarke, for one, never spoke to him again.

It was also the deciding factor for Sean O'Casey, a member of the IRB, though not its Supreme Council, who had never liked Hobson anyway, suspecting him of being the silent but effectual spirit behind the Volunteers' distrust of the Irish Citizen Army. Now this man 'whose warmest appreciation of Labour was a sneer' had handed the Volunteers over to Redmondites. O'Casey turned on the Countess Markievicz and forced an old-fashioned, all-out showdown. Had he realised it, Con shared his view of Hobson. Her old ally of the Fianna days had disgusted her by his refusal to help Labour during the lock-out and now, by siding with Redmond, he had put himself completely outside her pale.

But O'Casey had been wanting a public confrontation with Con for some time. He'd been infuriated by her attitude to the Citzen Army's new flag[1] which had been woven for them by the guild of embroider-esses of which Yeats' sister, Lily, was a member. It was a deep blue poplin and decorated with a plough around which glittered a collection of stars. O'Casey adored it; *The Plough and the Stars* was to be one of his best and most famous plays. But in *Drums Under the Window* he records that Madame merely glanced at it, said the design had no republican significance 'and returned to oiling her automatic'. That Madame had a gun is given recurrent emphasis both in pro- and anti-Markievicz writing, not only as being unusual – though plenty of men had them by this time – but as somehow shocking. Con never saw the logic in *not* having a gun; it was hers, she was a soldier in an army, and as a daughter of Lissadell she was more used to firearms than many of the men around her. When O'Casey writes about Larkin oiling a bayonet, he does so with tender amusement, 'a young boy with a new toy', but when Con does the same with a gun he is affronted – and so were others.

The flag's Plough was more significant than the Stars for the Citizen Army at this point; although they'd built up their membership to 1,000 it had been very heavy going, especially in recruiting rural workers, 'the Labour Hercules leaning on his club' is how O'Casey described them, and in 1914 a disheartened Captain White resigned. He was replaced by Jim Larkin and with this change in the leadership O'Casey felt strong enough to challenge Con. He called a meeting of the Citizen Army Council to which he proposed the motion:

> Seeing that Madame Markievicz was, through Cumann na mBan, attached to the Volunteers, and on intimate terms with many of the Volunteer leaders, and as the Volunteers' Association was, in its methods and aims, inimical to the first interests of Labour, it could not be expected that Madame could retain the confidence of the Council; and that she be now asked to sever her connection with either the Volunteers or the Irish Citizen Army.

Con left no record of the meeting; she refused to publicise personal matters and she knew, like everybody else, that O'Casey's dislike for her was personal. But she dealt nicely with the situation by saying nothing at all, just as she'd done when her position had been challenged at the inauguration of the Fianna. Some of the Volunteer leaders were her friends, she was using that friendship to build a bridge between them and the Citizen Army and she was not going to let O'Casey's class consciousness snap that vital link. She merely let her record speak for her and refused to resign.

[1] It flew during the Rising, was captured by a British soldier but eventually found its way into the National Museum in Dublin.

She was gambling as much as O'Casey was, and it was a close thing; the vote went seven to six in her favour. O'Casey was particularly miffed that she voted for herself while he, from some mistaken idea of chivalry, abstained. He promptly resigned.

Jim Larkin did not want to lose either of them and called a general meeting in which he appealed for O'Casey to apologise to Con and withdraw his resignation. O'Casey refused. At least, that is the version he gives. Another member at the general meeting recalls it differently and said that O'Casey accused Con of being a spy for the Volunteers, went on to say that he was afraid of no man and, going completely over the top, pointed at Larkin to add 'not even of him'. Larkin, who had been sympathetic to O'Casey up to that point, got to his feet 'and the question was no longer O'Casey versus Madame but O'Casey versus Larkin'. O'Casey left the Irish Citizen Army.

One cannot expect justice from such a man, but a bit of logic would be nice. In Chapter Four of *The Story of the Irish Citizen Army* he praises Con and Captain White for separating themselves from the antagonism towards the Volunteers and says: 'It is most probable . . . that the influence of these two Leaders of the Citizen Army Council would have evolved a working basis of genuine and useful unity between the two organisations.' Yet when she remains consistent and keeps on working for that unity, he asks her to resign. Then, in Chapter Ten, when, after his own resignation, he admits that active co-operation between the Volunteers and the Irish Citizen Army had come about, he gives the credit not to Con, who had worked so hard for it, but to James Connolly who, as O'Casey himself says, had seldom interested himself in the affairs of the Citizen Army up to that point.

There is no doubt the climate became easier for co-operation once its two most choleric men left the Citizen Army – Jim Larkin went off on his lecture tour of the States a few weeks after O'Casey's resignation. Tom Clarke always blamed a great deal of the trouble between the two forces on 'a disgruntled fellow called O'Casey'.

James Connolly took over the leadership of both the ITGWU and the Citizen Army. Sean O'Casey left the Irish battlefront for ever, though, rather touchingly, he completed his story of the Citizen Army – he probably needed the fifteen guineas badly – although the 1916 Rising and the Citizen Army's part in it took him completely by surprise, and began his career as a playwright and brooder over wrongs.

CHAPTER EIGHT

From the moment of their inception both the Irish Citizen Army and the Volunteers waited, with most of Ireland, to see what the British Government would do about them, hardly believing it as day after day went by without any attempt at suppressing them.

But, having proved incapable of suppressing the Ulster Volunteers, Asquith could hardly prohibit an exactly similar army in the South without provoking the very sectarian trouble he was trying to avoid. He made the only move he could and on December 6, 1913, banned the importing of arms and ammunition. The Irish Republican Brotherhood especially breathed more easily; it was unlikely that a government planning suppression would begin with an unenforceable measure like this. For the prohibition made no difference. In April 1914 Carson illegally imported his arms and, two months later, on June 26, 1914, the Volunteers of the South illegally imported theirs – and both sides bought them from a Germany only too happy to oblige any organisation likely to embarrass England.

The parallel goes even further; the men and women who ran the guns for the Irish Volunteers belonged to the same Anglo-Ascendancy class as Carson and his gun-runners and no more thought themselves traitors to England for doing so than he did. Darrell Figgis, an Irish writer based in London, had made the offer to Sir Roger Casement to go to Germany and purchase weapons. (Casement had now retired from the British Consular Service and was devoting his time to the Volunteers and IRB.) The Hon. Mary Spring Rice, daughter to Lord Monteagle and a cousin of the then British Ambassador in Washington, conceived the idea of bringing them over in private yachts to avoid detection, and Erskine Childers, the author of the 1903 classic spy novel *The Riddle of the Sands* – a superb yachtsman – carried guns over with another yacht owner, Conor O'Brien, godfather to the writer and Irish politician, Conor Cruise O'Brien.

Though Erskine Childers later joined Con in the republican cause – and died for it – he thought of himself at that time as a Home Ruler, although that designation covered a wide gamut of belief and Childers was on its extreme end in wanting Dominion status for Ireland.

On July 12, 1913, Erskine Childers, his American wife, Mary Osgood, Mary Spring Rice and her cousins Conor and Kitty O'Brien, in the *Asgard* and the *Kelpie*, made a rendezvous in the North Sea with a tug which carried Darrell Figgis, 1,500 Mauser rifles and 45,000 rounds of ammunition. The cargo was divided between the two yachts, and the *Kelpie*'s weapons were landed without incident at Kilcoole, County Wicklow in August.

But Bulmer Hobson, who was in Casement's confidence, and had been put in charge of landing *Asgard*'s cargo – this was just before he fell from the IRB Supreme Council's grace – had arranged a much more audacious scheme which, if it came off, would put up the Volunteers' score and attract recruits. The *Asgard* was to come right into Dublin Bay, to Howth on the north side, and in daylight. Though she was heavily overloaded and encountered a bad storm in the Irish Sea, Childers' navigation and seamanship brought *Asgard* into Howth not only on the right day but at the very minute when the Volunteers, who were to distribute the arms, arrived on the pier.

It is a measure of how much faith Hobson put in Con's training of the Fianna, and how deep the rift between him and Con had become during the lock-out, that he had detailed a detachment of the scouts to look after the ammunition – he felt he couldn't entrust it to the still very amateur Volunteers – and kept Con herself in the dark. True to IRB secrecy he kept many others in the dark as well; even the Volunteers had only the vaguest idea that this was not just another route march. But in not informing the Fianna's chief that he was using them on such an important assignment he was showing not only discourtesy but distrust.

Cathal Brugha, a young IRB member, was in charge of a number of taxis which would take a large part of the rifles into Dublin. Liam Mellowes and Seán Heuston led the Fianna boys who were pushing a heavy trek cart full of oak batons, at that point the only weapons the Volunteers had. One of them later told Nora Connolly what happened.

When we came near Howth two chaps came running towards us and told us to come on the double. The Volunteers were a bit fagged, but when they heard the word 'rifles' they simply raced. When we got to the harbour we saw the rifles being unloaded from a yacht. You ought to have heard the cheers when we first saw them! It was then the clubs were given out to a picked number of men ... They were to use them if the police attempted to interfere.

The rifles were handed out to the men, but there were more rifles than men, so the rest were sent into the city in motor cars. Most of the ammunition was sent in the same way, but our trek cart was loaded with it. None of it was served out to the men.

It was a wise precaution. Coastguards had spotted the unusual activity at Howth and alerted Dublin Castle. The taxis got through unnoticed but on the march back the Volunteers, each carrying a rifle, were stopped on the Malahide Road at Clontarf by the police and a detachment of the King's Own Scottish Borderers regiment. Had the Volunteers' rifles been loaded there would have been bloodshed. As it was, the police assistant commissioner who was in charge, was on shaky ground. In Ulster armed Unionists were parading through the streets of Belfast with impunity. Also, the government ban was against the *importing* of arms: was it legal to disarm men of rifles once they had been imported?

While Darrell Figgis, who had marched in with the Volunteers, was arguing the point with the assistant commissioner, most of the Volunteers managed to slip away across the fields to safety, still carrying their rifles. As quite a few of them were trade unionists they sought refuge in their old stamping ground of Croydon Park which was nearby. (One of Sean O'Casey's greatest complaints had been that so many trade union men joined the Volunteers.)

The Fianna boys pushing the ammunition-filled trek cart had been warned by the shouting that there was a stoppage ahead, and had swerved into a side lane to get away unseen and bury their treasure. Then, according to Nora Connolly, like the loyal boys they were, six of them went straight off to Con's cottage at Balally to tell their chief all about it, with a 'Guess what we've been doing'. Con had been holding a Fianna convention at the cottage, and among those who had come down for it were James Connolly's daughters, Nora, Ina and Agna, all members of the Belfast *sluagh* (troop). (Connolly's home was still in Belfast at this stage and he was commuting from it to his job at Liberty Hall.)

'Tell us about it and we'll know all the quicker,' Con said. She must have been hurt, not only at missing the excitement, but that the boys had been in an action of which she'd known nothing; generous woman that she was, however, she showed only pleasure for the achievement of her boys and Ireland. There was rejoicing at Balally camp that night.

Back in Dublin at that moment there was no rejoicing, only tragedy.

While the Scottish Borderers had been confronting the Volunteers on the Malahide Road, they had been given the order to load, and had not subsequently unloaded. They had been forced to march away without having disarmed the exultant Volunteers. By the time they reached the city, word of the landing had spread and a crowd, flushed with nationalist pride, had taunted them and, growing bigger and more insolent by the minute, had followed them back towards their barracks. As the Borderers reached the Liffey quayside called Bachelors Walk, the crowd, by now very large and excited, had begun throwing rocks and bottles at them. An officer, who had met the column on its way back from Clontarf and therefore appeared unaware that its rifles were loaded, ordered his men to face about and take up firing position. Whether the order to fire was given or not was to be much disputed later. The fact remains that a volley of bullets went into the crowd, killing three people instantly and wounding thirty-eight others, one of whom died later.

One of the dead was the mother of a soldier in the British Army. Nora Connolly remembered him weeping as she walked beside him at the victims' funeral which was made into an immense occasion, attended by representatives from nearly every nationalist group, military and civil.

The authorities were forced to act fast if rioting was to be avoided. A commission was set up which reported back within the fortnight and, even before then, the King's Own Scottish Borderers had been posted away from Dublin. Anyway, nine days after the shooting, war broke out in Europe and people's attention was diverted elsewhere.

Bachelors Walk had not been a massacre. What emerged at the enquiry was that it had been a badly-handled incident involving an unruly crowd, some sorely-tried soldiers and an ignorant officer.

But there had been no such 'incident' in the North. The point was not lost even on Irishmen and women most loyal to the Crown. Dublin Castle expelled a sigh of relief as the potential danger of the occurrence became dispersed, seemingly, among greater and more terrible events. But the memory of Bachelors Walk had not dispersed, it had become absorbed as one more entry on the tally of injustice and atrocity committed against Irish people by the British over seven hundred years of history.

As far as the Howth gun-running was concerned, Con ended up being involved with it after all. One of her Fianna scouts turned up on her doorstep at Balally the next morning with twenty rifles that had yet to be smuggled into Dublin. A taxi was procured, the rifles put in and the Connolly girls sat on them until they were safely at their destination. 'Agna,' said Nora, 'we'll go to the Volunteer office and ask Liam [Mellowes] does he want us to sit on any more rifles.' They spent the rest of their day helping out and got a rifle each as a reward. The Irish Citizen Army were given some of the Howth guns, though they also managed to acquire their own; some from a stonemason friend in England who sent them in hidden between slabs of marble, and some from the British Army 'with which their owners parted willingly or unwillingly'.

Ina Connolly later wrote:

When we heard that guns had been run in at Howth and us sitting pretty a few miles away, it nearly broke our hearts. How could we face up to Belfast and father and say we knew nothing and did less? It looked as if we were not to be trusted . . . 'Had I been a boy,' I said, 'I should not have been overlooked.'

It highlighted the Volunteers' attitude to women. Were they going to allow them equal status or were they not?

At the inauguration of the Volunteer movement at the Rotunda, back in November 1913, it had been made clear that they were not. Ominously, the women who attended that meeting found themselves escorted to a special Ladies' Gallery. There they sat and listened to speeches which talked about making an honest and 'manly' stand, about all who were 'manly, liberty-loving and patriotic', about how to 'realise themselves as citizens and men'. There were only a couple of references to the fact that Ireland had a female population at all. The Volunteer Manifesto mentioned 'that there will be work for women to do', and Eoin MacNeill had said: 'There would be work to do for large numbers who could not be in the marching line. There would be work for the women.'

What that work was to be was detailed later by one of the Volunteer committee, Michael Judge: '. . . there would be uniforms and rifles wanted . . . and the ladies could form a society and collect money for that, and put their hearts and souls into it'. Mr Judge was also a member of the Ancient Order of Hibernians, the Catholic equivalent of the Orange Order, and rabidly anti-feminist – they had acted as stewards at some of Redmond's Home Rule meetings and handled violently the suffragettes who had heckled for Votes for Women. It was Mr Judge who had written to the papers suggesting the 'slender, springy, stinging riding whips' for the backs of women daring to impede the visit of Prime Minister Asquith.

It was on those terms that, on April 5, 1914, one hundred women met in a Dublin hotel to form a female auxiliary force to the Volunteers, the Cumann na mBan (Irish Women's Association). Many of them, like Agnes MacNeill, Eoin's wife, were kin or friends of the Volunteer leaders and almost all were middle-class. Perhaps unsurprisingly, they saw themselves as subsidiaries to their men and formulated their constitution accordingly: to advance the cause of Irish liberty, to organise Irishwomen in furtherance of this object, to assist in arming and equipping a body of Irishmen for the defence of Ireland, to form a fund for these purposes to be called the 'Defence of Ireland Fund'. In other words, all the monotony and none of the excitement. Even so, their numbers grew rapidly – like the Volunteers they benefited from the new consciousness raised by the Howth gun-running and Bachelors Walk.

To Hanna Sheehy Skeffington and the Irish Women's Franchise League this was a backward step. They argued that as it was women who were raising much of the Volunteers' money, it was women who should use their strength as a bargaining counter. Just as Sean O'Casey was arguing that the Volunteers should acknowledge the rights of the working man in their constitution, Hanna was asking them to do the same for women. Neither made much headway.

Con agreed with them both:

> Today the women attached to the national movements are there chiefly to collect funds for the men to spend. These Ladies' Auxiliaries demoralise women, set them up in separate camps, and deprive them of all initiative and independence . . . take up your responsibilities and be prepared to go your own way, depending for safety on your own courage, your own truth and your own common sense . . .
> The two brilliant classes of women who follow this higher ideal are Suffragettes and the Trades Union or Labour women. In them lies the hope of the future.

True to her philosophy that any organisation with its heart in *one* of the right places should be encouraged, however, she conducted some delicate negotiations which resulted in the Inghínidhe na hÉireann forming its own branch of the Cumann na mBan, rather than being actually absorbed by it. Nevertheless the resourceful Inghínidhe disappeared from this point as an independent organisation, which was a pity although many of its leaders, along with many of the suffragettes, followed Con into the Irish Citizen Army. Con remained the only person who belonged to both camps.

It was the old, old problem. Did you free women first, or free the country so that it could free its women? Con and women such as Helena Moloney were quite sure: 'There can be no free women in an enslaved nation.'

On September 15, 1914, John Redmond personally committed Irishmen into the Great War on England's side. Speaking in the House of Commons he said: 'I will say that it is their duty, and should be their honour, to take their place in the firing line in this contest.' He went hotfoot back to Ireland to say just that.

At Woodenbridge on September 20 he spoke at a Volunteer parade.

> The war is undertaken in defence of the highest principles of religion and morality and right, and it would be a disgrace for ever to our country, a reproach to her manhood, and a denial of the lessons of her history, if young Ireland confined their efforts to remaining at home to defend the shores of Ireland from an unlikely

invasion, or should shrink from the duty of proving on the battlefield that gallantry and courage which have distinguished their race all through its history.

He was gambling that a generous gesture would help to ensure Home Rule on his terms once the war was over; that the chips he was gambling with were the lives of thousands of young Irishmen was irrelevant. One of them was his brother, Major Willie Redmond, killed in action in 1917 at Messines.

Afterwards it was suggested that Redmond, Dillon and the other Irish MPs had been seduced by too long a sojourn among the glories and ritual of the Mother of Parliaments. In England the Labour rank-and-file were making a similar complaint against their MPs whose working-class edge became blunted by the gentleman's club atmosphere of the House of Commons. But Redmond was both encouraging and responding to the mood of the times. The war would be over within the year, music hall stars sang 'We don't want to lose you but we think you ought to go', and throughout that golden summer of 1914 Britain and Ireland rushed to the recruiting stations, unwarned by the flare of our hindsight which lights up dead landscapes and dead men.

Redmond's speech split the Volunteers, whose original committee under MacNeill immediately repudiated it: 'Ireland cannot, with honour or safety, take part in foreign quarrels otherwise than through free action of a National Government of its own.' But when votes on the issue were polled in brigades all over Ireland only 13,500 men, out of 180,000, opted to stay with MacNeill and stick to their original purpose of defence and protection. These became the Irish Volunteers and, eventually, the Irish Republican Army (IRA), while the vast majority joined Redmond and became the National Volunteers. Numerous as these were, the National Volunteers didn't remain a force in politics for long; they were literally killed off in the trenches.

In the Cumann na mBan the vote went almost exactly the opposite way. Tame as it seemed to female activists like Con, its patriotism was not for England, and it had seemed so dangerously modern a movement to supporters of the Irish Parliamentary Party that they had discouraged their womenfolk from joining it. Shrugging off those who merely wanted to raise money for the British war effort, the Cumann na mBan became more militaristic and its Belfast branch, perhaps influenced by the example of the Connolly girls, began regular rifle practice and actually challenged their equivalent Volunteer branch to a shooting competition.

But it was still Liberty Hall which gave the greatest opportunity to women, thanks to the influence of the Countess Markievicz and James

Connolly, who never wavered in his appreciation of their intelligence and capability. During the Votes for Women campaign his support had earned the gratitude of the Irish Women's Franchise League, who called him 'the soundest and most thoroughgoing feminist among all the Labour men'.

In order to give employment to women, Con and Helena Moloney – with Connolly's encouragement – had set up a co-operative next door to Liberty Hall making shirts and underclothing.

Men and women of the Irish Citizen Army frequently marched together singing the Battle Hymn composed by the Countess Markievicz.

> Bless Thou our Banner, God of the Brave,
> Ireland is living, shout we triumphant . . .

As Con herself said, 'It may not be great poetry, but it *is* good propaganda.'

Women and men were in the same first-aid classes given by Dr Kathleen Lynn, one of the few female doctors in Dublin and very nearly the only one in sympathy with Liberty Hall. Her name bobs up again and again in the history of that time like some merciful lifeboat, looking after jailed suffragettes, hunger strikers, tending to the wounded and dying during the Easter Rising and, in 1919, founding the St Ultan's Infant Hospital, a wing of which was added later in the name of Constance Markievicz, her great friend.

Like the Irish Volunteers, the Irish Citizen Army in those early days used Con's *Fianna Handbook* as its training manual, particularly its chapters on drill and rifle exercise. It was the best source of training material available.

But with its lack of resources, the Citizen Army still found it difficult to get its men together. 'I can always guarantee that the Irish Citizen Army will fight,' said James Connolly, 'but I cannot guarantee that it will be on time.'

The Fianna on the other hand had become known for their discipline and dependability. Their skill at first aid was a by-word, learned in the hard school of the lock-out baton charges – the death of one Fianna boy, Patsy O'Connor, in 1915 was indirectly attributed to his being batoned in 1913 while giving first aid to another victim. When the Volunteers went on manoeuvres in the Dublin mountains it was the Fianna who acted as their guides. When a fire had broken out at Patrick Pearse's school, St Enda's, they stopped a panic by joining hands in a line to prevent the rush and conducted an orderly withdrawal.

114

Most of all, they were past masters in annoying the British Army and raising their own side's morale. Their anti-recruitment campaign was Con's special baby. As Margaret Skinnider said, they upset the stages of recruiting posts and heckled the recruiting sergeants. At nights, unseen, they papered Dublin with posters printed on the hand press at Surrey House reading: 'Irishmen, Beware. Enlistment in England's Armed Forces is Treachery to Ireland,' or, sometimes, 'Be True to Ireland, do not join the Baden-Powell Scouts.' They were continually torn down until Con managed to obtain bicycles for her guerrilla bill-posters and perfected a method of leaning the bike against a wall, clambering up on the saddle, and pasting the poster up out of reach.

Outside Liberty Hall hung a banner reading: 'We Serve neither King or Kaiser, but Ireland.' That too was torn down – on the orders of the commander of troops in Dublin – and went up again. Neutrality was sedition, but the British Government did not believe Irish nationalists were neutral. They lumped all of them, Volunteers, Citizen Army, Fianna and others, under the inaccurate heading of 'Sinn Féiners', a term which now took on the connotation 'Pro-German'. On December 4, 1914, military and police broke up Connolly's *Irish Worker* presses and suppressed the paper, at the same time banning Arthur Griffith's journal, *Sinn Féin*, and the IRB's *Irish Freedom*. Redmond applauded the action against these 'execrable little rags'.

At that moment Sir Roger Casement was in Germany with the knowledge of the Irish Republican Brotherhood and funds supplied by Clan na Gael in America, trying to get German support and arms for an Irish insurrection, and to recruit an Irish brigade[1] from among the Irish and German prisoner-of-war camps. The Germans gave vague assurances – and actually did send arms for the Rising – but all Casement's attempts were disastrous and, as it turned out, played no part in the eventual insurrection, except in so far as they convinced Casement himself, Bulmer Hobson and Eoin MacNeill that German help would eventually come and that no Rising could hope to succeed without it.

The inner circle of the Irish Republican Brotherhood never put much hope in Germany, but they were prepared to play her off against England just as Carson had when, in 1913, he indicated that he was prepared to accept help against Asquith's Home Rule from 'a powerful continental monarch'.

[1] Asquith had promised Irishmen enlisting in the British Army a brigade of their own, but Lord Kitchener, Secretary of State for War, was prejudiced against Southern Irishmen. The Unionist Volunteers had their own Division, but the Southerners were dispersed among different units, not being allowed their own flag or badge and, in some cases, being refused commissions.

James Connolly believed that if a German landing in Ireland guaranteed Irish independence, both from England and Germany, the Irish would be justified in supporting it. The war appalled him. He saw it as an imperialist capitalist plot. His only hope was that it would signal an uprising of the working classes in all countries of Europe, but as, one by one, European workers' movements flung themselves into it and international socialism disintegrated, he became bitter. 'The Germans are as bad as the British,' he told Pearse and Tom Clarke. 'Do the job yourselves.'

Con's stance appeared the most basic. She didn't give a damn for Germany, imperial or otherwise, but if it was fighting England it must be a Good Thing. Later on in the war a play called *An Englishman's Home* which had been having a long run in London, was brought to Dublin. It was crude propaganda, depicting the atrocities that would take place if the Germans invaded England. Con took a full force of the Fianna to its opening night, occupying the pit and the gallery while the rest of the theatre was full of British officers and their wives. The audience watched peaceably until the Germans came on stage, at which point the Fianna stood up and sang 'The Watch on the Rhine' in German as Con had taught them.

No wonder that of all the known 'Sinn Féiners' Con was the one the British authorities suspected most of having the deepest pro-German sympathies. She added a marching song to the Citizen Army's repertoire, an audacious doggerel called 'The Germans are winning the war, me boys'. She said openly and so often that she did not want the war stopped until the British Empire was smashed that, later, in 1916, the pacifist Francis Sheehy Skeffington, horrified by the losses in Europe, challenged her to debate.

Being Con, she accepted but she was disastrous. According to Louie Bennett:

> She reiterated the same few points in various, wild flowery phrases, and talked much of dying for Ireland. The Countess had the meeting with her ... Her supporters spoke in a bitter and sinister vein. I gathered they were willing to watch the war continue, with all its dreadful losses and consequences, if only it led to the overthrow of England ... Then Connolly stood up ... As well as I can remember he spoke strongly in favour of seizing the moment to fight now against England.

Hanna Sheehy Skeffington was also there to watch her husband's challenge and is kinder to her old friend, the Countess:

> He was pro-peace, she for a longer war, as she held Britain was being beaten. After a warmly contested word-duel, just before the vote was taken, James Connolly, who had been a quiet on-looker, suddenly intervened on Madame's side, swinging

the meeting round. When Skeffington laughingly reproved him for throwing in his weight at the end, he replied with twinkling eyes, 'I was afraid you might get the better of it, Skeffington. That would never do.'

This is Con at her least attractive; shrill, bloodthirsty and rather silly, and having to be rescued from an untenable position by male wisdom. It is this aspect of her which has stayed like a residue in male Irish memory, while so much of her goodness has been washed away.

But what should not be forgotten about Con is what she herself tried to forget – that she was English.

For her, to be Irish had been an option, not a condition, and she had taken it because Ireland was the underdog and her heart and mind had moved her towards it. She was a convert to Ireland and, like many converts, had to take up the extremist position in the new faith. Con had to despise England because she dare not do otherwise; it was not a pose put on for other people, but to convince herself. It is why, in the terrible Dáil debate of 1921 over the Treaty with England, when former colleagues were hurling abuse at each other, Michael Collins searched for and found the one word he knew would hurt her most, and screamed 'English' at her, who had been sentenced to death for Ireland's sake.

But the redeeming thing about Constance Markievicz is that she did not run true to the aridity of the stereotype which has since been imposed on her; when confronted on the personal level her compassion always overcame the doctrinaire. Long after the war, when faraway British soldiers had become present and hostile Black and Tans, feeling against Irishmen who had fought for England ran high, especially on Armistice Day when nationalists tore out the remembrance poppies worn by British Legion supporters. Passing one elderly man, Con took the poppy from his coat and threw it on the ground. 'That was for my son,' said the man. 'He was killed on the Marne.' Con bent down, picked up the flower and put it back in his lapel.

Chapter Nine

Ireland, unknowing, like it or not, had been committed to rebellion soon after war began. The date had been set for Easter Week 1916.

The men who took the decision were a military council within the Irish Republican Brotherhood, and at that point they told it to nobody, not even the outer casings of secrecy in the nest-of-dolls which was the Brotherhood and of which they were the central and most secret core. As they read history the time for Ireland to throw off England was now, while she was engaged in a world war, or never.

The two men at the heart of this group were Tom Clarke, the dynamiter and tobacconist, and his closest associate in the IRB, Seán MacDermott, a thirty-year-old barman. One by one they brought in others, among them Joseph Plunkett, a student, poet and son of Count Plunkett, Professor Thomas MacDonagh, a teacher at Patrick Pearse's school, and Patrick Pearse himself.

Eoin MacNeill, leader of the Volunteers, was not told and neither was Bulmer Hobson, who had done so much to rejuvenate the IRB. Both these men still saw the Volunteers as a purely defensive force and, as Tom Clarke guessed, would oppose a Rising.

The difficulty Tom Clarke and his inner ring faced was to keep everybody in the dark – too many previous rebellions in Irish history had failed through betrayal – and at the same time keep the Volunteers at action stations.

In a sense Patrick Pearse had taken the place Bulmer Hobson might have had if he had not become cautious and joined MacNeill in the wait-and-see brigade. Pearse had gone the other way, developing from a dedicated Gaelic scholar and headmaster – his foundation, St Enda's, was one of the most advanced schools in the country, teaching its children pride in themselves and their country – to an extremist after Tom Clarke's heart, and one of the things which shifted him along that course was the horror of the 1913 lock-out.

He had written at the time: 'The tenement houses of Dublin are so rotten that they periodically collapse upon their inhabitants, and if the inhabitants collect in the street to discuss the matter, the police baton them to death.'

His genius, and his supreme value to Tom Clarke, lay in his oratory. Pearse could transmute reality into myth and, more important, myth into reality. In July 1915, Clarke gave him his chance. The occasion was the funeral of an old hero of the 1867 Fenian Rising, O'Donovan Rossa, whose body had been brought back from the States, where he'd been living, for burial in Irish soil. Clarke wanted it made into a mass event, complete with march past and a volley over the grave that might provoke the authorities into a reaction which, in turn, would wake up the dormant Irish and justify his planned Rising in their eyes. But the British for once showed sense; military and police were kept off the streets that day.

Eva Gore-Booth and Esther Roper had come over to Dublin to visit Con and were sitting in an upstairs window of a friend's house to watch the procession of Volunteers, Citizen Army, Fianna and sympathisers complete with pipe bands and banners go by. Esther turned to Eva and said: 'Well, thank goodness, they simply can't be planning a rising now, not with such a tiny force.' In London, where she and Eva now lived, she had become sadly used to the apparently endless tramp of troops on their way to France. 'But,' she wrote later, 'I did not realise, as Connolly and the others did, the power that an intrepid failure has to rouse Ireland.'

Nor did she hear the spine-tingling speech Patrick Pearse made by the Rossa graveside. He said: 'They think they have foreseen everything, provided against everything, but the fools, the fools, the fools – they have left us our Fenian dead and while Ireland holds these graves Ireland unfree shall never be at peace.'

Originally, Connolly had not wanted the Citizen Army involved with the funeral. 'When are you fellows going to stop blethering about *dead* Fenians? Why don't you get a few *live* ones for a change?' but, after a talk with Tom Clarke, fell in with the plan and wrote an article for the literary souvenir of the funeral in which he, too, turned a dead Fenian into a live incitement to revolution.

Connolly's temper shows a dilemma that was almost splitting him apart. It is generally acknowledged that he was one of the greatest Labour leaders and theoreticians Ireland has ever produced. Everything he wrote and thought was born out of experience. He had been born into not just the working class, but the most deprived section of it, in County Monaghan, from which his parents had emigrated while he was still a child in order to survive. They had gone to Edinburgh where James had to start work at the age of eleven, going from one dead-end job to another, eventually being forced into the British Army as a way of staying alive. He had so loathed the experience – it is said he was given the duty of guarding an Irishman about to be executed for agrarian agitation – that he rarely talked about it. Its only compensation was free time in which he educated himself, a process that led to socialism and Marx. After his marriage to a domestic servant, Lillie Reynolds, who provided perhaps the greatest security of his life, he had returned to Ireland at the request of the Irish Socialist Republican Party and their promise of a wage of one pound a week, which they had not always been able to deliver. The Connollys had to live in the slums among poverty even they had not dreamed of. Nora Connolly, his daughter, said that in winter 'Mother could only light the fire at night time.' He'd worked with Maud Gonne against evictions, founded socialist newspapers, written and preached, but, just as his parents had done, he was forced to emigrate – this time to America – to keep his family of seven children alive, returning in 1902 to work for Larkin, women's rights, unions and every cause that needed him.

When the lock-out had ended by the men and women of Dublin being forced back to work on the employers' terms, he had become embittered not just against capitalism – he'd always had reason to hate that – but by British Labour's failure to support them long enough. He'd written:

> Aye, bitter hate, or cold neglect
> Or lukewarm love at best,
> Is all we have or can expect
> We aliens of the west.

The humiliation of being starved back to work had shattered the workers' confidence in themselves and their union. When the Citizen Army had begged them to join it and be counted, the response was dismal; nobody wanted to be openly identified with Liberty Hall. Connolly had to bear not only their indifference but that of practically every union official and Labour leader in Dublin. It was too shaky a foundation on which to build his hoped-for liberation of the working class.

Then had come the war with its retreat of European socialism and the failure of trade unionism to stand against it. Sean O'Casey said that when Connolly turned to nationalism Labour lost a leader. It would be more accurate to say that he was the leader Labour didn't follow; there was nowhere else for him to turn to.

He had always been a strong nationalist – one of the reasons he returned from the States was homesickness – and for a long time had seen the two political loves of his life as indivisible. 'We cannot conceive of a free Ireland with a subject working class; we cannot conceive of a subject Ireland with a free working class.' But which freedom came first?

It was exactly the dilemma Constance Markievicz, Hanna Sheehy Skeffington and others had faced over women's rights. Con had solved it immediately: Ireland first. Now Connolly, more painfully and more slowly, had been forced to the same conclusion. A free Ireland was the prerequisite for socialist victory.

In December 1914 he warned the government where he was heading: 'Our cards are on the table. If you leave us at liberty we will kill your recruiting, save our poor boys from your slaughterhouse, and blast your hopes of Empire . . . we will evoke a spirit that will thwart you and, mayhap, raise a force that will destroy you.' The authorities left him his freedom, hardly considering the Citizen Army as a 'force' that would destroy them, but they suppressed his *The Irish Worker* for which this had been an editorial – he had it printed and distributed in leaflet form, and in May 1915 began publishing *Workers' Republic* from Liberty Hall's printing press.

With the decision taken, he became frantic that it should be put into action while England's back was turned, before another Irishman died in its war, and before Ireland herself was partitioned.

This last fear had solidified on May 19, 1915, when the Liberal Cabinet was suspended and replaced by a Coalition Ministry which included no less than eight Unionists. Sir Edward Carson was Attorney General. That inveterate enemies of Home Rule had been awarded influential positions alarmed even the most moderate Redmondites, and the Volunteers received a surge of new recruits.

The new *Workers' Republic* carried a masthead from the French revolutionary Desmoulins: 'The great only appear great because we are on our knees: let us rise', and its contents, on street fighting, guerrilla warfare, and the history of revolt and its lessons, shouted aloud that the Citizen Army, for all its size, was out for insurrection or, at least, was prepared to sacrifice itself so that insurrection could begin. One of its articles was on the fight at the Alamo in 1821. 'It was one of those defeats which are more valuable to a cause than many loudly trumpeted victories. It gave spirit and bitterness to the Texan forces and, more important still, gave time to their comrades elsewhere.'

The complacency with which the authorities regarded all the marching and apparent bluster seems extraordinary now, but must have made good sense at the time, rather on the mistaken principle that someone who constantly threatens suicide won't actually go ahead and do it. Their use of the Defence of the Realm Act (DORA) was petty rather than wholesale and merely increased resentment. Civil servants were dismissed from their jobs for belonging to the Volunteers. Liam Mellowes was deported to England and Nora Connolly had to go after him and smuggle him back dressed as a clergyman. Francis Sheehy Skeffington was sent to prison for anti-war speeches.

There is no doubt that the Citizen Army had plans for a rising of their own, although exactly what they were remains unclear to this day. The only three who knew them were Connolly, and his second-in-command, Michael Mallin, and Con.

Constance became concerned about what might happen to Stanislas, who was still with her and frequently active in the Fianna, if she were arrested. It was something of a relief when a letter from Casi included 300 roubles for the boy's journey to his grandparents' home in the Ukraine. The Ukraine was not going to be much safer than Ireland, or, for that matter, the journey in between, but Stanislas arrived safely and Con was now completely free of ties.

She was hardly lonely. A French journalist who visited Surrey House wrote of it: 'The salon of Countess Markievicz is not a salon, it's a military HQ.' It was also open house. 'Nobody was denied a lodging,' said Padraic Colum, 'so long as she had a bed or a sofa or a few cushions. Many friends made a practice to get in by the window and spend the night in her house if they were in the neighbourhood. She never knew how many she was going to seat for breakfast.' Connolly was lodging upstairs and one or other of his daughters were always visiting and some Fianna were in permanent residence. The evening gatherings were wonderful. Hanna Sheehy Skeffington recalled how Con would issue last-minute invitations, saying: 'The gas is cut off and the carpets up, but you won't mind.' By the light of candles guests gathered. 'She had lovely furniture,' Frank Kelly, an officer in the Citizen Army, told Sean O'Faolain, 'and splendid pictures . . . we used to go into the sitting room and someone would sit at the piano and there would be great singing and cheering and rough amusement. She had lifted her lovely drawing-room carpet . . . and on the bare boards there was stamping of feet.' A young Volunteer called Michael Collins was a visitor and is remembered for reciting Emmet's speech from the dock at the top of his voice. Con would recite Keats to piano accompaniment.

There was little time for culture, but she still occasionally popped into the Arts Club and it may have been about this time that she made a telephone call from there which is still remembered because another member overheard it and complained to the committee that it was 'political'. The committee's response was to censure the member for listening in to a private conversation.

Citizen Army manoeuvres became increasingly belligerent. On

October 1915, a particularly foggy night, all its soldiers, male and female, staged a mock attack on Dublin Castle, the centre of British administration and a large complex of buildings which included a hospital. As a test of their efficiency they had been mobilised at short notice and didn't know whether the attack was to be real or simulated. 'Is this it?' everybody asked everybody else. 'Is this it?' It wasn't, but it went well, with different sections converging on the Castle from different directions. One section had been detailed to 'defend' the complex and a defending Citizen Army soldier was heard to remark to another: 'Imagine going through all this to help the old Castle, when I'd go through twice as much to pull it down.'

If the 'attack' did nothing else, it alarmed the detectives of the Special Branch known as G-men, because they belonged to G-division, the government's detective force. They followed the Citizen Army divisions, when it was over, to Emmet Hall at Inchicore where they were to celebrate their manoeuvre in tea and buns. It turned out to be quite a party and the G-men had to stay on watch until five a.m. when, one soldier remembered, 'we rejoined the police outside and were pleased to find that it had been raining while we were enjoying ourselves, so that the poor fellows were not dry. We then marched home.'

Connolly's impatience for insurrection also led to verbal attacks on the Volunteer leaders for not making a move, describing them as 'legally seditious and peacefully revolutionary'. He had begun to alarm Tom Clarke and his military council who were afraid he and the Citizen Army might stage a rising on their own, an act which would lead to the suppression of the Volunteers and ruin all their plans for Easter 1916.

On January 19, 1916, James Connolly disappeared. To this day it is uncertain whether or not he was kidnapped. Whatever it was, the military council of the Irish Republican Brotherhood was behind it. Patrick Pearse and Sean MacDermott had told him that 'he would have the Volunteers as allies if he waited. After "a terrible mental struggle" Connolly agreed.'

There must have been more to it than that because when Connolly arrived back at Surrey House three nights later, he told Con and Helena Moloney that he had been 'through hell'.

So had they. They had, after all, plans for their own rising and the disappearance of their leader at this stage was serious. Phone calls to his family in Belfast and to friends had established that it was a genuine disappearance. Con wanted to turn out the Citizen Army there and then, a decision which is almost invariably quoted as an example of panic or hysteria, although Desmond Ryan, the leading authority on the Rising, makes it clear that there had been an agreement between Connolly, his second-in-command, Michael Mallin and the Countess that if any one of the three were arrested, the remaining two would call out the Citizen Army to take up positions for a rising.

The Citizen Army's intelligence must have been good, however, because it soon became apparent that the IRB military council had something to do with the disappearance, and Con held her hand while Mallin bearded the council in its den and warned them that if Connolly was not returned quickly the Citizen Army would rise. Éamonn Ceannt, the Volunteers' Director of Communications and another member of the IRB military council, who was present, said: 'What could your few numbers do anyway?'

'We can die,' said Mallin, 'and it will be to our eternal glory, and to your shame,' a reply which would have won Con's admiration, and certainly won the council's.

The result of this incident was that Connolly was told the projected date of the Rising, which was to coincide with the arrival of a shipload of arms Casement had negotiated in Germany. From that moment on he was co-opted on to the military council and calmed down his editorials, at least to a certain extent.

The Director of Military Intelligence in Ireland, wrote on April 10, 1916: 'The general state of Ireland ... apart from the activities of the pro-German Sinn Féin minority, is thoroughly satisfactory. The mass of the people are sound and loyal as regards the war, and the country is in a very prosperous state, and very free from ordinary crimes.' But the G-men had become alerted by the general air of tension, even though their superiors – and Eoin MacNeill – recognised no tension beyond the ordinary.

Surrey House was raided along with other 'known Sinn Féin' houses. Con came back from a meeting to find her small printing press being carried out by the police, while boys and girls of the Fianna harassed them by 'comforting remarks', and nationalist songs.

Margaret Skinnider arrived from Glasgow, smuggling in detonators for Citizen Army use. She and Con went out to the Wicklow Hills and practised with them by blowing up a wall. Poppet, the Irish cocker spaniel, played a good nationalist role by tagging along with any soldiers of the Citizen Army out in the country carrying guns thereby giving credence that they were a hunting party.

Con also sent Margaret, a maths teacher, to draw plans of Portobello and Beggars' Bush Barracks, a job she accomplished without attracting attention, although two officers of the Irish Volunteers had already attempted it and failed.

It seems likely that the drawings she made were for a plan of all strategic points, drawn up for use by both Volunteers and Citizen Army, now in co-operation, and that Con was in charge of a large part of it. Nora Connolly remembered her finishing the last map and admiring her skill at the drawing board. Nora asked if anyone had been curious about what she was doing. 'Only once,' Con said, 'when an unexpected visitor who has nothing at all to do with the movement walked in one day and caught me . . . I said it was a housing scheme I was interested in.' That the explanation had been accepted was, said Nora, 'the advantage of being known as a woman of many interests'.

Obviously, whoever did or did not know the date for the Rising, the leading women of the Citizen Army did. Con, for instance, confided it to Margaret Skinnider who went back to Glasgow with the knowledge. When she tried to cheer up her Irish mother by saying, without giving away the date, that she thought there might be a rising soon, her mother shook her head: 'There never was an Irish rising that someone didn't betray it.'

Margaret returned to Dublin some time before Easter to take her part in the insurrection, to discover that Con had found time to make her a uniform 'of better material than her own'.

There had been a small conference among the women leaders, including Dr Kathleen Lynn, who was to be medical officer on the day, about what they should wear when they went out to battle – breeches or skirts? Breeches were obviously more practical, but should they add to the populace's shock at seeing the imperial world tumble about its ears the shock of women in trousers? Margaret Skinnider, who was to act as despatch rider on the day – on a bicycle – opted for breeches and so did Con, though she wore a skirt over them on pre-Rising occasions so as not to attract attention.

As a precaution, in case she was killed, she had her photograph taken in the uniform, minus skirt, complete with her hat and its cockade of feathers, and a revolver. She was by this time forty-eight years old. One of the Citizen Army men told Jacqueline Van Voris: 'She was lovely in uniform. I can remember seeing her marching at the head of the Citizen Army with Connolly and Mallin at a parade on Sunday afternoon. My God, she was *it*.'

Tension continued to rise. A Fianna boy bringing gelignite into Dublin had trouble delivering it to its destination and so naturally went to Surrey House for orders, somehow avoiding the watching G-men. He was later arrested, but the gelignite was never found.

On March 24, the police began raiding the offices of seditious journals, starting with *Gael*, published by the Gaelic Press. Luckily, Con was shopping in that vicinity, saw them and rushed to Liberty

Hall to tell Connolly that his printing press, tucked away in the Women Workers' Co-operative shop next door to Liberty Hall, might be next. Connolly found the police already in the shop searching through bundles of papers and held them at gunpoint. 'Drop those papers or I drop you.' The police left, promising to return. The danger was not just to the press, but that the raid might be extended to Liberty Hall which at that point contained the Citizen Army's very considerable arsenal.

It was decided to mobilise and the order was sent out at once. It is an indication of how efficient the organisation had become that within the hour 160 working men had dropped tools, coal sacks, trollies and were running through the streets towards Liberty Hall in their overalls. One section, who worked in a yard on the other side of the canal, had saved time by swimming over, and arrived dripping wet.

The police wisely retired without entering Liberty Hall and the event turned out to be merely a useful emergency drill. The Citizen Army had been prepared to fight and had turned up on time, complete with its women's ambulance corps and Fianna. It had also been an example in co-operation – the Volunteers had been put on the alert and stood by until two a.m. the next morning.

From that time on until the Rising, Liberty Hall was guarded day and night and James Connolly moved out of Surrey House to sleep on a bed in his office.

During the raid Con, having seen Liberty Hall temporarily safe, and suspecting the raid was a prelude to war, returned home to get into her uniform and collect her firearms. Nora Connolly went too, to fetch her father's carbine and bandolier of ammunition and sent them back with an attendant Fianna boy. Con had no mean arsenal of her own and armed herself with an automatic pistol, a Mauser and bandolier.

Just as they were leaving there was the unmistakable rap of police on the door. Con reduced her hall light to a glimmer and opened the door to two detectives who had come to tell her that under the Defence of the Realm Act she had been prohibited from entering County Kerry where she had been due to speak at a Fianna gathering in Tralee on the following Sunday. (Madame's speeches were too inflammatory; she had recently made one in Cork on March 6, ostensibly on 'The Sacrifices of Robert Emmet' which had turned into anti-recruitment propaganda.) Nora Connolly overheard the conversation.

'What will happen if I refuse to obey the order and go to Kerry? Would I be shot?'

'Ah now, Madame, who'd want to shoot you? You wouldn't want to shoot one of us. Now would you, Madame?'

'But I would. I'm quite prepared to shoot and be shot at.'

'Ah now, Madame, you don't mean that. None of us want to die yet. We all want to live a little longer.'

'If you want to live a little longer you'd better not be coming here. None of us are fond of you, and you make grand big targets . . .'

Connolly forbade her to go to Tralee in case she was arrested because she was 'too valuable'. Like the other leaders, she was immensely busy, and took her turn standing guard at Liberty Hall and also turned up there every afternoon with a bag of cakes for the other sentries' tea. She'd overdrawn her bank account for the next quarter by £45 and confessed, 'if this bally revolution doesn't take place soon I don't know how I'm going to live.'

She found time, too, to write a poem which was published in the last edition of the *Workers' Republic* on Easter Saturday, April 22. It ends:

> So we're waiting till 'Somebody' gives the word
> That sends us to Freedom or death;
> As free men defiant we'd sooner fall
> Than be slaves to our dying breath.

On Palm Sunday, watched by the Citizen Army drawn up in full formation in Beresford Place, the green flag of Ireland with its golden harp was unfurled over Liberty Hall. Connolly was immediately censured for flying it by his fellow officers of the ITGWU, whose headquarters this was as well; they demanded an explanation for the risk he was putting them all in. Connolly replied that no explanation was needed and that if the time came when the union objected to the Irish flag, he would resign from it. The flag was allowed to go on flying.

A busy evening ensued. Connolly's play *Under Which Flag*, which depicted an Irishman torn between joining England's army or Ireland's – and eventually choosing Ireland's, of course – was performed with the Abbey actor, Seán Connolly, playing the hero. He was killed on Easter Monday.

Behind the scenes Connolly was giving his last lecture on guerrilla warfare. It is said that he finished it with: 'The odds against are a thousand to one. But if we should win, hold on to your rifles because the Volunteers may have a different goal. Remember we're out not only for political liberty but for economic liberty as well. So hold on to your rifles.'

On Monday a Provisional Revolutionary Government was constituted and the Proclamation of the Irish Republic prepared for Liberty
Hall's printing press. 'Irishmen and Irishwomen! In the name of God
and of the dead generations from which she receives her old tradition
of nationhood, Ireland, through us, summons her children to her flag,
and strikes for her freedom . . .' It was signed first by Thomas Clarke,
then Patrick Pearse who was to be president of the provisional
government, Seán MacDermott, Thomas MacDonagh, Éamonn
Ceannt, James Connolly and Joseph Plunkett.

Among its assurances it contained a clear guarantee to women that
there would be equal rights and equal opportunities to all citizens.
James Connolly had insisted on this inclusion and told Hanna Sheehy
Skeffington just before the Rising that the signatories had been
'practically unanimous' in agreeing to it. 'Only one questioned it,' he
said. (Who that was remains unknown and, since he died with the
others, he has been forgiven.) Without her knowledge, Hanna Sheehy
Skeffington had also been chosen to be a member of the civil provisional government if the Rising continued for an appreciable time.

Con was approved by Tom Clarke and the others as a 'ghost' for
Connolly, one of the deputies for the leaders who were entrusted with
sufficient of the Rising plans to take over should the leader fall.

During the week officers of both the Volunteers and the Citizen
Army were given their orders for the Rising. Roughly, the plan was
to occupy strategic points in a ring around central Dublin; the GPO
in O'Connell Street and the Four Courts to the north of the Liffey;
the Mendicity Institution and the South Dublin Union, which commanded Kingsbridge railway terminus, in the west; the Jacobs Biscuit
Factory in the south; St Stephen's Green to the south-east; and
Boland's Mill in the east, covering the main road from Kingstown
(Dun Laoghaire) along which troops brought in from England would
have to march.

Smaller sections would help fill in the gaps and snipers were to
cover the rest.

The GPO was to be seized by a combined force of Volunteers and
Citizen Army under James Connolly, and the provisional government
established in it by Pearse, Clarke, Seán MacDermott and Joseph
Plunkett. Of the two other signatories to the proclamation, Thomas
MacDonagh, commanding the 2nd Battalion Volunteers, was at Jacobs
Factory, and Éamonn Ceannt in command at South Dublin Union.
Boland's bakery mill was to be the headquarters of the 3rd Battalion
Volunteers under brigade adjutant Eamon de Valera, and the Four
Courts of the 1st Battalion, under Edward Daly.

The Cumann na mBan and the Fianna were to act as messengers, nursing orderlies and stretcher bearers. None of them was given a commission in the Volunteers. In the Citizen Army many of the women soldiers were armed and Con, Dr Kathleen Lynn and Helena Moloney were commissioned. James Connolly told them that the moment the first shot was fired 'there will no longer be Volunteers or Citizen Army, but only the Army of the Irish Republic.'

Apart from the Citizen Army men in the combined force at the GPO most of the others, male and female, were to be centred on St Stephen's Green under Commandant Michael Mallin. The only woman officially posted at the GPO was Connolly's secretary from Belfast, Winifred Carney, who had come down to be at his side and type orders. She remained there to the last.

Also down from Belfast for the duration was Connolly's wife Lillie, who was to stay at Con's cottage at Balally in charge of the spaniel, Poppet.

The insurrection covered the provinces and orders were issued to battalions round the country. A rising in Ulster was considered hopeless and the Volunteers from those counties were to go to Galway and put themselves under the command of Liam Mellowes.

The officers knew their objectives: the rank-and-file were told to stand by for special manoeuvres on Easter Sunday.

There was no artillery deployed because there was none, but Connolly was convinced, mistakenly as it turned out, that none would be used against them on the Marxist principle that capitalists would not destroy property.

On the Thursday of that week Constance made a flag. The making was recorded in 1968 by Maura O'Neill Mackey, then a young member of the Cumann na mBan who was staying at Surrey House along with Laurence Ginnell, one of the few Irish MPs in sympathy with the nationalists, and his wife. For Maura, Constance was

the living embodiment of Kathleen Ni Houlihan . . . the loveliest woman I had ever seen and I was acutely aware of her immense vitality and personal magnetism. She taught us Morse Code and how to clean revolvers and other guns. We were trained to carry messages and under Dr Kathleen Lynn studied first aid – all the time being constantly urged by the Countess that one day we would be needed in Ireland's bid for freedom.

All that week the Countess had seemed 'on edge'. On the Thursday in question she . . . came down with what we recognised as the green bedspread from Larry Ginnell's bed. Poppet, Madame's pet dog, always had to play his part in whatever she was doing and kept jumping up and down pulling at the material until eventually he tore a piece out of the side. (This piece is still missing, as I pointed out in Kildare St. Museum [the National Museum in Dublin] when the Flag was formerly placed on view during the Golden Jubilee Commemoration.)

The gold paint Con hoped to use on the material had dried up, 'so she sent to the kitchen for a tin of mustard which, having moistened, she mixed with the paint . . . she commenced to paint the words "Irish Republic" on the material while we held it taut.'

The flag was taken to the GPO on Monday and flew over it until it was captured. It was eventually taken to London, but returned in 1966 by the then British Prime Minister, Harold Wilson, for the Golden Jubilee of the Rising.

Maura spent the Rising helping the wounded in the Four Courts area under the command of Edward Daly.

On the evening of Thursday, April 20, Bulmer Hobson overheard a conversation at Volunteer HQ which alerted him to the fact that a Rising was planned shortly. He went straight to Eoin MacNeill who insisted, though it was after midnight, on going to St Enda's and confronting Patrick Pearse. Pearse listened to their outburst and then said quietly: 'Yes, you are right. A Rising is intended.'

Scholarship seems to have made MacNeill into one of life's absent-minded professors, but it is still a mystery how he could not have noticed what was going on under his nose when girls of the Cumann na mBan, who'd been making up endless medical kits all week, suspected a Rising was at hand. How Pearse could have assumed that once MacNeill did know, he would fall easily in with the plan, is another. MacNeill was alarmed and outraged. As he left, he said: 'I will do everything I can to stop this, *everything* except ring up Dublin Castle.'

So he did, but not until after a lot of vacillating and consultation with Bulmer Hobson and The O'Rahilly, another who was convinced the Rising was madness. The deciding factor came on Saturday with the news that German arms were not coming and that Sir Roger Casement had been arrested. There had been a disastrous series of mishaps down in Tralee where the German ship, the *Aud*, carrying 20,000 rifles, a million rounds of ammunition and ten machine guns had arrived on schedule to find nobody waiting for her. After a long delay she had been forced to sail away again, only to come under the guns of a British naval force which took her under escort to Cobh Harbour. The *Aud*'s captain was determined that if the arms could not benefit the Irish, they certainly were not going to benefit the British, and neither was his ship. When he and his crew had safely disembarked, the *Aud* blew up.

Further along the Kerry coast, arriving separately by submarine, Sir Roger Casement and two other men had been put ashore also to find nobody waiting for them, had been discovered eventually and arrested.

That was enough for MacNeill. Men were despatched all over Dublin and the country to countermand the original orders and, to make doubly sure, on Saturday night he put a notice in the next day's papers which read:

Owing to the very critical position, all orders given to Irish Volunteers for tomorrow, Easter Sunday, are hereby rescinded and no parades, marches or other movements of Irish Volunteers will take place. Each individual Volunteer will obey this order strictly in every particular.

The effect of the countermand on Volunteers who had gone to bed on Saturday night keyed up for the next day was traumatic. The men and women who were prepared that night to go out and fight the following day – and the news of the *Aud* and Casement's capture had convinced them that this at last was it – were going to battle not just for themselves but to wipe out ancestral memories of fiasco and humiliation. Hobson, perhaps seen as a more formidable opponent to the IRB military council than MacNeill, was summoned on Good Friday, to an alleged meeting at a house in Phibsborough, which he entered only to find himself taken prisoner by armed men on the military council's orders. He was not released until Bank Holiday Monday, by which time everything had gone too far to stop. (Remembering O'Casey's comment on him that everything pertaining to Labour was a sneer, it is interesting that one of the first things Hobson says he noticed on his release was 'the Dublin mob, not joining Connolly, but systematically looting the shops'.)

In fact, things had already gone too far to do anything but fight or surrender. Alerted by the scuttling of the *Aud*, Casement's arrest, and the theft of 200 lb of gelignite from a quarry at Tallaght, Lord Wimborne, the Lord Lieutenant, was planning to raid Liberty Hall 'and other Sinn Féin arsenals' and round up the leaders 'who have countermanded their Easter Day parade . . . [and] are probably sitting in conclave plotting against us'.

Con had spent Saturday night at the home of Jenny Wyse Power, out of the way of possible arrest, and read the countermand there next morning. She rushed to Liberty Hall and found Connolly and Sean MacDermott.

'"What has happened?" said I. "MacNeill has cut the ground from under our feet," said he. I began to lament and question them, he cut me short with, "It will be all right, we are going on, it will only mean a little delay."'

The provisional government of the new republic spent Easter Sunday in Connolly's small office at Liberty Hall; by lunchtime they had decided that the Rising would go ahead on the next day, Easter Monday. The rest of the time was spent in trying to countermand the countermand, sending messages, drawing up new plans. 'It was,' wrote Con, 'the busiest day I ever lived through.'

Mostly it was women who carried the message to re-mobilise the Volunteers outside Dublin – Máire Perolz to Cork, Eily O'Hanrahan to Enniscorthy, Nancy Wyse Power to Borris and others to Dundalk, Tralee and Waterford – since they were least likely to be suspected on what was a dangerous, and in many cases futile, mission. Nora Connolly, who had dashed down from Belfast for orders after reading MacNeill's announcement, was sent back to proceed as planned.

Contacting the Citizen Army was a comparatively easy matter, and it seemed something approaching its full, but small, complement would turn up on the new Rising Day, but MacNeill's order had caused havoc among the Volunteers and how many could be depended upon to present themselves was anyone's guess.

By the time she got to bed that night – she and Winifred Carney stayed at the home of William O'Brien, Connolly's staunchest ally in the ITGWU – Con was so tired that, unloading her automatic, she was careless and sent a bullet through the bedroom door. Nobody paid any attention.

The next morning the four city battalions of the Volunteers and the Citizen Army paraded with full arms and equipment in front of Liberty Hall.

Con said goodbye to Tom Clarke. 'His life's work had borne fruit at last . . . We met for a few minutes just before the time fixed to march out. It seems queer, looking back on it, how no one spoke of death or fear or defeat . . . We then went downstairs, and each man joined up with his little band.'

Death and defeat were staring back at them from the littleness of those little bands. (Quite deliberately nobody seems to have counted them.) And one man did speak of it: Connolly muttered to William O'Brien as they said goodbye, 'We are going out to be slaughtered.' O'Brien asked if there was any hope. 'None whatever,' said Connolly.

A bugle sounded fall-in and the Irish Republican Army marched away.[1]

'Somewhere and somehow,' wrote James Fintan Lalor, the political

[1] Strictly speaking, according to James Connolly, the Citizen Army and Volunteers blended into the Irish Republican Army from the moment the Rising began. In fact, of course, the integration took longer and contemporary commentators still distinguish between the two.

theoretician shaped by the Great Famine, 'and by someone, a beginning must be made, and the first act of armed resistance is always premature, imprudent and foolish.'

Chapter Ten

What most of the IRA sections had to break down first, apart from a few doors, was incredulity.

It was just not the day for a revolution; it was Bank Holiday, the weather was glorious and people had better things to do.

Dublin had prospered by the war; it had brought new jobs and taken up the unemployed slack by gathering it into the British Army which, through its dependants' allowances, was providing soldiers' wives – the so-called 'separation women' – with the first regular income some of them had ever known.

Half the capital and most of the British officers appeared to have gone off to the Fairyhouse Races and their places taken by visitors coming into the city on day excursions. Dublin was full of crowds, springtime sunshine and an almost tangible security.

To the writer Elizabeth Bowen that April morning was the end of an era, especially for the middle and upper classes who had remained untouched by the lock-out disturbances.

> Battles were associated with battlefields, not yet cities. To that extent, in spite of the Great War, the Edwardian concept of civilisation still stood unshaken. It was held still that things should know where to stop – and also where not to begin. But also, Dublin had by now become a modern city – as such, she was destined to be the first to see the modern illusion crack . . . more than cracked, it shivered across; not again to be mended in our time.

Despite the Bank Holiday, the General Post Office in Sackville Street (now O'Connell Street) was open for business. When the mixed force of Volunteers and Irish Citizen Army wheeled in they found people buying stamps and a lieutenant in the Royal Fusiliers sending a telegram. He was taken prisoner, along with the sentries guarding the telegraph in the upstairs offices, and the customers hustled outside. As windows were broken to clear the line of fire and barricades of typewriters and furniture built up, the tricolour and Con's green and gold-mustard Irish Republic flag were raised over the tympanum. The Citizen Army took revenge for 1913 by flying O'Casey's beloved Starry Plough over William Martin Murphy's Imperial Hotel further along the street. The building was a roofless shell by the time the Rising was over.

Patrick Pearse went out to stand between the pillars of the GPO portico and read the Proclamation of the new Republic to an uncomprehending gathering of passers-by. The ink on it was hardly dry; the Liberty Hall printing press had been going all night to turn out some 2,000 copies. Connolly clasped his hand when he had finished and said: 'Thanks be to God, Pearse, that we have lived to see this day.' But apart from that congratulation, said one observer, the response was chilling.

Soon after the occupation a company of Lancers sent from Marlborough Barracks came dashing on horseback from the north end of the street. As they reached Nelson's Pillar just above the GPO, the Volunteers opened fire, killing four of them. The Lancers wheeled about and went back to their barracks, causing the Volunteers to hope that if the British were only going to use cavalry against them, Ireland had a chance.

Up at the Castle there had also been early bloodshed. A very small force of the Citizen Army, headed by the Abbey actor Seán Connolly, and including Helena Moloney, had rushed the gate to Upper Castle Yard and when the policeman on duty tried to shut it on them, Seán Connolly shot him dead. While the Royal Irish Constabulary outside the city were armed, the constables of the Dublin Metropolitan Police were not. Helena Moloney saved the life of another policeman who came round the corner at that moment by firing her revolver in the air, at which he retired.

This attack has consistently puzzled the Rising's hundreds of historians. If Connolly had pressed it home he would have found the Castle almost empty of defenders, and with Sir Matthew Nathan in his office as Under Secretary at that moment preparing plans to round up sixty or more 'Sinn Féin' leaders, unaware that rebellion had already begun. Desmond Ryan says the plan for the attack was to seal up the Castle by taking the guard room in its upper yard, seizing City Hall and the buildings facing the Castle gates, and that Connolly's force of sixteen could not have hoped to hold the Castle itself, weak as it may have been.

The original planning for the Rising, after all, had been based on an assumption that something like 5,000 Volunteers and Citizen Army would take part. MacNeill's countermand had reduced this to about 1,000 with a gradual reinforcement, as the news got round, bringing it to the region of 1,500.

The insurgents were actors extemporising a full-scale drama with a skeleton cast, sticking to a script which, without all the extras necessary to the plot, no longer made sense. But, even as originally planned, the action had been intended to matter more symbolically than militarily. The pity was that actual death was necessary to bring that symbolism home; and the deaths of the policeman, of Seán Connolly himself – shot later that day on the City Hall roof by a sniper – and of hundreds more, was hideously real. Early on that Monday, during a raid on the Magazine Fort in Phoenix Park by a small number of Fianna and Volunteers, the seventeen-year-old son of one of the Fort's officers was gunned down and killed as he ran to get help. 'Poor lad,' later said one of the Volunteers, 'we had no choice, he had to pay the penalty.' Elsewhere, cooped up and coming under fire for the first time, more than one Volunteer went berserk and had either to be restrained or killed by his fellows. Towards the end of the week, after fierce fighting in the Four Courts area during which it took the military two days to advance 150 yards, British soldiers ran amok, dragged civilians out of their houses and shot or bayoneted as many as fifteen.

For, if the Volunteers were coming under fire for the first time, so were many of the British soldiers, who were recruits still undergoing training and who, on Easter Monday, were considerably under strength. According to official figures there were only 111 officers and 2,316 other ranks in Dublin at that moment. To add to their panic, rumour was sweeping the city that all Ireland had risen, that German forces had invaded, 'that a large force of rebels intended to attack Portobello Barracks, which was held by only a few troops, many of whom were recruits ignorant as to how to use their rifles'.

They were also without the support of the Dublin Metropolitan Police who, since they were unarmed, were wisely withdrawn from the streets once it was realised what was happening – a factor that gave rise to a complication for both sides.

From the moment they realised they were not policed, looters fell to work. Bulmer Hobson, who had just been released, saw them. The Republic's soldiers in the GPO watched with horror as plate glass windows of confectionery shops opposite were smashed, showering sweets, chocolate boxes and slabs of toffee into struggling crowds of men, women and children. Desmond Ryan, one of those at the GPO, wrote: 'Old women from the slums hurl themselves towards the windows of a shoe store and almost walk through the plate glass, which shivers and breaks among the mob, dealing deep gashes and bloody hurts which cannot check the greedy and aimless frenzy.' Having tried shooting over the looters' heads, there had to be a sortie from the Post Office before they could be dispersed.

Apart from these essentially pitiable specimens, Dubliners reacted with disbelief, then irritation that their holiday was being spoiled and then with a curiosity that killed not a few of them as they wandered, sightseeing, into the firing line. More than one Volunteer, preparing himself for the battle of his life, found himself dug in the ribs by an inquisitive passer-by and asked what he thought he was doing.

As countermanded Volunteers heard that the Rising was going ahead without them, some hastily scrambled their equipment together and went to their original posts. Fifty-four men from Kimmage, bristling with pikes and firearms, boarded a tram to get there more quickly. Squashed passengers protested and the conductor ordered them off, so they commandeered the vehicle, making it drive to the city centre without stopping. When they had reached their destination they insisted on paying their fares.

The O'Rahilly, who'd been down in Limerick specifically to cancel the orders for the Rising there, found it was on when he got back and sped to join it, scrambling into the GPO and saying that as he had helped to wind the clock, he must be there to hear it strike.[1] He was killed by machine-gun fire on Friday, while helping to lead the evacuation from the now-burning building.

Major John MacBride, Maud Gonne's ex-husband, who had been in obscurity working as a corporation water-bailiff, had known nothing of the Rising, and had come into the city that Monday to attend a wedding. He responded to the news that there was fighting like the old warhorse he was, and joined Thomas MacDonagh at the Jacobs Factory where he distinguished himself leading dangerous raiding parties during the week.

Eoin MacNeill had cycled to a friend's house that Monday morning and was discussing what he thought was his successful attempt to call off the Rising, when fellow-Volunteers burst in to say it was on. For a while he still refused to believe it and then, with tears in his eyes, said: 'I will go home for my Volunteer uniform and go out and fight. My friends and comrades are fighting and dying and I must join them.' He changed his mind again, however, and although he tried to undo what he had done by discussing an appeal with Arthur Griffith in their joint names for all Volunteers to support the Rising, there was no way of distributing it, and it was too late.

When Margaret Skinnider cycled up to the south end of St Stephen's Green that Monday morning she found she had arrived

[1] 'Am I such a craven that / I should not get the word / But for what some travelling man / Had heard I had not heard?' / Then on Pearse and Connolly / He fixed a bitter look: / 'Because I helped to wind the clock / I came to hear it strike.' 'The O'Rahilly'. *Collected Poems*, W. B. Yeats.

before the Citizen Army. 'There were no soldiers in sight; only a policeman at the far end of the Green doing nothing.'

This would have been Constable Michael Lahiff, on duty near the monument dedicated to Irishmen who lost their lives for Britain while fighting against the Boers and subsequently known as Traitors' Gate. He was unarmed and that Easter morning he was shot and killed.

Since the story that it was Countess Markievicz who killed him was the first one mentioned to me in connection with her name by more than one well-read Irishman, it should be considered at this point.

The writer, Tim Pat Coogan, usually a meticulous researcher, as evinced by his books *Ireland Since the Rising* and *The IRA*, told me PC Lahiff was shot through the lungs and lingered for three days, attributing the act to Constance, though he agreed when pressed that he was unable to say how he knew it.

Martin Sheridan, the former *Irish Times* journalist, searched his memory for me of the time almost thirty years ago when the bust of Constance Markievicz, now on St Stephen's Green, was unveiled.

One of my ports of call in those days was a drinking den dignified by the name of the Irish Times Club and run by a genial tough old gaffer, an ex-RIC man named Charlie Long. One night in an uncharacteristic act of vandalism, the new *monumentum* was riven from its moorings and chucked into the lake in the Green (this sort of treatment has usually been reserved for relics of the Raj). The outrage was condemned by the *Irish Times* but not by Charlie Long, who was heard to mutter something about 'nice kind of people they're puttin' up statchas to these days – murderers of policemen'. Of itself, this proves nothing except perhaps that some body of opinion did exist which linked the Countess to the killing of Constable Lahiff. Pending the availability of further evidence, one way or the other, the only possible verdict is one of not proven.[1]

Nevertheless, that Madame shot a policeman in cold blood on Stephen's Green has become attached to, and now dominates, much of her memory. A great many Dubliners say they grew up knowing it, although the first detailed printed account appears to be in a book called *The Easter Rebellion* by Max Caulfield, published in London in 1965. It is a racy read, but rather long on picture-the-scene detail and short on attributed sources. He does not isolate the evidence on which he bases his account of PC Lahiff's death.

Within five minutes [of the Green's occupation by the insurgents], Constable

[1] Later Martin Sheridan kindly translated from the Gaelic for me some of the extracts relating to the Stephen's Green occupation in Professor Liam Ó Briain's book *Cuimhní Cinn* and found that 'what is important about this material is the way it illustrates her humanity and seems to contradict the legend of her killing the policeman'.

Michael Lahiff attempted to enter the Green by Traitors' Gate. He was told to go away but obstinately, if courageously, refused. Informed of his attitude, the Countess rushed to the railings and took aim with her Mauser rifle pistol. As she fired two men beside her also shot. Lahiff slumped to the pavement, hit by three bullets. 'I shot him,' shouted the Countess delightedly, 'I shot him.'

Not only does Constance 'delightedly' shoot the policeman but, according to Mr Caulfield, she also 'stormed' (not surprisingly, if the incident is true) at one of the other girls who was being fondled by a British prisoner. '"Is this what you call fighting for Ahland?"'; she is 'bloodthirsty' and generally appears not to please Mr Caulfield.

If Max Caulfield is correct in timing PC Lahiff's death 'within five minutes' of the Green's occupation – and this tallies with the entry about Lahiff in the *Sinn Féin Rebellion Handbook*[1] – it was not Con who shot him. She was elsewhere, as we shall see, and did not arrive until some time later and, when she did, it was alone and not, as Mr Caulfield describes her entry to the Green, with troops who were 'merely Boy Scouts and women; she nevertheless marched them in with the confidence of a woman whose ancestors had been conquerors.'

The Coroners' Inquests for 1916 which might give details were destroyed in the Civil War. And while it would take nearly a lifetime to read everything that has been written in connection with the Rising, I have so far been unsuccessful in tracing any book – even among those hostile to Con – which mentions the incident. Elizabeth Bowen, no great lover of Con, does not quote it in her history of the Shelbourne Hotel which faces the Green on its north side and which might have been expected to reverberate with the shock of one of the Ascendancy class, for which it catered, doing such a thing.

A broadcast on Radio Telefís Éireann about the matter elicited a phone call from Mr William Mullen, whose father was around at the time and thought she did, although he didn't see her do it, and another from Mr Edward Kruger, a member of the Fianna who was with her on the Green and is sure she didn't, although he was not with her all the time. Mr Breandán MacGiolla Choille, the former Keeper of State Papers, whose 'Intelligence Notes' are an extremely useful source of information on the time, kindly contacted me to say that in

---

[1] *The Sinn Féin Rebellion Handbook* was compiled by the *Irish Times* from various sources. PC Lahiff's name appears in the list of members of the Dublin Metropolitan Police Force killed. The entry also disposes of the rumour that he lingered for days in agony, merely saying: 'shot by the rebels at about 12 noon on the 24th April. He was hit three times before he collapsed. He was brought to the Meath Hospital where he died shortly after admission. He was 28 years of age and had 5 years' service.'

all his searches among the state papers he had not come across any such evidence.

At her subsequent court martial by the British, there was no mention of her shooting a policeman. It is not naïve, moreover, to suggest that Con never mentioning the shooting of PC Lahiff is a telling point in itself. Her almost helpless honesty is an important feature of her character, but she merely says she tackled 'any sniper who was particularly objectionable'. While she shot back at snipers with every intention of hitting them, her subsequent actions indicate an anxiety to save the lives of unarmed men, and she did so on at least two occasions during that week.

What is significant is how willingly the story that she shot an unarmed man has been received and the tenacity with which it has been remembered since. It may be that some flawed, unconscious logic has been going on in the male Irish mind. Two rules of gentlemanly warfare were broken at Stephen's Green on Easter Monday: a helpless man died and a woman displayed a joy in battle; therefore the woman broke *both* rules; QED, Constance shot PC Lahiff.

Con did not march to the Green with Michael Mallin and the Citizen Army contingent because she had another duty to perform first; it had originally been envisaged that she would act as liaison officer between Stephen's Green and the GPO and, once she and Dr Kathleen Lynn had seen the companies march from Liberty Hall, they drove off in a car packed with medical supplies. They reached City Hall about noon, the moment that Seán Connolly was making his raid on the Castle (and the moment, too, that PC Lahiff was being shot on Stephen's Green according to the *Sinn Féin Handbook*). There the two women unloaded part of the supplies, Kathleen Lynn stayed at City Hall and Con drove off with the rest to Stephen's Green. Máire Nic Shiubhlaigh, the Abbey actress, who was with the Jacobs Factory contingent, saw the car go past and the Countess waving her hat at them and yelling encouragement.

When she got to the park which is Stephen's Green, Michael Mallin altered her orders and told her he was so short-handed she must stay with him, and made her his second-in-command. The contingent had already broken into the park, were barricading the railings and were, literally, entrenching. Both Mallin and Con have been criticised for wasting time by setting their men to dig trenches which would become a death trap from bullets fired from the height of the surrounding buildings, especially the tall Shelbourne Hotel, which overlooked them. But the digging had begun before Con arrived and, anyway, the original plan had envisaged that the Shelbourne and other command points would be occupied by their own troops and Mallin was still banking on the arrival of fifty more men. The entire strength of the Green's contingent at surrender was, according to British Army estimate, 110 men and eleven women.

With that number they were supposed to command Grafton Street, Harcourt Street, Leeson Street and Kildare Street and the main approaches, one of them from Portobello Barracks. Sergeant Frank Robbins, for instance, had to hold Harcourt Street station and bridge with three men instead of a planned sixteen. He delayed the train to Wexford, which got to its destination four hours behind schedule, when, having been supplied with a permit to leave by Countess Markievicz, it brought confirmation of the Rising in Dublin to the Wexford Volunteers. But Frank Robbins had to abandon the station later.

Sean O'Faolain says that Constance, once she saw that they were not going to have the men to take the surrounding buildings, argued that it was stupid to remain on the Green and that they should have a line of retreat. It was decided the best place would be the solidly-built College of Surgeons overlooking the north end of the Green and a small party, under Frank Robbins, immediately took it. Desmond Ryan describes how it happened.

> Mallin advised Robbins to use guile taking the College. The doorkeeper was a rabid Carsonite who displayed a copy of the Ulster Covenant signed by himself in his room. Robbins had only three men and three women to assist him. One of the women was Madame Markievicz, very happily for the rabid doorkeeper as it turned out. He was arguing with a holiday drunk as Robbins and his party approached the College. Robbins made a swift rush for the door just as the drunk, after long and maudlin protests, had agreed to call back another day, and reached the door as it was slammed in his face in a panic. At the same minute a shot gun went off, missed Robbins by a few inches ... Robbins wedged his foot inside, followed by his revolver and a surly surrender accompanied a defiant refusal to show the party where a store of guns in the bulding was ... Robbins and his men were so enraged that they were seriously tempted to shoot him. Madame Markievicz intervened and told them to lock the doorkeeper in his bedroom with his wife and family.

They were released once the defences were secure. The Irish tricolour was raised over the College and stayed there for the rest of the week.

All the IRA contingents were now in place; necessarily they had been forced to take up static, defensive positions, but that in itself was an aggressive act which no authority could tolerate for long. Considering their numbers, plus the swiftness and, from here on, the efficiency with which the British moved against them, the miracle of the Rising is that it lasted as long as it did.

There had been an attempt to cut all wires to the Dublin Telephone Exchange in Crown Alley but, again through bungling caused by the countermand, at least one of the lines had been overlooked and the British were able to keep tabs on insurgent positions.

Of the women who rose for Ireland, it tended to be those in the Citizen Army who saw most action at first hand. The Cumann na mBan were kept firmly in their subordinate place by the Volunteers, though about sixty of them managed to persuade various male commanders that their nursing, signalling and cooking skills would prove necessary. Thirty of these stayed in the GPO throughout, only leaving under protest on Friday. Those few who were treated most like comrades-in-arms were the women who went to the Marrowbone Lane Distillery to join Con Colbert, one of Con Markievicz's earliest Fianna recruits, and therefore more likely to be sympathetic to women's participation.

In contrast, Eamon de Valera flatly refused to allow any of them to join him in Boland's Mill. It was a rejection which the Cumann na mBan were not to forget and which, considering his role in Ireland's future, boded badly for the freedom of its women. In 1937, during the Dáil debate on his proposed constitution, de Valera admitted that he had told the women who came to the Mill that he did not want them: 'I said we have anxieties here . . . and I do not want to add to them . . . I did not want them as soldiers in any case.' Hanna Sheehy Skeffington later swore that de Valera admitted sheepishly to her that he wished he had not acted in this high-handed way – but only because it had meant that some of his best men had had to spend time cooking.

His position is confirmed by Sheila Humphries, a member of Cumann na mBan.

De Valera was the only commandant who refused absolutely to have the Cumann na mBan in the posts. The result, I believe, was that the garrison there did not stand up to the siege as well as in other posts; some of them had an attack of the jitters and were liable to fire at anything.

Back at St Stephen's Green the Ascendancy, refusing to be done out of its customary tea at the Shelbourne, was taking it in the drawing room overlooking the Green, with sporadic rifle fire spattering against the hotel front. Some of the off-duty officers of both the Shelbourne and the United Service Club had begun taking pot shots at the rebels, and Con was returning their fire 'with frightening accuracy'. 'Not till a bullet entered obliquely through the bay window, shearing the tip of a rose petal from the hat of a lady seated against the wall, did the guests reconsider their choice of scene.' With Dublin cut off, most of them had to stay on in the overcrowded hotel and, noblesse oblige, undertake the duties of servants who slept out and had not been able to get back in.

With their retreat now safeguarded, the Citizen Army was still barricading the roads round the Green and still waiting for reinforcements which never arrived, although a few Volunteers and three Cumann na mBan girls wandered up and joined them at the irresistible invitation of Citizen Army soldier Bob de Coeur who stood at the gate saying: 'If you're any bloody good come in and fight for Ireland,' and a warning from the Countess that they could only expect a noose or a bullet for their pains. A commissariat and first-aid post had been set up in the Green's summer house under the command of Con's friends, Madeleine ffrench-Mullen and Nellie Gifford (Jim Larkin's 'niece' of 1913). Con herself was patrolling the Green, helping with the commandeering of carts and cars which were still unsuspectingly driving up, and returning sniper fire.

James Stephens, the writer and poet, lived nearby the Green and had been attracted by the disturbance, not knowing his admired Countess was in the thick of it, and arrived to witness a nasty incident when a man stepped on to the Green's footpath and

> gripped the shafts of a lorry [cart] lodged near the centre [of the barricade] . . . From nowhere armed men appeared at the railings and they all shouted at the man, 'Put down that lorry. Let out and go away!' . . . The man did not let out . . . Three shots rang out in succession. At that distance he could not be missed and it was obvious they were trying to frighten him . . . instead of going away he walked over to the Volunteers.

The man was warned again. '"Go and put back that lorry or you are a dead man."' He persisted. 'A rifle spat at him . . . the man sank in on himself and sagged to the ground . . . At that moment the Volunteers were hated.'

The man was a well-known Sinn Féiner and Con, furious, threatened to court martial the man who shot him.

That Monday night the weather turned chilly, preparatory for the rain which came next day. 'Countess Markievicz,' says Max Caulfield, 'curled up comfortably in Captain Mallin's car, an act of thoughtlessness for which she apologised the next morning when she learned how the other girls had suffered'. They had slept on seats in the summerhouse, according to Mr Caulfield, 'swept by a cold wind'. It was actually Dr Kathleen Lynn's car and Margaret Skinnider says that Con meant only to have a brief sleep in it before her turn on watch, but that she overslept – considering how little sleep she had

had in the last few days, it is not surprising – 'and couldn't forgive herself'.

That Monday night as the exhausted Irish Republican Army slept with even more exhausted sentries on guard, the British were organising. Still thinking they might have to repel a German invasion, they sent for reinforcements not only from Belfast, the Curragh and Athlone, but from England where four battalions of Sherwood Foresters, many of them still undergoing training, were mobilised for embarkation to Kingstown (Dun Laoghaire). Since the telegraph at the GPO was denied them, the message had to be sent via the Admiralty by wireless from a naval vessel in Kingstown harbour. By the next morning a cordon was being thrown round the city, and one hundred soldiers and a machine-gun unit from the Curragh had occupied the Shelbourne Hotel and the United Service Club.[1]

Con and the others found themselves under raking fire, and Michael Mallin got a bullet through his hat as he rescued a wounded colleague from the gate. Another Citizen Army man was killed. Madeleine ffrench-Mullen and the others were ordered to make a dash for the College of Surgeons and were fired on as they did so. At the Shelbourne they were watched with disapproval: 'Look at them running,' one lady said, 'with no hats on.' By seven a.m. everybody was in the College. They were now cut off, but they managed to hold the troops that were firing on them by firing back and, in due course, helped to restrict the passage into the city of the reinforcements from England.

At three-thirty p.m. that Tuesday came the boom of artillery fire as two of four 18-pounders brought from Athlone cleared the insurgents' barricade on the North Circular Road bridge half a mile away. Connolly had been wrong; the British were prepared to use shell against property. But Connolly had also said that the thunder of artillery would be a portent of victory as far as they were concerned. Although the sound brought fear, there was an odd *'nunc dimittis'* sense among the insurgents. Martin Sheridan was told that one of the comments was: 'Be Jesus, we've won.' The Fenian Rising had been avenged; there could be no humiliation for men and women who had evoked such a massive reaction from the British. They were being taken seriously.

On Tuesday afternoon, Francis Sheehy Skeffington, appalled by the fighting, was touring the city trying to stop looting. He was picked up and arrested with two journalists unconnected with the nationalist

[1] For a detailed account of troop movements during the Rising see Chapter IX by G. A. Hayes-McCoy in *The Making of 1916*, ed. Kevin B. Nowlan, Dublin Stationery Office, 1969.

movement, Patrick Mackintyre and Thomas Dickson. The three were taken to Portobello Barracks and put in the charge of Captain Bowen-Colthurst, who was later to be judged insane. Skeffington was taken on a raiding party that night as Bowen-Colthurst's hostage and was a witness to the captain shooting a boy in Rathmines whose only crime seemed to have been that he was coming out of a Catholic church. The next morning Skeffy and the two journalists were taken to a wall in the barracks and shot. Their bodies were immediately buried in quicklime and the bullet holes in the wall repaired. Bowen-Colthurst then led a raid on the Sheehy Skeffington home in the hope of finding some evidence against him which would justify the act, temporarily arresting Hanna and her son, aged seven.

After the Rising, Bowen-Colthurst's senior officer, Major Sir Francis Vane initiated a court martial of his captain which accepted the plea that he was guilty but of unsound mind at the time of the crime. Hanna's persistent demands for an enquiry resulted in a Royal Commission in August which apologised. She was offered compensation, but refused. Even among all the deaths still to come, Skeffington's held a particular horror which was to help work Irish opinion against the British.

At the three-storey College of Surgeons the windows were barricaded and holes made into the side walls to give access to other houses in the row. Margaret Skinnider said they were careful not to damage the College's museum and library. 'We destroyed nothing but the portrait of Queen Victoria.' The debutante who had once curtseyed to the Queen helped the others take the portrait down and make puttees out of it. Some of the younger Fianna boys had managed to track Con down; twelve-year-old Tommy Keenan and the boy who was going blind refused to obey Con's order to leave and stayed, occasionally sallying out through side entrances to get food and medicine for the wounded. Hunger was the problem; James Connolly sent three Cumann na mBan women to the College with ammunition and they managed to buy cheese and Oxo and to hold up a bread van, commandeering its contents for their own and the Citizen Army. But bread was getting generally scarce in Dublin – a fact that did not endear its already-hostile residents to the Rising.

On Wednesday Margaret Skinnider, getting impatient with inaction, insisted on accompanying a raid to set fire to a house behind the Russell Hotel in an attempt to dislodge the troops in it. Mallin had not been willing, 'for he did not want to let a woman run this sort of risk', Margaret Skinnider wrote. But she told him that as the Republican Proclamation stated that women were now equal to men 'women have the same right to risk their lives as men'. On the raid a sniper in the house opposite opened fire, killing seventeen-year-old Fred Ryan and wounding Margaret three times. She was dragged back into the College under fire by Councillor William Partridge where Con held her hand while Madeleine ffrench-Mullen probed for the bullets. She cried, but only because, she said, they had to cut off her uniform. Liam Ó Briain managed to get a nightdress for her from a flat they had broken through to. When Margaret was made comfortable, Con disappeared – she had gone out to get the sniper who had done the damage – and came back to tell Margaret she was avenged.

The College was now under almost continuous fire. Liam Ó Briain wrote:

> The noise was appalling, and it was increasing all over the city . . . I was near him [Mallin] and the Countess while they were speaking together. She said she was getting anxious – anxious about not having a bayonet or a sword or some 'stabbing instrument', so as to be ready for them if they should break in . . .
>
> I didn't often see the Countess during those days and I don't know where she was usually to be found; on the roof, I suppose, or wherever she thought most dangerous or most favourably situated for fighting. The sight of her and her presence in their midst was a wonderful inspiration and encouragement to the men. They never called her anything but 'Madame' and there wasn't one of them who wouldn't have given his life for her.

They were encouraged on Thursday by the discovery of the College's hidden arsenal – sixty-four rifles in perfect condition. But they knew elsewhere things must be going badly; there was continual bombardment in the direction of the GPO where flames and smoke could be seen billowing into the air. Fire was spreading along the blocks of buildings facing the Post Office and gradually encircling it. Connolly had been hit twice, once in the arm and, more seriously, in the ankle, but was refusing to leave.

Nora, his daughter, back from the North, had gone to see her mother at Con's cottage and found her in a state of near collapse from reading a newspaper report which said her husband was dead.

Another woman casualty was Margaretta Keogh of the Cumann na mBan who was killed in the South Dublin Union trying to go to the help of a wounded Volunteer.

The Mendicity Institute had been completely surrounded on Wednesday and Seán Heuston, one of Con's original Fianna, and his men had been playing a deadly game by catching the grenades hurled through the windows and hurling them back. Two Volunteers had been killed and two badly wounded. Outnumbered and exhausted, Heuston had eventually surrendered and the British besiegers had been infuriated to find that their enemy consisted of only twenty or so men.

Of the reinforcements from England two battalions got through to Dublin without difficulty, but the 2/7th and the 2/8th of the Sherwood Foresters (the Robin Hoods) did not, coming under heavy fire from de Valera's tiny outposts which managed to kill or wound 230 of them, including all the officers of one company.

The architect of the military build-up that week was Brigadier-General W. H. M. Lowe, who found himself engaged in severe street fighting which was without precedent in the history of the British Army. It was, of course, nothing to what it had been facing in France, but its nature was different and, therefore, awkward to counter.

One of his actions, either miscalculation or revenge, was to direct two of his 18-pounders at short range at Liberty Hall, which was also attacked by the naval gunboat, the *Helga*, which came up the Liffey and moored by the Custom House to open fire. The building was empty, apart from a caretaker who prudently retired when the bombardment began. In government eyes Liberty Hall had always appeared to be the headquarters of Irish intransigence and now paid the penalty. Despite sustaining some Gruyère cheese-like holes, the walls stood up well but the interior was wrecked.

By Friday the GPO roof was on fire.

Until almost the end [wrote Desmond Ryan], the Cumann na mBan shared the dangers, the fire, the bullets, all the ordeals of the fighters, in the most dangerous areas, on the barricades, through the bullet-swept streets and quaysides, carrying dispatches, explosives and ammunition through the thick of the fray, assisting in the hospital, cooking and, in some cases, approaching the British military posts to deliver warnings from Pearse that the Red Cross posts of the insurgents had been fired on by the British snipers, while in the end it was a woman who marched out to initiate the final negotiations.

This was Elizabeth O'Farrell who, with Julia Grennan and Winifred Carney, had refused to leave the GPO wounded when the other women were ordered away. Along with what was left of the Post Office contingent they made the perilous evacuation, in which the O'Rahilly and others were killed, to houses in Moore Street, where they again came under heavy fire and were cut off, and the decision was taken to negotiate for a surrender, 'to save the men from slaughter', William Pearse, Patrick's brother, told Desmond Ryan, 'for slaughter it is'. Elizabeth O'Farrell carried a white flag to the nearest British barricade and spent the rest of that day, and Sunday, in negotiation and touring the various insurgent positions under military escort, delivering the signed messages of surrender to their commanders from Pearse and Connolly.

The British had by now perfected the etiquette of military negotiation with a female; when, back on Tuesday, the City Hall contingent had been forced to surrender after coming under terrific fire, Dr Kathleen Lynn, as the only officer there, negotiated it, to the astonishment of the captors 'who were at first unsure as to whether their code of conduct would allow them to accept surrender from a woman'.

It is a measure of Constance's infamy among the authorities that, while accepting Pearse's surrender, Brigadier-General Lowe asked for her by name, unable to believe she was not in the GPO with the rest of the leaders.

All that the College of Surgeons knew on Saturday night was that firing in the city was gradually dying down, though not the firing at them. Whatever else Con did that week – and her own account of it is surprisingly brief – she established a pleasant legend about herself at the Shelbourne where, I was told, you can see the College of Surgeons roof from the Constitution Room at the top of the hotel. At noon every day of the Rising week, they say, 'for humanitarian reasons', Con would hoist a flag which brought about a truce between the two forces, stopping the firing just long enough for a hotel employee to nip across into the park and feed the ducks.

On the Saturday night Con and Michael Mallin were preparing a plan to retreat unseen from the College with their contingent, make their way into the countryside and carry on a form of guerrilla warfare from the hills. Many years later, after Eva's death, Con told Esther Roper about that last night in the College of Surgeons.

Through the night those assembled there prayed for the dead and the living. A great peace was over them, waiting for the end. Constance wanted to join in the prayers, but at first they could not understand why a non-Catholic should wish to take part in Catholic prayers. In her earlier life religious observances had not meant much to her. I think she hated to belong to a church that represented the richer rather than the poorer people . . . But now, face to face with death, she was deeply impressed by the reality of spiritual things to these men and women among whom she had lived. As she shared their prayers there came to her a vision of the Unseen, which wrought such a change in her that from that moment to her, too, the things that are seen became temporal and the things that are unseen, eternal.

It was the moment she decided to become a Catholic. Not long afterwards, in prison, she wrote a poem dedicated to her fellow soldier, Councillor William Partridge, who was generally beloved in the Citizen Army and who died after his imprisonment for the Rising.

Around the tall black Cross. One hope, one prayer
Filled all our hearts, one perfect holy Faith
Lifted our souls. As we knelt humbly there,
Your silvery voice, soft as a dying breath,
Was answered by a hundred strong and clear,
Craving a grace from her whom all hold dear –
'Mary! be with us at the hour of death.'

On Sunday morning as the Mass bells rang, Elizabeth O'Farrell
was driven by a British officer to Grafton Street and from there walked
to the College of Surgeons carrying a white flag and Connolly's order
to surrender. Bullets were still whistling around Stephen's Green but
there was nobody to be seen. Constance roused Mallin, who was
asleep, and he ordered all the others in from the tunnels to the
surrounding houses to read the order to them.

Almost all the women started crying. But amongst the men there was commotion
and uproar; some of them cursing, some shouting that it was wrong to surrender,
that they should fight to the death . . . The Countess was among them and calmed
them. She said the same thing to everyone: 'I trust James Connolly – I trust
Connolly.' Were it not that the order had come specially from Connolly, she and
some of the others would have fought to the death . . . After a while all eyes turned
to the door . . . Then we saw him, the English soldier – a cigarette in his mouth,
unarmed, clean-shaven, neat, indifferent, *insouciant*. A sort of murmur ran through
the men: here in our midst was one of those who for a week had been trying to
kill us and whom we had been trying to kill. One of us, Joe Connolly, raised the
pistol he was holding. But the Countess was watching him and seized his hand.
'Don't, Joe. It would be a dreadful disgrace now. We told them we were surrendering.'

They surrendered officially to Captain de Courcy Wheeler, who
was married to a kinswoman of the Gore-Booths and who offered
to drive Con to the Castle. She refused, saying that as she was
second-in-command she must walk with the men.

On the march to the Castle they were targets for the hostility which
had met other surrendered insurgents, some of whom had been
attacked by 'separation women'. As they passed Trinity College, says
Liam Ó Briain, an elderly servant yelled, 'Shoot every one of them.'
There were unfavourable comments on the fact that Con was wearing
breeches.

It is doubtful if Con heard; she and Mallin were discussing something of immediate interest – whether they would die by shooting or
hanging.

The Rising for the rest of Ireland had been wrecked by MacNeill
but it went ahead in north County Dublin under Thomas Ashe, who

employed guerrilla methods that approximated to those used later in the Black and Tan war, in Galway under Liam Mellowes, and in County Wexford.

Figures of total losses vary but are considered to be at least 450 killed, 2,614 wounded and nine missing, the vast majority of these in Dublin city.

Of British troops, seventeen officers were killed, forty-six wounded; ninety-nine other ranks killed, 322 wounded and nine missing. The Royal Irish Constabulary (outside Dublin) had thirteen killed, twenty-two wounded. The Dublin Metropolitan Police: three killed and seven wounded. Insurgents and civilians totalled 318 killed and 2,217 wounded.

Damage to property was estimated at £2,500,000.

The whole thing was a drop in the ocean of blood about to wash over the Somme. It had, it is true, tied up thousands of troops that were needed elsewhere and frightened the British Government nearly out of its wits. But it had confirmed most Dubliners in their belief that extreme nationalism was dangerous and its adherents mad. The centre of Dublin was in ruins to prove it. And Nelson still stood on his pillar near the smoking Post Office, intact except for a bullet chip out of his nose until 1966.

CHAPTER ELEVEN

And what was it all for? Why couldn't they have waited for the Home Rule which must have come in eventually and peaceably?

Bulmer Hobson had once put all the reasons for not having a Rising to Patrick Pearse in a Dublin restaurant. Pearse had listened to him and then, infuriatingly, had risen from the table saying: 'I cannot answer your argument, but I *feel* that we must have an insurrection.'

James Stephens had looked with revulsion at the dead men and dead horses lying around Stephen's Green and had hated the Volunteers, but when he wrote his book on the Insurrection later in 1916 he was seeing the reason for it as Con, and James Connolly and Pearse and the others had seen it and as the logical Hobson never could:

> If freedom is to come to Ireland – as I believe it is – then the Easter Insurrection was the only thing that could have happened . . . If, after all her striving, freedom had come to her as a gift, as a peaceful present such as is sometimes given away with a pound of tea, Ireland would have accepted the gift with shamefacedness and have felt that centuries of revolt had ended in something very like ridicule. The blood of brave men had to sanctify such a consummation if the national imagination was to be stirred . . . We might have crept into liberty like some domesticated man, whereas now we may be allowed to march into freedom with the honours of war.

In other words, setting aside the ransom through blood, the Calvary – and it was no coincidence that Easter had been chosen for the Rising – English rule had literally made Ireland sick, starving her, depriving her of her youth, forcing her to swallow humiliation, and the most ideal Home Rule was useless in expunging the poison; what was necessary was a strong emetic.

If the rebels had done nothing else, they had purged themselves. 'At least Ireland was free for a week.' As they were rounded up, exhausted, hungry, in some cases wounded, they exuded a spiritual well-being, which the authorities should have recognised as dangerous because it left their fellow-countrymen who had stood and watched, even those who had strongly disapproved, feeling vaguely contaminated in contrast.

One of these was John Dillon, MP, Redmond's deputy. He had witnessed the Rising at uncomfortably close quarters, being marooned with his family in their home in North Great George's Street, only a few hundred yards away from the GPO. Even in his revulsion, Dillon shared enough Irish racial memory to feel a stirring of national pride, but it was as a politician first and foremost that, on Sunday while the contingents were still surrendering, he wrote to Redmond begging him to impress on Asquith the expediency of showing mercy.

> You should urge strongly on the government the *extreme* unwisdom of any wholesale shooting of prisoners. The wisest course is to execute *no one* for the present . . . If there were shootings of prisoners on any large scale the effect on public opinion might be disastrous in the extreme.

The government had put all Ireland under martial law and sent Major-General Sir John Maxwell to deal with the situation with a free hand. Sir John was under pressure from the strong reaction against the Rising in Britain, from Unionists, and in Ireland itself, which still believed it to be a German-inspired plot. The *Times* editorial on April 26 demanded strong measures against 'declared rebels in collusion with our enemies'. On the 28th, the *Irish Times* said: 'Sedition must be rooted out of Ireland once and for all. The rapine and bloodshed of the past week must be finished with a severity which will make any repetition of them impossible for generations to come.' And the *Irish Independent*, the journal of William Martin Murphy, Larkin's and Connolly's old enemy, not surprisingly declared that those responsible for the 'insane and criminal rising of last week were out, not to free Ireland, but to help Germany . . . had not a shred of public sympathy . . . deserve little consideration or compassion'. It did, however, ask for leniency towards the 'innocent, ignorant, misguided and irresponsible . . . young fellows who'd known little of what they were committed to'.

Redmond, of course, had been in London and in a statement in the House of Commons on the Friday – which was to damn him later – expressed on behalf of the majority of the people of Ireland, 'detestation and horror of these proceedings'.

In private he recommended mercy to Asquith who recommended it to Maxwell, but neither man showed sufficient vehemence to deflect Maxwell from what he considered his duty. Part of that duty, after all, was to the troops who had helped quell the rebellion, many of them Irish themselves – the Royal Irish Regiment, for instance, had been involved in the fierce fighting at the South Dublin Union – and to Irish soldiers in France, 90,000 of whom were fighting the very nation that Pearse's Proclamation had described as 'gallant allies in Europe'.

Some 3,500 men, including Arthur Griffith and Eoin MacNeill, and seventy-nine women, among them Winifred Carney and Helena Moloney, were rounded up under arrest and of these 1,836 men and five women were interned in England, while the rest were released.

A total of 170 men and one woman, the Countess Markievicz, were tried by court martial.

At dawn on May 3, Patrick Pearse, Tom Clarke and Thomas MacDonagh were executed.

On May 4 came the executions of Edward Daly, Michael O'Hanrahan, William Pearse and Joseph Plunkett. The shooting of Daly, O'Hanrahan and William Pearse indicated that the scale of reprisal might be massive, since they had not been signatories to the Proclamation and had taken no part in the plans for the Rising. Willie Pearse seems to have been included merely because he was Patrick's brother and had loved him too well to leave him to face danger alone. Joseph Plunkett was another matter. He had been the youngest signatory of the Proclamation, but as he was dying from TB anyway and had been forced to spend most of the week in the GPO lying on a mattress, his death had poignancy, especially as he had been allowed to marry his fiancée in his cell on the night before his execution. She was Grace Gifford, sister of Nellie who had been with Constance at Stephen's Green and their mother, a Unionist, blamed their involvement in the whole thing on the 'evil influence of Countess Markievicz'.

On May 5, John MacBride, Maud Gonne's ex-husband, faced the firing squad although he had not been a signatory nor a planner and not even in command of the contingent he fought with. Like all the others he made a brave end, telling his court martial that he had stared down the barrels of too many British rifles in the past to be afraid now.

On May 8, it was the turn of Éamonn Ceannt, Michael Mallin and the two Fianna boys, both nineteen, Seán Heuston and Con Colbert. Heuston said before he died: 'Whatever I have done, I have done as a soldier of Ireland and I have no vain regrets.' The priest attending his execution said that afterwards his face looked 'transformed and lit with a grandeur and brightness I had never noticed before'.

On May 9, Thomas Kent, a Cork Volunteer, was executed.

On May 12, James Connolly and Seán MacDermott were shot. James Connolly was strapped into a chair for his execution because he could not stand on his shattered ankle.

'They will be the last,' Maxwell promised, commuting seventy-five other death sentences to varying terms of penal servitude. But by then it was too late.

153

'What was General Maxwell to do,' George Moore is supposed to have asked, 'give the rebels prizes for good conduct?' And by his lights, Maxwell had been lenient, considering that it was wartime and that the Rising was seen as an act of treachery. Looking back with a dispassion achieved by the distance of seventy years, liberal Irishmen and women will now admit that to execute fifteen men was not unreasonable for the time and that another government might have made it more; it was the choices for execution and the manner in which they were carried out that proved the British so psychologically crass.

The courts martial had been held in secret and nothing was known of the executions until the announcement afterwards, so that the delay between each group of shootings was like waiting for an aching nerve to be hit again or, said one Irishwoman, 'like watching a stream of blood coming from beneath a closed door'. And also from behind those closed doors came the priests bringing news of the courage with which the men had died.

Day after day Irish opinion was jerked further and further away from its original mooring as the disaster of the Rising was superseded by a recognition that these had been good, some of them admired, men, and that they and the others had for a week held off twenty times their number.

Dillon's patriotism overcame him; ramming the facts of Sheehy Skeffington's death down the throats of House of Commons members on May 11, even before the executions of Connolly and MacDermott, he added that he was proud of the rebels' courage

> and if you were not so dense and stupid as some of you English people are, you could have had these men fighting for you . . . it is not murderers who are being executed: it is insurgents who have fought a clean fight, however misguided, and it would have been a damned good job for you if your soldiers were able to put up as good a fight as did these men in Dublin.

The commuted death sentences on Constance and Eamon de Valera were welcomed but did nothing to stem the anger growing in Ireland and in America – where it was especially fierce – and even in liberal England on behalf of which the *Manchester Guardian* denounced the shootings as 'atrocities'. George Bernard Shaw was writing:

> My own view is that the men who were shot in cold blood, after their capture or surrender, were prisoners of war, and it is therefore entirely incorrect to slaughter them . . . An Irishman resorting to arms to achieve the independence of his country is only doing what Englishmen will do if it be their misfortune to be invaded and conquered by the Germans in the course of the present war.

De Valera's sentence was commuted because he had been born in the USA and there was some question that he might be an American citizen. Con's was commuted 'solely and only on account of her sex'. F. S. L. Lyons in writing of this sees fit to add 'to her great indignation', thus turning this woman's misery into something like comic relief amid a male tragedy. Nor is he the only one to make it seem slightly ridiculous that Con expected to die and did not.

Certainly Con had nerved herself to face the execution squad, as all the leaders had, and, like them, regarded it as a fitting finish. When Lillie Connolly had been taken in the early hours of May 12 to say goodbye to her husband in his cell she had wept, 'But your life, James, your beautiful life,' and Connolly had answered, 'Hasn't it been a full life, Lillie, and isn't this a good end?' And on the same night Seán MacDermott had written to his family: 'You ought to envy me.'

Only seven months previously the Germans had set a precedent by executing the English nurse, Edith Cavell, for assisting wounded and refugee soldiers to escape in Belgium. Since her own offence against the British had been so much greater, Con had every reason to think that they would respond in the same way. There was a body of opinion which believed they should; Lord Powerscourt, the Provost Marshal, for instance, was begging the authorities to shoot her. Esther Roper always believed it was only Asquith's personal intervention which saved Con, and in view of the outcry over Nurse Cavell's death, it is likely that he wanted to avoid bringing such opprobrium on his own head.

With the other women and most of the leading male insurgents she was sent to Kilmainham Jail, but from the first Constance was isolated from the others without news of what was happening. On her third morning there she heard the fire of rifles from the courtyard and knew that executions were taking place, but not on whom. She heard the shots which killed Pearse, Clarke, MacDonagh, Plunkett, Daly, Willie Pearse, O'Hanrahan and MacBride. The sound of those volleys haunted her to the end of her days and she was turned sick by the single shots which followed them, the dispatch, in case they had not died immediately.

She herself was court martialled on May 4; like the others without legal representation. The first witness against her was a seventeen-year-old page boy from the University Club, Stephen's Green, who said that he had seen her drive up

in a motor car. She gave orders to a Sinn Féiner after he had shut the gate of Stephen's Park. She then drove up towards the Shelbourne Hotel – I saw her again about 1.15 p.m. She was then behind one of the monuments in the Green, she had a pistol in her hand which she pointed towards the club and fired.

Although it made no difference, Con could not bear such sloppy evidence, and proved by cross-examination of the boy that from his position he could not possibly have seen what he said he did. She declined to cross-examine Captain de Courcy Wheeler who was the second witness and swore to the fact that she was armed on her surrender and had said she was second-in-command.

The accusations against her were of taking part in an armed rebellion and in the waging of war against His Majesty the King . . . with the intention and for the purpose of assisting the enemy, to which she pleaded Not Guilty; and of attempting to cause disaffection among the civilian population of His Majesty, to which she pleaded Guilty.

Asked if she had anything to say, she said: 'I went out to fight for Ireland's freedom and it doesn't matter what happens to me. I did what I thought was right and I stand by it.' She was taken back to her cell.

The following night, the English soldier on duty outside her cell waited until the prison was quiet, unlocked her door and entered to give her a cigarette and smoked another with her, allowing her to ask questions and giving her the names of those who had died so far. Esther Roper says Con never forgot the man's kindness and always wanted to thank him, but didn't know how to find him and didn't dare try in case she got him into trouble.

In the morning, after she had again heard a volley from the courtyard – this one was MacBride's execution – an officer came in to read the finding and sentence of the court martial. The court recommended the prisoner to mercy solely and only on account of her sex. General Maxwell had confirmed the death sentence and added, 'but I commute the sentence to one of penal servitude for life.' The officer, who was young, was embarrassed and mumbled the words. Con made him repeat it, this time clearly. She was alone; she knew her comrades were dying and she was facing life imprisonment. Not surprisingly, she said: 'I wish you had the decency to shoot me.'

She was moved to Mountjoy Prison – known ironically to its inmates as 'The Joy' – again to solitary confinement. The press snatched a picture of her as she sat waiting for the move in a lorry with a wardress, and the photo was published in the *Daily Sketch* on May 10 with three more showing Pearse surrendering and MacBride and others being marched away. The caption read:

which is clever of the *Sketch* psychologists because to anyone else the faces just look tired, and Con's in particular is vulnerable in its thinness.

It was in Mountjoy that Eva and Esther Roper found her. Their anxiety had been terrible. On Sunday, April 29, Eva had read a report in the *Lloyds Weekly News* which gave a circumstantial account of her sister's body being found dead on Stephen's Green; since then she had been running around to highly-placed friends to try to get news. As the two women arrived in Dublin on May 12, having wangled a permit to visit Con, they saw newspaper hoardings: 'Execution of James Connolly.' 'James Connolly shot this morning.' At Mountjoy they were shown into a room which had a barred window opening on to a passage which ended in another grille and on the far side of this Con's face at last appeared, 'looking ghost-like', wrote Esther. They had to talk across the passage with a wardress patrolling between.

> After greeting us, Con asked almost at once whether Connolly had been shot. We had been warned that on no account must we answer this question. Though no word was spoken she must have seen the answer in our faces, for with tears running slowly down her cheeks, she said, 'You needn't tell me, I know. Why didn't they let me die with my friends?'
>
> It was a terrible moment. Under all other circumstances in prison she kept gay and brave. This was absolutely the only time I ever saw her show emotion there . . . Soon she drew herself up and said, 'Well, Ireland was free for a week.'

Later on she asked: 'Why on earth did they shoot Skeffy? After all he wasn't in it. He didn't even believe in fighting. What did it mean?' She was greatly concerned about Michael Mallin's wife, who had five children and was now expecting their sixth. Mallin had been secretary of the Silk Weavers' Union, not a well-paid job, and Con asked Eva and Esther to find his wife and make sure she was all right. 'She did not think of herself,' wrote Esther.

Her first letter, on May 16 from Mountjoy, to Eva confirms this. It is perhaps one of the most prosaic and the most gallant ever written.

> Dearest Old Darling, It was such a heaven-sent joy, seeing you. It was a new life, a resurrection, though I knew all the time that you'd try and see me, even though I'd been fighting and you hate it all so and think killing so wrong. It was so dear of Esther to come all that long way too . . . Now to business. Hayes and Hayes are

agents for Surrey House . . . The house is very untidy as I had no time to put it straight after the Police raid.

She gives elaborate details of what furniture, pictures, etc., she wants stored: 'Don't store furniture with Myers, he was a brute to the men in the strike.' She worries about her unpaid bills, to her grocer, baker, butcher, oilman, all of whom Eva is empowered to pay with Con's money.

I owe two coal bills; one to Clarkin, Tara St. the other to a man I forget in Charlemont St., on the R-side if you face the bridge but close to the chemist at the corner where the trams cross. I owe also a trifle to Gleeson of O'Connell St. for a skirt and to the Art Dec. Co., Belfast. But there's no hurry about any of these – they are quite accustomed to waiting. Don't pay anything without being sure the bill is really mine as people have tried on queer tricks getting things on credit in my name before now.

You dear old darling, its such a bore for you. I feel rather as if I was superintending my own funeral from the grave . . . I left a green canvas suit case and a small red dressing case and a brown bag with Peter Ennis, Caretaker of Liberty Hall [he who had been forced to retire from the bombardment, which in all likelihood blew up the cases and the bags with the rest of the Hall's interior.] . . . I dare say Peter's been arrested, but he wasn't mixed up in anything so he may be out. I left my bike knocking around the Hall too.

I miss poor Poppet very much and wonder if he has quite forgotten me. Poor Mrs Connolly, I wonder where she is and if you got him from her . . . I do feel so sorry for her. She was so devoted to her husband. Also she had four children at home, and only the two older girls working. With regard to Bessie Lynch [who helped out at Surrey House] what I had in mind for her was to start her washing in a small way after the War. She is a beautiful laundress. Of course she would want another girl with her to do accounts, etc. but you could let her know I haven't forgotten and that the 10/-a week is only to keep her safe and happy till something can be arranged.

Poor Bridie Goff my servant ought to get a months wages at least. She was arrested with me . . . If you can't find Bessie advertise for her in the evening paper.

I nearly forgot the little Hall in Camden St. Mr Cummins pawnbroker S. Richmond St. is the landlord. If things quiet down [some words censored here] I'd like to go on paying the rent for them as hitherto. A little boy called Smith living in Piles Buildings could find out . . .

I feel I'm giving you such a lot of worries and bothers, and I feel too, as if I hadn't remembered half. Anyhow its very economical living here! and I'm half glad I'm not treated as a political prisoner as I should feel so greatly tempted to eat, smoke and dress at my own expense. In the mean time I live free, all my debts will be paid and I suppose after a time I will be allowed to write again or see a visitor. I don't know the rules but try to get in touch with Mrs Connolly, Mrs Mallin and Bessie Lynch. I would be sorry for any of them to be hungry and I would be sorry too if they thought I had forgotten them, for they were friends . . .

Now darling don't worry about me, for I am not too bad at all; and its only a mean spirit that grudges paying the price. Everybody is quite kind and though this is not exactly a bed of roses still many rebels have had much worse to bear. The life is colourless, beds are hard, food peculiar, but you might say that of many a free person's life, and when I think of what the Fenians suffered and of what the Poles suffered in the Sixties I realise that I am extremely lucky. So darling don't worry your sweet old head. I hope that I shall see you again some day and shall live in hopes ... I can see your faces when I shut my eyes. Yrs. CdM. Number 8374

> Name: Constance G. de Markievicz
> HM Prison, Mountjoy Female.
> Dublin.

As it turned out she need not have bothered to make arrangements for storing her furniture. When Eva and Esther got to Surrey House they found that it had been ransacked by the military looking for incriminating evidence, and that what they had left undamaged, the looters had finished off. Furniture was broken, papers, ornaments, books, pictures lying smashed on the floor. 'A beautiful leather dressing-case ripped across by a bayonet and so on. The garden had been dug up in search of arms, but nothing had been found.' A few things were saved, but Constance Markievicz never had a proper home of her own again.

Eva and Esther were warned not to linger in the streets for fear that Eva's great likeness to her sister would get her shot by soldiers who were still trigger-happy. 'For hours on end we tramped the streets until our search for the Commandant's wife was successful and we were able to carry out Constance's earnest wishes.'

Since there was no likelihood of another visit to Con for some time, the two women went back to London to campaign with many others for Sir Roger Casement who was now in the Tower of London accused of treason. There is no doubt that he was technically guilty and that the trial was fairly conducted. But in view of his impressive past work for humanity, the fact that he considered himself an Irish citizen, that another execution would redouble the feeling against them in Ireland and America, it would again have been sensible on the part of the authorities not to carry out the inevitable death sentence. But they did. After a rejection of his appeal, Casement was hanged at Pentonville Prison on August 3. What had increased Irish bitterness was that British Intelligence in an attempt to condone the hanging, had privately circulated the so-called 'black diaries' apparently belonging to Casement which showed that he was a homosexual. They were condemned by his friends as forgeries, but there is every probability that they were not. Outraged Ireland remained unconvinced, however: an Irish patriot could not be homosexual.

Dublin was a numbed place to be that summer. 'Something would happen,' Grace Plunkett told R. M. Fox, 'and I would think "I must tell so and so", then I would remember that he, like the others, was dead.' Some families had suffered double blows: Grace had lost her husband of a few hours, and her sister, Muriel, who'd been married to another executed leader, Thomas MacDonagh, was now a penniless widow with two children. (Muriel herself was drowned the following year.) Kathleen Clarke's husband had been executed and so had her brother, Edward Daly, and under this distress she had lost the child she was expecting.

But with so many men in prison in England, it was up to the women to make sure that the cause for which the Rising had been fought did not die with its leaders. Kathleen Clarke became president of the Irish Volunteer Dependants' Fund, since the most immediate need was to raise money for the wives and children left destitute. A grimly determined committee was formed which included Áine Ceannt, widow of the executed Éamonn, Muriel MacDonagh, Sheila Humphries, niece to The O'Rahilly, Lila, sister of Con Colbert, Eily, sister of Michael O'Hanrahan, and Margaret Pearse, mother of Patrick and Willie.

They found a valuable ally in Hanna Sheehy Skeffington, who had once condemned the Cumann na mBan for its subservience to a male cause. In her fight to bring her husband's murderer to trial she went to raise sympathy in the United States where she also spoke to over 250 meetings on Ireland's claim to independence.

American support, financial and moral, was crucial at this stage. Cumann na mBan sent an envoy, Min Ryan, to give the States its view of the Irish situation; Nellie Gifford, Nora Connolly and Margaret Skinnider, now nearly recovered, joined her, all of them demanding that Ireland be considered one of the small nations deserving liberty, one of the issues over which the Great War was being fought.

Back home the wives and children of the dead and imprisoned men were a form of living propaganda, and at the Masses for the executed held in nearly every parish collections were taken at the church door for the Fund. There were huge meetings to demand the release of prisoners, especially those – the majority – who had been interned without trial. When General Maxwell asked the Bishop of Limerick to remove from the parishes priests who had been pro-insurgents, he was refused. The Celtic Revivalists added their weight; anyone with aspirations to poetry, and even those who had none, rushed for pen and paper to express their emotion in verse; 'our part,' wrote Yeats, in *Easter 1916*, 'to murmur name upon name'. He could not agree with some of the participants; Con, for instance, he described in

> That woman's days were spent
> In ignorant good-will,
> Her nights in argument
> Until her voice grew shrill

and MacBride, his beloved Maud's ex-husband, as

> A drunken, vainglorious lout.
> He had done most bitter wrong
> To some who are near my heart.

He could not even agree with the cause: 'For England may keep faith.' But he knew that all of them

> Now and in time to be
> Wherever green is worn,
> Are changed, changed utterly:
> A terrible beauty is born.

In less immortal words, but kinder, AE wrote a poem for private circulation, beginning: 'Their dream had left me numb and cold / But yet my spirit rose in pride' and devoted a verse to Constance:

> Here's to the woman of our blood
> Stood by them in the fiery Hour,
> Rapt lest some weakness in their mood
> Rob manhood of a single power.
> You, brave on such a hope forlorn,
> Who smiled through crack of shot and shell,
> Though the world cry on you with scorn,
> Here's to you, Constance, in your cell.

Less and less of the world was crying on her with scorn. Nora Connolly and Margaret Skinnider were singing her praises in America, Eva and Esther Roper were speaking to every meeting they could about her; and in Ireland her stock had risen to an incredible height when Father Ryan, of the Franciscan Capuchin Friary in Church Street, Dublin, who had brought out much of the news from Kilmainham about how nobly the rebels were dying, also brought praise of Con and said how beloved she was in his Church Street district where 'she often came here to assist personally the poor and destitute'. Petitions were organised to try to obtain political status for her imprisonment. And in August 1916 the committee and members of the Cumann na mBan at their annual convention elected Con their president.

The only person unaware of all this adulation was Constance herself. She, too, had been moved to verse and a wardress at Mountjoy was in possession of a poem on flimsy paper, which subsequently gave rise to speculation as to whether Connolly and Constance had been lovers.[1]

> You died for your country my Hero-love
> In the first grey dawn of spring;
> On your lips was a prayer to God above
> That your death will have helped to bring
> Freedom and peace to the land you love,
> Love above everything.

It is highly unlikely that there was anything more between James Connolly and Constance Markievicz than mutual respect and complete political understanding. Their friends attested to the fact that she never called him anything but 'Mr Connolly'. True, he stayed in her house but so did a lot of other people, *and* at the same time. She was deeply fond of Connolly's wife and daughters, as they were of her, and Nora, who was with her often enough to suspect something had it been going on, never spoke of Con in anything but the highest terms. When she wrote the poem she was at her lowest ebb, lonely and grieving for her dead friends, and if for a moment that loneliness and grief spilled out in romantic emotion, not just for Connolly but for all of them, then it is not to be wondered at.

If Con didn't know what a focus for rebel sympathy she had become, General Maxwell did and he set about getting her away by writing to the Home Office:

> It appears to be desirable that the Countess Markievicz should be removed from Mountjoy Prison, Dublin, to some prison in England. From censored letters it appears that sympathisers know how she is getting on in prison and that in some way information is leaking out ... This lady is the only prisoner convicted for rebellion who is now in Ireland.

Just then Constance found an ally, a sympathetic apprentice wardress from County Wexford who took the risk of smuggling out two letters written on bits of toilet paper which were sent to Eva, telling

---

[1] Anne Marreco, who quotes the poem in *The Rebel Countess*, came to the conclusion that they were not.

her that she was to be moved to England – the Home Office had acted on Maxwell's recommendation.

Darling, I am alas! going into exile. Make a point to try and get in to see me. I believe you could by influence. Do you know Seddon? and is he an MP. He and I were great allies in the Strike, and he might be willing to help. I know he liked me personally. He might get the Labour people to put questions anyhow. Remember, I don't mind being in jail, and if it's better for the cause I'm prepared to remain here. My only desire is to be of use to those outside in the long tedious struggle with England. Nothing else matters to me . . . Shall be quite amiable – am not going to hungerstrike, as am advised by comrades not to. It would suit the Government very well to let me die quietly. I want to work for the Army, that's all. I look forward to seeing you the whole time. Put on your prettiest hat when you come! My family must be quite amusing about my latest crimes! . . . Very very best love. Am going to Aylesbury. Let friends there know.

It was unsigned.

On another scrap of loo paper she mentioned that she was glad that 'M' (most probably her daughter, Maeve) had been 'amused, not shocked', presumably by Con's part in the Rising.

The tone was as bright as ever but the thought of incarceration, possibly for her lifetime, in England daunted her. As she said, 'the Joy' was not a bed of roses, but at least outside the walls lay her world and she could hear its traffic and the call of its newspaper boys. She was transferred in June.

Aylesbury Prison was tough, especially the criminal section where Con was confined and there is little doubt that Con's title and reputation marked her for grimmer treatment than the others. Helena Moloney, Winifred Carney and Nell Ryan were also interned there but had political status and Con was not even allowed to be seen greeting them when they waved over a wall. The three Irishwomen made a formal appeal to the Home Office to be treated as convicts, giving up all privileges in order to share Con's lot alongside her, but their request was 'disallowed'. Instead Con was isolated among the thieves, prostitutes and murderesses.

She grew to be sorry for her fellow prisoners, realising that poverty had led to crime in most cases, but in a prison where syphilis was rife, the lack of hygiene alarmed her.

The dinners were served in two-storey cans, used indiscriminately among 200 women . . . A great many of the women were known to be suffering from venereal disease and at the time an attempt was made to keep their tins separate. This was dropped after a while. There was no proper accommodation for washing these 400 tins. I used to do 200 with another convict. We did our best to get them clean in a big terra-cotta bowl on the kitchen table and to dry them on two towels. Sometimes the water would not be hot, sometimes there was no soap or soda and then you could neither dry nor clean the tins ... I could give you endless examples of English cleanliness. It may be summed up as follows: Brasses, floors, doorknobs, all that jumps to the eye immaculate, but dirt and carelessness behind the scenes. I have seen vermin found in the baths.

None of this could be said in her letters of course, but she campaigned against prisons in speeches and articles for the rest of her life.

She became concerned especially about one woman who was doing seven years for shooting her lover who had announced he was going to marry somebody else when she'd told him she was carrying his child. The baby had been taken away from her when he was twelve months old because of the rule that no child between one and fifteen years be allowed in prison. Con begged Eva to try to get her out and Eva put a campaigning friend on to the case. The woman was released, given a job and reunited with her little boy.

Con's greatest ally was a rough, tough, indomitable Irish–American prostitute, May Sharpe, known as 'Chicago May'. This lady's memoirs rate the Countess Markievicz as the grandest woman she had ever known. At one point the prisoners, during chapel, were asked to pray for British military success. Con, Chicago May and a German woman serving a sentence for spying, refused.

For spite [wrote Chicago May], they made the three of us women carry enough gruel around the prison to feed the entire two hundred convicts. We had to carry immense, heavy cans up winding stairs. While we were doing this, the Countess recited long passages in Italian, from Dante's Inferno. The place looked like Hell, all right, with the lights dimmed and musty-smelling bags tacked across the windows, as a precaution against bombing.

In this connection, Esther Roper tells a story which shows how well she understood Constance. In Aylesbury at that time was a Mrs Wheeldon, a suffragette who had been convicted – in Esther's opinion, unjustly – for attempting to assassinate Lloyd George. Passing Mrs Wheeldon in a corridor, Con congratulated her on trying and, telling Esther about it later, added some 'lurid' remarks on the politician concerned.

I said to her, [wrote Esther] 'You know very well you wouldn't hurt a hair of his head yourself. Now what would you do to him if he was wounded and on your own doorstep?' 'Take him in and look after him, of course,' she said promptly, but not too pleased to have been made to admit the undramatic truth. Her hatred never went beyond words: they, I admit, were emphatic and bitter enough at times. But if I had had the misfortune to be her enemy, I would have trusted myself, personally, to her without hesitation.

Refusing to pray for Britain was about the only time Con made any difficulty for the prison authorities. She obeyed the rules absently, as if her mind was elsewhere, and the worst the prison governess found to say about her was that, though scrupulously clean, she was an untidy dresser. Possibly this was because she was losing weight so badly that her convict's dress hung on her like a tent. She wrote to Eva:

I saw myself – for the first time for over 3 months the other day. It is quite amusing to meet yourself as a stranger. We bowed and grinned, and I thought my teeth very dirty, and very much wanting a dentist, and I'd got very thin and very sunburnt. In 6 months I shall not recognise myself at all, my memory of faces is so bad. I remember a fairy tale of a Princess, who banished mirrors when she began to grow old. I think it showed a great want of interest in life. The less I see my face the more curious I grow about it, and I don't resent growing old. It's queer and lonely here . . . One thing I should enjoy getting out for, and that would be to see the faces of respectable people when I met them!

Appalling as the food was, there wasn't a day when she wasn't hungry and she was to say of that time: 'We had a certain community of hatred that gave one mutual interests and the mutual sport of combining to pinch onions, dripping or rags!' and when Esther was visiting she told her: 'All prison does for people is to teach them to use bad language and to steal. I was so hungry yesterday that I stole a raw turnip and ate it.'

Once again she found a sympathetic wardress who would smuggle out letters to Eva for her and in these scraps she gave a grimmer picture of conditions, not to worry her sister but to provide her with ammunition by which the cause of all prisoners could be used against Britain.

The doctor here [Fox] is a devil. She is going to be Governor but rules are so strict she can't hurt me in any way . . . Don't count on my getting out for ever so long. Unless a real fuss is made [Home and America] I don't see any reason why they should let me go. You should get 'questions' asked on anything you can think of and start grievances – company one's in – starvation etc and try and make them publish trials . . . They don't want a continuous fuss. Let me know the trades union conditions for workrooms' *temperature*. The trades unions should have a visitor or Inspector here. They should start jail reform. The people here are all poor people and they should see to them. Best love and kisses to you both. I love being in poetry and feel so important! Yrs for Ever.

The last sentence was a reference to a book by Eva, *The Death of Fionavar*. Con had illustrated it, finding time somehow during the busy winter of 1915–16. After a couple of months in Aylesbury she was allowed a notebook in which to sketch and write, though each page was carefully numbered so that none could be torn out and used for a nefarious purpose.

Her first visitors were official, the Duchess of St Albans and Lady Battersea whose good works included visits to convicts but, since the Duchess had known Con in her youth, it was an awkard interview which the Countess did nothing to relieve.

'What are you doing now, Constance?'

Constance said she had been scrubbing when she had been summoned to the visiting room.

'That is rather hard work,' said the Duchess.

Constance said it wasn't.

'Well, you don't *like* scrubbing out your cell?'

'Why not. Wouldn't you?'

The Duchess changed to a standard question. 'Do you say your prayers every night, Constance?'

'Yes, of course,' said Con. 'Don't you?' There was silence.

'Well, goodbye, Constance. I suppose you wish you were out of this place?'

'Yes,' said Constance, 'wouldn't you?'

'The questions which should be asked me and all political prisoners at a visit,' wrote Con in a furious, illicit note to Eva.

What do you weigh? What was your normal weight? What do you get to eat? Can you eat it? How much exercise do you get per day? How often do you get clean underclothes? Are you constipated? Can you get medicine? What temperature is the room you work in? What is your task, i.e. how much must you do in a week?

She was not allowed to receive a visit from Eva and Esther until September, three months after they had seen her in Mountjoy. She wrote afterwards:

I did love seeing you and Esther so. I hope she got her hat all right. Yours was very nice and you don't know what a picture the two of you made, all nice soft dreamy colours. (Moral: Always visit criminals in your best clothes – Blue and grey for choice, if it's me!)

Apparently their talk together at this visit was listened in to, and the woman Governor of Aylesbury wrote a confidential report on it. She said that Constance had talked much of Maíre Perolz – this was a friend of hers who, when Con had been forbidden by Connolly to go to Tralee and speak there just before the Rising, had gone and delivered Con's speech instead. Con told Eva, it seems, that Madame Perolz was to be given one of her dresses to wear 'like Elijah's Mantle' and was to 'keep things going and keep the clique together'. She begged to see Maeve, her daughter, though this was not allowed, whether by the prison authorities or by the Gore-Booths themselves is uncertain.

About the only thing Aylesbury did for Constance was give her time to reflect. The exercise did not alter by one iota her political convictions but it did a lot for her spiritual health. On that last night in the College of Surgeons she had undergone a deep mystical experience which the men and women around her had been able to express through the ritual of their Catholic prayers in a way that her own, half-believed Protestant Church upbringing had denied to her. At Kilmainham, waiting for a firing squad, she had asked the chaplain, Father Ryan, to be with her at the end and, although the end was to be eleven years later, it was a promise he kept. At Mountjoy she had registered as a Roman Catholic and asked the chaplain there, Father McMahon, to start giving her instruction although – and this was typical of her – having seen the essence of the faith during that strange moment in the College of Surgeons, she was impatient with the details of its dogma. Father McMahon's encounters with her are amazingly reminiscent of the priest's in Evelyn Waugh's *Brideshead Revisited* with Rex Mottram.

> I can't understand Countess Markievicz at all [Father McMahon told Hanna Sheehy Skeffington after one session]. She wants to be received into the Church, but she won't attend to me when I try to explain Transubstantiation and other doctrines. She just says, 'Please don't trouble to explain. I tell you I believe all the Church teaches. Now Father, please tell me about the boys.'

She shocked him even more when she described Lucifer as 'a good rebel', but Hanna Sheehy Skeffington said that she believed 'that was part of her habit of leg-pulling authority'. Now the Catholic chaplain to Aylesbury took up the thankless business and found Con more receptive, though she refused to enter the faith formally while she was in prison.

Every night at six o'clock, after lock-up, she would sit still and try to establish communication with her sister, 'and it worked. I got to her.' Eva also got through to her, as she said in her poem, 'Comrades, To Con':

> The peaceful night that round me flows,
> Breaks through your iron prison doors,
> Free through the world your spirit goes,
> Forbidden hands are clasping yours.

167

The wind is our confederate
The night has left the doors ajar;
We meet beyond earth's barred gate,
Where all the world's wild rebels are.

Con trained herself to see beauty around her, in the starlings quarrelling on her windowsill for crumbs, or a black beetle or 'a wedge-shaped flight of wild geese over us as we were exercising, making their weird cackling cry and they brought me home at once'.

Yeats wrote of her again in 'On a Political Prisoner'.

She that but little patience knew,
From childhood on, had now so much
A grey gull lost its fear and flew
Down to her cell and there alit,
And there endured her fingers' touch
And from her fingers ate its bit.

Did she in touching that lone wing
Recall the years before her mind
Became a bitter, an abstract thing,
Her thought some popular enmity:
Blind and leader of the blind
Drinking the foul ditch where they lie?

Not a lot, actually. She wasn't bitter either. 'Remember,' she wrote to Eva, 'no one has it in his power to make me unhappy.' Or, if they did, nobody ever knew it, not even that Christmas 1916 when all the internees, including the three Irishwomen at Aylesbury, were sent home and she was left alone.

The return of the internees was a Christmas amnesty from Lloyd George, now Prime Minister, in an attempt to sweeten the Irish temper, but the home-coming of nearly 2,000 men and women who, if they had not been extreme nationalists before, had certainly become so during their imprisonment, only exacerbated the situation. And so did Lloyd George himself. Back in August 1916 Lord Kitchener, the Secretary for War, had been drowned when the ship on which he was travelling to Russia had struck a mine, and Lloyd George had taken over his position, at the same time adopting the Irish problem as his own. As War Secretary he had proved brilliant and, by equally clever manipulation of the popular press, had made the British population believe that if anybody could win this protracted and dreadful war for them, he could. He had capitalised on this and, in an unholy alliance with the Unionists, Bonar Law and Sir Edward Carson, had managed to collapse Asquith's coalition and replace it by a five-man war cabinet with himself at its head.

On the Irish front he had been holding separate talks with both Redmond and Carson over the matter of partition, clandestinely getting each to agree to the exclusion from Home Rule of six Ulster counties; Derry, Antrim, Down, Armagh, Tyrone, and Fermanagh. This was a greater exclusion than Redmond wanted, but for the sake of Home Rule for the other twenty-six counties he agreed. Since Carson had wanted all nine counties excluded from Home Rule and kept for the British Empire he, too, was making a concession but he, too, agreed.

In keeping the talks with each man separate, Lloyd George also kept them in ignorance of the fact that while Redmond had received the impression that partition was to be only temporary, Carson had been given to understand that it would be permanent. It seems impossible that even Lloyd George's serpentine mind could have convinced itself that this arrangement had any lasting value; as it turned out it didn't even tide him over to the end of the war – on July 11, 1916, a Cabinet member, Lord Lansdowne, announced to the House of Lords that this form of partition would be 'permanent and enduring'. Redmond, although he did not lie down, was politically dead from that moment and the return of the angry internees in December was another nail in his coffin. It would only take the end of the war, and the resulting return of thousands of Irishmen from the front to discover that their country had diminished to twenty-six counties, to bury not only him, but his Irish Party and the entire constitutional movement.

The danger became apparent even to Redmond in a by-election held in Roscommon early in February 1917 when Count Plunkett, father of the executed Joseph, stood as an Independent candidate against the pro-parliamentary man in what had traditionally been a Redmondite seat. Plunkett's platform was vague, almost a protest against the manoeuvring of Lloyd George; his only claim to any policy at all was that he would make an excellent representative for Irish independence at the forthcoming International Peace Conference when the war ended and that he was the father 'of his dead boy and that two more sons were suffering penal servitude' for their part in the Rising. The result caught everybody, nationalists, Home Rulers and Lloyd George, unawares. He won twice as many votes as Redmond's man. Afterwards, and only afterwards, at a victory celebration, did Plunkett announce that he would not be taking his seat in 'a foreign parliament', i.e. the House of Commons, 'for it is in Ireland that the battle of Irish liberty is to be fought.'

Here, at last, in hard electoral terms was the volte-face of Irish opinion, brought about by the courage of dead men, the suffering of women and mishandling by the government; Ireland was awash with a new force that only needed harnessing.

What is more, the machinery that could do it was at hand – Sinn Féin. Arthur Griffith, its author, had been as little responsible for the Rising as Eoin MacNeill. True, Sinn Féiners had fought in it, but they had done so as Volunteers or Citizen Army men and women; once it had begun Griffith, moved by its heroism, had tried to join it, but had been asked by the leaders in the Post Office to save his efforts for propaganda in the future. Luckily for his political reputation, he had been arrested and interned in the crude sweep the British had made of suspicious characters. The same wholesale misunderstanding had, both in Britain and Ireland, dubbed the Rising as the 'Sinn Féin' rebellion and everyone who took part in it as 'Sinn Féiners'.

Now, as he emerged weak and blinking from internment, it was to find that he had a huge and receptive audience for his programme of self-reliance, though this same audience was now transmuting that self-reliance into republicanism and had less enthusiasm for his original idea of a dual monarchy. Moreover he discovered that his allies were no longer dreaming idealists, but hard-headed fighters whose leadership had been proved in the internment camps, men like Eamon de Valera and the young man who had once recited Emmet's speech from the dock at Con's house, Michael Collins.

On May 9 there was another chance to test the political water at a by-election in South Longford, an even greater parliamentary strong-hold than Roscommon. This time the election committee chose a candidate who could not even make a speech because he was still serving a penal sentence in Lewes jail for his part in the Rising, Joe McGuinness, and there is no doubt that the man who pushed Plunkett into nominating him was Michael Collins who wanted not only to see how far the electorate was prepared to go, but a candidate who stood a long way out from the moderation of Arthur Griffith, with whom he had been having some 'fierce rows'. The fact that McGuinness refused to stand did not worry Collins; he put him up as a candidate anyway, again with little more coherent policy than was displayed on McGuinness' electoral poster, showing a convict and a slogan: 'Put Him In To Get Him Out'.

Joe McGuinness, whose refusal to stand had been based on the republican ethic of having nothing to do with British parliamentary procedure, suddenly found himself an incarcerated but elected MP. He had won, after a recount, by thirty-seven votes, in its way a more amazing victory than Plunkett's.

The campaign to release the 122 Irish rebels still in English prisons, among them Eoin MacNeill who, considering that he had done so much to stop the Rising, had received a bewildering life sentence at his court martial and was serving it in Dartmoor, was becoming increasingly vociferous. Questions were being asked in Parliament, town council after town council were passing resolutions asking for their release, the Cumann na mBan was circulating foreign countries with details of their unjust treatment, especially that of Countess Markievicz. Lloyd George, at that moment organising a convention to try to solve the Irish question, decided to create a favourable atmosphere for it by releasing the lot. The men were freed on June 16, 1917.

On Sunday, June 17, the Home Office informed Eva that convict G–12 of Aylesbury Prison could be collected, and taken home. Máire Perolz, Helena Moloney, and Dr Kathleen Lynn, all of whom had come over to greet the men coming out of prison, stayed on in order to welcome her. Esther and Eva begged and borrowed the prettiest summer outfit they could and 'soon Constance, herself again, thin but beautiful, in a blue dress instead of that twice too large, hideously ugly garment supplied by a paternal government, left that prison for ever.'

She had gone into imprisonment fourteen months before, thinking she must die for Ireland. The intervening period had weakened her body but it had restored her mind which was now joyously prepared to live for Ireland; in many ways, as it turned out, it would be the more difficult thing to do.

CHAPTER TWELVE

Con, struggling through waving flags and cheering, singing people, in order to board the boat at Holyhead, called out: 'Which is the right side for us to get on?' A grinning, coal-smeared face looked out of the ferry's engine-room and said, 'It's always the right side if you're on it.'

On the boat the crew hovered solicitously around her, providing her with a breakfast of grapes and peaches.[1] At Dun Laoghaire there was another crowd waiting for her 'delirious with excitement and pleasure'. But even that did not prepare her for the welcome she was accorded by Dublin when she reached it on that Thursday, June 21, 1917. So much of the city had turned out to see her that it was nearly frightening, 'like plunging into the waves of the Atlantic', said Esther Roper. Lamp posts were decorated with tricolours and cheering small boys, work had been abandoned and the traffic diverted for the triumphal procession, which was led by a pipe band, followed by marchers representing all Con's organisations, followed by Kathleen Lynn's car driven by a uniformed Volunteer with Con standing up in it so that the people could see her, which was more than Esther, following in the car behind, could do in the press. It was a long time before they could even set off, and when they did the progress through the city took hours.

Even the male prisoners who had returned a few days before had not received the outpouring of patriotic love which now centred on and almost overwhelmed this lone female; with de Valera the last surviving leader of the Rising.

To Con, still trying to catch up with a year's changes, it seemed that only alchemy could have transmuted the hostile groups which had jeered her to prison into the masses who were now cheering her out of it.

She had no home to go to; the procession was heading straight for her spiritual home, Liberty Hall. But what remained of it was a

---

[1] *Prison Letters.* 'Alas,' wrote Esther Roper, 'these friendly people were all drowned later on when the boat was torpedoed.'

roofless, shattered building in which the only reality, Esther felt, was the figures in mourning, the widows of Easter Week who had come to welcome their old friend.

Even though she rarely put down their subtleties on paper, Con's perceptions were acute; she may have realised even at that moment how the state of Liberty Hall symbolised the condition of Labour in Ireland, that not only was James Connolly physically dead but not one scrap of his spirit remained in that wreck of a place. Suddenly she was very tired and could not even make a speech. She appeared at one of the windows and told the cheering crowd, 'I am going home now to rest in order that I may start work at once.'

The 'home' was Dr Kathleen Lynn's, where she stayed quietly for some days. 'Only a mean spirit grudges paying the price,' she had said, but, however ungrudgingly, a price had been paid; fourteen months of bad food, bad treatment and willing herself to bear up under them, perhaps for years, had drained something even from her vigour. Hanna Sheehy Skeffington told Esther Roper that in her opinion Con's terms of imprisonment shortened her life.

There was one thing more to be done before she started work; on June 24 at Clonliffe College in the presence of friends, who included Mrs Mallin, she was received into the Catholic Church and given the baptismal name of Anastasia. In many ways it was one of the most radical actions of her life, most of which, after all, had been spent in a society where 'They are Catholic, you know' was said in the same way that the anti-semitic said 'They are Jews, you know', hinting at the unbridgeable chasm which lay between the upright and normal on this side and the alien and vaguely unclean excesses which lay on the other.

To her socialist friends it looked like a reactionary move to join a Church which condemned practically everything they stood for, but Con saw no anomaly; if the Catholic Church did not stand for the equality of the masses who belonged to it, then it should. Eventually she was to commit this thinking to paper, but in the meantime she followed her own rule: if an organisation which had possibilities was not going in the way you considered it should, then you joined it to ensure that it did. Her biographers and others regard her conversion as a way of identifying more closely with the people she wanted to represent, of wriggling herself more deeply into the soil of Ireland. No doubt that was part of it; if she wasn't Irish now then she never would be; but Con was ahead of her time – and her biographers – in attempting to reconcile two apparently warring ideologies in a theory which has only comparatively recently emerged in the Catholicism of the Third World and is known as 'liberation theology'.

Con began to pick up the threads. In the time she and the men had been in prison, it had been the women who, as Cathal Brugha was to say later, 'kept the spirit alive, who kept the flame alive and the flag flying'. Now, sometimes willingly, sometimes a bit reluctantly, they were moving aside to let the men take over again. The National Aid Fund [1] had achieved importance not just in helping prisoners and their dependants, but in finding employment for men who had lost jobs by their participation in the Rising. It was decided that it could not be run on the women's voluntary basis but needed a full-time secretary and one of the men interviewed was young Michael Collins. 'The women members of the trust did not view him in too favourable a light,' one of Collins' biographers wrote. 'He seemed to them to be altogether too cocksure, seated on the edge of a desk, swinging his legs. But he created, nevertheless, an impression of certainty.' Undoubtedly there was a recognisable professionalism in Collins which marked everything he did; he reminded them of Seán MacDermott, the executed leader – he was, in fact, Collins' idol – and, anyway, they were pressured to accept him by the other men who had been interned with him in England and who knew him to be a leader himself. Although he didn't say so in such company, Michael Collins, who had been with the GPO contingent to the end, thought the Rising 'was bungled terribly, costing many a good life', and now saw a situation ripe for advancement – Ireland's and his own. He got the job at £2. 10s. od. a week which was, he said, 'not to be sneered at'.

Con, however, was determined that, while Ireland's freedom was always the main objective, women should play an equal part in gaining it. With her as its president, the Cumann na mBan began to regard itself as something more than simply an adjunct of the Volunteers. For the very first time, their policy statement that year, 1917, contained a clause which related directly to women and pledged the members to follow 'the policy of the Republican Proclamation by seeing that women take up their proper position in the life of the nation'. They also declared that all funds they collected were to be devoted 'to the arming and equipping of the men *and women* of Ireland'.

One thread, however, obstinately refused to be picked up; it had snapped in too many places: the devastation of Liberty Hall had indeed reflected the state of Irish Labour.

Just before he was executed, James Connolly had been aware how incomprehensible his part in the Rising would seem to his fellow

[1] By 1917 the Irish Volunteer Dependants' Fund had merged with the Irish National Aid Association to become the Irish National Aid and Volunteer Dependants' Fund, and was commonly referred to as the National Aid Fund.

socialists: 'They will forget I am an Irishman.' But the real danger, as it turned out, was in their forgetting his socialism and how he had allied it to nationalism. 'The cause of Labour is the cause of Ireland,' Connolly had said when he raised the green flag over Liberty Hall. 'The cause of Ireland is the cause of Labour.' Acquiescing to Home Rule merely meant the transfer of British capitalism to Irish capitalism: 'And, says the town worker, after we have crushed the Saxon and freed Ireland, what will we do? Oh, then you can go back to your slums, same as before . . .' he once wrote. If Labour took no part in freeing Ireland, it would have no chance to shape its new freedom and would find itself as badly off as before.

The man who became the power in the ITGWU, and therefore in the Irish Labour movement, after Connolly's death was the one in whom he had confided, as he marched away from Liberty Hall to begin the Rising, that there was no hope whatever of its success, William O'Brien. How deeply that prophecy of failure, and the failure itself, affected O'Brien is not measurable. Certainly, O'Brien no sooner inherited Connolly's mantle than he cast it off, leaving nationalism to Sinn Féin and concentrating only on building up the union's strength, a task in which, for the next few years, he and the ITGWU president, Thomas Foran, succeeded brilliantly, bringing up its membership to something like 100,000 by 1923. Between 1918 and 1930 the Irish Labour Party and the Irish Trade Union Congress formed a single organisation.

Lip service was paid to James Connolly's memory, but the Irish Citizen Army was in disarray as Liberty Hall became increasingly dominated by men who resented the link between it and the union. Despite all the emotion for the executed men of the Rising, the 1916 Irish Trade Union Congress in August had pointed out that only half the members of the Citizen Army were ITGWU men, a repudiation which showed it was not endorsing what Connolly had always envisaged as the fighting arm of the workers. On the 1917 anniversary of his death, it was mainly the Citizen Army women who made sure he was commemorated. They posted replicas of the Easter Proclamation around the city and then, when the streamer which said: 'James Connolly Murdered May 12, 1916' was removed at the insistence of the police, Helena Moloney made another and she, with half-a-dozen other women, barricaded themselves on the shattered roof of Liberty Hall to display it. The police had to break down a door and shovel away a pile of coal before they could get to the second banner and tear it down.

On July 19, 1917, a by-election in East Clare was won by the Sinn Féin candidate, a thirty-five-year-old teacher of mathematics of whom little was known except that his battalion had fought well in the Rising and that he, like Collins, had distinguished himself by his behaviour in prison, Eamon de Valera. The seat had been made vacant by the death of Major Willie Redmond, brother to the leader of the Parliamentary Party and was being contested by Patrick Lynch, KC, a popular local candidate and a former Crown prosecutor. De Valera fought a lofty and professional campaign while his supporters, mostly Volunteers, fought for him equally professionally but less loftily, passing the word that Lynch had 'defended one half of the murderers in Clare and is related to the other half'. Feelings ran high. The wife of a Munster Fusilier, for instance, challenged every Sinn Féiner with her husband's drawn sword. Constance's republican speeches on de Valera's behalf at Ennis, the capital of Clare, brought on an attack by soldiers' relatives, and the Labour League of Ennis, all stout Sinn Féiners, had to form a cordon to allow her escape down a side street. She loved it. It was like old times.

It was another landslide for Sinn Féin, de Valera winning 5,010 votes against Lynch's 2,025. A week later W. T. Cosgrave, another released prisoner, later to be President of the Executive Council of the Irish Free State, was also elected on the Sinn Féin ticket, at Kilkenny.

But what was the Sinn Féin ticket? Whatever it was, it could obviously sweep the country, but what was it? Under Arthur Griffith, the man who had virtually copyrighted the name, it still stood for Empire and monarchy, yet de Valera and the others had stood for the principles of the Easter Rising to which such ideas were anathema. De Valera in one of his speeches had quoted the Proclamation and added: 'To that government, when in visible shape, I offered my allegiance and to its spirit I owe my allegiance still.' It was decided that the matter should be cleared up once and for all at Sinn Féin's convention, the Ard Fheis, in October.

In the meantime the Countess Markievicz was being honoured. De Valera, Cosgrave and Laurence Ginnell, who had resigned his seat in the House of Commons to devote himself to the nationalist struggle, were with her in Kilkenny when her name was put on its roll of honorary citizens. She was photographed with them all, and nobody looks less like a rebel than Constance in a long coat and soft, fichu collar, holding a bouquet.

Soon afterwards she became the first woman to receive the freedom of Sligo, her home town, and in his speech bestowing that distinction, the mayor said that they were also paying a tribute to a family of which she was the most distinguished member. But that same family is not mentioned as attending any of the many functions at which she spoke that weekend, and Con stayed the nights in a hotel. Nor did Con accept the honour on their behalf; middle-class Sligo was made aware of why she had fought in the Rising. 'I became a rebel,' she told it, 'because the older I grew and the more I thought and the more I used my eyes and the more I went around amongst the people of Ireland, and particularly Dublin, the more I realised that nothing could help Ireland only to get rid of England, bag and baggage.' She was accepting the honour they gave her as a member of the Irish Citizen Army, a proud friend of James Connolly. She mentioned 1913 and then finished by saying: 'In appealing to the Peace Conference we are appealing not only on the grounds of sympathy but on logical grounds, and on these grounds we are going to have the support of the nations.'

Like de Valera at this stage, she was advocating Sinn Féin as a constitutional movement out to achieve Irish independence by appeal to the Peace Conference after the war, not by revolution. 'No one is preaching rebellion,' she wrote to Eva. De Valera was stressing that the Volunteers were once again what they had been originally, 'the best protection that England could not come and rob them' of their rights.

None of this reassured a government daily receiving reports that Sinn Féin and Volunteers were increasing their membership, that drilling was taking place with increasing efficiency and pride and that a marching song which had gained popularity in 1916, 'A Soldier's Song', was becoming an unofficial national anthem. Arrests began for drilling and 'seditious' speeches. By September 1917 there were over thirty Volunteers in Mountjoy on such charges, chief of whom were Austin Stack, commandant of the Tralee Volunteers, and a top Irish Republican Brotherhood member, Thomas Ashe.

Con had managed to snatch a conversation with two men, Liddy and Brown, while they waited under arrest at Limerick station on their way to Mountjoy.

I said, 'Think it over before you hunger-strike, for they will let you die, and it would be fatal for the Cause if you gave in to save your life.' I told them that there was no need for them to strike, and that it was terrible suffering, and in fact tried to persuade them not to, but the one idea that is in every one of their minds is, 'We are soldiers pledged to Ireland and we can fight in jail as well as out, and die in jail as well as out, and it is up to us to do it.' I think the English are trying to goad us into another rising, to wipe us all out . . .

With the tide running strongly for Sinn Féin her advice was sensible, but it was also subjective. Hunger strike was the one thing in the world Constance was afraid of. 'I don't know how they find the courage to do it . . . I don't feel a bit sure that I could do it. It's different from fighting somehow, it is so cold-blooded.' She would not urge anybody to do a thing she shrank from herself.

The prisoners, however, had insisted that they should be given the status in Mountjoy of prisoners-of-war, an illogical stance if Sinn Féin was in fact a constitutional movement, but the sheer formlessness of Sinn Féin encouraged individual interpretation and was, in any case, a threat that the movement might run out of steam. More blood sacrifice – or in this matter, as Con had pointed out, cold blood – must be made for Ireland. When they were refused prisoner-of-war status, the men hunger-struck. Apparently forgetting the revulsion caused when the system had been used on English suffragettes, the authorities obliged by forcible feeding. Thomas Ashe died a few hours after the tube had been forced down his throat on September 25.

At the inquest it was revealed that for fifty hours previously he had been deprived of bed, bedding and boots and left lying on the floor of his cell. The coroner's jury, which contained some Unionists, censured the Castle authorities for not acting more promptly when Ashe's condition had been brought to their notice.

'Dr K.L. [Kathleen Lynn] thinks that it was the forcible feeding that did it, that they forced some into his lungs,' wrote Con.

The funeral was reminiscent of O'Donovan Rossa's, except that it was much bigger and that in turning out for it in their thousands, Dubliners were consciously defying the British Government. The crowd that followed the hearse to Glasnevin on September 30 was estimated between 30,000 to 40,000 and was attended by practically every organisation in the city, most of them wearing the tricolour colours of orange, white and green. Even a large contingent of Redmond's Volunteers attended. Constance led a force of the Citizen Army in uniform.

A volley was fired over the grave and Michael Collins delivered the only oration, shortly and effectively: 'That volley which we have just heard is the only speech which it is proper to make over the grave of a dead Fenian.'

It was Collins, too, who had made the arrangements for the funeral, backed by the Irish Republican Brotherhood of which he was now a principal member, and displayed his immense professionalism once more; a film taken of the Volunteers firing over the grave was developed in the cars during the return journey and was viewed in Dublin that same night.

Helplessly, the authorities accorded the remaining prisoners political status.

Constance made scores of speeches that autumn arranged for her by Sinn Féin as one of their biggest crowd-pullers, but two at least she made on her own account. One was for her old Citizen Army friend and the man who had awakened her to her new faith, William Partridge, who had died as a result of his imprisonment for the Rising. She wore the same Citizen Army uniform she had been dressed in at Stephen's Green, the tunic of which had belonged to Michael Mallin. The other was in the remote town of Athea, County Limerick, where Con Colbert had lived. Despite its isolation, people poured in from the surrounding districts so that her address, which was characterised by 'terseness and lucidity' was punctuated 'by deafening roars of applause from the vast multitude gathered around the platform . . . this lady certainly has the courage of her convictions'.

But wherever she went during that strenuous schedule, she made one thing clear. She was Sinn Féin, but she was also socialist. More often than not she was in Citizen Army uniform – she had been promoted to Major – and she brought James Connolly into the forefront of her speeches. Inherent in all her pleas for Irish freedom was freedom for its working class. In public, and no doubt in private, she begged Labour to take the place Connolly had won for it by his death in the fight for the new Republic. Sinn Féin was in an inchoate situation which could be shaped still from inside and out; it was even possible that the ingrained conservatism of the Irish working class could, by strong Labour leadership, have had its new-found national-ism harnessed to a policy of social and political change, although that would not have been easy.

As it was the Irish TUC, incorporating the Irish Labour Party, either failed to understand Connolly's form of republicanism or deliberately ignored it. The ITGWU's withdrawal from the national struggle caused a rift which severed Labour's only formal link with the republicans and, in turn, cut the republicans off from existing Irish socialism.

The link between the ITGWU and Constance Markievicz remained strong, however; during her imprisonment her financial affairs had been put into the hands of her brother, Sir Josslyn Gore-Booth, who had been told that 'the convict's property is badly in need of administration and is subject to much loss', which is not surprising in view of how much she gave away. 'I never knew,' Hanna Sheehy Skeffington said, 'a person with less sense of property or less attached to possessions.' When she emerged from Aylesbury she was penniless until her allowance was restored, and it was the ITGWU which stepped forward to put funds at her disposal.

Nevertheless, when she entered Dublin's Mansion House on October 25, 1917 for the three-day Sinn Féin Ard Fheis, with over a thousand other delegates, she was carrying James Connolly's banner virtually single-handed.

Typically, she went straight into the attack. Eoin MacNeill was present and up for election to the executive, and she opposed him strenuously or, according to pro-MacNeill sources, 'viciously'. He had changed his mind too many times, she pointed out, had ruined the plans for the Rising with his countermand; it would not be safe for Sinn Féiners to trust their lives to such a man. From this remove it is difficult not to sympathise with Con's view, and equally difficult to understand the loyalty MacNeill still inspired among Irishmen, for it does not seem to have been only in a desire for unity that so many now rushed to his defence. De Valera, while still in prison, had risked a flogging when, suddenly glimpsing MacNeill, he had ordered his men to stand to attention and 'Eyes Left' in the salute to a senior officer. Nora Connolly, now over in the United States, was writing more in sorrow than in anger in *The Unbroken Tradition* that MacNeill's mind was of 'the academic order – not the type to which revolutionists belong'. MacNeill's Celtic scholarship held an attraction which left Con cold, but which perhaps connected the others to some primitive Irish innocence they would not willingly abandon in these new politics, and they were ready to tuck his vacillation into a twilit subconcious, forgiven but not quite forgotten and never, ever spoken about. Con brought the matter into the open air and forced de Valera to clear it by stating his conviction that MacNeill had not acted 'otherwise than as a good man'.

With relief at the solidarity, MacNeill was elected on to the executive with a massive 888 votes. Mentally Con shrugged: the matter was over, but the illogic of the situation was that no such forgiveness was extended to Bulmer Hobson who remained in the wilderness.

The soul of Sinn Féin was worth winning – whereas at the beginning of 1917 there had been 166 Sinn Féin clubs representing 11,000 members, by the Ard Fheis it had grown to 1,200 clubs and a membership of a quarter of a million – and there were undercurrents in the battle to control it which had not yet polarised. De Valera, for instance, had renounced the Irish Republican Brotherhood as no longer necessary. The time for secrecy was past. Con agreed; conspiracy had always been alien to her and the problems it had caused in Easter Week had confirmed her view. In this she had an ally, Cathal Brugha, who, although a physically small man, had shown such gigantic courage in the Easter fighting – wounded in twenty-five places, he had held off a British attack on the South Dublin Union, singing 'God Save Ireland' while he did it – that he had earned himself a place in the new pantheon.

But to Michael Collins conspiracy was the breath of life and he was ruthless and brilliant enough to manipulate it almost any way he pleased. He was emerging as the leading figure in the reconstituted IRB and, always a political realist, was at this moment putting its power behind de Valera. A split personality, he had won the adoration of his companions in prison, but they had summed up his most disliked feature, arrogance, with the phrase: 'Collins thinks he's a big fellow.' Friends and enemies – and he was to make plenty of both – were to forget the derogatory origin of the title and he became 'the Big Fellow' not just because of his size but through his presence which exuded power 'through some uncomfortable magnetism of the very air, a tingling of the nerves'. At the Ard Fheis he circulated to IRB members a list of candidates he wanted supported.

There were three natural nominations for the presidency of Sinn Féin, Count Plunkett, Arthur Griffith and Eamon de Valera, and with a display of unanimity and magnanimity which won all hearts, both Plunkett and Griffith stood down in favour of the rising star, de Valera. Lord Longford's biography, however, makes it clear that this was not a spontaneous gesture; Griffith, at least, had been manoeuvred into it.

> About a week before the convention de Valera met Griffith over coffee . . . The discussion with Griffith was friendly, but de Valera was firm. He insisted if he went forward he could win, since the new Sinn Féin was largely a Volunteer movement. But it would be better if there were no contest. Griffith agreed and decided not only to withdraw his name, but to propose de Valera.

De Valera, therefore, was unanimously elected president, Arthur Griffith got the next largest amount of votes (1,197) and became Vice-President with Father Michael O'Flanagan, a radical priest and Sinn Féiner (780). Honorary Secretaries, Austin Stack (857) and Darrell Figgis (510); Honorary Treasurers, W. T. Cosgrave (537) and Laurence Ginnell (471). There were twenty-four executive members including Cathal Brugha (685), Constance (617) and Michael Collins (340).

The trickiest question facing the convention was in its policy for self-government, since, apart from the fact that it should *be* self-government, the delegates and executive possessed among their numbers varied and conflicting ideas. De Valera had worked out a formula which pleased everyone. Sinn Féin would aim at securing international recognition for her independence at the Peace Conference, and then, 'having achieved that status the Irish people may by referendum freely choose their own form of government'.

He added:

This is not the time for discussion on the best forms of government. This is the time to get freedom. Then we can settle by the most democratic means what particular form of government we may have. I only wish to say in reference to the last clause that there is no contemplation in it of having a monarchy in which the monarch would be of the House of Windsor.

The convention sighed with relief. A simple clear formula was what it wanted. That it was a postponement of basic issues, they knew; that it carried the seeds of civil war, they did not even dream.

There were such seeds in the reorganised Irish Volunteers. Collins, as its new Director of Organisation, Diarmuid Lynch, Director of Communications and Seán McGarry, General Secretary, were all IRB men and, like much of the rank and file, were prepared to use force again to bring about a republic. Here again the election of de Valera to the Volunteers' presidency reassured the moderates and Cathal Brugha, really a fierce believer in force, said on his appointment to Chief-of-Staff that they did not intend to meet English rule by assassination.

At that point, however, de Valera was handling his two horses with skill in making it seem to the watching public that they were in harness. He managed to satisfy Constance that his heart was in the left place politically and she proposed his name as Chief at the Fianna convention, another post to which he was unanimously elected.

Women, too, were pleased with him. Their resolution clarifying Sinn Féin's guarantee of equality between male and female members had been adopted at the convention, and four women, Con, Kathleen Lynn, Kathleen Clarke and Grace Plunkett, had been elected to the executive. The suffragette *Irish Citizen* congratulated Sinn Féin, but commented: 'It was regrettable to notice so few women delegates.'

At the first Sinn Féin executive meeting in December Countess Markievicz was appointed to head its Department of Labour along with her socialist friend, Cathal O'Shannon, and Irish Labour felt itself well represented on the new movement.

Jim Larkin in America, however, recognised the danger both in the States and Ireland of Labour's withdrawal from the nationalist fight. 'The Sinn Féin movement here is anti-Labour,' he wrote to Foran of the ITGWU, 'and for the Socialists they think they are anti-Christs. They have tried to impress the American public that the Revolution was a Catholic Revolution.' He did not approve of what the Irish-women, who had gone over to America on propaganda tours, were doing.

I must call attention to the fact that Mrs S. [Hanna Sheehy Skeffington] is just an apologist for the Sinn Féin crowd . . . Nora C. [Connolly] follows the same line

... they make out that Arthur G. [Griffith] is a God-given saint and statesman; that nobody in Ireland did anything but Sinn Féin. Connolly and the other boys all recanted Socialism and Labour and were good Sinn Féiners. My God, it is sickening.

In another letter he wrote: 'What are O'Brien and the rest doing in allowing the Griffith gang to monopolise all the credit for the effort? ... Are they all turned to Sinn Féin? ... Have our section any representatives on the alleged Provisional Government?'

In March of 1918, John Redmond died, saddened and beaten. He had attended a convention called by Lloyd George to thrash out the problems of Home Rule once and for all, but since Irish opinion was fast moving beyond Home Rule anyway, since Sinn Féin boycotted it and since there was no movement on the question of partition, it failed.

The immediate result of his death was a by-election in his old seat of Waterford, the second of three Sinn Féin fought early in 1918.

None of the seats was particularly representative of an Irish cross-section, and in Waterford Sinn Féin were facing a sentimental vote for Redmond's son, who called it a party of 'anarchy and destruction'; nevertheless Sinn Féin lost them all. But, just as it looked as if its apparently unstoppable progress was running out of steam, the British Government, with perfect timing, stepped in to speed it up again.

The successful spring offensive by the Germans on the Western Front created a desperate need for thousands more British soldiers and, therefore, to extend conscription to Ireland where there was still a reservoir of men which remained unconscripted so far. Lloyd George was warned and was aware of the trouble extending conscription to Ireland could make for him, so he did two things at the same time. One was to introduce a bill which gave his government power to introduce conscription to Ireland, and the other was to dangle before unsmiling Irish eyes a promise to bring in a form of Home Rule before conscription was implemented. Both Home Rule – and Lloyd George's promises – were now so irrelevant that Irish attention from the start was focused on the conscription issue. Nothing Lloyd George could have done could so successfully have combined every disparate element in Ireland against him; even the Irish MPs registered their protest when his bill was passed on April 16 by leaving the House and returning home to make common cause with Sinn Féin. A committee of Irish bishops registered a protest at 'an oppressive and inhuman law which the Irish have a right to resist by every means that are consonant with the laws of God', and discovered themselves to be bedfellows with Labour, which had also risen in nationalist solidarity.

On April 23 the Irish Trades Union Congress organised a one-day general protest strike which effectively paralysed Ireland, except in Unionist Belfast. For this female co-operation was vital, since the threat of politically-enforced conscription was combined with an actual economic/industrial conscription whereby employers were encouraged to fill jobs left vacant by men with boys or women in order to give subsequently unemployed men no choice but the British Army.

Con organised Cumann na mBan, the Franchise League and the Irish Women Workers' Union to hold a flag day and to sign a pledge not just to resist conscription, but to promise not to fill men's jobs. It was the right move at the right time but the trouble was that their slogan, 'No woman must take a man's job', was to be remembered in an Ireland which never had full employment as a concession that men had the prior right to work.

Irish contempt for the authority of the British Government had never been deeper or more widespread and the authorities became seriously alarmed at the unrest. Again the government made two simultaneous moves to deal with the situation. On May 11 it dispatched a soldier, Field-Marshal Lord French, to be Ireland's new Lord Lieutenant – a man who must have been dismayed, though not surprised, to find there his sister, Charlotte Despard, a veteran suffragette, demonstrating against him. Secondly, it seized on an excuse of a German plot to move against the Sinn Féin leaders in order to shut them up.

The basis for the excuse was thin and certainly did not involve Sinn Féin as an organisation; the old Fenian, John Devoy, in America was in constant touch with Germany in an effort to get arms for Ireland, and one of Casement's ill-starred Irish Brigade had actually landed, and been arrested, in Galway with a message from Germany – on Germany's initiative – to Michael Collins which would, in any case, have been ignored at that stage of the game. Austin Chamberlain, a member of the Cabinet, confessed that the evidence for a 'German conspiracy' might be insufficient for a jury, but it would be sufficient for America, which had been in the war against Germany since the previous year.

Between midnight and dawn of May 18 the G-men of Dublin Castle instituted a gigantic round-up of persons known to them as prominent in the Sinn Féin movement, among them the Countess Markievicz, Maud Gonne who had recently returned to Ireland from France, Kathleen Clarke, Arthur Griffith, W. T. Cosgrave, Eamon de Valera, Joe McGuinness and Count Plunkett. Those of them who, like Con, were on the Sinn Féin executive knew it was going to happen; Michael Collins had begun building up a spy network which reached into Dublin Castle itself and had been given a list of the wanted men and women and the date of their arrest. The executive met that night to decide whether to run, fight or let themselves be taken. Darrell Figgis, who was among them, wrote: 'I am stirred by pride in my comrades and our comradeship of those days. No one thought of himself or herself and all our debate was directed to the effect on the country.' They decided to allow their capture; for one thing, Arthur Griffith was contesting an election in East Cavan and the propaganda value of their arrest would swing the vote in his favour. (Which it did.) As Con later wrote to Eva: 'Our arrests carry so much further than speeches. Sending you to jail is like pulling out all the loud stops on all the speeches you ever made or words you ever wrote.'

Michael Collins left the meeting to rush round and deliver other warnings, then went to the house of Seán McGarry which, he knew, had already been raided and was therefore relatively safe, and slept the rest of the night in it. Somebody had to be left at large to keep the organisation going; it is significant that, whether the others had decided it or he had decided for himself, Collins was that man. Cathal Brugha was also left at large and so, as both men had high dual roles in Sinn Féin and the Volunteers, the shaping of events was left to two men who, despite differences over the IRB and differences yet to come, were proponents of militancy and, at that point, uncompromising republicans.

Con, accompanied by Poppet the spaniel, who went everywhere with her, left the meeting to hurry to Maud Gonne's house and warn her that she was on the list of arrestees. Then she went on towards Rathmines where she was living, but she was arrested before she got there by two detectives accompanied by six soldiers; Poppet was arrested as well, which was fair because the dog had just about as much to do with a German Plot as his mistress. Con was told she would be taken to Holloway and at the mention of England was swept with longing to see her sister again.

The following Sunday was hot. In their London flat Eva and Esther Roper were sitting and thinking about Constance:

. . . we had no news whatever as to her movements [Esther wrote]. Suddenly, for no reason whatever, I felt I must go to Euston Station to meet the Irish Mail. I was reluctant to say so, for Eva was tired out. However, I did so. She asked 'Why?' I was obliged to reply, 'I have no reason whatever, only I feel I must.'

The two of them set off at once. 'The station was hot and quiet when we got to the arrival platform and I felt exceedingly silly.' When the train came in and nobody familiar appeared to get off, she felt sillier. Then she saw, coming down the platform, first a cocker spaniel, then a couple of soldiers with rifles, and finally the Countess Markievicz. There was a brief, joyous reunion before Con was driven off to prison, Poppet was left in Eva's custody and the strange little incident was over. 'I tell the tale just as it happened,' said Esther, 'I am not in the least psychic nor have I ever had a similar experience.'

It was as well the sisters met then because Con, along with Maud Gonne and Kathleen Clarke, was interned without trial and both they, and potential visitors, had to sign an undertaking not to discuss politics, which the three women refused to do. Nobody from outside was allowed to see them.

All the arrests caused an outcry and none more than Kathleen Clarke's. Even the Irish MP, Tim Healy, wrote: 'It should have been enough for them to shoot her husband and her brother, without depriving her children of their mother.' Maud Gonne was haunted by the memory of her young son, Seán MacBride, running after the Black Maria that had taken her away. She was refused permission to sign a cheque in order to provide for him. Con worried about her two friends – and in the case of Kathleen Clarke, overdid it. Mrs Clarke, her nerves raw with worry for her five children, and prickly with resentment at what she suspected might be patronage, turned on her: 'Little and inoffensive I may be, but my charge sheet is the same as yours.' After that, she said, Markievicz 'shut up'. Close allies though they were, there were inevitable moments of irritation with each other and while one's sympathy is with Kathleen Clarke, it is understandable if Con was showing off as the experienced old lag – she had earned the right in Aylesbury's hard school. The snub did not make a scrap of difference to her; every letter praised Kathleen's courage and continued to worry about her health.

At first the three women were kept isolated, but after much protesting were eventually moved into adjoining cells and were allowed to be sent food, clothes, books and approved newspapers. Through Eva, Con procured fruit for Kathleen Clarke, who was having trouble eating. After that her requests were for brushes, paper and water-colours – she thought the smell of oils in the cells might be too much for her friends – and did a lot of painting.

I wish I knew how long they meant to keep me, so as to know what to get in. The whole thing is really laughable. My companions I think of as 'Niobe' and 'Rachel' as they are the two most complete and perfect – though now, alas! mournful – mothers that I ever met. It's really very bad luck on the kids to lose *both* parents . . . I am quite well off, for a wonder, so you can buy me any book you can think, and also some stockings with thick soles. I passed yours on to Mrs C. [Clarke] who came with nothing but what she stood up in.

When they heard of the election of Arthur Griffith (then in Reading jail) for East Cavan, the Irishwomen cheered. 'Such a victory! Our arrests did it! For we were not at all certain; in fact, most doubtful, of the result.'

She reiterated to Eva that there was no basis for their internment. 'First let me tell you and our common enemy the Censor that there is no German plot!' and at one point decided that the authorities suspected her of German affiliations because, just before she was arrested, 'kidnapped' is how she put it, she'd had German measles. She was consistently rude about the Censor, signing off her first few letters with '*Auf Wiedersehen*' just to annoy 'that diabolical long nose' who was reading them. The prisoners had to restrict their writing to 'domestic and business' subjects. 'I would like to remind the sweet rulers of this Empire,' wrote Con, 'that they have constantly affirmed that "Ireland is a domestic question".'

As always the letters were cheerful; she would not give the Censor the satisfaction of believing her to be anything else, nor Eva the anxiety; but there are frequent mentions of Casi and Stasko (Stanislas, her stepson) from whom nothing had been heard since the upheaval of the Russian Revolution the year before, which show her worry for them.

In Ireland arrests were multiplying. By autumn 1918, as Sinn Féin pointed out, there were 500 people imprisoned under the Defence of the Realm Act on charges ranging from singing 'A Soldier's Song' to giving their name in Gaelic when accosted by a policeman. Hanna Sheehy Skeffington suddenly turned up as a prisoner to join the three in Holloway because she had returned from her propaganda tour of the United States without a passport. They were all glad to see her, especially Con – she and Hanna had not met since before the Easter Rising. Hanna was able to give them all the news of her American tour which had included a personal interview with President Wilson, to whom she had handed a petition from Cumann na mBan, signed by Con as its president, and other distinguished Irishwomen, appealing to him 'to include Ireland among the small nations for whose freedom America was fighting'. As Hanna told Con, 'I was the first Irish exile and the first to wear there the badge of the Irish Republic.' After the exchange of information Hanna went to her cell and started a hunger strike, which procured her release within a few days.

Limerick, in a protest against Constance's imprisonment, gave her the freedom of the city and W. B. Yeats, for all his disapproval of her politics, signed the document. But not everyone was going over to Sinn Féin; though the government was holding its hand in enforcing conscription, it had instituted a campaign for voluntary recruitment and succeeded in gaining more than 11,000 recruits in eleven weeks. However, the matter shortly became academic as the Germans began suing for an armistice.

In October Maud Gonne, who had been unwell, was released to a London nursing home.

With the coming of the Armistice on November 11, 1918, a general election was called for December and a one-clause act ten days later permitted women to stand as Members of Parliament. (The right to vote had been given to men over twenty-one and women over thirty years of age the previous January.) Pressure had been brought to bear on the government not to extend this facility to Ireland by both Unionists and Irish parliamentarians, unsuccessfully.

Casually, Con wrote to Eva: 'By the way, shall you stand for Parliament? I wouldn't mind doing it as a "Shinner", as an election sport, and one does not have to go to Parliament if one wins, but oh! to have to sit there and listen to all that blither.' She was less uncommitted than she seemed; Cumann na mBan, with which she was in touch, were urging Sinn Féin to put forward women candidates. The reply it was given was non-committal and amazing: the issue would depend on whether or not it would be according to law. This, at the same time as they were putting out an election pamphlet reminding women voters of those two law-breakers Patrick and Willie Pearse, by saying: 'Save Ireland by voting as MRS PEARSE will vote,' and promising that 'as in the past, so in the future the womenfolk of the Gael shall have high place in the Councils of a freed Gaelic nation'.

The pro-suffrage *Irish Citizen* commented: 'It looks as if Irishmen, even Republicans, need teaching in this matter.'

However, in the end Sinn Féin decided to be brave and put up two women candidates – it was the only party in Ireland to run any – one was Connolly's secretary, Winifred Carney, who had distinguished herself in the Easter Rising in the GPO, and the other was the Countess Markievicz. Winifred was to stand for the Victoria division of Belfast, an unpromising seat, and Con for St Patrick's in Dublin, a working-class constituency which knew her well.

It would have been nonsense not to have nominated Con; well-known republicans were thin on the ground, in addition to which Sinn Féin had decided to contest Unionist areas in North-East Ulster with candidates who were also standing elsewhere. De Valera, for instance, was standing in three seats including his by-election victory, East

Clare, and East Mayo where he faced – as well as he could face anybody seeing that he was in prison – John Dillon, now leader of the Parliamentary party.

For Sinn Féin it was an election under the most difficult conditions possible; of seventy-three of its candidates, forty-seven were in prison, all papers sympathetic to it had been banned and the others were under censorship, its director of elections was arrested three weeks before polling day, and it was still being dubbed 'pro-German' by its opponents. This was not a time to offend the women who had already proved their value in working for the by-elections.

Despite the restrictions there was no doubt that this was a national plebiscite on Ireland's independence. Half of Sinn Féin's election manifesto was blacked out by the Censor, but the vital words: 'Sinn Féin aims at securing the establishment of that Republic' remained.

After much agonising and changing of minds, Irish Labour made its decision – which in the long run proved disastrous to it – not to contest. It was persuaded, says Dorothy Macardle, 'in order that the National forces might be kept solid and united in this crisis, although organised Labour was far from satisfied with the social outlook of Sinn Féin'. It may be that it felt it could be complacent because, as Dorothy Macardle also points out, 'The majority of the working men and women of Ireland were members of Sinn Féin or the Volunteers or Cumann na mBan, and, as the disciples of James Connolly, held that the freedom of the nation and the freedom of the working classes must be pursued as one undivided aim.' Presumably its trust was in de Valera who, at the 1917 Sinn Féin Ard Fheis, had said: 'When Labour frees this country – helps to free it – Labour can look for its share of the patrimony.'

For Connolly-followers like Con there was no option but support for Sinn Féin, and in any case to her nationalism was the chicken which would lay Labour's egg.

Holloway Prison allowed Con a large sheet of paper for her election address, but little time: she scribbled it down so fast she was afraid it didn't make sense and, in any case, wouldn't get past the Censor. (De Valera's didn't.) It was straightforward enough:

> As I will not procure my freedom by giving any pledge or undertaking to the enemy you will probably have to fight without me. I have many friends in the constituency who will work all the harder for me. They know I stand for the Irish Republic, to establish which our heroes died . . .

That she was asking her constituency to do what nobody in the

British Isles had ever done before – vote for a woman in a general election – was not mentioned. She was an Irish person appealing to Irish people.

Very few constituencies throughout Britain were being asked to vote for women. Of 1,623 candidates standing for 707 seats, only seventeen – just over one per cent – were women. This was not because they were reluctant to stand but because local parties were reluctant to nominate them; even the English Labour Party, supposed champion of women's suffrage, was putting up only four. The Conservatives made their one female nomination late, and only then because their candidate for Kennington, Lambeth, died during the campaign and his widow was hastily adopted in his stead. Christabel Pankhurst was standing for Smethwick as the Women's Party candidate, certain that the electorate was sufficiently tired of male-dominated, war-ridden politics to respond to her slogan: 'Give women a chance.'

There was a general fear among politicians that the newly-enfranchised women would vote for female candidates regardless of policies and the outcome would be a woman's party versus a man's party. All the old anti-suffrage arguments were revived; that women, being shielded from the reality of the crass, cold world did not deserve the vote whereas men, who had to make their way and support their families, did; that the House of Commons was not 'a fit and proper place for any respectable woman to sit in'.

All Con's friends and supporters turned out to work for her, the Irish Women's Franchise League, Sinn Féin, Volunteers and Cumann na mBan held meetings in the St Patrick's Division. In writing to thank Hanna Sheehy Skeffington and the others, Con said: 'It's been so good for the country having no leaders. They have all had a chance to learn how to think and act. Leaders can be such a curse.'

Polling day was December 14, but the result of the poll was delayed to allow the service vote to come in. Despite this, many soldiers did not receive their postal voting papers by the close of poll, which helped Sinn Féin, still suffering from the 'pro-German' slur, an image that did it harm when, just before the end of the war, the Holyhead ferry had been torpedoed by a German submarine, with the loss of all those who had been so kind to Con on her return from Aylesbury.

The results amazed even Sinn Féin. The Home Rule party, which had dominated the political scene and public opinion for so long, and which had held nearly seventy seats in the Commons at the dissolution of Parliament, had only six seats; twenty-six had gone to the Unionists and Sinn Féin had gained seventy-three – one of them the St Patrick's Division of Dublin.

CHAPTER THIRTEEN

Hardly anyone, then or later, looked on Constance's win as a cause for female celebration, or a personal tribute to her.

To the British Government it was merely part of the detritus of the Sinn Féin landslide.

To the amazed, jubilant crowds outside Sinn Féin headquarters in Harcourt Street, waiting for the results to come in, it was just one more miracle in a series of miracles.

> Harry Boland would come to the window and in the silence that immediately fell would call out 'Countess Markievicz is in' or 'Seán T. O'Kelly has been elected' or 'Alderman Tom Kelly beats them both in Stephen's Green.' Then the crowd would demonstrate to its heart's desire . . . Never had a nation so much reason to make a cautious demand and never had it made a more daring one. As the figures poured in and Sinn Féin won with huge majorities it seemed as if with their bare hands the ordinary men and women had seized the cordon of bayonets around Ireland and thrust them aside to call their sovereignty to the world.

To the English suffragettes, knowing Sinn Féin policy would not allow Con to take her seat, it was frustration at being denied the sight of the first elected woman walking through the Members' entrance of the House of Commons. And Irish suffragettes, though pleased, were sad that 'Under the new dispensation the majority sex in Ireland has secured one representative. This is the measure of our boasted sex equality.'

To English historians Constance Markievicz became an annoying footnote to the following year's by-election of Lady Nancy Astor who, they have to explain, was the first woman to sit in, but not be elected to, Westminster.

And to Irish historians it is a mere mention in an event which changed the political face of their country.

In fact, Constance's win was a considerable personal achievement and should not be taken for granted. Every other woman candidate in Britain was wiped out in that general election of 1918, including Winifred Carney and even, although by only a small margin, Christabel Pankhurst.

Unnoticed by Irishmen, to whom subsequent elections in Britain become academic, is the fact that in the next general election, 1922, no women were elected, though thirty-three were candidates. Indeed, the next three women elected to Westminster, including Lady Astor, all got in on by-elections by what became known as 'the widow's route'. Lady Astor, on her husband's translation to the Lords in 1919, stepped into the seat which had been his, and the two others, in 1921 and 1923, also took over their husbands' constituencies.

Elizabeth Valance points out:

> These women had not pushed themselves politically. They had in each case loyally helped their husbands and in doing so had won the affection and acknowledgement of the constituency. They had not sinned against the female virtue of modesty. Their candidacy was the extension of their acceptable role as wives ... Their husbands had, as it were, legitimised their political aspirations and this 'halo effect' of male acceptability was perhaps, at the time, essential.

So Con was not only the first woman to be elected to the British Parliament, she was also, for some years to come, the only woman to be elected in her own right, and deserves better than to be treated as an unexceptional part of an exceptional phenomenon. She was facing an Irish Party opponent, William Field, who had held St Patrick's for twenty-six years, and polled 7,835 votes to his 3,742 in a three-way election in which an Alderman J. J. Kelly also stood as Independent, polling 312 votes.

Certainly she was standing on what proved to be a landslide ticket, but to counterbalance that she was facing the anti-feminist prejudice which had defeated her sisters in England and which existed even more strongly in Catholic Dublin, especially as the Church she had so recently joined was opposing women in politics. As early as 1909, the *Irish Ecclesiastical Record* had stated: 'Allowing women the right of suffrage is incompatible with the Catholic ideal of the unity of domestic life.'

And of course, if she had stood for another party she would not have got in; but neither would de Valera, who had defeated John Dillon. If she had stood for another party she would not have been Markievicz.

Constance made it look easy; her only recorded comment on the result was to Eva and very laconic: 'My election was a foregone conclusion. I must know a lot of those who voted for me', but it goes to the heart of the matter. Her fame in her constituency was not only as a Sinn Féiner, but a woman who had stood by them in 1913, who had become known by word of mouth through a hundred personal acts of kindness and generosity. Nearly 8,000 men and women voted for the Countess Markievicz because she embodied the policy they wanted in the person they trusted to pursue it. It was what the purists of the suffragette movement had hoped to achieve. It had, after all, been a woman's victory of the very best kind, because the fact that she was a woman had not mattered.

And the fact that Constance, during her convalescent stay with Eva after her release, paid an incognito visit to the House of Commons Members' cloakroom to see her name under her allotted coatpeg, indicates that she was more pleased by the distinction she had earned for herself in the despised English history books than she let on.

However, there were some months to go before she was freed. She began to worry that the success of the election would encourage Britain to keep its prisoners longer 'out of spite'. She was also concerned that the influenza epidemic which had broken out would affect Eva – 'I shudder to think of you out in it' – and Kathleen Clarke, who was getting feebler. She wrote that she had great plans for her constituency, especially its women, and asked to be sent books on economics.

In the eyes of republicans, the election results exactly qualified Ireland's case for inclusion on the Peace Conference agenda. President Woodrow Wilson in his Fourth of July address had said that the settlement of the question of the small nations would be 'upon the basis of the free acceptance of that settlement by the people immediately concerned, and not upon the basis of the material interest or advantage of any other nation . . . for the sake of its own exterior influence or mastery'.

In the meantime, the republicans felt they had a mandate to set up their own parliament, the Dáil, and proceeded to do it.

In its euphoria, Sinn Féin overlooked one ominous and significant fact: that while its own popular vote had been 485,105, Redmond's old party had still gained a total of 237,393. An awful lot of people had voted *against* an Irish Republic.

The first Dáil Éireann met at Dublin's Mansion House on January 21, 1919. All Irish MPs (or rather TDs: Teachta Dála, Member of Dáil Eireann) returned in the recent election were invited to attend, but only the Sinn Féiners took their seats, and of those only twenty-four could actually do so. To the name of Constance Markievicz and thirty-five others the answer was given: '*Fé ghlas ag Gallaibh*' (Imprisoned by the foreign enemy).

In fact, twenty-six names were read out and answered to, but two of the answers were faked. (The record was later amended.) Michael Collins and his equally daring friend, Harry Boland, were in England helping Eamon de Valera out of Lincoln Prison in an escape involving forged keys and breath-stopping moments and every other element of a *Boy's Own* adventure. De Valera went into hiding.

The British Government didn't react. It was probably relieved to be rid of him. It didn't even, at that stage, prohibit Dáil Éireann as an illegal government. Lloyd George was, in fact, facing a situation for which he was completely unprepared; his own coalition Cabinet, now dominated by Conservatives, had only met for the first time on January 10.

Despite its Lilliputian size, Dáil Éireann was conducted with dignity, and members of an international press sat in the bunting-draped gallery to watch it.

Presided over by Cathal Brugha in the absence of de Valera, the Dáil declared for a Republic, elected de Valera as President and appointed delegates to the Peace Conference in Paris. Ireland's Declaration of Independence was read in Gaelic and English, and a democratic programme based on Easter Week's proclamation was passed unanimously. The proceedings, which were mostly in Gaelic, did not even last two hours. 'Speaking in a difficult language and one to which the orator is not born is a great shortener of proceedings,' sneered the *Daily Mail*.

The sheer monumental daring of what it was doing, plus the fact that it was doing it in Gaelic, may have obscured for this new government the fact that, urged on by Collins and Brugha, it was committed to a Republic first and last.

Sinn Féin under de Valera had always stood for a Republic, though he was later to rail at the Dáil declaration as 'a strait-jacket'.

Also obscured in the Dáil proceedings was the Democratic Programme, or, more accurately, what had been left out of the Democratic Programme. For this, it seems, Irish Labour had suddenly stood up on its hind legs and demanded a *quid pro quo* for its magnanimity in not contesting the general election. An Irish delegation was about to set off to the forthcoming International Labour and Socialist Conference at Berne and wanted to show that, though it was not represented in the Dáil, it had influence over it; thereby gaining from the Conference support for Irish independence. Accordingly, an able Labour leader, Thomas Johnson, had drawn up a programme which went further than Pearse's legacy and reached out to James Connolly's, and was radical enough to bring against it the forces of reaction.

When Michael Collins saw it he immediately summoned those members of the Irish Republican Brotherhood whom he considered 'broadly representative' and read the declarations out to them one by one. One of those present, P. S. O'Hegarty, said indignantly that the sections all tended to 'the principle that responsibility for the well-

194

being of a citizen no longer rested on himself but the State' and, he added, it made his gorge rise.

'Collins then said that he would suppress the "Democratic Programme" and he did so; but next morning, the day of the Dáil's assembly, the others refused to go on without a Democratic Programme, and the draft was handed over to Seán T. O'Kelly, who finally produced what was put before the Dáil.' Some of what O'Hegarty calls 'the worst doctrinaire jargon' was taken out, but it was still a radical document, pledging in the name of the Republic 'the right of every citizen to an adequate share of the produce of the Nation's Labour', and that 'no child shall suffer hunger or cold from lack of food, clothing or shelter, but that all shall be provided with the means and facilities requisite for their proper education and training as Citizens of a Free and Gaelic Ireland.' 'A passage,' says the historian, F. S. L. Lyons in *Ireland Since the Famine*, 'to which later generations were to look back in irony and anger.'

Constance Markievicz would have approved of the wording, and of Labour's attempt to muscle in on Sinn Féin policy, but she was still in prison.

English newspapers tended to think the whole thing was a farce, but one French historian who was watching that first Dáil from the gallery saw that what had been done was in its way as grave as the Declaration of Independence for Americans – an act from which the nation could not withdraw. 'And those who knew it,' he wrote, 'divined that a new epoch was beginning, and one that would be terrible.'

It had already begun. Even as he watched, nine men from Tipperary were lying in wait, as they had been for five days, for a cart full of explosives bound for Soloheadbeg quarry near Limerick Junction. It approached the ambush on January 21, the day Dáil Éireann convened, and when the two RIC policemen guarding the gelignite refused to surrender it, they were shot dead. The killing had been a deliberate act of independent policy by the Tipperary Volunteers who, like all Volunteer brigades, had seen the impetus go out of their force now that the threat which had fuelled it – conscription – was over. Men were deserting the Volunteers and leaving the cause of Irish freedom to the politicians, to the chagrin of many of their officers who had no faith in the constitutional approach which even former fire-breathers like the Countess Markievicz were now espousing.

As Vice-Commandant Seán Treacy, who had led the Soloheadbeg raid, put it: 'If this goes on we'll have to kill someone and make the bloody enemy organise us.'

Although there had been skirmishing before this, the two constables were the first British dead at Irish hands since Easter Week. They were both Catholic, both popular locally, and their death caused horror among English and Irish alike and was condemned at Mass by clergy all over Tipperary the next Sunday. So great was the horror that the Dáil executive was given automatic credit in Ireland for having known nothing about the killings, nor having wished them.

Dublin Castle, as usual, lumped the leaders of the Dáil and the Volunteers together as Sinn Féin and therefore responsible for the killings, and it is hard to blame them when men like Collins and Brugha belonged to both organisations. How much these two were responsible for the increase in violence, it is still difficult to say.

It may be that individual Volunteer, or Irish Republican Army battalions, desperate to arm themselves, were acting on their own initiative. Nevertheless on January 6 Michael Collins had been down in Cork organising its brigades and a few days after the killings at Soloheadbeg, another attack took place to gain weapons in Cork, at Macroom, and a soldier was seriously injured. We know, from his letters to Austin Stack, then still in prison, that Collins always thought force was going to be necessary and that the 'political and theoretical' side of Sinn Féin was not 'fully alive to the developing situation'. In this he was backed by Cathal Brugha whose name was on a directive in *The Volunteer* journal on January 31, stating that every Volunteer was entitled to use 'all legitimate methods of warfare against the soldiers and policemen of the English usurper, and to slay them if it is necessary to do so to overcome their resistance'.

Whoever's policy it was or was not, the killings and raids became more numerous and the counter-reprisals became more repressive in the dreary spiral towards war.

In Holloway Kathleen Clarke's condition became such that the authorities decided to release her, and Con was left alone. 'Weren't you shocked when you saw her?' she asked Eva in her letter. '. . . For the first time in my life I was thankful to see the back of a dear friend.' She made a joke of her solitary state: 'It is so funny being alone . . . I quite forget she is not here and I start talking with her occasionally,' but she felt it badly. She was almost infuriatingly cheery about her own health, refusing to admit to Eva – or even to herself – that it wasn't excellent, but there is little doubt that if she had not imposed that rigid refusal to give way on herself she too, like Maud Gonne and Kathleen Clarke, might have lived into her nineties.

She received, along with the other elected Sinn Féiners, the letter sent to all Westminster MPs from 'Yours faithfully, D. Lloyd George', informing her that His Majesty would open Parliament on February 11 and hoping that she might find it 'convenient to be in your place'. Since he wouldn't let her out of prison and, anyway, the letter did not arrive until February 18, she felt he was not sincere, and passed a happy hour composing a vitriolic reply.

But the 'flu epidemic, which was to give the coup de grâce to thousands who had survived the last four miserable years, was now reaching into the prisons; Pierce McCann, a Sinn Féin MP, died of it in Gloucester Prison, forcing Lloyd George, who wanted no more Irish martyrs, to release all his detainees.

Constance came out of Holloway on March 10, 1919, spent a few days' recuperation with Eva, visited her coatpeg at Westminster, and entered Dublin on the 15th to a welcome which surpassed even the one she had received two years before on her release from Aylesbury.

I was met by deputations of everybody! We motored in to Dublin to Liberty Hall. Last time was nothing to it. The crowd had no beginning or end. I made a speech and we then formed up in a torchlight procession and went to St Patrick's. Every window had a flag or candle or both. You never saw such excitement.

A similar reception had been planned for de Valera, now out of hiding, including a ceremonial presentation of the keys of the city to him by the Lord Mayor, an honour only accorded in the past to an English sovereign. That effrontery, however, Dublin Castle was not prepared to overlook, and banned it along with all meetings. To Michael Collins' disappointment – he had arranged it – de Valera refused confrontation at that stage and cancelled the celebrations. In view of the reinforcements arriving in Dublin in case there was trouble for the authorities, he was right. H. W. Nevinson of the *Daily Herald* wrote: 'I watched the English Garrison preparing as for another Easter Week. All day long our soldiers paraded the streets . . . Guns and cavalry paraded . . . Tanks and armoured cars rumbled about, while overhead flights of aeroplanes buzzed in battle formation.'

The second session of Dáil Éireann was held on April 1. De Valera was elected Príomh-Aire (President). He read out the list of his Cabinet: Arthur Griffith for Home Affairs; Count Plunkett, Foreign Affairs; Cathal Brugha, Defence; Eoin MacNeill, Industry; W. T. Cosgrave, Local Government; Michael Collins, Finance. And Countess Markievicz as Minister of Labour.

To England her appointment merely added to the Ruritanian element of what the *Times* correspondent called 'the stage play at the Mansion House'.

Eamon de Valera, however, took himself, everything he did, and especially this, his first ministry, very seriously indeed; yet this most cautious of men, preparing a government for which he wanted international recognition, was willing to do what no other head of state in

Western Europe had done and appoint its first woman Cabinet Minister and, by giving her that particular position, the first woman Minister of Labour in the world.

A woman, Alexandra Kollontay, had been made Commissar for Social Welfare in the Soviet Government of 1917, but Social Welfare, like Health, Pensions, Education, are universally regarded as 'women's areas' whereas Labour ministries are male preserves, and only put into female hands in very special circumstances. Britain did not see a woman in a government post until 1929 when Margaret Bondfield was appointed by Ramsay MacDonald – as Minister of Labour. It was not until 1933 that a woman appeared in a United States Government and then it was Frances Perkins who held the post in Franklin D. Roosevelt's New Deal administration – as Minister of Labour.

That Constance, Margaret Bondfield and Frances Perkins were all 'firsts' and all held the same rank is no coincidence.[1] In each case, de Valera's, MacDonald's and Roosevelt's, there was an urgent need to woo the respective country's Labour and the solution was to appoint an outstanding woman who had devoted herself to the cause of the industrial working class, in the belief that men of the Labour side were more prepared to support women in a position of responsibility.

De Valera was wooing Labour hard in 1919, sending a plea for recognition with Cathal O'Shannon and Thomas Johnson to the International Labour and Socialist Conference at Berne and receiving its support for Ireland, which called on the Peace Conference 'to make good this rightful claim of the Irish people', and was later in the year to promise that the Irish worker would 'find no clash between his interests as an Irishman and his class interests as a worker'.

What is surprising is that subsequent historians have not seen Constance's appointment as the event it most certainly was in feminine advance, merely mentioning her name in the Cabinet list, in most cases, without comment.

Less surprising, perhaps, is the lack of comment on this revolutionary breakthrough at the time.

Her colleagues accepted her as if it were the most natural thing in the world, and Ireland itself had become used to her. Anyway, so many extraordinary things had happened and were happening that it was as if giants were roaming the land, and the presence of a giantess among them was no greater wonder.

Constance's given explanation for her appointment is interesting: 'I took a gun to their heads,' she told Kathleen Clarke. 'I said I'd go over to Labour if they didn't.' Certainly, de Valera could not at that

[1] I am grateful to the Rt. Hon. Shirley Williams for pointing this out.

stage have afforded to lose one of his most popular TDs, nor have countenanced a break in his unity, but it is doubtful if he, or Con herself, believed she would carry out the threat. What is significant is that she made it; it is the first, and welcome, sign that she was becoming aware of the necessity for political in-fighting. It coincides with the disenchantment, shown in her letters to Eva, with 'leaders'. She had gone into the battle for Irish freedom full of ideals, to discover that the men around her, while equally idealistic, were out to make their careers from that battle and, once the freedom was won, to control it. She was to be outclassed in ruthlessness and lust for power, but, at least, she was becoming aware that such things existed.

To sum up, Constance was perhaps the only person de Valera could have chosen who was acceptable to both nationalists and Labour in the Labour Ministry – 'I belong to both organisations,' she said, 'because my conception of a free Ireland is economic as well as political' – *and*, let it not be forgotten, the women's movement. With re-arrest hanging like a Damocles' sword over every member of the Dáil, Cumann na mBan might yet again have to keep nationalism viable, as it had after the Easter Rising, and de Valera was willing to compliment it by electing its president to office. Besides all this, Con was a good choice in herself.

She had told Eva that she was 'full of ideas', and she was an innovative woman; at that stage de Valera was choosing a Cabinet which was as high on ingenuity as it was to be low on opportunity.

The problems facing the new Cabinet were certainly gigantic. Although the British Government did not formally prohibit the Dáil until September 10, 1919, individual members were in constant danger of arrest and from May onwards it became a Dáil-on-the-run, meeting in secret, shifting its base, hiding its papers and all against a background of accelerating terror. It was a situation demanding nerve, flexibility and, if anything was to be achieved, administrative ability. Constance Markievicz had been born for it. She was about to have the time of her life.

Chapter Fourteen

The war about to begin in Ireland was precipitated by terrorist acts against police, barracks and magistrates, whether sanctioned by the Dáil or not – and for many months the Dáil kept quiet on the matters. Had the government responded by some realistic settlement at this stage, it might well have separated moderates, in and out of Sinn Féin, from extremists. It chose not to and, when it did, it was, as usual, too late. The sense of outrage at Soloheadbeg and Macroom and other places where such attacks took place dissipated under the military repression which followed. After a raid for rifles on a military column in Fermoy, County Cork, in which one soldier was shot dead and three others seriously injured, the British soldiers' reprisals wrecked part of the town, including the house of the jury foreman who had condemned the original IRA raid as 'an appalling outrage'.

De Valera, Con and others repeatedly declared that the English Government was seeking to goad Ireland into open rebellion. 'What was really happening,' said Robert Kee, 'was that the Volunteers were goading the government into goading the people into rebellion.'

The year of 1919 was just a limbering-up for the full-scale terror and counter-terror which marked 1920 and 1921. Nevertheless the efficiency with which the IRA was to conduct its guerrilla war began to show itself, especially in Dublin where Michael Collins was getting spies of his own infiltrated into the Castle and had organised a group of men into what became known as 'The Squad', dedicated to eliminating G-men and others he considered dangerous.

Michael Collins himself, in his capacities as Minister of Finance, Director of Organisation for the Volunteers and unofficial Chief of Intelligence, had four offices at any one time and into most of them was built a secret room, cupboards and escape routes, which he was forced to use more than once.

Since the Dáil had not yet been suppressed, he led one life as a hunted man and another as a Minister of State, getting his picture in the papers as such, and announcing the ambitious project of the Dáil Éireann National Loan by which it was hoped to raise £250,000 in Ireland alone. (Within the year the sum reached was over £357,000.)

The money had to be lodged in various hiding places and bank accounts which would escape the attempts of the British to locate it. At that time Dublin Castle employed an elderly official, Alan Bell, who was proficient at tracking down such funds. Collins had him shot, which greatly facilitated the safeguarding of the Loan.

Considering that its Members and Ministers were usually only one jump ahead of the police, the Dáil programme to make British rule redundant was over-ambitious; that it achieved as much as it did is remarkable. In the main such achievement depended on the commitment, the daring and the ability of the various department heads. Michael Collins was conspicuously successful, so were W. T. Cosgrave and his young assistant, Kevin O'Higgins, in the Ministry of Local Government. A system of Dáil Courts was set up under Austin Stack (Minister of Justice) and Robert Barton (Agriculture) to settle land disputes and, later, civil and criminal cases, which in many instances supplanted the British legal system whose judges more than once found themselves in court with nothing to do.

How successful Constance Markievicz's Ministry of Labour was can be judged by the fact that many men have preferred to believe that she was incapable of having run such an efficient department and have credited that efficiency to her deputy, Joseph McGrath. Mr McGrath was undoubtedly an able man – he proved as much by becoming a wealthy tycoon later in the Irish Free State – but since he did not become her deputy until November 1920, was arrested in the December and did not get released until the following July, it is stretching anti-feminism somewhat far to believe that he was the guiding light of a department which flourished from March 1919.

Documents are disappointingly scarce (destroyed by enemy action) and the minutes of the Cabinet meetings, preserved in the State Papers office, Dublin, are terse to the point of non-committal, presumably to avoid giving too much away if they fell into the wrong hands.

What is significant about the latter is the way the Ministry of Finance business gradually forces its way to the top of nearly every agenda; inevitable, perhaps, in that it held every other department's purse strings and that Michael Collins was more successful in avoiding arrest than the others. Also, he gained ascendancy because de Valera had decided, somewhat to everyone's dismay, to go to America at this point (June 1919). There was alarm at his leaving, just when there was so much to be done, and some – though not his colleagues, who never doubted his courage – believed he was running away from the front line. Collins was especially aghast at his chief's proposed absence, but de Valera's decision points up the fundamental difference between two men who shared similar qualities. De Valera was 'highly intelligent, charming, compassionate, vindictive, volcanic and cold, vicious and generous' – all adjectives which at one time or another described Collins. But of the two, it was de Valera who saw Ireland, and himself, in an international context. He had a gravitas which Collins lacked; nobody could dream that the President would ever leap on a colleague and wrestle him to the ground in the aggressive play that Collins – though at other times he hated to be touched – indulged in. Collins might be brilliant with figures, but it was de Valera who, it was said with awe, understood Einstein's theory of relativity. Collins was the consummate politician and manipulator; de Valera was the statesman.

By May 1919 it was becoming clear that, despite frantic lobbying, the delegates to the Paris Peace Conference were not going to give Ireland's claim a hearing. President Wilson had bowed to Lloyd George on the matter because he needed Lloyd George's support in setting up his dream of a League of Nations. De Valera would go to appeal for justice to Ireland from the American people and to float an Irish loan in the USA. Collins gave in and arranged the trip. On June 8, the President of the new Republic, an old cap dragged down over his eyes, was smuggled aboard SS *Lapland* at Liverpool and began his first official international visit as a stowaway being violently seasick for eight days.

He had delayed his departure in order to greet three members of the American Commission on Irish Independence, who had previously tried unsuccessfully to get Dáil Éireann a hearing at the Peace Conference, and arrived in Ireland in May to see conditions for themselves.

Considering the importance of American public opinion, it would have been politic for the British to have held their hand a little: instead they turned it into a ham-fist.

> During our visit to Ireland [the Commission reported], we witnessed numerous assaults in public streets and highways with bayonets and clubbed rifles upon men and women known to be republicans, or suspected of being in favor of a republican form of government. Many of the outraged persons were men and women of exemplary character and occupying high positions in the business and professional life of the country.

They also witnessed de Valera being forcibly prevented from entering the Mansion House for a Dáil Éireann meeting, and that same meeting being raided in a search for Collins and Robert Barton, whom Collins had helped escape from Mountjoy a few weeks previously.

Constance played a large part in making sure the Commission got information she considered vital, and was later personally thanked for it. She gave them evidence on the way women were being treated in the prisons, of attacks on women and children in the streets, police interrogation of children, infant mortality, destitution and hunger, and made sure the members of the Commission paid attention to the labour situation with the result that they reported back:

Ireland has the best organised and most coherent labor movement in the world. It is being thwarted and suppressed by the army and constabulary. Wages of unskilled workers are below a line which means to them hunger, cold and privation. The wage of skilled labor is far below the minimum for decent existence . . . The heads of the National Irish Labor Party . . . are, without exception, ardent republicans, fully alive to their rights and insisting on selfdetermination for Ireland. They have all been the innocent victims of atrocities against their own persons in the jails of Ireland and England.

They were horrified to discover, through being in her company, that the Countess was shadowed everywhere and that threats were made against her.

The problem of police interrogation of children was her first assignment for Dáil Éireann. After the Soloheadbeg raid, the fifteen-year-old brother of Sean Treacy, who had led the raid, and the eleven-year-old son of one of his farm workers had disappeared into RIC custody and remained missing for ten weeks. Con's committee enquired into the detention of them and others, and was able eventually to procure the children's release.

In the meantime she organised her department, appointing Alderman Tom Kelly, TD, a good Labour man, as her deputy, should she be captured. She instituted a system of Conciliation Boards for industrial arbitration, had surveys made with a view to establishing guidelines for wages and food prices, set up a general employment agency to find work for jobless Volunteers and Cumann na mBan, arranged for a boycott on British goods, initiated a campaign in support of Irish industrial development and began a fund for a James Connolly Memorial Workers' College.

Employers and staff who submitted to the Ministry's arbitration were surprised that women turned up to give it. One of Con's letters mentions that Mrs Áine Ceannt had just returned from one such mission: 'She was most successful and thanked by both sides – I like to set women on to these jobs. She and Lily [illegible] are on the Panel of Judges for St Patrick's.' Her correspondence is workmanlike. One letter to an erring colleague tartly points out: 'It is the custom of this office to acknowledge letters as soon as they are received.'

The impatient Collins criticised those departments which fell below the standard of his own. 'Stack,' he is supposed to have hissed at the

Minister of Justice, 'your department is a bloody joke.' But he found no fault with Con's.

They were not unlike in finding danger a stimulant and even turning it to their advantage. During one of the first cases of arbitration in which the Irish Women Workers' Union was involved, the owner of a rosary-bead factory and his staff were being presided over by Alderman Tom Kelly at the Sinn Féin office in Harcourt Street, Dublin, when Con arrived to tell them that she had received intelligence – either from her own spy network or Collins' – that the military would be raiding the place in a quarter of an hour. The employer and union went on disagreeing. 'Ten minutes,' announced Con. Still no agreement. 'Five minutes,' said Con. It became not so much a question of justice, as nerve. The employer gave in and fled.

Among the day-to-day bureaucracy were two necessities for them all; keeping a low profile to the authorities and keeping a high one, as leaders, to the general public. Between her appointment in April and June 1919, Con not only gave evidence to the American Commission, she went on a speaking engagement to Glasgow and appeared at meetings in Ireland, most of which were proscribed and had to have the location switched at the last minute.

Typical of these meetings – and one that was to have repercussions – was the lecture by Countess Markievicz arranged for May 17 at Newmarket, County Cork, under the auspices of the Irish Citizen Army. It was banned because it might 'conduce a breach of the peace, promote disaffection, and make undue demands on the military and the police'. With so much to do, the last thing Con wanted was arrest; on the other hand, she never turned down a call from the Citizen Army. She made her arrangements and did not arrive in Newmarket until nearly midnight, to find a large crowd and a brass band waiting for her. Con's speech reinforced a policy which had been proposed to the Dáil by de Valera just before he left for the States, advocating the social ostracism of the police. 'Their history,' he had said, 'is a continuity of brutal treason against their own people . . . They must be shown and made to feel how base are the functions they perform and how vile is the position they occupy.'

In a manoeuvre that became a local legend, Con then changed clothes with a willing – and brave – volunteer, Madge McCarthy, and was driven off through the cordons to Drominorigle where she gave another speech the next day, while Miss McCarthy, watched by the RIC, went to a Newmarket hotel to spend the night.

Four weeks later, on June 13, Con was arrested in Dublin for that Newmarket speech and found herself surrounded by a small army of thirty tin-hatted, bayonet-carrying soldiers and an equal number of police on her way to Cork to face trial. It was no coincidence that only a few days before her arrest the American Commission's report on Ireland had been published. Both the delegates and the *Irish Citizen* accused the British of arresting her because of the importance of her evidence to the Commission; the British denied it, without explaining why they had delayed the arrest for so long.

Constance was sickened to find herself arrested when she still had so much to carry out, and more sickened still by being accused of telling the Newmarket audience to 'treat the children of the police as spies, ostracise them, treat them as lepers, and refuse to sit near them in church or school'. It is hardly likely that a woman who had insisted on feeding a blackleg's child would say such a thing, and Con denied it absolutely. As usual she refused to recognise the authority of the court, but she got up to say 'for the benefit of her friends' – the court was packed with sympathisers – that she would never advocate the persecution of policemen's children: she would leave that to the police. No child should be hurt or made unhappy; she asked her friends in the name of Éamonn Ceannt, who was a policeman's son and who died for Ireland, to respect children, and called for three cheers for the Irish Republic.

The judge gave her four months without hard labour in Cork female prison.

It was Con's third successive summer in prison and the strain was beginning to tell – local press reports said she looked worn and pale at her trial. However, Eva was ill so Con's first letter to her from Cork Prison said:

> I am so sorry that I just got arrested, for I know how that will worry you. But you needn't bother, for I am in excellent health and spirits . . . This is the most comfortable jail I have been in yet. There is a nice garden, full of pinks, and you can hear the birds sing. I have heaps of friends here [County Cork] who send me in lots of very good food.

In another she said of the Newmarket business: 'I transferred my hat, coat and the long blue Liberty scarf you gave me years ago, to a girl. These police, who swore they knew *me*, followed *her* round Newmarket, while I looked on and laughed, so you see what liars they are!'

As ever, she used her imprisonment to catch up on reading; Eva sent her Strindberg's poems which she enjoyed. She liked to read history ('history plus economics equals politics') and found G. K. Chesterton's *History of England* 'so human and so unexpected'. She did a lot of gardening and took comfort from what beauty there was:

> The moths here are so lovely. They come fluttering in through the bars at night, every shade and every shape, such big ones all splotched over with orange and red,

205

great white soft things, and wee ethereal ones, all opalescent and shimmering, moonlight colours. One I got today was like the waves of a pale, twilight sea, another was like a creamy shell. I try to save their lives.

The number of soldiers who guarded her constantly surprised her and she found herself sorry for them, having joined up to fight 'the Hun' and finding themselves guarding 'one patriotic woman'. She found them 'all so small and so young' that they ought to be at school instead of 'idling about with iron hats and fixed bayonets . . . It's an awful life for a young man . . . They all want to be demobilised, but if they were . . . there is not enough work already, so Lord knows what they'd do . . . I think one of the reasons why they are making wars is to dispose of revolutionary man-power.'

Nora Connolly, who visited Con several times, also wondered at the number of young soldiers on duty and echoed the remark of a woman who lived near the prison, 'Yerra, God help ye, all that turnout for one lone woman.'

Just before her arrest, with acute political sense, Con had 'hustled' her supporters in St Patrick's constituency to get ready for the municipal elections which were to take place in January 1920. They were to be fought under a system of proportional representation which, the British hoped, would undermine the Sinn Féin vote by giving fairer representation to minorities. Constance had supported the idea because she believed otherwise (and was proved right). 'It's going to work out just the other way,' she told Eva, 'you watch . . . My getting locked up has done more to bring women out into the open than anything else. The shyest are ready to do my work when I'm not there.'

In an effort to get news of her husband and Stanislas, Con had used William O'Brien of the ITGWU to approach Litvinov, the official Soviet representative in Britain, with a request that he make enquiries. Somehow the answer got through to Eva who passed it on to Con who wrote:

Do, do write quick and tell me what you know about him . . . I don't suppose he [Stanislas] is a Bolshevik and I daresay he is in a rather awful position. He hated politics and wars so, poor boy . . . I've not heard of Casi either for so long, he was in Kiev, rather a bad place just now, and he might just as easily be a Bolshevik as anything else. Fine ideas always attracted him and he would be quite capable of being enthused into thoroughly enjoying wearing a big beard and waving a Red Flag. He was always torn in two between his artistic appreciation of the rich and Princely people, and just as strong an appreciation of the wrongs of the people and the beauty of self-sacrifice.

Even here he was a bit of an anxiety for he would lunch with the Enemy [i.e.

the Dublin Castle set] and sup with the Enemy and between the two make a wild rebel speech. He was absolutely sincere all the time, here it was only rather compromising, in Russia both sides would be stalking him with guns. Do try and find out from S. whats happened to them all, I don't like to write. In the Old Russia it would have got them all on to a black list, even to correspond with a rebel like me.

Soviet Communism at that time had, as Arthur Koestler pointed out in *Arrow in the Blue*, sounded 'good, just and hopeful' and Con, while not being doctrinaire, still felt an optimism for it that gradually faded. She was to say of herself and other Irish socialists: 'We're fighting for the working class. Call us what you like.'

Con was released from Cork Prison on October 16, 1919 and went rushing back to Dublin and her ministry. The *Watchword of Labour* wrote: 'Everyone rejoices to welcome back to the restricted liberty of ordinary Irish life the cheerful and invigorating personality of Madame de Markievicz. Four months of prison life have not damped her spirit or quenched her flaming idealism.'

'Restricted liberty' was right. Dáil Éireann had finally been suppressed in September so its sessions and Cabinet meetings had to be held at varying secret locations with escape routes. Armed police suppressed the annual convention of Cumann na mBan due to be held at the Mansion House three days after Con's release, so it had to be held 'elsewhere'. Collins' raising of the Loan was proving so successful that to be found with a receipt for it in one's pocket was as dangerous – and arrestable – as being found with a gun.

Alderman Tom Kelly, Con's deputy who had run the Labour department during her incarceration, was deported without any charge being made against him and in the same swoop an attempt was made to find Con at Kathleen Clarke's where she stayed occasionally. While still on the run, she wrote to Eva:

What on earth is the meaning of their latest move? Old Kelly always describes himself as a 'Man of Peace' and it is an admirable description. Was it not lucky that I was away? I hear that Mrs Clarke asked to see the warrant and that the detective in charge said there was none. She then asked what I was charged with and they said they did not know ... they searched the house to her amusement.

She made them look everywhere and waste a lot of time! ... you might try and find out with what awful crime I am charged this time! It's enough to make anyone curious. Wasn't it a shame to stop the Aonach? [The Annual Christmas trades fair had been suppressed.] It is just a fair and nothing more ... It's political to the extent that it is organised to help Irish Industry and trade to hold their own against English, German or any other foreign industry ... Of course this is treason, as the Enemy wish all Irish men and women to emigrate or starve ... All this fuss may be to upset our organisation for the elections, and to prevent our people in the slums learning the intricacies of P.R. [Proportional Representation] but I don't think that the enemy will gain much. The situation appeals to the imagination of the people and they love the excitement. They are not afraid and they have a great sense of humour . . . I am going to keep quiet for a bit and then dodge them and go about as usual, as there is much to be done.

Ellen Wilkinson once pointed out wryly that what every woman politician needs is a wife, the all-round helpmeet of the male politician, but Constance was luckier than most in that she had one, or several, in Dublin itself. The women of Dublin gave her shelter, prepared meals for her, lied to the police on her behalf, the Cumann na mBan did her typing, the Fianna ran her messages and, at moments of greatest danger, the Dublin crowd opened up and swallowed her so that the soldiers and G-men should not get her. She was running terrible risks, but enveloped in so much love, at the age of fifty-two she bloomed as never before. 'Age dropped from her completely,' says Sean O'Faolain, '. . . she had found within herself in her last prime summer, more of the pure vigour of nature, than at any time in the height of her youth and beauty.'

It's awfully funny being on the run [she wrote to Eva]. I don't know whether I am most like the timid hare, the wily fox or a fierce wild animal of the jungle. I go about a lot, one way or another. Every house is open to me and everyone is ready to help. I fly round town on my bike for exercise and it's too funny seeing the expression on the policemen's faces when they see me whizz by. There are very few women on bikes in the winter, so a hunted beast on a bike is very remarkable.

Being so well known was a hazard; on one occasion she was keeping her head down and hurrying through a crowd when a friendly docker on top of a tram recognised her and began to bawl out his gratitude to her for all her work during the lock-out. Wincing, she had to beat a hasty retreat.

Christmas was spent on the run but she managed to enjoy it: 'I had two Xmas dinners at the two extremes of Dublin, and quite a cheery time.'

That she was full of bounce is illustrated by Desmond Ryan:

William Norman Ewer of the *Daily Herald* had asked me to come to the Café Cairo to recover from a three days' controversy he had been conducting with Madame de Markievicz over the lunch table in a restaurant attached to Liberty Hall. [Con's letters to Eva from Cork prison had shown that she thought the Labour *Daily Herald* was going to the right, and she had accordingly weighed in to its distinguished correspondent.] . . . Madame proceeded to denounce several famous British pacifists and Labour leaders as hypocrites and double dealers. Whereupon to the joy of the whole restaurant Ewer opened fire upon Madame and told her what he thought of herself and her arguments ... This delighted Madame, who arrived the two following days in the hopes of converting so forceful and fiery a pacifist. The argument had somewhat exhausted Ewer so he asked me if I knew of a nice peaceful Café where he could smoke his pipe in safety from Madame de Markievicz for a day or so until he thought of some argument which would silence her for ever. It had been a great battle between Madame and Ewer and he was being invested with a halo all unknown to himself as the only man who had ever laid out the Countess in argument. At first in the Café Cairo Ewer thought he had found his peaceful haven and he smoked his pipe so much at peace that he began to miss the fierce rhetoric and persistence of Madame.

More women than ever before stood for the borough and district councils in the January 1920 elections – forty-three were returned. Constance was disappointed by the fact that 'I could not get any woman to stand in either of the wards of St Patrick's', nevertheless she gave a lot of her time to speaking for women in other areas.

I spoke five times for various women in the elections and had some very narrow shaves. At one place I spoke for Joan, and they sent an army, just about an hour too late. At another, I wildly and blindly charged through a squad of armed police, sent there to arrest me, and the crowd swallowed me up and got me away. The children did the trick for me.

Just how much the police wanted to catch her is indicated by a directive issued on January 14 by Chief Commissioner W. E. Johnstone:

The Countess Markievicz has, according to the newspapers, made two appearances at unannounced meetings in the City ... I must again impress on all who superintend the grave importance of securing this woman's arrest, and, to this end, force sufficiently strong to secure her arrest must be held in reserve at each Divisional Headquarters tonight and tomorrow night. The moment an unannounced meeting is discovered a message must be sent by the quickest method available to the nearest Divisional Headquarters and to the G. Division, Dublin Castle. The police on the spot must act firmly and promptly, as the Countess never remains at a meeting for more than a few minutes and may possibly be heavily veiled and, therefore, difficult to recognise.

Despite the ban on Sinn Féin, it won control of eleven out of the twelve cities and municipal boroughs in which the election had been fought. On the day after the results were announced, another policeman, this time an assistant commissioner, was shot dead on Collins' orders in the centre of Dublin. In Thurles, County Tipperary, a Police Constable Finnegan was killed a few yards from his home. (In both cases the coroner's jury brought in verdicts of wilful murder.)

This brought the total number of Irish police killed since the general election of 1918 to fourteen, with over twenty others wounded.

The effect of the killings, combined with the social ostracism of the RIC advocated by de Valera and Con, led to resignations on a large scale. If the ex-policemen were not to regret their decision to leave – after all, they were Irishmen – something had to be done to find them jobs, and Con set about doing it. She sent out directives to all Sinn Féin clubs asking them to help find the men employment, and set up a special job agency for them in Dublin.

In June came evidence that the police authorities were assisting the defection of their own men by giving them orders which they could not stomach. A constable from Listowel, Jeremiah Mee, reported that a Divisional Commander, Colonel Smyth, had told them that there was to be a new offensive which would beat Sinn Féin at its own tactics: 'When civilians are seen approaching, shout "Hands Up!" Should the order be not immediately obeyed, shoot and shoot with effect. If the persons approaching carry their hands in their pockets, or are in any way suspicious, shoot them down.'

They were assured that whoever they shot they would not get into trouble. Hunger strikers would be allowed to die in jail – 'the more the merrier'. Any man, they were told, who wasn't prepared to wipe out Sinn Féin was a hindrance rather than a help and had much better leave the job at once.

PC Mee left, wrote down what he had heard and took his evidence to Arthur Griffith, who sent him to the Labour Party offices later for questioning by, among others, Michael Collins and the Countess Markievicz. Collins did not believe him, suspecting him of being a police spy. (Colonel Smyth was nevertheless shot down and killed a month later by the IRA.) But Con, who impressed Jeremiah Mee by her 'dignified bearing and direct, businesslike manner', trusted him, and it turned out she was right. She took him on at her office, which was at 14, Frederick Street, to help run the agency for ex-RIC men, and it is from Mee that we get one of the few glimpses of Con's Ministry of Labour at work. He told Anne Marreco that it was no coincidence that her department was the only one unraided; Con was a martinet about security.

The office itself was on the second floor bearing a sign 'Apartments To Let', though the young ladies working in it asked such impossibly high rents that genuine would-be flat-hunters were put off. Not more than one person at a time was allowed to leave the premises and no staff allowed to approach it if there was someone loitering in the street who might be watching. All documents were taken away at nights to special hiding-places. In the daytime, in the inner office, the young ladies, if raided, rushed to the several pianos which furnished the place, and pretended to be teachers of music. There were bridges of planks at the back windows enabling a quick getaway – during one false alarm when two armoured cars and lorries stopped outside the entrance, Con slid out of the window like an acrobat.

With increasing attacks on personnel and barracks, and with mounting resignations from the RIC, the authorities began recruiting in England and Ulster to swell the ranks. By mid-April 1920 some four hundred men, many of them ex-soldiers, had arrived from England to find that there was a shortage of complete RIC uniforms. At an inquest on a young man shot dead by police, it was noticed that two of these new constables wore khaki trousers. Accordingly they were given the nickname of a famous hunt in Southern Ireland, which became a synonym for terror, 'The Black and Tans'. It is legend in Ireland that they were the sweepings of English jails; in fact, says F. S. L. Lyons, they were

> for the most part young men who found it hard to settle down after the war, who had become used to a career of adventure and bloodshed, and who were prepared to try their luck in a new sphere for ten shillings a day and all found. Their ruthlessness and contempt for life and property stemmed partly from the brutalisation inseparable from four years of trench warfare, but partly also from the continual and intense strain imposed upon them by service in Ireland. They were vulnerable to every kind of sudden attack by bomb or rifle-fire and since their opponents seldom wore uniform and could vanish into the empty countryside or into the crowded streets of the cities, it is not surprising that the 'Tans' should before long have come to regard the whole population as hostile, which, certainly, once it had experience of the methods of the new police, it very soon became.

Though the Tans' reputation was bad, much of it was earned for them by 'the Auxies', an auxiliary division of the RIC which consisted mainly of ex-British army officers, who received a pound a day and topped their dark-blue uniforms with Glengarry caps. Their own commanding officer, Brigadier-General Crozier, eventually resigned, alleging that their drunkenness and insubordination shamed him.

The combined force of police and military in 1920 and 1921 has been estimated in the region of 40,000 and they faced an IRA which, while theoretically numbering about 15,000, was nearer, according to Michael Collins, to 3,000 who could fight effectively. On the other hand, the IRA's advantage lay in the loyalty of the local population; where it did not command the hearts and minds of civilians, it inspired enough fear to ensure that nobody gave it away. Spies, informers and the merely disobedient were shot and their bodies left in the open to encourage the others.

This, in turn, suggested to the leaders of the opposing force the enterprise of carrying out murders in the guise of IRA. In March the newly-elected Lord Mayor of Cork, Thomas MacCurtain, was shot dead in his own house by a gang of masked raiders. However, there was enough evidence to convince the local population that the raid had been engineered by the Royal Irish Constabulary; the coroner's jury brought in an angry verdict of murder against David Lloyd George, Lord French (the Lord Lieutenant), the Chief Secretary, and District Inspector Swanzy of the RIC. Though he retreated into Ulster, DI Swanzy was later tracked down and shot.

In Dublin, some Dáil Éireann headed paper was stolen; and in May, Con was one of those who received a piece of it on which was written:

> An eye for an eye
> A tooth for a tooth.
> Therefore a life for a life.

I have just received what is commonly called a 'Death notice from the Black Hand gang in the police' [she wrote to a friend]. I think there is no doubt that they are plotting to murder us, and before doing so they are taking precautions to manufacture evidence to prove that we assassinated each other ... Luckily we are not nervous and have the strength to go on just the same as before. One is a little more careful to try and be ready to die and that is all.

Her friends were convinced the authorities were out to kill her and they, in turn, so alarmed Eva that when she and Esther Roper were in Italy later that year, Eva procured an audience with the Pope, and begged him to use his influence to alleviate her sister's danger.

Despite the risk, Con refused to miss a single meeting of any organisation of which she was an official, nor did so, although increasingly she was forced to go about in disguise; her stage experience came in handy and the disguises, as long as she kept her mouth shut, fooled everybody. Stooping to camouflage her height, her greatest success was as an old woman. One of the Fianna executive remembered a meeting being interrupted by the ring of a bell. When he answered, he saw only an old woman. He asked 'this oul' wan' what she wanted, and an unmistakable voice said gaily, 'Tally, didn't you recognise me?' She could not, says Van Voris, disguise her accent.

She was at Liberty Hall for a meeting of the Irish Citizen Army Council when word came through that she must leave immediately; the place was about to be raided. Her old friend Frank Robbins, who had been with her at Stephen's Green, and another man, were told that she must be taken safely out of the building no matter what. 'When she was handed over to us we saw a very old woman, dressed in old-fashioned clothes and wearing an old Victorian bonnet. Her make-up gave her the appearance of a feeble old lady anywhere between seventy-five and eighty years of age.'

The younger Connolly girls frequently acted as the feeble old lady's grandchildren in order to get her from place to place. Nora Connolly recalled such an excursion with two children, one of them her young sister, hanging on to Con's arms, and crossing a road where there was a policeman on duty:

> I was too tense to do or say anything, but Madame played her part wonderfully. First she stepped off the pavement, and then she stepped back again. Finally the policeman took compassion on the poor old lady and started escorting her across O'Connell Street, his hand on her arm. The two young ones followed behind, their eyes wide as saucers. When they got to the other side, the policeman left her outside Nobletts, and he patted her on the shoulder as much as to say, 'You're all right now, Granny.' When I got across the street, I saw the unholy mischievous glee in her eye, and her foot doing a little jig under her skirt. That was Madame for you.

She extracted fun where she could because there was less and less about. Yeats called them 'dragon-ridden' days and got it right again.[1]

Photographs of the time show the aftermath of street clashes with untidy bodies lying in the road, passers-by with their hands up in the air, views of a silent Dublin with soldiers on the roof of the Four Courts, holding rifles against the skyline. Men in Glengarry caps peering into clothing, mail vans, bicycle baskets.

It is not too fanciful, either, to see the fear emanating from that army of occupation, surrounded by sullen, Irish faces, waiting for the ambush or the bullet in the back. They knew that, despite the suppression of all republican newspapers, news of every move they made circulated more quickly by word of mouth than publication, that every man and woman on their wanted list had a hundred allies, ready

[1]Now days are dragon-ridden, the nightmare
Rides upon sleep: a drunken soldier
Can leave the mother, murdered at her door,
To crawl in her own blood, and go scot-free;
The night can sweat with terror as before
We pieced our thoughts into philosophy,
And planned to bring the world under a rule,
Who are but weasels fighting in a hole.

to divert them away from patrols and barricades, that whoever killed a policeman or soldier would, in these people's eyes, become a hero. The reaction to their fear was hideously predictable and inside the heavily guarded prisons an increasing number of suspects were tortured for information.

The local county council elections held in June 1920 showed the counter-reaction; Sinn Féin swept the board everywhere but the Unionist-dominated counties of Ulster, Antrim, Derry, Armagh and Down. Isolated RIC barracks began to be abandoned and British authority largely disappeared in places in the South and West of Ireland, to be replaced by the writ of the underground Dáil. The republican courts and police kept a remarkable order, even to ensuring the safety and land of Unionists, and punishing wrongdoers. Liam Lynch, the commandant of Cork No. 2 Brigade actually tracked down and brought to justice a group of armed men who had taken advantage of the situation to rob a bank at Millstreet, stealing £20,000 – all of it recovered and returned to the bank.

Losing political authority, the government brought in more and more troops in an effort to establish military control, but English soldiers could not do the job that the old and now fading RIC, with its local knowledge, had performed. At the beginning of August troops raided a meeting at Cork Town Hall, thinking they were rounding up a republican court; in fact they had, unknown to them, captured five senior officers of the IRA, including Liam Lynch himself, who gave a false name. The men were released a few days later because the military still did not know their real identity – the only man held was the new Lord Mayor, a face they *did* recognise, Terence MacSwiney. MacSwiney began a hunger strike which was not only to kill him but, in the repercussions of his death, a great many more.

In Dublin raids intensified and in one of them Constance made a getaway in a taxi with a trunk containing important Ministry of Labour papers perched on top of it. 'Where to, ma'am?' asked the cabby. 'Anywhere,' said Con, racking her brains for a safe hiding place, not for herself, but her documents.

The taxi drove out to Harold's Cross and back. 'Where to now, ma'am?' asked the cabby. 'Anywhere,' said Con; every friend who could be entrusted with the papers was likely to be raided. Once more the taxi drove to Harold's Cross and back. Then Con was inspired. She directed the taxi to a second-hand shop opposite Lissonfield House, headquarters of the Black and Tans. The trunk with its papers was put into the shop front window by the shopkeeper, a friend of hers, and marked 'For Sale £3', an enormous sum in those straitened times. Sean O'Faolain who, among others, retailed the incident said that for days she had to pass the shop in terror that someone would buy the trunk, but they did not and eventually a new home was found for it.

She took appalling risks in an effort to find out what atrocities were going on so that she could send details to de Valera and friends in the States. Despite a strict curfew she would follow the military: 'Night after night they wake people up and carry off someone, they don't seem to mind who. Some of the people that they took lately did not belong to our crowd at all. When they could not find Mick Staines they took his old father (aged 60) and his baby brothers!'

Men she knew were being killed in raids (theirs or the military's) and she had moments of acute depression. Jeremiah Mee said that when the news came in of a republican death she would sit in her office chair, smoking cigarette after cigarette in silence and then, with a supreme effort, would pull herself together and carry on as if nothing had happened.

She almost admitted how tired she was getting to Eva: 'It is rather wearying when the English Man Pack are in full pack after you . . .'

The fact that she was arrested again, and this time outside Dublin, may have saved her life. She had been on a much-needed weekend holiday to the hills with young Seán MacBride, Maud Gonne's son, accompanied by a Frenchman, Maurice Bourgeois, who was ostensibly in Ireland as a journalist but who, according to Robert Brennan, was an agent observing the Irish scene for his government. 'When he arrived,' wrote Brennan, who had directed Sinn Féin's elections in 1918, 'he was rather hostile to Sinn Féin. The memory of 1916 still rankled. The Rising had been a stab in the back for the Allies.' Being arrested was to change Bourgeois' attitude.

It is very bad luck [Constance fumed in a letter to Eva]. I went for a weekend holiday with Seán and the motor car he was driving broke down all the time! We had to spend Saturday night at a place somewhere in the Dublin Mountains, I at a farm house, he and a French journalist at an inn. Coming back the same thing happened. Engines, horn and lamps all being out of order. The Police pulled us up because of the tail lamp not being there, asked for permit – he had none, so they got suspicious and finally lit a match in my face and phoned for military. All the Kings horses and all the Kings men arrived with great pomp, and many huge guns and after a weary night in Police station, I found myself here [Mountjoy] on Remand, till to quote their own words, they 'decide whether they shall bring a charge against me or not'. It sounds comic opera, but its the truth.

As for Bourgeois, he told Brennan he was

thrown into a filthy cell and when I protested several bullies in uniform threatened to beat me up and shoot me. When I produced my diplomatic passport, they said they were about to provide me with a passport to hell and they reviled France and the French people in the most revolting language!

It was two days before he managed to get word to the French consul to secure his release. 'When I met him,' Brennan reported, 'he was still white with rage over the treatment he had received. He had ceased to be anti-Sinn Féin. Indeed, he became one of our stoutest champions.'

Con's treatment was worse; she was kept in solitary on remand in Mountjoy for ten weeks without charge. Her small, cramped writing at this time, very different from her usual expansive scrawl, shows her desperation at being away from the fight and facing more imprisonment. She told Eva that she was studying Gaelic hard, but even about that she railed:

> I wish I knew why Grammarians always search the world and dictionaries for the words you want least in a language and give them you to learn, and leave out the words that you want every day. I can talk about hawks and flails, scythes, rye and barley, magicians, kings and fairies; but I couldn't find out how to ask for an extra blanket or a clean plate or a fork. I suppose I shall find out some day.

Whether she wanted to be or not, she was safer inside the Joy than out. The principle on which Terence MacSwiney, now in Brixton Prison in England, was forcing himself to starve – 'It is not those who can inflict the most, but those that can suffer the most who will conquer' – was applying to Ireland. Despite the viciousness on both sides, it was the suffering of innocent Irish people which was getting through to the outside world.

Inflamed by the death of a popular officer from an IRA expanding bullet, the town of Balbriggan in County Dublin was fired by the Black and Tans, and two of its citizens bayoneted to death. After similar incidents elsewhere, the populations of towns and villages expecting reprisals began a nightly exodus from their homes to sleep in the fields, and the pathos of such scenes was reported by correspondents with effect not only in Europe and the States, but in England. Journalists like C. P. Scott, editor of the *Manchester Guardian*, and H. W. Nevinson of the *Daily Herald*, began a shift of English public opinion, even in the Cabinet itself, which tended to think that if it took these methods to govern Ireland, it would be better not to govern it at all.

In order to appear in American eyes, at least, to be responding to the situation, Lloyd George's Cabinet had spent much of 1920 tinkering with what was ironically known as the 'Better Government of Ireland Bill', which was basically a re-vamping of the old Home Rule idea, but this time with the important difference that it gave final recognition to the partition of Ireland. Two Irish Parliaments were to be set up, one for the six counties of Ulster in which there was a Unionist majority, and another for the twenty-six remaining counties. Both would be subject to the government in London, both to take an oath to the British Crown, and if, within fourteen days of the day fixed for the opening of either of the two Parliaments, the majority of its elected members had not taken the oath, it would be dissolved and the role of British Government resumed in its place. The Southern Irish called it shortly, 'the Partition Act'.

Sir Edward Carson and the Ulster Unionists did not like it; partition was not what they were after, and especially a partition which gave them only six of Ulster's nine counties.

With the cold logic that ran through his bigotry, however, Carson accepted the loss of Donegal, Cavan and Monaghan as a matter of inevitable mathematics. By leaving out the Protestants of those three counties, he avoided bringing into 'the Northern Province an additional 260,000 Roman Catholics'.

Such Roman Catholic minority as were now stranded in the new Province had their vulnerability brought home to them. In a reaction against the IRA terrorism, and whipped up by the Orangemen, Protestants began rampaging through Catholic areas in a series of pogroms which were to reflect the intensification of war in the South by their increasing dreadfulness.

IRA prisoners on hunger strike were beginning to die, but the one who hypnotised world attention was the young Lord Mayor of Cork, Terence MacSwiney who, by effort of will, dragged out his dying for seventy-three days. Doctors waited to feed him but, it is said, even when he went unconscious his teeth clamped to stop them. A week after his death on October 25, despite an international campaign for mercy, an eighteen-year-old student, Kevin Barry, who had taken part in an ambush of military in King Street, Dublin, in which a soldier was killed, was hanged in Mountjoy.

Whether this death stung him into reprisal, or whether they were just causing him bother, Michael Collins decided to direct his lethal attention to a group of secret servicemen known as the 'Cairo Group' because they were British officers who had been recruited in Cairo in Egypt for the special task of wiping out Collins and his men. Sixteen had arrived in Dublin posing as commercial travellers and were living in rented flats and hotels around the city. Collins had gradually located all of them and, on what became known as 'Bloody Sunday', November 21, 1920, he sent eight groups of men to their various lodgings where they were gunned down. One of fourteen killed that day turned out to be an innocent officer of the Royal Army Medical Corps who was shot by mistake in the Gresham Hotel.

'I found out,' Collins said later, 'that those fellows we put on the spot were going to put a lot of us on the spot, so I got in first.'

The revenge by Black and Tans was swift and extremely bloody. That same afternoon they invaded the sports ground of Croke Park where a Gaelic football match was in progress and fired into the crowd and players, killing twelve people and injuring sixty others.

Con heard the shooting from her cell in Mountjoy which was not far away and wrote to Eva: 'The Croke Park affair lasted 40 minutes by my watch, and there were machine guns going . . . It's a miracle that so few were killed.'

That night two of Collins' men and an apparently innocent visitor to Dublin, the nephew of the Roman Catholic Archbishop of Perth, Western Australia, were 'shot while attempting to escape', a euphemism which may actually have been true, though Collins found evidence that they had been badly beaten up before they died.

On the night of December 11, the city of Cork exploded into flames after curfew when a combined mob of Auxiliaries and Black and Tans poured into the town, looting and wrecking, inflamed by the activities of the Cork IRA which, under Tom Barry, Commandant of No. 3 Brigade, were inflicting severe punishment on them. The damage done was estimated at between £2 to £3 million. Chief Secretary of Ireland, Sir Hamar Greenwood, attempted to tell the House of Commons that the citizens of Cork had, for some reason, tried to destroy their own city, but both a military enquiry and a British Labour Commission uncovered such damning evidence against the British troops that the Cabinet decided that to publish a report would be 'disastrous to the government's whole policy in Ireland'.

In prison Constance heard about Cork and the official explanation but, knowing the city well, she formed her own conclusions. 'Some men have a wonderful capacity for lying! What puzzles me is why they don't do it better. For instance, it was so silly to assert that the City Hall caught fire from Patrick St. . . . a broad river and many streets lie between the two areas.'

She had been court martialled and the charge trumped up against her, she told Eva, was 'conspiracy' in forming the Fianna Éireann which had, as she pointed out, been performing openly for eleven years.

I asked them could they point to one 'cowardly attack' on the armed forces of the Crown by little boys. It was an awful performance; after being shut up alone for two months to be suddenly brought before 8 'judges' plus prosecutors, bewigged barristers, enemy witnesses, etc., and surrounded by bayonets, it was very bewildering.

She was sentenced to two years' hard labour. She commented: 'For starting Boy Scouts in England B. Powell was made a baronet! . . . I bet he did not work as hard as I did from 1909 till 1913.'

She gritted her teeth to face her sentence as best she could by starting a rock garden in the prison yard and settling down to read the lives of Tolstoy and Danton.

At the end of 1920, Eamon de Valera returned to Ireland from the United States, where despite a punishing tour, his success was merely qualified; he had raised over five million dollars for the Irish National Loan and had kept Ireland's cause continually before the American people, but he had not been able to obtain official recognition for his country from them. He had hoped to stay on and try further, but the situation in Ireland was so obviously out of hand that he felt compelled to return.

He was smuggled back into Dublin on December 23, 1920; it shows how long he had been away – eighteen months – that he was surprised to find that his first visitor, Cathal Brugha, had a gun in his pocket. However, his comparative freshness to the Irish scene and his lack of involvement with its bloodier side, enabled him to fulfil a role which had been notably lacking during the last year, that of a moderate. In the States he had taken a hard line on the Ulster question, referring to it as a rock on the road to freedom which must be blasted out of Ireland's path but now, with the Government of Ireland Bill on the statute book and partition in effect, he seemed willing to consider a dividing up of all Ireland into Swiss canton-like units of which Ulster would be one, or a federal system of government. He recognised that England had a legitimate fear that an independent Ireland might be used as a foothold by a hostile foreign power and took pains to show that the fear was groundless: 'If England can show any right with which Ireland's right as a nation would clash, we are willing that these be adjusted by negotiation and treaty.'

To his confidants like Harry Boland, Michael Collins' old friend, who by now had given his loyalty to de Valera after spending time with him in America, the President of Ireland made it clear that he was not a doctrinaire republican.

He told Boland that if he presented Lloyd George with the ultimatum that Dáil Éireann had been given a mandate for a republic and nothing else, it would simply put Lloyd George into a position of being able to force a new Irish Party into existence.

By preparing himself as the nice guy, with Collins obligingly playing the part of the heavy, he hoped to keep both moderates and extremists in Sinn Féin and the IRA happy and at the same time give Lloyd

George the opportunity – which the Prime Minister by this time badly needed – to open negotiations.

In view of what happened later, it was ironic that the British Cabinet assumed that Collins was in fact the real behind-the-scenes leader in Ireland and was thwarting de Valera in his effort for peace. 'De Valera and Michael Collins have quarrelled,' Lloyd George told his cabinet in April. 'The latter will have a Republic and he carries a gun and he makes it impossible to negotiate. De Valera cannot come here and say he is willing to give up Irish Independence, for if he did, he might be shot.'

On what he based his assumption that Collins and de Valera had quarrelled is uncertain, but he was right in that there was a growing distrust between the two men. De Valera had returned to find Cathal Brugha and Collins at loggerheads, mainly because Brugha resented the Big Fellow's effortless dominance and, while de Valera had done his best to calm both men down without taking sides, there is little doubt that he, too, found Collins a threat, or at least Collins thought he did. On his return from America, de Valera had suggested that Collins should take his place there on a similar tour, so that 'we will not have here, so to speak, all our eggs in one basket'.

His motives may have been of the best, but Collins distrusted them. 'The Long Whoor won't get rid of me as easy as that,' he said.[1]

Under the new Government of Ireland Act there had to be elections in May for the 128 seats of the Southern Irish Parliament it provided for. Sinn Féin had no intention of going into a Southern Irish or any other British-dominated Parliament; it used the occasion as a poll for the second Dáil Éireann. The fact that in every single one of the 128 constituencies – except for Trinity College, Dublin, which, as usual, elected four Unionists – Sinn Féiners were returned unopposed, convinced Britain that, even allowing for IRA intimidation, the majority of the Irish in the South were behind the republicans.

Constance Markievicz was re-elected but now, instead of being the only female representative in the Dáil, there were, to her delight, five other women TDs, Ada English, Mary MacSwiney, sister of the dead Lord Mayor of Cork, Kate O'Callaghan, Kathleen Clarke, and Margaret Pearse, the mother of Patrick. The last four were, in fact, all relatives of men killed since 1916. Of the 124 Sinn Féin TDs twenty-three were in prison, like Constance, thirty were internees, three were escapees from prison, thirty-six were on the run from arrest and four had internment orders taken out against them.

---

[1] 'Whoor' or 'hure', as it is locally pronounced, has no sexual connotation, being merely dismissive abuse.

With so many enforced absences the Dáil was not to meet in full until August, but its very existence was, whatever its intention, an implicit recognition that partition was a fait accompli. 'From that moment,' wrote Winston Churchill, now Secretary of State for the Colonies under Lloyd George, 'the position of Ulster became unassailable.'

In Mountjoy, Con was joined by one of her Cumann na mBan girls, Eithne Coyle, who had been sentenced to one year for possessing documents relating to the banned Cumann na mBan and the plan of a barracks. She had been working in Roscommon, ostensibly for the Gaelic League, but actually as a courier for the IRA, cycling round the countryside noting troop movements.

Like so many Cumann na mBan her work in the war had been invaluable and, as the prosecutor at her trial indignantly pointed out, she had remained undetected for so long 'because she was a woman'. She found her President labouring, as few Ministers of Labour ever have, on her prison rock garden. She remembered how a group of visiting justices kindly asked the Countess if there was anything she needed. 'Dung,' said Con, which shook them; though several sacks of manure duly arrived for her later.

As 1921 went into one of the most glorious summers anyone could remember an apparently unfailing sun shone on an Ireland where sudden, and often very hideous, death was becoming commonplace.

It was a wonderful and unforgettable summer, that of 1921 [wrote Con's friend of her debutante days, Elizabeth, Countess of Fingall]. Such long evenings over the quiet country where there was a Curfew now at 11 o'clock and motor Curfew at 7 o'clock, so that the country seemed to belong to the lambs and birds . . . But people were ill at night, and babies frequently choose to be born during those hours, knowing nothing of Curfew . . . The Doctors drove in fear, and messages summoning them must be carried on foot by the poor, who have no telephone. And such messengers made terrifying journeys and were sometimes shot 'by mistake'.

Trains were derailed, landmines exploded, pitched battles took place in the streets killing passers-by, a twenty-one-year-old girl was killed when shots were fired at a cricket match being played on Trinity College pitch between the Gentlemen of Ireland and the Military. An elderly Unionist Irishwoman was deliberately 'executed' by Cork IRA for giving information about them to the authorities. The Tans shot priests, women and children.

A low estimate of the number of civilian casualties between January 1 and July 11, 1921, came to 707 killed and 756 wounded.

As the climax to an operation to cripple the British civil administration and in which income tax offices all over the country had been destroyed, the beautiful eighteenth-century Custom House in Dublin was burned down. It was an effective show of strength on the part of the IRA but, beside losing one of Ireland's finest buildings, five of the raiders died in the resulting battle and seventy more were captured.

Both sides began privately to admit that they were coming to the end of their tether. The IRA was losing ammunition, manpower and, in some places, sympathy, which they could not regain. Michael Collins publicly said the burning of the Custom House was a success, and secretly admitted he did not think the fight could go on for longer than another three weeks. The British Cabinet was facing the fact that to quell Ireland it would need thousands more reinforcements and the introduction of blanket military law with its corollary of execution for anyone and everyone who was a member of Sinn Féin and the IRA which, as General Macready, GOC Ireland, pointed out to the Cabinet, would mean shooting a hundred a week.

Lloyd George quailed at the cost in money, men and, more especially, international prestige.

At three o'clock on Sunday afternoon, July 24, 1921, Constance was informed that a truce had been declared pending negotiations between Ireland and Britain, and emerged from Mountjoy, blinking, into what was to be her last perfectly happy summer. Even that was shadowed by an indication of what the future held for Ireland's women and Labour; although she had been made Minister of Labour once again, her department no longer carried Cabinet rank. Along with Fine Arts, Education and a few others, it had been demoted. The two sides of Irish life which Constance had represented in her post had proved their utter loyalty to the cause of independence – Labour had collaborated by refusing to stand in the elections so as not to divide the vote and had struck against British military troop movements; Cumann na mBan and other women had rendered such service that the war could not have gone on without it. They had served their turn and would go on serving it.

The new women in the Dáil protested. Mary MacSwiney warned of the precedent the move created. 'She would have been appalled,' wrote Margaret Ward, 'if she had been able to look into the future; over fifty years were to elapse before the Irish Government again had a woman in the Cabinet.'

Whether Con fought against the demotion of her ministry with the same acuteness with which she had gained it, is unknown. If she did, she lost the battle. Certainly in public she held her tongue and gave as much to her downgraded department as she had in its greater days.

Once again, every consideration was subservient to the cause; for one thing it would have been loutish to have spoiled the relieved joy with which Ireland was welcoming its breathing space, for another nobody dared show a rift in the united front which the negotiators had to carry to London to bring about the treaty for which the country was holding its breath.

Chapter Fifteen

The two great opposing political parties in Ireland today, Fine Gael and Fianna Fáil, were not founded on differences of class, race, social or economic theory, religion, or anything else that would make them comprehensible to the rest of fallible humanity, but on whether their originators favoured, or did not favour, a piece of paper – the Treaty between Great Britain and Ireland signed in December 1921. Fine Gael's[1] roots are pro-Treaty: Fianna Fáil's anti-Treaty.

To say that the Treaty was followed by a civil war may be stating the obvious to many; but there are a surprising number of people who don't know it, not only in modern England, but in Ireland itself. As late as 1973, Maria McGuire could write that the nuns who taught her history in school never mentioned it: 'When we came to the twentieth century, we learnt of the glorious rising of 1916, which had ended in the execution of its leaders. Strangely, the lessons stopped at 1921; we did not learn about the Civil War of 1922 and '23.'

The Treaty and its aftermath are a prism which so deflected the perceptions of Irish people that it is virtually impossible to find a contemporary account that is not distorted by it. Hindsight can pinpoint the errors that were made, but to understand *why* they were made needs some compassion for men who believed they were acting from the highest motives, even if what transpired was the jockeying for power which has become the dreary cliché of any country that attains freedom from a conqueror.

They faced what has been called 'the shock of success'. Irish revolt had been so securely damned for seven hundred years that to find it had succeeded to the point where the age-old oppressor was prepared to come to terms, placed on the people who had won it a responsibility for which they were not really prepared.

These very people, on whose personalities so much was to depend, were a brilliant job lot, thrown together by the Rising but who, because of imprisonments, trips abroad and the need, for security reasons, to meet as rarely as possible, had not been welded into a unit. Neither

---

[1] At this point known as Cumann na nGaedheal, it became Fine Gael in 1933.

were they used to any opposition but the enemy's; they had been elected in a democratic abnormality which undermined the right of anyone to stand against them as disloyalty to the cause.

De Valera, in particular, had come to believe he *was* Ireland. (The fact that he later dominated Irish politics for forty years gives him some belated justification.) 'He appeared to have no doubts that he had been "born to be king" – not, of course, an expression he ever used,' said his most loving biographer. And he himself said with terrifying simplicity: 'When I want to know what the people of Ireland want, I examine my own heart.'

He knew that the people might have been fighting for a republic but that they were unlikely to get it; in preliminary talks which he himself had conducted with Lloyd George, it had become obvious that, with the British Empire still very much intact, the government were not going to allow its closest, and therefore its most strategically vulnerable, possession to make a crack in it in case the entire edifice came tumbling down. 'We are not doctrinaire republicans,' he told the Dáil. He did not, of course, admit as much to Lloyd George. In fact, during those early talks Eamon de Valera showed that he was one of the few men in Ireland, or in the world for that matter, who was up to Lloyd George's weight. The British Prime Minister said of the meetings between them that it was like being on a merry-go-round one horse behind de Valera and totally unable to catch up.

Lloyd George offered Ireland – the twenty-six counties of the South – a form of dominion status which was curtailed by an insistence on free trade and defence stipulations, and demanded that it recognise the existing powers and privileges of the Parliament of Northern Ireland, which 'cannot be abrogated except by their own consent'. No republic and no unification. The terms were unacceptable, but they were a start; de Valera rejected them and went home, keeping the negotiating line open.

During the hiatus, in July 1921, he was sitting on the side of his bed when the word 'external' flashed through his mind. 'External associate,' he thought, would exactly clarify Ireland's desired position. To make it clear to his colleagues he drew a large circle representing the British Commonwealth; inside it were five smaller circles representing the self-governing countries of that group of nations. Ireland he sketched as a circle outside the large circle, but touching it. Ireland would be associated with the Commonwealth but not a member, and therefore would not have to recognise King George – this was a cardinal point – as its own titular head, but only as head of the Commonwealth with which it was freely and externally associated.

It was a subtle idea – too subtle as it turned out for the thinking of

225

the time, though it was later to become the basis on which African and Indian states became wholly independent while still linked to Britain.

The new negotiating team was chosen with care. Arthur Griffith would be the chairman; he had been a loyal supporter of the new Sinn Féin since 1917, nevertheless, he had to be watched; because of his dual-monarchy ideas, he might be prevailed upon to accept the Crown as the head of Ireland if he were put under pressure. When it was announced that Michael Collins was also to go, the English automatically assumed that he, with the fearsome image they had of him, the 'gunman', the extreme republican, would provide the counter-balance to Griffith. In fact, this was not so. Collins was already contemplating acceptance of the Crown. He was the supreme realist who knew, nobody better, how enervated Ireland had become by the Tan War, though this knowledge may well have blinded him to how much the same war had weakened Lloyd George's own political position, to say nothing of the international outcry that would go up if the war began again. Collins was also reluctant to go to the London talks which surprised de Valera, since he had been piqued at not being included in the original negotiations. But Collins had decided in advance that whatever was agreed, 'Either way, it will be wrong.'

Two lawyers, Eamon Duggan and George Gavan Duffy, were included as 'mere legal padding', to use de Valera's term.

The real counter-balances to Griffith were Robert Barton, a staunch republican who was at the same time a Protestant landowner, and, as chief secretary, Erskine Childers, the man who had run the guns to the Volunteers at Howth in 1914, and had since become de Valera's most ardent supporter. The admiration was mutual. De Valera later said that if he could have chosen the character he would most liked to have modelled his own on, it would have been Childers'.

Interestingly, Mary MacSwiney, now a prominent member of the Dáil, was considered by de Valera as a possible delegate, but because of the attitude 'of Griffith and Collins to women in politics', he did not propose her name.

De Valera's decision not to go himself has mystified everybody ever since. Collins interpreted it as de Valera wishing him to make concessions which de Valera himself, as President of the Irish Republic, could not in all decency make. De Valera felt that his influence with his extremists would be the greater if he had not been a party to the negotiations, which is much the same thing.

That, with hindsight, was the first mistake. The second was to make the delegates plenipotentiaries, that is, carry full power to make the agreement and sign it; although, to be fair to the Dáil and de Valera, it was made perfectly clear to the delegates verbally and in writing that 'the complete text of the draft treaty about to be signed will be submitted to Dublin and reply awaited'.

Off they went, to begin the talks in London on October 11, 1921. They carried with them the confusing concept of 'external association' of a *united* Ireland which had to have the assurance from Lloyd George that 'such association would secure for it the allegiance of the present dissenting minority' (the Unionists of the six counties of Ulster). That much was clear. If they broke off negotiations it was to be because they were being refused the unification of their country – something that would gain them sympathy from the watching world. What was less clear was how such an assurance could be received from Britain which had already proved itself impotent against men like Carson.

The joy in Ireland, which seemed to regard the war as good as over, was another pressure on them. Killing had stopped immediately truce was declared. But there were still 3,300 men interned and forty women in prison, among them Con's friend in Mountjoy, Eithne Coyle who, after Constance's release, had missed her so much she cried for a week. Eventually Eithne and the other Cumann na mBan women in Mountjoy got so 'fed up' that they managed an escape over its wall on Hallowe'en night. Eithne was smuggled to Maud Gonne's house before going home, and was visited there by Constance who lent her £5, a kindness she never forgot.

The greatest stain on the summer, however, was in Belfast where they had their own Bloody Sunday, July 10, when Orange mobs showed what they thought of the truce by burning down 160 Catholic houses, killing fifteen of their occupants and injuring another sixty-eight, a forerunner of attacks which killed hundreds.

Since February 1921 Con's Ministry of Labour had been instructed to co-ordinate a general boycott against Belfast manufactured goods as a protest not just against the violence but against Protestant employers who effectively discriminated against Catholics by asking all their workers to sign a declaration of loyalty to the British Government. While it is difficult to think of any other material way the Dáil could have shown its displeasure, the boycott nevertheless pointed up the division between the twenty-six counties and the six, and reinforced bigotry. The effectiveness with which Con ran the campaign is evidenced by the fact that Michael Collins was able to use the nuisance value of the boycott as a bargaining factor in his talks in London. Much of its grass roots work was done by women, who were praised for it in several Dáil debates, persuading shops not to stock goods manufactured in Belfast and issuing blacklists of firms handling Belfast goods. As Margaret Ward says: 'Woman the consumer had become woman the activist.'

Con came down hard on any religious discrimination by Catholics against Protestants, as shown by her letter as Minister to a Catholic quarry manager in the North:

> It has been reported to us by Mr McCartan that he has received a notice from you ordering him to dismiss a Protestant workman from his employment . . . We wish to state that the Government of Dáil Éireann cannot stand for intimidation and for the penalising of men because of their religion, and unless this intimidation is stopped we shall have to put the matter into the hands of the Republican Police.

In October she was free, for the first time in four years, to preside over the Cumann na mBan Convention, the largest ever, attended by delegates representing nearly 800 branches.

It was now a very different organisation from the one that had been set up to assist the Volunteers in 1914. Nobody in 1914 had dreamed that such assistance would entail being under fire, risking life and imprisonment by breaking curfew, assessing enemy military installations, smuggling weapons, and all this often in areas under martial law, where fear of reprisals, especially against women, was daunting. Hanna Sheehy Skeffington and others were already compiling an account of what women had suffered during the Tan Terror; undoubtedly many women had been raped or sexually assaulted, but the subject was so taboo that the victims were unwilling to give evidence, except in rare cases.

The new Cumann na mBan was young – a large proportion of its membership was in its twenties – and regarded itself as the comrade rather than the adjunct of the IRA, able to take its own political decisions. At the Convention, for instance, the members supported unanimously a proposal that all citizens, male and female, over the age of eighteen should be allowed to vote in any plebiscite or election 'in which the honour and fate of Ireland shall be at stake'.

Con was proud of it. She told the delegates: 'Cumann na mBan will be a name that will go down to your children and your children's children,' but she warned them against the prevailing belief that the fight was over. '. . . Go out and work as if the war was going to break out next week . . . if the enemy sees any weakening the whole thing is up.'

She was not immune from the general relaxation, however:

> It is heavenly to be out again and to be able to shut and open doors [she wrote to Eva]. It is almost worth while being locked up for the great joy release brings. Life is so wonderful. One just wanders round and enjoys it. The children and the trees

and cows and all common things are so heavenly after nothing but walls and uniformed people.

Another great relief for her was to get a letter from Casi, telling her that he and Stanislas were well, though they had endured a great deal in the 1914–18 war and the Russian Revolution. Casi was in Warsaw now, working as a legal adviser and commercial counsellor to the American consulate; his home had been burned down by the Bolsheviks and the family scattered. Stasko (Stanislas) had seen five years' service with the Imperial Marine Guard followed by two years as 'a hostage of the Bolsheviks'. It was the first time husband and wife had been in contact since 1916. Con's reply, that of a friend rather than a wife, shows how far they had grown apart in their differing adventures.

She gave him news of mutual friends:

> I never go anywhere that someone does not want to know, have I heard from you ... I am so glad that you have been successful with plays, and only hope that you are fairly comfortable. I've often been very unhappy thinking of all you and your people must have suffered ... Most of the pictures and some of the furniture is safe up to this. Lots of things were stolen and destroyed in 1916.
>
> A one-act play of mine was played last night with great success ... If this truce goes on, you ought to come over for a bit. I know a lot of Irish now, you will be surprised to hear. Now goodbye for the present. Do write to me again soon. Yours ever, Constance de Markievicz.

It is as if her attention is elsewhere; like the rest of Ireland's, it was directed at the negotiations taking place in London.

To encompass the complexity of those 1921 Treaty talks has required the writing of entire books.[1] Reading their accounts has the morbid fascination of watching a chess game being played simultaneously on three boards – each side had to consider not only the subject under discussion but the effect on their own extremists and world opinion – with political or actual death apportioned to the losers. Three of the Irish delegation would be dead by the end of the following year, two of them by violence.

Basically, clever as the Irish plenipotentiaries were, they were outclassed in political manoeuvring by the men they were dealing with, two of whom, Lloyd George and Winston Churchill, would have come high on any world list of manipulating statesmen. Such men

---

[1] Perhaps the best is *Peace by Ordeal* by Frank Pakenham (Lord Longford), Sidgwick and Jackson, revised edition, 1972. See also *Michael Collins and the Treaty* by T. Ryle Dwyer, Mercier Press, Dublin, 1981.

could detect the chink in any armour and lance through it with pinpoint accuracy. The Irish contingent had not been provided with the long spoon necessary to sup with them.

Very roughly, both Michael Collins and Arthur Griffith committed the fatal mistake of being seduced into individual private talks with Lloyd George in which both gave away more than they intended or realised. Both ignored the de Valera-like warnings of Erskine Childers; Griffith in particular regarded Childers as an Englishman – even an English spy – and he hated Englishmen.

As the days and nights of negotiation went on, they found themselves confused by obfuscating orders from Dublin, and mentally and physically exhausted. Finally, when Lloyd George had worn them down to a position which he knew to be just about acceptable to his own side, he rushed them. 'Sign now or it is war.' They signed, and they did not check back with Dublin before doing so.

'Will anyone be satisfied at the bargain? Will anyone?' wrote Collins immediately afterwards. 'I tell you this, early this morning I signed my death warrant. I thought at the time how odd, how ridiculous – a bullet may just as well have done the job five years ago.'

The Treaty *was* his death warrant; nevertheless, it was more than generations of Irishmen and women over the past seven hundred years could have thought possible. Ireland was to have its own Parliament and Executive, enjoying the same constitutional status as the Dominion of Canada. 'It was,' said Kathleen Clarke later, 'the biggest Home Rule Bill we have ever been offered.'

But the new Irish Free State, as it was to be called, was still divided from Ulster; in order to placate both the Irish delegates and the Ulster Unionists, Lloyd George had suggested the subtle device of a Boundary Commission which was to adjust the frontier between the six counties of the North and the twenty-six in accordance with the wishes of each county's inhabitants. Obviously areas such as Catholic-dominated Tyrone and Fermanagh would want to transfer to the Free State, leaving a very small Protestant division which, Collins was convinced, would prove economically unviable.

There was also the very thing de Valera had stipulated there must not be, an oath of allegiance which all members of the Irish Free State Parliament had to take:

I ... do solemnly swear true faith and allegiance to the Constitution of the Irish Free State as by law established and that I will be faithful to H.M. King George V, his heirs and successors by law, in virtue of the common citizenship of Ireland with Great Britain and her adherence to and membership of the group of nations forming the British Commonwealth of Nations.

The Treaty was, Michael Collins said, a mere stepping stone, the freedom to achieve freedom, and in this, in the long run, he was proved right. On the matter of partition he was proved disastrously wrong; the Boundary Commission was a farce which ran for years until, in 1925, the Free State Government came to a financial agreement with the British, and the Catholics of Northern Ireland were 'thrown to the wolves'.

The fact that the President of their country and its Dáil had no chance even to look at the terms before the Treaty was signed, and that it was published in the newspapers at eight p.m. on December 6, the same day that it had been signed, whether the President or the Dáil had read it or not, was such a monumental blunder on the part of the Irish negotiators that it looked, and still does, like wilful insult. The kindest interpretation was that they had been hypnotised by Lloyd George into forgetting that there was such an instrument as the telephone.

De Valera refused to accept the Treaty. The Dáil debate on the subject which began on December 14 and went on for weeks, makes painful reading even now, not only because it presaged civil war and the death of several of the speakers, but because of their manifest agony at being divided against each other.

Arthur Griffith, as chairman of the delegation, moved the acceptance of the Treaty: 'We have brought back the flag; we have brought back the evacuation of Ireland after 700 years by British troops and the formation of an Irish army. We have brought back to Ireland her full rights and powers of fiscal control.' It was, he said, 'equality with England'.

Erskine Childers opposed it. He analysed the Treaty clause by clause in an effort to show the Dáil that under it 'the authority of the British Government will inevitably appear in the Irish Constitution ... The King, representing the British Government, or the Governor-General, will have power to give or refuse assent to Irish legislation.'

Kevin O'Higgins made an equally able speech, but for the other side. He told the Dáil that Lloyd George had threatened the delegation with 'terrible and immediate war' and that they were not entitled to plunge Ireland into it. Robert Barton and Gavan Duffy, who had signed the Treaty, explained that they had done so with reluctance but that, having done so, they could only recommend it to the Dáil.

But as the debate wore on, it became less cerebral as men and women came forward to whom the idea of an Irish Republic had not just been a symbol but the brief which had entitled them to kill for it.

There was no chance of reasoned debate when ancestral passion,

231

reaction and exhaustion, hatred of England, dread of responsibility, respect for the patriot dead, loathing of war, 'Every circumstance that could cloud vision and distort judgment was present,' says Dorothy Macardle who was there.

In the National Library of Ireland there is a letter written by the dying Terence MacSwiney in Brixton to Cathal Brugha which shows the heavy legacy that had been inherited by the republicans.

What I suffer here is more than repaid for by the fruit already reaped – if I die I know the fruit will exceed the cost a thousand fold. The thought makes me happy and I thank God for it. Ah, Cathal, the pain of Easter Week is properly dead at last. God bless you again and again and give you and yours long years of happiness under the victorious Republic. With all a comrade's love.

Weighed down by it, Brugha's speech against the Treaty was especially bitter.

One by one the women deputies rejected the Treaty. To read some accounts of the debate, it might be thought that they did so out of loyalty to their dead men: Margaret Pearse's two sons, Kathleen Clarke's husband, Mary MacSwiney's brother, Kate O'Callaghan's husband who had been shot in front of her. Their opponents used their loss to discredit their arguments, imputing mental instability due to their grief, but Mrs O'Callaghan spoke for them all in denouncing these smear tactics and saying that 'no woman in this Dáil is going to give her vote merely because she is warped by a deep personal loss'. Mary MacSwiney's long, uncompromising speech had some telling points:

I stand here for the will of the people, and the will of the people of Ireland is their freedom, which this so-called Treaty does not give them. The will of the people was expressed in December 1918. The will of the people was expressed in the manifesto which sent every one of you here. And I ask any one of you voting for this Treaty what chance would you have if on the twenty-fourth of last May [the election] you came out for Dominion Home Rule?

It was irrefutable that the Dáil had been elected on the Sinn Féin republican ticket.

Only two people in the entire debate spoke for working-class interests. One was Liam Mellowes, Con's helper in setting up the Fianna, and the other was the Countess Markievicz. Both of them suspected that the Treaty would merely perpetuate capitalism under another flag – and in that they proved themselves prophets.

It had already become obvious that the Treaty suited right-wing interests; it was being backed by the Irish Republican Brotherhood, and William Martin Murphy's *Freeman's Journal* was welcoming it with open arms. What had particularly set the alarm bells ringing in Con's head was that the proposed new Dáil of the Irish Free State was to have an Upper Chamber and that in London Arthur Griffith had given a guarantee to see representation in both chambers by Southern Unionists, a class, Con's own class, which, she said in her speech, had always

> combined against the workers . . . used every institution in the country to ruin the farmer, and more especially the small farmer, and to send the people of Ireland to drift in the emigrant ships . . . I object to any government whereby a privileged number of classes established here by British rule are to be given a say . . . in the form of an Upper Chamber, as against all, I might say, modern ideas of common sense, of the people who wish to build up a prosperous, contented nation. But looking as I do for the prosperity of the many, for the happiness and content of the workers, for what I stand, James Connolly's ideal of a Workers' Republic . . .
> [Interruption: 'A Soviet Republic!']
> . . . A co-operative commonwealth! – these men are to be set up to uphold English interests in Ireland, to uphold the capitalists' interests in Ireland, to block every ideal that the nation may wish to formulate . . . I know what I mean – a state run by the Irish people for the people. That means a government that looks after the rights of the people before the rights of property. And under the Saorstát [the Free State] I don't wish to anticipate that the directors of this and that capitalist interest is to be at the head of it. My ideal is the Workers' Republic for which Connolly died. And I say that this is one of the things that England wishes to prevent. She would sooner give us Home Rule than a democratic Republic. It is the capitalists' interest in England and Ireland that are pushing this Treaty to block the march of the working people in Ireland and England.

She became emotional, but so had almost all the speakers. She was making her speech on January 3, the Debate had gone on for three weeks and bitterness and division were widening. She mocked and enraged Michael Collins by repeating the ridiculous rumour, then in circulation, that he had designs to marry Princess Mary and get himself made Governor of the New State.

But she ended touchingly: 'I have seen the stars, and I am not going to follow a flickering will o' the wisp . . .'

Four days later the Dáil voted on the Treaty; sixty-four for approval, fifty-seven for rejection. Frank Gallagher, who was there, wrote: 'The painful silence was soon broken in every part of the Chamber, and not only women, but stalwart men, sobbed and wept like children.'

De Valera and his cabinet resigned. Kathleen Clarke, seconded by Liam Mellowes, proposed de Valera's re-election as President. This time the vote was even closer, but the motion was lost by two votes. It was an ambiguous constitutional position. The Dáil had been elected as a republican government and now, on a motion by Michael Collins, Arthur Griffith became its new President, promising that he would keep it in existence until an election could be called to decide whether or not the people wanted the Irish Free State. While Griffith was being elected, de Valera and the anti-Treatyites walked out and what little dignity the Dáil retained disintegrated into vituperative screams:

Collins: Deserters all! We will now call on the Irish people to rally to us. Deserters all!
Ceannt: Up the Republic!
Collins: Deserters all to the Irish nation in her hour of trial. We will stand by her.
Markievicz: Oath breakers and cowards.
Collins: Foreigners – Americans – English.
Markievicz: Lloyd Georgeites.

Collins became Minister of Finance, W. T. Cosgrave, Local Government, and Richard Mulcahy, who was Chief of Staff of the IRA, Minister of Defence. The latter was an Irish Republican Brotherhood member, and had spoken for the Treaty because, he said, he saw no alternative. His appointment in Cathal Brugha's place left the Army leaders ominously divided.

But another ominous sidelight on the Treaty debate is the way the concerted opposition of the women members had infuriated the pro-Treaty men.

When, early on in the debate, Con suggested an adjournment because Michael Collins was tired, which he obviously was, he became so angry that she had to withdraw the remark. It is true that the women were raising the ghosts of dead men which the pro-Treatyites could not face, but there was another element of something like blame, which was to grow into the feeling: 'If it hadn't been for the women . . .'

As near as dammit, P. S. O'Hegarty imputed the later trouble to women. He pointed out that on January 7, 1922, when the Dáil had accepted the Treaty, Michael Collins offered an olive branch to de Valera, 'to come behind us and help us to get the best out of the Treaty'. Says O'Hegarty:

For a moment, time seemed to stand still . . . de Valera said nothing . . . But while he hesitated Deputy Mary MacSwiney, fearing lest he might meet Collins' generous speech half-way, got on her feet and said: 'No, we won't go in with you, nor help you in any way . . .'

It was men like him who nicknamed the anti-Treatyites 'The Women and Childers Party'.

The fact that Cumann na mBan immediately and overwhelmingly rejected the Treaty, the first nationalist organisation to do so, confirmed the belief among the pro-Treatyites that activist women were out to scupper the Treaty. So, when a motion was put forward in the Dáil on March 2, 1922, asking for the franchise for the coming election to include women on the same terms as men, that is, to give the vote to women over twenty-one, it was defeated. That debate was nearly as acrimonious as the one on the Treaty had been. Pro-Treaty men who favoured women's suffrage kept quiet, while the anti-feminists on their side took over. Joseph McGrath, for instance, Con's former deputy at the Ministry of Labour, who had now succeeded to her job, talked about 'the women in men's clothing' which Con challenged as a 'dastardly remark'.

Arthur Griffith said the Dáil had no power to alter the franchise, anyway it would take too long to make a new register (which would have had to include young men newly of age who could be expected to vote against the Treaty) and, finally, that Britain would refuse to recognise the validity of such an election.

Con's speech was dignified: Equality for women, she said, was one thing she had worked for since she was a young woman.

That was my first bite, you may say, at the apple of freedom and soon I got on to the other freedom, freedom to the nation, freedom to the workers ... I have worked in Ireland, I have even worked in England, to help the women obtain their freedom. I would work for it anywhere, as one of the crying wrongs of the world, that women, because of their sex, should be debarred from any position or any right their brains entitle them to hold.

The pro-Treatyites made conflicting objections – that this was not the time to raise such a matter: why had women waited so long to raise it. 'Before, war measures were the only measures that were attended to,' said Con in reply, 'and, naturally, the women did not push forward at the time when asking for their rights might have delayed people in a house where they would be in danger of murder.'

Reason, however, was deserting the Dáil in its division. When Con had got up to speak another deputy rose. Con said she had been on her feet first. He replied: 'An O'Keefe will never yield to a Gore-Booth.'

The motion was defeated. To the women it seemed that, as Con later said, 'if they are good enough to take part in the fight, they are good enough to vote', but, having fought the British, they were now denied a full franchise because the British wouldn't like it. It made them cling more strongly than ever to the ideal of the republic with its equal citizenship which had been promised to them in the 1916 Proclamation.

Once again, the good opinion of the USA was seen as essential by both sides, and both sides tried to procure it by sending delegations to it on a speaking tour. De Valera asked Con if she would be one of the chief speakers for the republican cause with Father O'Flanagan, Austin Stack, J. J. O'Kelly and Kathleen Barry, the sister of the nineteen-year-old student, Kevin, who had been hanged by the British. She left on April 1, 1922, and may well have been glad to get away for a bit. Certainly America was glad to see her; she had become famous, and not just among the Irish–Americans, as some sort of amalgam of Joan of Arc and Grace O'Malley, the Irish pirate queen who was a thorn in Elizabeth I's side. The fifty reporters and photographers who boarded the *Aquitaine* when she docked at New York seemed surprised to find that she wasn't wielding a sword.

> Despite her martial achievements she is not a martial looking person [wrote the New York *Evening World*], . . . frail, rather, and almost deprecatory except when she is talking about the Irish Republic. Very tall and slender, she has the stoop characteristic of so many women of her height. Her soft, waving ash-brown hair is done in the quaint psyche knot at the crown of her head, her eyes behind the eye-glasses are clear blue, and there is a dash of pink in her thin cheeks. Her smile is charming. Back of everything she says one feels emotion like a flame.

Another paper said she was 'obviously one of the soft, sweet, unyielding sort', and another that she was 'quixotic and shrewd, mystical and wayward, a figure to kindle the imagination'.

If America took to the Countess Markievicz, the Countess Markievicz took to America. (AE once said she should have been born there.) She loved its get up and go, its food, its coffee, the vastness of its distances, and its chewing gum – she adopted the habit so enthusiastically, chain-chewing in the same way that she chain-smoked, that her companions had to beg her to desist[1] – even its prisons. Almost the first thing she did in New York was to get permission to visit Jim Larkin in Sing Sing where he was serving five to ten years for 'criminal anarchy', a sentence that somewhat reflected the anti-Bolshevik hysteria that had enveloped the country after the Russian Revolution, since, apart from some extremely inflammatory speeches, his crime was in publishing 'The Left Wing Manifesto' in the journal *Revolutionary Age*. The two revolutionaries, the convict and ex-con, exchanged news over a roast chicken lunch after which the warden, recognising

[1] The best account of Con in America is contained in *The Rebel Countess* by Anne Marreco, who gained much of her detail from Kathleen Barry.

a connoisseur of prisons, took Con on a guided tour of Sing Sing, which she compared favourably with British prisons she had known. (Larkin served only three years, being released on a free pardon from the Governor of New York in January 1923, and was deported back to Ireland.)

The tour that had been arranged for the republican women – the men had a separate schedule – was punishing, even for the young Kathleen Barry, but Con at fifty-four seemed to take it in her stride. They went from New York to Philadelphia, on to Detroit, a quick trip to Canada and back, Ohio to Cleveland, into north-west Minnesota, glimpsed the Mississippi, on to Montana, across the Rockies to Washington and Oregon, San Francisco – 'You would never know there had been an earthquake and fire so short a time ago' – Los Angeles, where they found the tropics, took the Santa Fé trail and saw the Arizona Desert, went east to Massachusetts, Cincinnati, Chicago, Boston and, finally, back to New York, all in two months.

At every town and city Con spoke to capacity crowds and punched home the same message – the necessity for a free and undivided republic, the impossibility of accepting partition, the lack of support in Ireland for the Free State, the nonsense of an oath of allegiance for people who had fought for a republic.

Con's emotional appeals brought the house down, bringing in as they did the Star Spangled Banner which, she said, had been Ireland's inspiration: '. . . Your stars on their blue ground; stars shining to us in the dark night of our trouble tell us how you have suffered for freedom.'

Though they more than once followed hard on the heels of the Free State delegation, the women raised huge sums for the republic – in Philadelphia alone the audiences pledged subscriptions worth 50,000 dollars.

It was while she was in Philadelphia, attending a reception in the Belleview Stratford Hotel that the Countess spotted an ex-prostitute on the other side of the room, gave a yelp of joy and ran over to hug her old companion from Aylesbury Prison, Chicago May, to the great pleasure of May and to the amazement of what May called 'the swells'.

Mostly they preached to the converted, though one reporter, with a hazy idea of Ireland's politics, gave Con a shock by asking her if she approved of its present provisional government. She leaped out of her chair, shouting, 'My God, man!' then controlled herself, sank back, lifted her presentation bouquet of roses to her face, smiled and apologised.

About the only coolness she encountered was at Akron in Ohio, which had just been visited by the Free State delegation who had told the organisers of Con's visit something so shocking about her that they were reluctant to repeat it. When Con pressed them to reveal it, they said the 'unmentionable charge' was that she was virtually a Communist. Con laughed.

Nevertheless, she enjoyed Akron which, as she told Eva in a letter, took her fancy because, like so much of America, even

> the poor houses ´. . . were among greenery. I love the way they build cities here. So few rows of gaunt bare houses all joined together in dismal uniformity as we have at home . . . each with trees round it and on its little plot of green grass . . . The bathrooms are a joy, and even the small houses have them: walls and all of shining white tiles, and cupboards built in to the walls, so convenient.

She was critical of Butte, Montana, however, despite the fact that she and Kathleen were met with 'a band and an army. All Sligo seemed to be there.' What distressed her was a copper mine.

> *It was awful.* Of course the manager showed us the show parts, great passages well ventilated and the wonderful machinery, but we saw few men working. I insisted on going into hot places and seeing men working with pick and with drill.
>
> I saw a man drilling the copper ore without the water appliance to keep the dust down and breathing in copper dust eight mortal hours every day. This is nothing but murder, as the dust sticks in the throat and eats into the *trachea* and they die *for sure* of a terrible form of consumption . . . They told us few men live to be old in Butte, Montana.

As her train wound through and over the Rockies – 'I wonder that the engineers are not national heroes. They certainly ought to be' – she wrote a letter to her stepson, Stanislas, from whom she had heard at long last.

> You know I've had a pretty stiff time of it, about three years and a half, and some of it was awful. I did what I could to help you and I think that some of the people whom I got to intercede for you may have been a little help . . . Jim Larkin . . . had already promised to try and get certain Bolshie friends of his to try and get you set free. He is in prison here, I think because he was too revolutionary and made wild speeches. But he's awfully decent and promised to do all he could to get you out . . . You rail against the Bolshies. I know little about them, but one thing I do know that our people suffered far worse from the English; and what I begin to believe is that all governments are the same, and that men in power use that power for themselves and are absolutely unscrupulous in their dealings with those who disagree with them . . . I do long to see you again. You were always as dear to me as if you had been my own son . . . Of course, if we get things fixed up right in Ireland, I am sure we shall want men like you, who know languages and that I could get you a good job. Now goodbye darling boy, and much love from your loving Mother.

Kathleen Barry told Anne Marreco that Con bought present after present, including some Hudson Bay furs, for 'my little daughter' – Maeve was now twenty years old. But one of the bonuses of her trip was that, when she arrived in London, she was reunited with Maeve, though the fact that both had changed since their last meeting is shown by Maeve having to ask Kathleen Barry which woman in a group was her mother.

Two days before a monster meeting in Madison Square Garden in New York, which was to mark the end of the trip, Con arrived in Boston. The *Boston Telegraph*'s leader writer wrote:

> Tomorrow a remarkable woman will visit Boston. While there has been, unhappily, division of opinion as to the better method for Ireland to adopt in securing her freedom, no one has ever disputed the intellect or ability or vision or valour of Countess Georgina Constance Markievicz . . . Men may differ with her in opinion, but no one can deny that history will recognise her as one of the great women in the world. Rightly she has been termed Ireland's Joan of Arc . . . men and women and children who have the opportunity to see this woman tomorrow should not let it pass, for in future years those who have gazed on the face of Countess Markievicz will proudly boast of that distinction.

CHAPTER SIXTEEN

'Things are awful here,' wrote Constance to Eva, after her return to Ireland from America in June 1922. 'There are more people being killed weekly than before the truce.'

Most of them were dying in what the Unionists now called Northern Ireland but which was still Ireland to the vast majority of people throughout the country. The IRA units in the north-east, partly to protect the Catholics from the increasing pogroms, partly to obtain arms, and partly to try to de-stabilise the Northern Ireland Government, were raiding, sniping, and disrupting railways. After two Ulster special constables were shot dead, a horde of their comrades in armoured cars raked Catholic streets in Belfast with machine-gun fire on May 31. By the end of May it was estimated that Protestants killed in the six counties numbered eighty-seven, Catholics 150. The Catholic Hospital, the Mater Misericordiæ, in Belfast, was like a war hospital, full of bullet- and shrapnel-wound cases, among them several children, and later that week an armed mob of Orangemen surrounded it, firing through the windows while doctors and nurses crawled from bed to bed trying to protect their patients. Terrified Catholics began to leave in their thousands, some to the South, some to Glasgow where, adding to the already high rate of unemployment, they caused questions in the House of Commons which Lloyd George replied to by the statement that there were '60,000 men in Ulster suppressing rebellion'.

Sir Henry Wilson, an archetypal Ulster diehard, who had been involved in the Curragh Mutiny, was now military adviser to the Northern Ireland Government and was pouring verbal petrol on the flames by virtually threatening invasion on the South. 'If serious trouble arises on the frontier between the Six Counties and the Twenty-Six Counties, I hope that the government will not restrain the military from crossing the frontier in their own self-defence.'

In the South the IRA had split, setting brother against brother in the pro- and anti-Treaty divide. A large section had put its trust in its old, much-loved leader, Michael Collins, and was reorganising itself into the Irish Free State Army, under Richard Mulcahy.

But a large section insisted on remaining the Irish Republican Army, and had set itself up 'to guard the honour and maintain the independence of the Irish Republic' under Rory O'Connor, Liam Lynch – the only member of the Supreme Council of the IRB who had voted against the Treaty – Liam Mellowes and others. In a press interview in March, Rory O'Connor repudiated the authority of the Dáil. The fact that he did it from 23, Suffolk Street, Dublin, which was the headquarters of an anti-Treaty party which de Valera had just formed, Cumann na Poblachta (League of the Republic), gave validity to the prevailing pro-Treaty view that de Valera was at the back of it. In fact, the new IRA, or the 'Irregulars' as its soldiers were called by pro-Treatyites, was beyond any political control, even de Valera's, and not even in complete control of itself. There were skirmishings and shootings and stand-offs between the two armies which arose because men had become used to acting on their own initiative and emotions.

Denied official funds, local brigades of Irregulars raided post offices and banks to keep themselves armed and eventually there was a co-ordinated break-in all over the country of Bank of Ireland branches which raised £50,000, needed, said Rory O'Connor, to pay debts incurred before the cleavage. The commandants were instructed to give receipts.

There was also a need to show defiance; on April 13 the Dublin Brigade, with Seán MacBride, now one of its new young commandants, occupied the Four Courts, which, as a united army, it had held against the British in Easter 1916, announcing it as its new headquarters. Windows were barricaded and a tunnel made in case of retreat, just as in the good old days. The next day other buildings were occupied, including Kilmainham Jail.

So Con had returned to a city which in its own centre represented the divided country and in which the occasional exchange of rifle fire cut through the sounds of everyday life.

Just before she had gone to the States, Con had made her home with the Coghlan family in Frankfort House, Rathgar. She had come to know them when the eldest daughter, May, aged fourteen, became a clerk in her Ministry of Labour. Mrs Frances Coghlan, May's mother, was a strong republican and managed, despite her nine children, to take great interest in politics. Con was a woman after her own heart and she made her welcome and comfortable, while May became her devoted assistant. Con found the atmosphere of the house, and the presence of its children, congenial and settled back in until she had time to find a home of her own.

There is no doubt that at this point she had put her military days behind her; when she had told her Cumann na mBan to 'go out and work as if the war was going to break out next week', it had been a tactical manoeuvre to make sure the British saw no sign of weakening on the Irish side. Had the Anglo–Irish war broken out again after the truce she would have joined in with all her might, but now that the opposition to all she believed came from Irishmen, she had no thought of trying to defeat them in any other way than politically. While she had been away de Valera and Michael Collins, in a desperate attempt to avoid bloodshed, had devised a pact which would enable both their sets of followers to go to the poll under the banner of Sinn Féin. By the time Con set foot back in Ireland the election was only a few days off – June 16 – and Con had no time to do anything other than trust de Valera and prepare for it.

The pact was a patched-up business. De Valera and the 'Women and Childers Party' had tried hard to get a postponement so that the election would not be fought on an out-of-date register, but Griffith had refused to hear of it. Michael Collins, however, had agreed that the new Constitution of the Irish Free State arising out of the Treaty would be published in time for people to know exactly what they were voting for, and that the Sinn Féin candidates should stand on a national coalition panel, the number of candidates representing the two factions to be in the same proportion as the Treaty vote in the Dáil. After the election there would be a coalition with an elected President, a Minister of Defence representing the army and five pro-Treaty ministers with four anti-Treaty. It was not very democratic, but it might avoid war.

Neither side distinguished themselves in the run-up to the election. De Valera, in particular, was making speeches which still sound like hysterical incitements to civil war, even though he and his apologists later said they were warnings of what could happen if the worst came to the worst. Since he later proved himself a politician with a Machiavellian grasp of events, both his friends and his enemies insist on attributing to him some deep design, but it seems more likely that he was merely reacting none too well to a situation which was almost totally out of his control.

Arthur Griffith and Michael Collins, in drawing up the new Constitution, did their best to accommodate the republicans; reducing the position of the King to a cipher, dropping the oath and refusing to recognise the special position in Ulster, but it departed too far from the Treaty and Lloyd George and Winston Churchill insisted on it being brought back into line. The Irish people were not told, however, of the changes made by the British Cabinet, and the final constitutional draft was not published until the morning of polling day, complete with the clauses republicans found so objectionable, including the oath of allegiance.

The situation was further complicated by the fact that Labour, having appealed to both sides to avert war and deciding that the Treaty was the best that could be salvaged from a bad job, at last decided to stand in its own right, so did Independents and so did Farmers, the more prosperous members of the agricultural community who were pro-Treaty.

Two days before the election Michael Collins reneged on his pact with de Valera. In a speech in Cork, which was immediately headlined by the pro-Treaty *Freeman's Journal*, he virtually told the electorate to ignore the coalition panel. 'I am not hampered now by being on a platform where there are Coalitionists,' he is reported to have said. 'I can make a straightforward appeal to you – to vote for the candidates you think best of . . . You understand fully what you have to do, and I depend on you to do it.'

The anti-Treatyites rightly regarded this as treachery and made much of it in an attempt to invalidate the result of the election, though it is doubtful if it really made much difference.

When the results were announced on June 24, 1922, the pro-Treatyites had won fifty-eight out of 128 seats, the anti-Treatyites only thirty-five, Labour had won seventeen, Independents seven, Farmers seven and four Unionists had held Trinity College, Dublin, as usual. A breakdown of votes showed that 239,193 went to the pro-Treaty side, 133,864 had gone to the anti-Treaty, but the largest amount, 247,226, had gone to the remainder, Labour, Farmers and Independent. Among those who lost their seats were the Countess Markievicz, Kathleen Clarke and the mother of Patrick Pearse.

Ireland had voted for peace.

Why it didn't get it was partly due to an act of violence for which Michael Collins was responsible but for which the anti-Treatyites carried the blame.

If Con was shocked by her defeat in St Patrick's, she didn't have time to dwell on it, because on June 22, 1922, Sir Henry Wilson was shot and killed at the door of his London Belgravia home on the orders of Michael Collins, and the consequences were too rapid and too dreadful to repine for the loss of a seat.

That Collins could have sent two men to do such a thing at this time argues that there was a streak in his character that his biographers would prefer to overlook. He did not seem to find it necessary to disabuse the British Cabinet, or his own, of the belief that the act had been committed by the republican side. Immediately he was under pressure from Lloyd George and Churchill to show good faith by reducing the garrison in the Four Courts, or else the Treaty would be regarded as abrogated. Collins played for time, but the kidnapping by the Four Courts men of one of his own generals – in return for the arrest of one of their officers – forced him to act. Two 18-pounder field guns were borrowed from the British Army – and eventually were reinforced by two more – and in the early hours of June 28, opened up on the Four Courts from the opposite side of the Liffey.

The bombardment, a declaration of open war, had its echoes further away than Dublin. In Paris Maud Gonne heard of it, and came rushing over to Ireland, in an attempt to make peace, not knowing that her son, Seán MacBride, was one of the Four Courts' two hundred-strong garrison. She gathered together a formidable committee of women from the ranks of suffrage, such as Hanna Sheehy Skeffington, Labour, pro- and anti-Treaty, and appealed to both sides. 'Mother was in favour of accepting the Treaty,' Seán MacBride told me in an interview in 1985. 'I fell out with her over that. But she changed as soon as the executions started.' The republicans were willing to cease hostilities as long as they held on to their arms, but Arthur Griffith, Maud's friend for so many years, refused to negotiate: 'We are now a government and we have to keep order.' They did not meet again.

Con was woken up in Rathgar by the bombardment, went immediately to the city centre and found that the Cumann na mBan had already mobilised and were keeping open the lines of communication between the Four Courts and the east side of O'Connell Street – the side that had not been destroyed in Easter Week – where the Dublin Brigade and other republicans were occupying various hotels under Oscar Traynor, moving in to the Gresham, the Hammam, and Moran's as frightened, hastily-dressed visitors and tourists moved out. Opposing snipers occupied the roofs on either side of the street which, in minutes, was being swept by rifle fire. It was Easter Week all over again; she could no more have stayed out of it than she could stop herself breathing. She reported for duty at Moran's, where the Cumann na mBan were organising a kitchen and first-aid centre in the basement.

De Valera was twenty miles outside Dublin when he heard the news. The attack on the Four Courts had come just two days before the Dáil was to meet. He went to his office for an impromptu meeting of republican delegates and issued a statement in support of the garrison 'the best and bravest of our Nation' and appealed: 'Irish citizens! Give them support! Irish soldiers! Bring them aid!' Then he joined up at the same office were he had enlisted as a Volunteer in 1913, this time as a private in his old battalion, known as 'Dev's Own'.

After two days of being shelled the Four Courts caught fire and the garrison surrendered, while behind them centuries of records shrivelled to ash. But the fight was not over – it had merely transferred to O'Connell Street around which, as in Easter Week, a cordon was tightening. They held out for eight days.

Many years later one of the fighters recounted this story of Con:

Coming on towards evening the fighting was mostly a snipers' battle. There was a sniping post on the rooftops at the top of Henry Street. It was a well-placed, well-manned post. The snipers in it – there were two or three of them, taking over from one another so that their fire was continuous – made my position in the shelter of the cornice as dangerous a one as you could find.

I was due for relief, and I wasn't sorry for that. But when my relief came, who was it but Madame. Played-out as I was after two or three hours up there under continuous fire, I didn't like the idea of a woman taking over that position. But Madame just waved me to one side with that imperious air she could put on when she wanted to have her own way. She slipped into what little shelter there was, carrying with her an automatic Parabellum pistol – the kind we used to call a Peter the Painter.

I couldn't rightly say how long she was up there, for I was so tired that I drowsed off to sleep. But when I woke up, the first thing I noticed was something different in the sound of the firing. The steady, continuous rattle of fire that I had learned to pick out from the sound of rifle and machine gun fire up and down the street had ceased; the snipers' post in Henry Street was silent.

As the net tightened and buildings caught fire, the various garrisons in O'Connell Street made a run for it. 'There was no point in remaining just to make a bigger bag of prisoners for the Free Staters,' one of the Cumann na mBan, Máire Comerford, said. Cathal Brugha stayed behind to cover the retreat with thirteen men and three women, Kathleen Barry, Linda Kearns and Muriel MacSwiney, the young widow of Terence. Before she left, Máire Comerford remembered Brugha as 'a much more gentle person ... gallantly encouraging everyone'. At last Brugha called his small force to surrender.

The surrendered men stood in a lane behind the hotel which was crowded with soldiers and men of the Fire Brigade [wrote Dorothy Macardle], ... asking one another, 'Where is Cathal Brugha?' Suddenly they saw him in the doorway, a small, smoke-blackened figure, a revolver in each hand raised against the levelled rifles of the troops. Enemies and friends called out 'Surrender!' But shouting 'No!' Brugha darted forward, firing, and fell amid a volley of shots.

Linda Kearns, a trained nurse, held his severed artery between her fingers as he was driven to hospital. He died two days later.

'I was tired, tired, tired and broken-hearted,' said Máire Comerford.

'I went down to the country, far away from Dublin. All I wanted to do was rest.' O'Connell Street was once more in ruins.

Brugha's widow, Caitlín, asked that only women of the republican movement form the guard of honour at her husband's funeral; it was a protest against 'the immediate and terrible' civil war which had been made by the government upon republicans. As the death toll mounted in the succeeding months, the unenviable task of burying the dead with full military honours was undertaken by Cumann na mBan who, 'with eyes shut and faces screwed to one side, fired a volley over the graves with revolvers or automatics'.

Collins was congratulated by a friend after Brugha's death for having dismissed 'an annoying insect'. Collins' reply was a rebuff. 'Yet I would forgive him anything. Because of his sincerity I would forgive him anything . . . When many of us are forgotten, Cathal Brugha will be remembered.'

A month later, the man who had been his dearest friend, Harry Boland, who had gone over to de Valera's side and was helping to reorganise the Republican Army in Leinster, was arrested in his bedroom in the Grand Hotel, Skerries, and was shot in the stomach as he walked forward, demanding to see a superior officer. 'When he was dying, his sister, Kathleen, asked him, "Who murdered you, Harry?" He would not tell. All he said was to bury him beside Cathal Brugha.' Again, Collins grieved.

On August 12, Arthur Griffith, anguished and overworked, fell down dead. Ten days later the armoured convoy in which Michael Collins was travelling along the Macroom–Bandon road was ambushed, and Collins killed. It is a measure of the man that when the news reached Kilmainham Jail, filled with republican men and soldiers imprisoned on the orders of the Free State, there was a heavy silence. 'I looked down,' said the IRA Commandant General, Tom Barry, 'on the extraordinary spectacle of a thousand kneeling Republican prisoners spontaneously reciting the Rosary aloud for the repose of the soul of the dead Michael Collins.'

And that was just the opening of a war in which killing brought grief and confusion to the killer – not that it stopped him killing again. But the deaths of Griffith and Collins cut away the tangled loyalties at least for the young men who now assumed leadership in the Free State Government, W. T. Cosgrave, President, Kevin O'Higgins, Home Affairs, and Richard Mulcahy, Minister for Defence and Commander-in-Chief of the Free State Army, who armed themselves with emergency powers and decided to save their state from disintegration and anarchy with a sternness which horrified even their own supporters.

With the collapse of resistance in Dublin, the anti-Treaty IRA fight moved into the south of the country where Liam Lynch, its Chief-of-Staff, conducted a guerrilla war and attempted to hold a line stretching from Waterford to Limerick, finding that the old days had gone and that many of the common people who had been prepared to nurture and hide the IRA when it had been fighting the British withdrew their support in a war against fellow-Irishmen. More than ever, the IRA had to rely on the unstinting allegiance of Cumann na mBan.

'The civil war was a mixture of hideous tragedy and raving farce,' Martin Sheridan told me. 'I once met an old ex-Free State Officer who told me about an action that was supposed to have taken place somewhere in West Offaly. The local republicans had quite pointlessly seized an old castle in the back of beyond. The neighbouring Free State garrison was ordered to oust them. They proceeded to do so, bringing with them their field kitchens but no food. The republican occupants had plenty of food but no fire. Under a flag of truce a civilised arrangement was made whereby the two sides exchanged the necessary facilities.'

The sense that they were helpless in this tragi-farce and acting out the greatest Irish joke of all for the entertainment of their enemies in the North and in Britain, was exacerbated by the refusal of the elected republicans, like de Valera, to recognise the new Dáil, arguing that the second Dáil had never been dissolved, and the setting up of a completely ineffectual government of their own based upon it. The IRA took little notice of it, and Kevin O'Higgins responded to it:

> We will not have two governments of this country, and we will not have two armies in this country. If people have a creed to preach, a message to expound, they can go before their fellow-citizens and preach and expound it. But let the appeal be to the mind, to reason, rather than to physical fear. They cannot have it both ways. They cannot have the platform and the bomb.

He was backed by the Catholic hierarchy who, on October 10, 1922, issued a pastoral letter, withdrawing the sacraments from those who carried on, said the bishops, 'what they call war, but which, in the absence of any legitimate authority to justify it, is morally a system of murder and assassination of the National forces'.

In the prisons, where thousands of men and women were now being held without trial – or political status – ordinary prisoners were given communion while the republicans would be 'lambasted' with the contents of the pastoral letter. The priests were particularly hard on the women who, in order to have their confession heard, had to accept the bishops' pronouncements, although very few agreed to such terms. Con's friend from Mountjoy, Eithne Coyle, was told that the bishops were always right. When she retorted that they had not been right when they burnt Joan of Arc, the priest was so angry he almost hit her.

Kevin O'Higgins' very reasonable pronouncements against the republican stance were backed up by less judicial action. On November 10, Erskine Childers, who had taken no part in the fighting, although he had carried on a militant publicity campaign against the Free State, was arrested for carrying a pistol, which, he pointed out, had been given to him by Michael Collins. His friends despaired for him; O'Higgins' pronouncements against 'the Englishman' in the Dáil showed a particular resentment against Childers, whose mother was Irish. A writ of habeas corpus was applied for on his behalf.

Nobody had yet been executed under the new regulation against carrying arms, but on the day of Childers' trial – held in camera – four young IRA men were shot for possession of revolvers. Questions from shocked Labour deputies elicited the response from O'Higgins that they had been executed lest it should be said that the first victim was chosen because he was a leader and an Englishman, a statement that showed Childers' death warrant was as good as signed.

On November 24, with an appeal and the habeas corpus writ still pending, he was shot.

De Valera's secretary, Kathleen O'Connell, wrote in her diary that de Valera was heartbroken. 'Childers executed. Oh God! How can we ever raise our heads again. Oh, the shame of it, shot by Irishmen. Poor Childers who had worn himself out in the service of Ireland.'

The effect of the deaths of Childers and the others was that the republicans now began to take reprisals 'officially', in the sense that Liam Lynch ordered them, and de Valera could do no more 'than pluck at his sleeve'. Two pro-Treaty Dáil deputies were shot at in a Dublin street, and one was killed.

The Free State Government responded. Four men who had been in Mountjoy without trial since the surrender of the Four Courts, were woken up in the middle of the night and told they would be shot as soon as it was light. One of them was Rory O'Connor, who had been best man at O'Higgins' wedding, and another was Con's loved Liam Mellowes. Mellowes' letter to his mother, written just before the execution, showed that the chaplain had refused[1] him the last

---

[1] C. Desmond Greaves says Mellowes did make his confession at the last moment in his *Liam Mellowes and the Irish Revolution*, Lawrence & Wishart, London, 1971.

sacraments because he would not accept the bishops' pastoral but, 'I believe that those who die for Ireland have no need for prayer.' He died, like Erskine Childers, forgiving his enemies.[1]

If Con committed to paper her personal agony over the death of so many friends and the civil war generally, it is not available. But she didn't need to: she aged.

The devoted ex-RIC man, Jeremiah Mee, from her Ministry of Labour days, said that when he first knew her she was 'handsome, athletic, bright-eyed and keen' but that when he saw her four years later at a meeting in Sligo she 'was a careworn woman, broken, dispirited and sad'.

After the sniper fight in O'Connell Street she had collapsed and, probably for the first time in her life, had to be treated as an invalid. Like Máire Comerford, she was heartsick. She had always liked to believe that things were simple, that all her geese were swans and that nearly everything wrong with Ireland was the fault of the British enemy; now all that pretence was swept away and she had found herself shooting at Irishmen. She never used the gun again.

Indomitable as she was, she was soon breathing fire, stumping Ireland, Scotland and England to explain the republican cause at meetings, defying, decrying and lampooning what she called 'the domestic enemy', attributing all evil to it and all goodness to her own side, but she didn't really believe it. 'Sometimes,' she was to admit to Esther Roper as she lay dying, 'I long for the peace of the Republican Plot.'

Like so many who worked with him in those days, she placed her hope for the future on Eamon de Valera, though even he, she thought, was 'too honourable to understand crooks'.

In fact, her view of the situation in Ireland was clearer and more realistic than his. De Valera had a frighteningly naïve conception of what Ireland should be (frightening, because he was going to be in a position to put it into practice):

. . . People who valued material wealth only as a basis of right living, of a people who were satisfied with frugal comfort and devoted their leisure to the things of the spirit; a land whose countryside would be bright with cosy homesteads, whose fields and villages would be joyous with sounds of industry, the romping of sturdy children, the contests of athletic youths, the laughter of comely maidens; whose fireside would be the forums of the wisdom of serene old age.

[1] Childers gave his son the daunting task of approaching everyone who signed the death warrant with his forgiveness. That same son eventually became President of Ireland.

Con had lived closer to the poor than he had, and among the urban poor, a class which de Valera seems to have overlooked. She knew that athletic youths would emigrate without employment, that happy, romping maidens had illegitimate babies and ended up sentenced for killing them, or for prostitution; she had met them in prison. She wrote:

> Life for the poor is a calvary spent in the weary and hopeless ranks of the unemployed when 'Home' has become the farcical name that custom gives to a one-room tenement where a hungry mother awaits, trying to comfort starving and shivering little ones, where the last stick of furniture, the last blanket, has been pledged for food in a desperate attempt to put off the cruel day when they must creep into that hell devised by a capitalist government – the workhouse.

She knew the poor did not devote their leisure to things of the spirit; they had children who grew up uneducated, 'helpless and incompetent, their health broken and their minds stunted and who fill our jails and workhouses'. It was an understanding of humanity that de Valera, with his Catholic puritanism, was never to comprehend.

No Gaelic idyll would change it, and the Free State Government certainly wasn't going to.

De Valera was opposing the government – and what was obviously the mass wish of those who had voted in the last election – because he took his own sublime view: 'The majority has no right to do wrong.'

Constance Markievicz was opposing it because she saw the majority of its people was being done wrong to. Every day bought confirmation of the nightmare James Connolly had foreseen and which Con and Liam Mellowes had voiced in the Treaty debate; that the only difference in the suffering of the poor was that it now took place under a green flag.

Her best hope that things might be changed was in Jim Larkin, who, though still in Sing Sing at the signing of the Treaty, had issued a manifesto throwing his weight on the republican side: 'We propose carrying on this fight until we make the land of Erin a land fit for men and women – a Workers' Republic or Death.' His antipathy to the Treaty was based on his distrust of Arthur Griffith and, says his biographer, 'this coupled with his warm admiration and respect for Eamon de Valera, cemented his stand on the Republican side. Still to Larkin the end remained a Workers' Republic, and Labour was the force which would regenerate the nation.' He was out of touch with the Labour Party in Ireland which had taken no official stand on the Treaty.

However, when Larkin was released and arrived in Ireland in April 1923 to find a fullscale civil war going on, he was horrified and immediately called for peace: 'Two armies were contending for power in the nation,' he declared at a gigantic Labour Day celebration in Croke Park, 'but I am speaking to the greatest army of all of them, and it is the working classes who are going to bring peace.' Unsuccessfully he began trying to persuade the republicans to 'come into the nation'; the greatest crime was that Irishmen should raise their hands against Irishmen, and not that Ireland was not yet a republic.

Yet in two months the Irish Labour Party was riven by a non-killing but nevertheless vicious civil war of its own between Larkin and William O'Brien, who, having worked hard on the Transport Union in Jim Larkin's absence, was not prepared to give up power and had, according to Larkin's friends, 'rigged' its annual congress against him.

'That the Irish Labour Movement should split at all was most unfortunate,' says Emmet Larkin, 'but that the split should have come when it did was nothing less than catastrophic.' The British employers had broken the resistance of the miners in 1921 and were forcing their workers to accept wage cuts amounting to £10 million a week. Irish workers were facing the grim knowledge that their turn was coming, and it did.

Dockers, agricultural labourers, coal trade employees, grain men, seamen, firemen and carters, one by one their unions opposed the shilling a day reduction imposed on them, and one by one were forced to give in. Larkin, too, gave in and went to Russia for a while. In his absence he was expelled as a member of the union he had created.

The Labour movement failed to make an impact on Irish politics. at a crucial moment, and never quite recovered, leaving the underprivileged to find such betterment as they could through other means and other parties.

Larkin stood for revolution, O'Brien for reform and not only did the two ideologies war with each other, but the deep conservatism of rural Ireland and the reluctance of working-class leaders to oppose the Church with socialist doctrines in a country where, at one time, the word 'liberal' could be dyed deepest red, left the deprived in continuing deprivation.

Because Con espoused so many causes, she was jeered at for not thinking deeply about any of them and, of course, the mud stuck. But she had the genius to know that if Connolly's teachings were to take any root in Irish soil it would have to be with the compliance of the Church, and she began work on a brave attempt to reconcile the two orthodoxies in a pamphlet which she was to publish in 1924, titled *James Connolly's Policy and Catholic Doctrine*. Sean O'Faolain called it an 'amazing ragout' and at the time he was writing, 1934, that is what it seemed. But a modern priest, espousing the poor in South America, for instance, would find it unsurprising.

It is a long pamphlet and, basically, what she says in it is that the Catholic Church did not *have* to support capitalism, though in effect it did, because not only was it against its original brief, but members of its own hierarchy held beliefs which were inimical to capitalism. She quoted the encyclical of Pope Leo XIII and various Irish churchmen to support her arguments, using the writings of Connolly to expand on points where, she felt, they had misunderstood him. She had already stressed in a previous pamphlet, *What Irish Republicans Stand For*, the Gaelic-ness of Connolly's ideal state and emphasised – knowing the Church's terror of Russian Communism – that it was not state socialism, but a much more de-centralised co-operative common-wealth, although it would include nationalisation of railways and canals, free state education which would allow for the teaching of religion – Con's writing at this point prefigures comprehensive schooling – and a state or, at least, co-operative backed bank. She wanted, as Connolly had wanted back in 1896, a forty-eight-hour week, graded income tax on anything over £400 a year to provide pensions for the aged, infirm, widows and orphans, universal suffrage and a minimum wage.

Some of the tenets – free maintenance for all children, for instance – were hardly likely to come about in hers or any conceivable lifetime, but it was still a harder look at life's necessities than de Valera's happy, romping Gaels.

Nationalism constantly coloured Constance's ideas, as it did Cumann na mBan's for too long a time and as it still does for feminists on both sides of the religious divide in Northern Ireland today, but there is no doubt that in many things she was ahead of her time, and – in some cases – ours. Even back in February 1920, when she was a Minister of Labour on the run, she found time to write an article for the *Irish Citizen* on criminal assault cases in which children were involved and quoted one of many trials which she had attended:

The sergeant, who had charge of the case, helped the child out with her horrible evidence, and ... the child signed her name ... The prisoner pleaded guilty to common assault, and the magistrate brought in a verdict accordingly with a fine of £5. One left that court with the feeling that something was very wrong somewhere, and one knew that the something wrong was the lack of women dealing with these little children ... The poor little witnesses must be terrified with so many enormous policemen surrounding them, and will give almost any answer to suit the case ... Let women be appointed as magistrates and solicitors to deal with children's cases.

She did not lose faith in God nor de Valera, but her distrust in any other form of government was beginning to show. She wrote to Eva:

The tragedy of Christ's life to me is far greater today than it was during the few terrible last hours of suffering. For every church and every sect is but an organisation of thoughtless and well-meaning people trained . . . and controlled by juntas of priests and clergy who are used to doing all the things that Christ would most have disliked. And yet I don't know how this can be avoided, for without organisation Christ would be quite forgotten, and all organisation seems in the end to go the same road: and if it does not go in for graft and power it just fizzles out. That is what is wrong too with all public bodies and governments, and what the world has got to think out is some scheme by which power can be evenly distributed over every person in the world and by which the foolish and uneducated can no longer be grouped in unthinking battalions dependent on the few pushers, self-seekers and crooks and made slaves of and exploited.

The first Lord Acton put it more succinctly: 'Power tends to corrupt and absolute power corrupts absolutely,' but they were both confronting the same eternal, insoluble problem.

Apart from these attempts of Con's, about the only constructive action to emerge from the republican side during the civil war was the Women's Prisoners' Defence League which had as its President Charlotte Despard, and its secretary that indefatigable defender of prisoners, Maud Gonne, who this time had a personal interest since both her son, Seán MacBride, and his fiancée, Kid Bulfin, were among something like 12,000 people – about 400 of them women – that the Cosgrave government had imprisoned under emergency powers which recalled the harshest days of the Tan war. A man could now be executed for having in his possession any plan, document or note prejudicial to the safety of the state. During the seven days from January 13, 1923 to the 20th, eighteen men were executed in various parts of the twenty-six counties. The eventual total was seventy-seven, as against the forty who had been executed by the British after Easter Week and during the Tan war.

The Women's Prisoners' Defence League (WPDL) did more than any other organisation to publicise the repression of the Free State to the outside world. The women, all related to prisoners, held eloquent Sunday meetings in the rubble of O'Connell Street to protest against the increasing overcrowding and brutality in the jails, they mounted vigils outside prison walls, they traced missing men and women and were generally an embarrassment to the government, which responded by trying to break up the meetings with hoses – and at one point, bullets.

Eventually Maud Gonne herself, always a target for the cameras with her beautiful face and widows' weeds, was arrested and held without charge in Kilmainham with others like Dorothy Macardle, the Republic's future historian, Grace Plunkett, Nora Connolly, Mary MacSwiney, Lily O'Brennan, Kate O'Callaghan, Máire Comerford and Eithne Coyle – the last two had been fired on in prison for waving to comrades in the exercise yard and Máire was wounded in the leg.

All of them went on hunger strike, as did most of the men, at one time or another. On the nineteenth day of Mary MacSwiney's and Kate O'Callaghan's strike, it was decided that the other female prisoners should be moved to North Dublin Union, which had been converted into a jail to take the overflow, if necessary by force. The women prisoners of Kilmainham held a meeting; they were worried about Mary MacSwiney's and Kate O'Callaghan's physical condition and didn't want to leave them behind alone. They decided to resist the move unless Mary and Kate were released and eighty-one took up position on the top landing. Dorothy Macardle wrote that they gave themselves orders:

> We were to resist, but not to attack; we were not to come to one another's rescue; no missiles were to be thrown; above all for the patients' sake, whatever was done to us, no one must cry out. Then we knelt and said the Rosary . . . Then we stood up three deep, arms locked and sang, as we do every evening, some of Miss MacSwiney's favourite songs.

Ten minutes later an agitated matron came up the stairs, begging the girls to give in because the military police were coming for them: 'God pity you, girls,' she said, 'you are going into the hands of men worse than devils.'

It took five hours to get the girls into the lorries to take them away. They clung to railings as they were kicked, had their thumbs twisted and their heads punched. When some were prised off they were kicked about like footballs. There was some sexual abuse, one woman had her dress cut off and was subjected to 'great indignities'. The wardresses were in tears, but when one of them intervened she was cut across the face.

Kate O'Callaghan and Mary MacSwiney were released the next day.

The determination and ruthlessness which the government was prepared to use to restore order, the hostility of the Catholic hierarchy, the condemnation of reasonable men like AE – he had written a letter in the *Irish Times* on December 26, 1922, begging the republicans to give in – 'I do not like to think of you that the only service you can render Ireland is to shed blood on its behalf' – and the lack of support from ordinary people, broke the republicans' resistance. When, in

April 1923 the IRA Chief-of-Staff, Liam Lynch, was killed it was obvious that the end had come.

On May 24, de Valera sent a message to 'Soldiers of the Republic, Legion of the Rearguard!' in which he told them the Republic could no longer be successfully defended. 'Further sacrifice of life would now be in vain . . . Military victory must be allowed to rest for the moment with those who have destroyed the Republic.'

It cannot be said that hostilities ceased – the IRA had dumped its arms, not surrendered them – and among the most intransigent the war was never going to be over, but peace of a sort came in with a whimper.

Nearly 4,000 people had died, damage to property was in the region of £30 million and enough bitterness had been banked to last generations.

Seen from this distance the Cosgrave-O'Higgins administration is unlikeable, but it had many achievements, two of which were remarkable in the circumstances; in 1923 it set up an unarmed police force, the Garda Síochána (Civic Guard) and in August of that same troubled year, it held a general election. It didn't make life easy for the Sinn Féin republican candidates, many of whom were on the run and who, if they appeared on an election platform were arrested. De Valera was taken when he appeared to speak at Ennis in August and spent nearly a year in prison; nevertheless he was elected and so were forty-three others of his party. The government gained five more seats, bringing them up to sixty-three but Labour, thanks to its internal problems, had been reduced to fourteen.

Constance Markievicz was back in her old seat in an election which, if it proved anything, showed that the voting public still wanted peace but had not liked the price of getting it.

Since the republican deputies were still recognising only the second Dáil and were refusing to take their seats in the Dáil of the Free State, it did not make much difference to Con, although she worked hard for her constituency in everything but actual representation, and joined the Women's Prisoners' Defence League in their protestations against the still-overcrowded prisons.

In November 1923 she was arrested, and it is ironic that for this, her last period of imprisonment, all she had been doing was collecting signatures with Hanna Sheehy Skeffington for a petition to release the male and female hunger strikers and making speeches from a dray. 'Honour bright,' she wrote to Eva, 'I was engaged in no work that was not visible to the naked eye and all my activities were passivist and within the law.'

The Sinn Féin *Daily Sheet* protested at Con's internment and said that the only possible reason for it could be 'Madame's chief offence . . . the popularity she enjoys with her constituents'.

She was getting on to fifty-six years old and for her own honour, and to show sympathy with her fellow-prisoners, she had to face an ordeal she had most dreaded – a hunger strike. She did it with her usual courage and wrote to the worried Eva that it had been nothing at all.

> The worst part of it was looking forward to the possibility of having to do it. I did not suffer at all but just stayed in bed and dozed and tried to prepare myself to leave the world. I was perfectly happy and had no regrets. It is all very odd and I don't understand it but it was so. I just seemed to be sliding along in a happy sort of dream. When Derrick[1] came to me he woke me up with a jump and it was like coming to life again and I wanted to live and I wanted others to live. I am telling you this because . . . I want you to realise what it was to me, that for just one moment when I was making it imperative on me when telling the police of my decision, I had the sort of shrinking that one has before taking a header into a cold sea; just a want of faith in the unknown but that was all . . . And by the way it has cured my rheumatism for the moment.

In fact she didn't stay in bed; hunger-striking with her was a young girl from Sligo, Baby Bohan, who had refused food for thirty days but who lived to tell Anne Marreco many years later that nobody was a more tender and devoted nurse than Constance. She cooked for her, spent hours sitting on the sick girl's bed, supporting her with her own body to ease Baby's backache and, because it was so cold in the converted poorhouse of the North Dublin Union which was now their prison, put her mittens on the girl's shrunken hands.

In December all the women prisoners and many of the men were freed.

The girls helped each other out through the gates. 'We were flattened,' said Sheila Humphries, The O'Rahilly's niece. 'We felt the Irish public had forgotten us. The tinted trappings of our fight were hanging like rags about us.'

The feeling that they were forgotten was prophetic; the civil war had caused such pain and humiliation that the national consciousness was understandably beginning to wrap itself in a protective amnesia. What had probably not yet occurred to the women – although there

[1] This was probably Tom Derring who, with D. L. Robinson, had organised the men's hunger strike in Kilmainham but who, after the death of two of the strikers and the intervention of Cardinal Logue, decided that nothing could be gained by more deaths and was allowed to tour the camps and prisons with instructions to stop the fasting.

were already indications of it – was that the leaders on *both* sides, while attributing blame to each other, would also put some of it on them.

Chapter Seventeen

A different Terrible Beauty to the one hymned by W. B. Yeats was born in Ireland around the year 1916.

As the world turned upside down, a large section of Irishwomen, like women elsewhere, managed to shake loose from the structure that had held them in place. For a moment the two sexes were offered the chance of a new and maturer relationship.

Whatever sphere these women entered, whether they fought for the vote, the underprivileged, or their country, they displayed the capability for equality, for partnership rather than subservience. Above all, they showed they could hold down jobs just as well as men.

But they were challenging an order much older and more deep-seated than British rule, and they were defeated.

Irishwomen got a free country and they got the vote. But in 1937 they were also to get a new Constitution, framed for the most part by Eamon de Valera, which put them firmly back in their traditional role. It gave them an Orwellian 'some-are-more-equal-than-others' equality 'with due regard to capacity, physical and moral, and of social function'.

*Article 40.*1: All citizens shall, as human persons, be held equal before the law. This shall not be held to mean that the State shall not in its enactments have due regard to differences of capacity, physical and moral, and of social function.

*Article 41.2/*1: In particular, the State recognises that by her life within the home, woman gives to the State a support without which the common good cannot be achieved.

 2/2: The State shall, therefore, endeavour to ensure that mothers shall not be obliged by economic necessity to engage in labour to the neglect of their duties in the home.

*Article 45.4/*2: The State shall endeavour to ensure that the inadequate strength of women and the tender age of children shall not be abused, and that citizens shall not be forced by economic necessity to enter avocations unsuited to their sex, age or strength.

In other words, women should not neglect their household duties by going out to work. 'I do not care what women's organisations there are . . . I am going, as long as I live, to try and work for that,' said de Valera.

Dragged down by the inertia of other women and divided by the Treaty and party lines, the feminists were unable to fight it. In 1952, thirty years after Independence, there were fewer women in elected politics than in 1922, and their impact and effectiveness was undoubtedly less.

This is not to say that Irishmen were more virulently anti-feminist than others: they weren't. Britain's political record is hardly better. The syndrome was general in every country involved in the First World War and the reaction to it was the same; women's help was accepted during the emergency and rejected when it was over. Internationally the male establishment started trying to push back women into the Pandora's Box from which they had so unfortunately been allowed to escape.

But there is no denying that the lid of that box was shut tighter and locked more securely in Ireland and that feminists had a harder job – and still do – to dislodge it. Divorce, abortion and – until very recently – contraception have been denied them, which may sound fine to a world that is beginning to think it has had too much of all three, but their absence has given thousands of women, who would have liked a choice, no alternative to appalling personal tragedy.

Not until the 1970s did the Employment Equality Act make job restriction on married women illegal – until then women in the civil service, local authority and health board jobs had to resign on marriage. In the years between 1963 and 1973 only three women served on an Irish jury and the rules which held them back were only changed in 1975 by a Supreme Court in which no woman had ever sat as a judge, just as no woman had been a judge either in the High or Circuit Courts.

Several factors contributed to this lagging behind; a conservative rural society, a reactionary Catholic Church, a high level of unemployment and poverty, the peculiar grouping of parties brought about by the Treaty. But buried among these are glimpses of another reason; during the civil war Ireland felt itself wildly out of control, and there were elements which were prepared to blame that feeling on uncontrollable women.

'Wild' was the adjective that came increasingly into use, and it was used interchangeably to describe the suffrage leaders, the Labour women, Cumann na mBan and any other female that did not keep her mouth shut and caused a fuss. There is no doubt the republican women were the most vocal and the least prepared to compromise, but there's little doubt that they had more reason than men to fear – even if they did not articulate that fear – a repressive future if the republic did not transpire immediately. And they were right.

It was to be expected that Kevin O'Higgins would refer contemptuously during the civil war to 'hysterical young women who ought to be playing five-fingered exercises or helping their mother with the brasses', and that in 1924 P. S. O'Hegarty would write that during the civil war, 'Dublin was full of hysterical women,' and added:

> Left to himself, man is comparatively harmless. He will always exchange smokes and drinks and jokes with his enemy, and he will always pity the 'poor devil' and wish that the whole business was over . . . It is woman . . . with her implacability, her bitterness, her hysteria that makes a devil of him. The Suffragettes used to tell us that with women in political power there would be no more war. We know that with women in political power there would be no more peace.

What was less predictable – although perhaps it should not have been – was how quickly some men of their own side jumped on the bandwagon of condemnation once they began to lose.

A captured IRA man, John O'Dowd, for instance, wrote that he had no use for republican politicians who were 'using the fighting men as pawns' and lamented that 'de Valera and the wild women are hopeless'.

And Eamon de Valera himself, in a conversation as recently as 1976 with Jacqueline Van Voris – which gave Margaret Ward the title for her most excellent book – looked back over his career and said: 'Women are at once the boldest and most unmanageable revolutionaries.' Always a man to pick his words, the 'unmanageable' indicates the alarm he and other men felt at the new force displayed by women, the fear of loss of power, of control. No matter if the women were on their side, they were threatening a male fortress which had to endure beyond party politics – dominance. The women had the bit between their teeth and if it was not removed, God only knew where they would bolt to.

Well, the bit was removed, the dust died down, and Ireland settled into what Margaret Ward calls 'a conservative, inward-looking, rural society'. Frank O'Connor, indignant at the repressive censorship which overtook his country, put it more rudely:

> Irish society began to revert to type. All the forces that had made for national dignity, that had united Catholic and Protestant, aristocrats like Constance Markievicz, Labour revolutionists like Connolly and writers like AE, began to disintegrate rapidly, and Ireland became more than ever sectarian, utilitarian – the two nearly always go together – vulgar and provincial.

It did not suit post-war Ireland to inflame its female population with stories of the courage, capability and bloody-mindedness of women who fought in the Tan war and civil war and, with exceptions such as R. M. Fox's *Rebel Irishwomen* and Sean O'Faolain's biography of Constance, very little literature was devoted to them in the next thirty years, as if they had become something to be ashamed of. Either they were dismissed with a pat of thanks, or they became the Lady Macbeths of histories like O'Hegarty's. More often they disappeared altogether, as women who have not adhered to what men consider the norm are prone to do.

Rosemary Cullen Owens, in her book on the Irishwomen's suffrage movement, *Smashing Times*, quotes Hanna Sheehy Skeffington as saying that women historians would have to chronicle the fight for the vote, the Ladies' Land League, Cumann na mBan, etc., 'for men, least of all Irishmen, will never bother about it'. And it is only recently that any serious attempt – by women historians – has been made.

In the meantime Countess Markievicz became chief scapegoat of the scapegoats. She was, after all, a natural for the role, having embraced every cause with which the wild women concerned them-selves. Moreover she was easier to externalise and cast off than most because she was 'foreign', a member of the Oppressor class whose high voice accented Ireland into 'Ahland'; nor did her marriage and motherhood fit the desired pattern.

The real Constance disappeared and a join-the-dots picture in which only the points of her character most antipathetic to men, her voice, her hyperbole, her militancy, the breeches, the gun, became accepted as her real image.

Besides Sean O'Casey, Yeats did as much as anyone to fix this cartoon in the public mind, but again, it has been suggested, Con was the scapegoat for his beloved Maud Gonne and what he considered to be her ungracious decline from greatness when she refused to hang about in noble poses and rolled up her sleeves to cope with the issues of the day.

> Have I not seen the loveliest woman born
> Out of the mouth of Plenty's horn
> Because of her opinionated mind
> Barter that horn and every good
> By quiet natures understood
> For an old bellows full of angry wind?

Both of them qualify for his jibe: 'A Helen of social welfare dream/ Climbed on a wagonette to scream.' No matter that the wild women were appealing for justice and compassion for prisoners and the underprivileged.

And to return to the *canard* of Con shooting the unarmed policeman during the Rising, it is interesting that the man who actually *did* shoot such a one – the actor Seán Connolly when he and his Citizen Army men were trying to take Dublin Castle yard – gets a favourable mention from Yeats in his poem 'Three Songs to the One Burden'.

> Who was the first man shot that day?
> The player Connolly
> Close to the City Hall he died;
> Carriage and voice had he;
> He lacked those years that go with skill,
> But later might have been
> A famous, a brilliant figure
> Before the painted scene.

Seán Connolly, of course, expunged his guilt – if guilt it was – by dying on the same day as the policeman he shot; certainly no opprobrium for the killing seems to attach to his memory on the principle that war is hell and all's fair in it – unless, of course, you are a woman.

The trouble with all this fear-filled rubbish is that it is obscuring a figure history cannot spare, the first, and most able, woman politician in Britain and Ireland, a courageous soul and one of the nicest human beings God ever made.

Writing in 1965, Elizabeth Coxhead complained of the 'curious ambivalence' which underlay such lip-service as was paid to Constance Markievicz.

> Maud Gonne? [she asked ironically], Yes, she was so lovely and gracious you'd forgive her anything. But Constance Markievicz, no; hers is not the image of Irish womanhood we want to present to the outside world. The crude, charmless, virago-picture almost imposes itself – and then one meets one of her comrades in arms, . . . and it is like coming out of a dark tunnel into the strong, sweet air of her own west coast.

And as she moved towards her death through the hardest years of her life, the sweetness did not lessen, but grew.

The first and most important task from 1924 onwards was to try to rebuild the shattered republican morale. She bought herself a second-hand Remington portable typewriter and tapped out article after article on the glories of Easter Week – saying remarkably little about her own part in it – extolling republican ideals and castigating the Free State. She had published in 1923 *What Irish Republicans*

Stand For, now she brought out her *James Connolly's Policy and Catholic Doctrine*.

In April 1924 she rallied the Cumann na mBan with her presidential address at its annual convention, outlining a scheme of reorganisation, looking forward, not back. 'No one knows when we may be attacked again or when we may see our chance to strike again. Peace is beautiful and we want peace; but we cannot shirk the fight if it is the only way to win.'

Margaret Ward wrote: 'The Countess still possessed the unerring instinct she had shown during the 1921 Convention to strike the right note in strengthening the resolve of her members and giving them hope that they would eventually triumph.' Nevertheless, it was noticeable that she devoted a large part of her speech to unemployment and methods of providing work. This was vital. The long-term effects of the Tan war and the civil war, and the international economic climate had done disastrous damage to trade and industry; bankruptcies were on the increase, while such jobs as there were went to Free Staters. Allocation of grants to public bodies for work such as road improvement, for instance, was conditional on preferential employment to ex-soldiers of the Free State Army. Every person employed in local government and the civil service – which was where many Cumann na mBan found their employment – had to make a declaration of allegiance to the Free State Constitution.

Refusing to take it, republicans found themselves boycotted. Hanna Sheehy Skeffington lost her job as a teacher in a Dublin technical college, doctors were unable to return to their profession. Máire Comerford had to set up as a poultry farmer and tried to live on five shillings a week. Eithne Coyle went to help her sister in a boarding house. Others without even these resources were thrown back on accepting the charity of people like Maud Gonne and Charlotte Despard who were subsidising, out of what remained of their own money, workshops for women in their own home, Roebuck House.

> There is starvation on every side [Con wrote to Stanislas], not only among the very poor, but among people who were quite well off . . . All the small businesses here are heading for ruin, and the farmers are in a bad way. The list of bankrupts is something appalling. The list of highly paid officials for whom jobs are made by those at present in power is daily increasing. To meet these expenses the old-age pensioners have been docked 1s per week off their pensions, as well as their bag of coal per fortnight. Taxes are awful, food prices are daily rising and rents are wicked . . . If I saw any chance at all I would say, come over and look around . . . But just now you don't know what may happen. Anything might happen to me, for one thing. I am living in a friend's house, and personally have nothing to complain of as the money I have keeps me.

Even so, she could probably have afforded a place of her own on her allowance, but as she was busily giving it away to those who needed it more, she stayed on in her single room in the Coghlans' large Frankfort House happily enough. One of her friends in the slums had, like so many at that time, got into severe arrears with the rent and the family was in danger of being put on the streets. AE told O'Faolain that even in 1927, the year of her death,

> she got out a ring her mother had left her – one of the few possessions she had stuck to . . . She pawned or sold the ring and got £70 or £60 for it – it must have been a fine ring – and so cleared off the rent. She never lent money. She just gave it away, like that.

The clothes she wore were old and looked as if they had come from some jumble sale – there is a photograph of her looking nervously exhausted and clad in a lamentable cardigan, which seems to be stuffed with newspaper, hanging over her blouse and skirt.

It was in this state that Casi found her when he returned to Dublin in the summer of 1924. Sean O'Faolain rather doubtfully repeats a rumour that, as the marriage was so manifestly over, Casi had come to ask for a divorce but that 'when he saw and spoke to her, however, all his old affection, all his old respect, revived, and . . . he simply could not do it'. But since O'Faolain records that the visit took place in 1919, some time after Con's release from Holloway – Casi was in Eastern Europe then and could not possibly have made the trip – such evidence is shaky. Nevertheless, though they spent some affable evenings together exchanging histories and remembering old times, once that was done there was little they had to say to each other. Their home was gone and so was the Olympian Dublin of the Celtic Dawn. Such mutual friends as they still possessed were scattered or ruined. The new government had introduced a Public Safety Act which increased its powers of arrest and imprisonment without trial. There were floggings of prisoners. Because of its distinguished resident, Frankfort House was raided from time to time without result 'but I suppose they want to keep their hand in,' Con wrote bleakly to Eva. Very fondly husband and wife said goodbye to each other and Count Markievicz returned to Poland.

However, Casi had told her that he was managing to earn a small income and having some success in Warsaw by writing plays, and, perhaps inspired by that, Con also turned dramatist. In September 1924 she organised a Republican Players Dramatic Society to raise funds and within a year they produced a dozen plays, two of them by Con of which the titles *The Invincible Mother* and *Blood Money* reveal the republican message. To echo what she had once said of her Battle Hymn, they might not be good plays, but they *were* good propaganda.

She began turning up again at AE's At Homes, which were still surviving, and there, one evening, Mary Colum met her again and was shocked when she compared the woman before her with the one she had known in 'her vibrant maturity'.

> At that time . . . she would on occasions get herself up in a Paris frock and, when few others in Dublin used cosmetics, put powder and rouge on her face. A remark of hers to me when I was a young girl, I always remembered, for it had a real feminine vanity: 'I am not interested in men, for I have had the pick of too many men.' But now no trace of beauty remained; she was like an extinct volcano, her former violent self reduced to something burnt out . . . haggard and old, dressed in ancient demoded clothes . . . the familiar eyes that blinked at me from behind glasses bereft of the old fire and eagerness.

'Was she so ugly then?' I asked, during our interview, of Mrs Louie O'Brien, who was the middle child of the Coghlans' nine children, and still, in 1985, remembered vividly the years Constance Markievicz spent in her home. 'No,' said Mrs O'Brien promptly. 'She was beautiful. Not at all like Madame MacBride [Maud Gonne], her face – Madame Markievicz's – was thinner, and she didn't care what she wore, she wore any old thing, but she was beautiful.'

Her disregard of convention was a constant source of embarrassment to the Coghlan children. Her room at Frankfort House looked out over the Coghlans' garden and she had been unable to keep her green fingers off it, growing flowers, strawberries and raspberries, paying the Coghlan children one penny for every dozen snails they collected, and insisting that they go and collect manure from the road outside after horses had gone by. 'We felt it was so shameful,' said Louie. 'There were Protestants living all round us, and this reinforced the Irish peasant image, no matter it was a Countess who'd told us to do it.'

As she was once again beginning to tour the country to make speeches at by-elections, and there were so many strikes, she expended thirty pounds and bought herself an ancient Ford car which had a crank start and every so often fell to bits. It became the joke of Dublin, but Con loved it, driving it furiously, proudly proclaiming that it would go up long hills in top, and studied the 'Bible' of its manual so that she could do the repairs herself. The Coghlan children would blush for her, and themselves, when the Countess stripped off her skirt – she did not have so many skirts that she could afford to get one dirty – and slid under the car, wrench in hand, to perform another repair miracle, wearing just bloomers on her lower half. It was a habit which became so well known that a man who came on a driverless car on a lonely road, spotted the long, feminine legs and scarlet petticoat sticking out from underneath it and called out, 'Hello, Constance.' Sure enough, the Countess Markievicz, with grease-spotted nose, looked out at him.

She used the car to go out in the hills to do some painting – she'd returned to watercolours, as oils were too expensive. But more often than not the Tin Lizzie was full of young Fianna boys or Coghlans. '"Children," she'd say,' Louie O'Brien remembered, 'and we'd all scurry into the car and go to the hills or into Woolworth's while she went into Sinn Féin headquarters. She loved children.'

She was enormously busy. In June 1925, she was co-opted on to the Rathmines and Rathgar Urban District Council and was regularly at its meetings, as conscientious over the problem of whether pigs should be kept within 100 feet of a dwelling, as she was in trying to prevent anti-republican discrimination in jobs. The meetings were frequently stormy as Con fought for public swimming baths, for facilities for the poor, the sick, the young and the old. She must have felt sometimes that she was the working classes' only champion. In one of her letters to Stanislas, she complained about the Larkin–O'Brien split: 'Both parties are more concerned with fighting each other and trying to ruin each other than in helping the workers.'

Much of her time was spent on the Fianna which, like Cumann na mBan, needed reorganising. Sensibly, the new emphasis was away from gun practice and towards physical training and education, with lessons in Gaelic, literature, history, archaeology, art, music, games, botany, first aid and woodcraft; naturally drilling and signalling were included, but the drilling called down the wrath of the Free State Government, which regarded any movement that retained Countess Markievicz as its Chief Scout with suspicion.

She had been hoping to start the Clan Maeve – the female equivalent of the Fianna scouts – in Ireland, and had actually done so in Scotland during her speaking tour there in 1923, but conditions at home were against the founding of a new nationalist youth organisation; the government was doing its best to suppress the original.

In December 1925, under the new Treasonable Offences Act, twelve Fianna boys were arrested in Wexford on the charge that they 'did assemble together for the purposes of being trained and drilled'. One, a fifteen-year-old, was released but the others were brought to trial two months later.

Con was furious. The Fianna had helped Ireland gain her independence and it was the supreme betrayal of that achievement that

266

Baden-Powell's Boy Scouts were allowed to use public grounds to drill in, as well as being allowed revolver and musketry practice, while her beloved Fianna were not. She went down to Wexford to appear as a witness in the trial.

When she was sworn, she added to the conventional oath: 'I will swear the truth on my allegiance to the Irish Republic.' The judge remarked to her: 'You must act with propriety.' The Chief Scout replied: 'I always behave with propriety, for I am a most proper person, I assure your honour.' You can almost see her winking at the public gallery packed with hooting and applauding Fianna. The defence case rested on the submission that the boys had merely been drilling to get ready for the march to Liam Mellowes' grave on December 13, and that if everyone who marched in a funeral procession was arrestable under the Treasonable Offences Act, the prisons would not be big enough to hold them. The jury returned a verdict of 'Not Guilty' and the Chief Scout and her boys emerged from the court amid shouts of 'Up the Republic' and 'Up de Valera'. But those were not to be the last Fianna Scouts arrested.

The year 1925 showed that the tide was very slowly turning in favour of the republican Sinn Féin. They had won two by-election seats from the government's pro-Treaty party Cumann na nGaedheal, and now had forty-eight elected deputies who still absented themselves from the Dáil, recognising a *de jure* Republic and Dáil which did not exist *de facto*. They had their own government and cabinet but it was making no impact on public affairs, and increasingly making them appear like children playing house. They had lost control of the IRA which, at that year's convention, adopted a constitution which in effect made it independent of the toy republican government.

Nothing in that year of 1925 demonstrated their powerlessness more clearly than the result of the Boundary Commission in November. This had been set up under the Treaty to decide on the border between Ulster and the South, and both Michael Collins and Arthur Griffith had been sure – and assured – that it would lead to the eventual unification of Ireland by making the Northern Ireland territory non-viable, since plebiscites would establish that the majority of inhabitants in Tyrone and Fermanagh, as well as smaller parts of Derry – including the city of Londonderry itself – South Down and South Armagh would wish to be included with their fellow nationalists in the Free State. But Collins and Griffith were dead. With their attention distracted by their troubles in the twenty-six counties, the Cosgrave–O'Higgins administration put its faith in the Commissioner who was to represent their interest in the deliberations with a British and a Northern Ireland appointee; this was Professor Eoin MacNeill, the man Constance Markievicz had distrusted ever since he had cancelled the Volunteers' orders for the Easter Rising.

'He has changed his mind too many times,' she had told the Sinn Féin Ard Fheis in 1917, adding that it would not be safe for Sinn Féiners to trust their lives to such a man, only to be howled down by, among others, Eamon de Valera.

No plebiscite was held; instead during the summer of 1925 the Commission examined some thousand 'witnesses' out of a population of a million and a quarter. MacNeill allowed no intimation to reach his colleagues in the Free State Ministry on what lines the Boundary Commission's report was being prepared. Perhaps nothing that he could have done would have prevailed on Sir James Craig, the Prime Minister of Northern Ireland, to yield an inch of ground, but if there had been MacNeill was not the man to do it.

On November 7 the *Morning Post* carried a leaked report which said that the Boundary Commission's findings would give only strips of land in Fermanagh and Armagh to the Free State, while Ulster was to retain everything it held within its present boundary, with the addition of some rich land in the nationalist-dominated county of Donegal. There was immediate outcry in the South, though neither the Free Staters nor the republicans could believe it.

However, in what Robert Kee calls 'an embarrassingly late protest', MacNeill's resignation from the Commission confirmed the truth of what the *Morning Post* had said.

Had she felt like it, Con would have been justified in saying 'I told you so', but, like the rest of Ireland, she was too distressed to want to.

In fact, the Boundary Commission report was never published nor implemented. Cosgrave, O'Higgins and others went to London and negotiated an amendment to the Treaty in which the old border remained *in situ* in return for a revocation of payments which the Treaty had laid down should be paid by the Free State to Britain.

So one of the greatest hopes which Collins, Griffith and the others had held when they signed the Treaty had come to nothing, the nationalists in Tyrone, Fermanagh, Derry, South Down and South Armagh inevitably felt they had been sold, and nationalists, North and South, refused to reconcile themselves to the fact that Northern Ireland was a separate country – and still do. The basis for the indissoluble problem had been laid.

The abstaining republican deputies were in no position to do anything. They sent out a bat's squeak of protest:

In the name of the Irish nation and the Irish race, in the name of all who have stood, and will stand unflinchingly for the Sovereign Independence of Ireland, we, the duly elected representatives of the Irish people, by our names appended hereto, proclaim and record our unalterable opposition to the partitioning of our country.

But the disaster of confirmed partition underlined how weak their position was. They could rail until they were black in the face that the Cosgrave administration was a usurper, but it was ruling and – the matter of Northern Ireland apart – was doing so effectively. True, the polls were showing a swing towards republican Sinn Féin, but it was unlikely that even the most sympathetic electors would continue that trend; as time went on they would want constituency members who could protect and help them in the legislative clinches. Sinn Féin were having to cut back on activities and staff through lack of funds and the publication *Sinn Féin* was virtually their only voice to the outside world. They were going round and round in a maze of their own making. The only way out meant breaking their own rules and blundering through their own carefully-constructed hedges.

The IRA virtually disregarded them, but even if it did not they were in no position to use it – one civil war was enough for anybody's lifetime.

Apart from recognising the Dáil of the Free State by the very act of entering it, to re-enter mainstream politics involved facing the fact that, in order to go into the Dáil at all, they must take the oath of allegiance to the British Crown. With the deviousness of a great political mind, de Valera decided to ignore the first obstacle and concentrate his opposition on the second: the oath.

At the Sinn Féin Ard Fheis in March 1926, he moved the resolution: 'That once the admission oath of the Twenty-Six-County and Six-County assemblies is removed, it becomes a question not of principle but of policy whether or not Republican representatives should attend these assemblies.'

Immediately there was what Con called 'an unholy row'. There were wild scenes as Father O'Flanagan opposed de Valera with an amendment saying that it was incompatible with the fundamental principles of Sinn Féin 'to send representatives into any usurping legislature set up by English law in Ireland'.

De Valera's motion was defeated by 223 votes to 218.

Con had voted *for* it. She wrote to Eva:

Dev, I say like a wise man, has announced that he will go into the Free State Parliament if there is no oath . . . I myself have always said that the oath made it absolutely impossible for an honourable person who was a republican to go in, and that if it were removed it would then be simply a question of policy with no principle involved whether we went in or stayed out . . . Some unlogical persons are howling.

> They stand for principle and for the honour of the Republic and prefer to do nothing but shout continually 'The Republic Lives'.

She knew the Republic did not live and that it had no chance of living until the Free State and its Treaty could be dismantled piece by piece from within its own constitutional interior.

The civil war had matured her; if glory was to be achieved, it would have to be by the ballot box, by constitutional opposition and debate. For her, the day of the gun had disappeared into the darkness that had killed Liam Mellowes, Cathal Brugha and Erskine Childers and sprinkled Ireland so lavishly with the graves of other Irishmen shot by Irishmen.

When in May 1926 de Valera broke with the extreme Republicans and formed the more moderate party, Fianna Fáil, Con joined it too.

'She was not a great political leader,' said the *Irish Times* seven years after her death, and through the process of denigration this has now become debased into the modern opinion I have heard expressed that she was a mere follower, dominated by male ideas, and that she stumbled blindly into Fianna Fáil out of her admiration for de Valera.

In the sense that she did not lead men then she was not a great political leader – very few women in the world's history have achieved such a position, and certainly not in Ireland. Constance Markievicz did not particularly want to lead anybody; she mistrusted power – 'I don't believe in leaders myself,' she said more than once – and in her prison letters found comfort in the incarceration of herself and other rebel figures because it would give people the chance to think of themselves. She wrote:

> If they would only learn to watch and heckle their leaders, aye, and distrust them, fear them even more than their opponents . . . but, alas, it's always their impulse to get behind some idol, let him do all the thinking for them and then be surprised when he leads them all wrong.

But there is a world of difference between not wanting to lead and blindly following. The only thing Con ever followed was her own conscience, and it took courage to allow it to lead her away from the safety of family and caste. Her ability bobbed her up on to the executive of every organisation she ever joined, and in the forming of the Fianna and raising the morale of an entire generation of Irish children she displayed a brilliant originality. The admiration she expressed for James Connolly and Eamon de Valera sprang out of her conviction – and relief – that she had found instruments who would bring into being her own ideals. The fact that de Valera eventually betrayed nearly every feminist principle she held was one of her very few errors

270

of judgment but she can be forgiven for not suspecting a man who at that time was making all the right noises.

It has proved difficult for Constance's biographers to show her thought processes through her own words; Sean O'Faolain solved the matter by coming to the general conclusion that she didn't have any, that she was a creature of instinct.

Con was a propagandist, not an apologist, but she took the banality out of her platitudes about honour, truth, idealism, Ireland, by believing them and, better still, living them. Yeats begged:

> God guard me from those thoughts men think
> In the mind alone;
> He that sings a lasting song
> Thinks in a marrow-bone.

Con thought in the marrow-bone and the depth of subtlety of that process shows not so much in her song, as in her actions in upholding every organisation reflecting her ideals of nationalism, socialism and feminism and then in trying to weave them together; she took some feminism into Sinn Féin at a time when it had none and at the same time influenced it towards republicanism, she wove feminism and the working class together by bringing suffragettes into the kitchens of Liberty Hall during the lock-out and by her unvarying support for women workers, and by her activity for the Fianna and the Citizen Army she urged the working class into nationalism.

Perhaps the most difficult decision of all was the one she took at the end of her life to join Fianna Fáil. Again she left her action to speak for her reasoning, but it was through reason and not as an acolyte to de Valera that she made it. She had been involved in the new policy from the first. As far back as January she had written to Stanislas that she was very busy because she was in the midst of 'the re-adjustment of all our political activities'. Nor was it a decision she could take lightly because to do it meant leaving her beloved Cumann na mBan – membership of Fianna Fáil contravened the constitution of Cumann na mBan – with which she had worked closely ever since its inception and of which she had been the president for ten years. 'Madame was no fool,' said Eithne Coyle, '... she had more than average intelligence to realise all the implications involved.'

It was because she did indeed realise all the implications that she left Cumann na mBan for Fianna Fáil; the day of physical force revolution was finished. Men, women and children of her constituency were starving and she was doing nothing for them by staying out in the political wilderness waving a green flag. Once the oath of allegiance was removed she could go into the Dáil and shout for them, untie Ireland from Britain and begin the long job of building Connolly's Republic.

It hurt her to do it, probably no other action in her life hurt her more, but also no other political action demonstrated the clarity of her foresight.

By staying in the political wilderness Cumann na mBan – and the IRA – may have retained their high republican purity, but increasingly it was the purity of a lake made sterile by acid rain. They continued to shadow box with a disappearing British foe and failed to confront the real enemy on their doorstep. 1931, for instance, was to find Cumann na mBan boycotting British sweets and mounting a campaign to 'Buy Irish', without being able to fight for the higher wages that would enable people to do so. And in the 1937 debate on the anti-feminism in de Valera's constitution, Cumann na mBan's voice was silent; it was preoccupied with protests against the celebration of George VI's coronation.

Nevertheless, the severance between Con and Cumann na mBan was dreadful for both. 'It nearly broke our hearts to lose her,' said Sheila Humphries. 'We did not even want to accept her resignation which, under our constitution, we were obliged to do. Alas, nobody won her.'

As for Con, she decided she must not look back. She made a gesture towards her new life by keeping up with new trends and having her hair bobbed. 'I don't see why old women should not be as comfortable as young,' she wrote to Stanislas and added that during the winter she had been wearing the red leather boots made for her all those years ago when she had first met him in Poland. 'And they are the smartest pair in Dublin.' But she sounded lonely as she ended, 'I'd love to see you again . . . Now goodbye, dearest boy, and do take care of your health. You know you were rather delicate as a kid. I wish I could look after you and spoil you for a while. Your loving mother.'

She was at least making up for lost time with Maeve whom she now saw fairly regularly. 'Maeve spent a day here on her way to Sligo and helped me pull the car to pieces. She loves machinery and is very clever at it. She is very tall and pretty and full of life and charm.' And on another occasion: 'Maeve blew in on her way to Sligo and commandeered the car. I love the queer little musical instrument she has and the way she has of lilting it to all sorts of silly little songs . . .'

She met her mother whenever Lady Gore-Booth came to Dublin, but she never saw her brother, Josslyn, 'and never want to', she told

Stanislas in a rare display of inner feeling. A friend, she said, had gone to Sligo to get Joss when she had been condemned to death after Easter Week (presumably to ask him to use his contacts in an effort to prevent his sister being shot, as Eva was frantically doing) '. . . but he would not come up. I have seen him once since . . . They are no worse than anyone else, and I suppose it's very embarrassing to have a relation that gets into jail and fights in revolutions that you are not in sympathy with.' Nevertheless, she said, Eva 'is the only real relation I have left'.

But on June 30, 1926, after Con had been strangely depressed for some days, she received a telegram from Esther Roper to say that Eva had died after a short illness.

Everything went from under Con. She didn't go to the funeral. She told Eithne Coyle: 'I simply cannot face the family.' In fact, she was ill. In her last letter to Eva she had written: 'It is such an age since I saw you, and that beastly Channel and the long, long journey costs such a lot and I never have any time or money somehow.'

A few days after, she had a collision in her car which just missed being a serious accident but 'I just had an extraordinary feeling that Eva was there and that it was all right.'

A while later she went to London to see Eva's grave and sat quietly in Eva's room and talked to Esther about the time when she had been in prison in Aylesbury and the two sisters had tried to get in touch every evening through telepathy.

And I got to her and could tell how she sat in the window and I seemed to know what she was thinking. It was a great joy and comfort to me. When I got out I lost this in the bustle and hurry of life, but now, just the last few days, I seem to get in touch again.

Before she returned to Dublin she told a friend that she hated leaving Esther, who had been Eva's spiritual sister: 'I feel so glad Eva and she were together and so thankful that her love was with Eva to the end.'

Esther thought Con had looked very ill, but she denied there was anything wrong with her, although during the winter she had told Stanislas that she had been 'very sick' and then, in the next breath, assured him her health was now wonderful.

Hanna Sheehy Skeffington and other close friends were concerned that she looked so tired, but she refused to slow down and threw herself into work for the Fianna, the Republican Players Dramatic Society, Fianna Fáil and her constituents. Geraldine Plunkett Dillon, taking some baby clothes to the St Ultan's orphanage run by Dr

Kathleen Lynn, discovered the Countess down on her knees, scrubbing its floor.

In January 1927 Lady Gore-Booth died. Con worked harder than ever. It was an appalling winter, poverty was on the increase, and there was a fuel shortage. Occasionally, one of Con's rich friends sent up turf from Kerry, or Con would drive out into the mountains to collect some, and then distribute it around the neediest in the slums, lugging the bags up the tenement steps on her back. One day after a delivery she returned to her car to find the little boy who had been left to guard it in tears because people had been taking the turf and he had been unable to stop them. 'It's all right, Sammy,' said Con. 'It's for them. If they didn't need it they wouldn't take it.'

She temporarily adopted a family which lived in one room, when the mother and children caught influenza, nursing them and cooking breakfast before the father went to work, until his wife was back on her feet again.

'She seemed perfectly happy,' Louie O'Brien said, remembering that there were still cries of 'Children' and trips out in the rattletrap car. But a friend entering her room at Frankfort House one evening found her sitting quietly, watching the rain outside, with tears running down her cheeks.

There was to be a general election in June 1927 so the spring was spent in the usual round of campaigning, driving from meeting to meeting to make speech after speech. She was still capable of being naughty and occasionally took her dog Shuler – Poppet had gone to his last kennel – with her when she wanted to heckle an opponent, encouraging him to howl during the speeches. But it was as if she was operating on some reservoir of energy stored in another time and now running out.

One day, just before the election, she was cranking the rattletrap when the starting handle slipped and broke her lower arm. While it was being set, all she said was: 'Glory be, it's not my jaw, I can still talk.'

Considering how new a party it was, Fianna Fáil did well, winning forty-four seats. The Government Party, Cumann na nGaedheal, had been reduced to forty-six and, had its opponents wanted to form a coalition, which was not envisaged, it could have found itself threatened.

On June 23, on the opening day of the Dáil's new session, the republican deputies walked up Kildare Street to Leinster House, where the Parliament had established itself, armed with counsel's opinion that they were at least legally entitled to go inside. A photograph of the group as they approached the gates includes Con, still wearing a sling and looking elegant for once, though very thin, with a cloche hat framing her face.

Before they could go into the chamber they were stopped by the Clerk of the Dáil and were told they could not enter unless they took the oath, 'a little formality'; after an argument, which they lost, they had to leave, and the doors of the Dáil were locked against them. They returned to Fianna Fáil headquarters in O'Connell Street and de Valera issued another statement pledging 'that as long as they were representatives of the people they would never take an oath of allegiance to a foreign king'. He talked of plans for its removal, amendments, referenda.

But beneath all the nobility of principle and elaborate manoeuvring lay stony facts. Had they gone to the electorate as an effective party prepared to take its place in the Dáil, they could have won more seats. In the Dáil they had a better chance of abolishing the oath than out of it. And, above all, at any moment some emergency could arise which would *force* them to go in, oath or not. Such an emergency was about to take place.

On July 10, Kevin O'Higgins, the Deputy Prime Minister, was assassinated returning to his home in Blackrock after Mass.[1] Almost immediately a fearful Free State Government introduced another Public Safety Act of such severity that it threatened civil liberties. Even more dangerously, as far as Fianna Fáil was concerned, it brought in electoral amendments which would disqualify a candidate from even standing unless he or she agreed to take the oath of allegiance. Either de Valera threw in his hand, reverted to civil war, or he was wiped out as a political force. He threw in his hand.

Con was no fool. She knew that sooner or later she would have to face the decision. Take the oath, or throw her trusting constituents to the wolves. But only the year before, at a meeting in Sligo when she had been reunited with Baby Bohan, now recovered from the hunger strike, she had told her: 'How could I ever meet Paddy Pearse or Jim Connolly in the hereafter if I took an oath to a British king?'

The way Eamon de Valera resolved the dilemma warrants his description by F. S. L. Lyons as 'the constitutional Houdini of his generation'. In August he returned to the Dáil, picked up the Bible which was lying by the book containing the oath and carried it to the far side of the room. He then went back to the book, covered the oath with some papers and signed his name. 'I want you to understand that I am not taking any oath

---

[1] The three men who shot him were IRA but, according to Peader O'Donnell, who had then been on the IRA executive, interviewed in the *Irish Times* on October 7, 1985, they were acting against orders so as to create an incident which 'would bring about a confrontation'.

nor giving any promise of faithfulness to the King of England or to any power outside the people of Ireland,' he told the Clerk in Irish.

But by then Constance Markievicz had solved the problem for herself by dying.

She did not have the sleight of mind with which de Valera could shuffle principles and sworn commitments around until they were stacked to his satisfaction. Her idea of honour would have baulked at trickery like covering up the oath with paper, however enabling it might have been. It would have killed her anyway, so she died before she had to, at the age of fifty-nine.

What was physically wrong with her is not quite clear. Elizabeth Coxhead said she had cancer, an opinion Louie O'Brien rejects because, she said, Con had seemed so fit until nearly the end. The doctors who operated on her said it was appendicitis, although almost immediately they had to perform a second operation.

Whatever it was, it is difficult to believe that Con's determination could not have overcome it if her old love of life had still been there, but it had been weakened by the civil war, the violent death of too many people and too many hopes, the loss of her sister and the brutality of political necessity. It may have been easier to suspend the will to live and leave a constitution, weakened by incessant smoking, unending activity and too much imprisonment, unable to fend for itself.

Early in July she attended a Fianna executive. A colleague noticed that she seemed unwell and suggested he take her home, but 'she was a peculiar woman. She'd sit a meeting out even if she dropped dead.' He whispered to the chairman to cut the agenda short, and then accompanied her back to Frankfort House in a tram. Dr Kathleen Lynn was called at once, looked at her and asked: 'What hospital do you want to go to?' 'The cheapest,' said Con. 'I'm a pauper.'

She was put in the general ward of Sir Patrick Dun's Hospital. The first operation seemed to be straightforward, but suddenly there came the announcement of another for peritonitis. An emergency radio message was broadcast for her family to come at once. In London Esther Roper, and in Warsaw Casi and Stanislas, set out at once. Maeve was already by her mother's side.

The moment Esther approached the screened-off bed she knew there was no hope, but Con was as brave and alert as ever. 'You know,' she told Esther, 'Eva has been by my side ever since I came in here, and now you are on the other I am quite happy.'

Esther felt Con's surroundings were too hard and asked why she had not mentioned the operation so that they could have found her a good nursing home, but Con said that if it was good enough for ordinary Dubliners it was good enough for her.

There were six others in the ward, Esther noticed. 'They looked poor as well as suffering ... they would hardly speak lest they should disturb her.' An old lady who was being discharged popped her head round the screen: 'Please God I'll see you again in Dublin, but if not there, in Heaven, Madame dear.' The Matron told Esther she could stay because they did not expect the Countess to live out the night.

The hospital's board room had been given over to a group of Con's friends to keep a vigil, Dr Lynn, Helena Moloney, Máire Perolz, May Coghlan. Sheila Humphries had arrived in a pink Paris dress because Con liked to look at pretty things. Outside in the rain a bigger crowd kept another vigil as the Dubliners prayed.

Con survived the night; it is thought she was struggling to wait for Casi and Stanislas. When they eventually arrived, with a box of roses, she said: 'This is the happiest day of my life.' She refused to let Esther open the box for her and did it herself 'though her weak hands shook as she opened it', and took out a card with an inscription from them. 'Look,' she said, 'don't they know how to do things?'

Esther went out into Dublin on some errands for Con to find that the whole city seemed to know who she was and what was happening. 'People I had never seen came up to me to ask about her, men, women and children.' One woman wept as she said: 'She thinks what's good enough for us is good enough for her. Please God she'll get better.' The tram conductor handing Esther her ticket asked anxiously: 'Will she get better, do you think?'

True to his promise to her when she had been under sentence of death in Kilmainham, Father Ryan was with Con at the end.

On the last day she said: 'But it is so beautiful to have had all this love and kindness before I go.'

She died in the early hours of July 15.

'It was as though joyous martial music had been suddenly silenced,' said Dorothy Macardle.

The Free State refused permission for Con's body to lie in state at either the City Hall or the Mansion House, so it was taken to the Rotunda, not civic property, and it was estimated that 100,000 people filed past the coffin as the Fianna stood guard over it.

Even Dublin had never seen a bigger funeral. Although flowers were expensive, there were eight lorry-loads of them; among them was a nest of three fresh eggs which a countrywoman had promised Con in hospital, thinking she would live, and wanted her to have anyway. Seven bands, contingents from Sinn Féin, the Fianna, all the women's organisations and unions, the ITGWU, Fianna Fáil and

277

Citizen Army marched through streets lined with enormous crowds. 'A champion was passing,' said Nora Connolly.

Due to the emergency caused by the assassination of O'Higgins, the Free State was harassed by the fear that such a vast demonstration of affection might turn into violence, and so detectives followed Con to her grave as they had followed her for so much of her life.

De Valera was a pall bearer and spoke the oration at Glasnevin cemetery, but there was no volley as they lowered the coffin, covered by her Citizen Army uniform, into the grave; the Free State had sent one hundred soldiers with rifles to make sure that Countess Markievicz was accorded no such honour.

EPILOGUE

On a summer's day in 1985 two friends and I made the lovely drive from Dublin north-west across Ireland to Constance's childhood home, Lissadell in County Sligo.

If we hadn't known better, we might have thought that Bord Fáilte (the Irish Tourist Board) had conspired with the many authors of novels in which the Big House symbolised the social decay of the Ascendancy class in Ireland, and had created an amalgam of them in all their dilapidation at Lissadell – weed-choked drive, diminished acreage, crumbling masonry were there in perfect representation. The house and its family have fallen on bad times.

The Gore-Booths, however, do not lack courage. Constance's remaining niece, Miss Aideen Gore-Booth, was giving a party of Irish schoolchildren a guided tour which, having paid our one pound each, we joined. Noticing our late arrival, Miss Gore-Booth welcomed us: 'I have three rules,' she said in the high, upper-class English accent which might have been Constance's. 'Please keep together, don't touch anything and enjoy yourselves,' in one breath summarising what her ancestors had told the native Irish since the time of Elizabeth I.

Sublimely ignoring the cracks in the walls, the mould on the painting in the hall, Miss Aideen showed us the china which had been made to celebrate the Act of Union in 1800, the figures Casi had painted, the Sarah Purser portrait of Con and Eva as children, the whale-killing implements acquired by Sir Henry, the address of gratitude to Sir Robert from his tenants for keeping them alive through a famine. There were some photos of Con and the odd relic of Eva, but when the two girls in silk kimonos fled from the evening light of Lissadell they took their spirit with them, for none of it remains.

When the tour was over my friends and I stood in the doorway and watched the children, released from good manners, get on their bicycles and ride off whistling and shouting towards the shore. It was just a house they left, interesting, but not too much, that somebody had built in another age. It was not necessary and it did not occur to them that they should even shake its dust off their trainers. They were

279

nice children, and why should they say 'the hell with it'? But they didn't have to; a daughter of the house had done all that on their behalf a long time ago.

GLOSSARY

Bean na hÉireann (*Woman of Ireland*): journal of the Inghínidhe na hÉireann.

Citizen Army: *see* Irish Citizen Army.

Cumann na mBan (*Irishwomen's Association*): set up in 1914 as a ladies' auxiliary to the Irish Volunteers; later the female wing of the IRA.

DMP Dublin Metropolitan Police, the British-controlled, Irish-manned, unarmed police force in Dublin city.

Fenians: derived from Fianna, the name of the old warrior caste of heroic Ireland, adopted for the nationalist movement renewed in the 1850s by the Irish Republican Brotherhood.

Inghínidhe na hÉireann (*Daughters of Ireland*): the nationalist women's group founded by Maud Gonne in 1900.

Irish Citizen Army: founded by Jim Larkin and James Connolly in 1913 as the 'fighting arm of the workers', later to combine with the Irish Volunteers in the Irish Republican Army.

Irish Party or Irish Parliamentary Party: the constitutional Home Rule movement led by the Irish MPs in the British House of Commons.

IRA (*Irish Republican Army*): officially declared on the day of the Easter Rising in 1916 and combining the Irish Citizen Army and the Irish Volunteers. Split by the civil war in 1922 over the Treaty, part of it became the Army of the Irish Free State.

IRB (*Irish Republican Brotherhood*): the secret nationalist organisation founded in 1858 which was behind Irish rising against the British and was revived to organise the Easter Rising of 1916 which finally led to independence.

ITGWU (*Irish Transport and General Workers' Union*): founded in 1908 by Jim Larkin; the most influential union in the Irish Labour movement.

Irish Volunteers: the nationalist military force founded by Eoin MacNeill in 1913 to offset the rise in the North of the Protestant, anti-Home Rule Ulster Volunteers.

IWFL (*Irish Women's Franchise League*): founded in 1908 by Hanna Sheehy Skeffington; the Irish counterpart of the Pankhursts' militant Women's Social and Political Union (WSPU) in England.

IWSLGA (*Irish Women's Suffrage and Local Government Association*).

RIC (*Royal Irish Constabulary*): the British-controlled armed police force which operated in all areas outside Dublin.

TD (*Teachta Dála*): Member of Dáil Éireann (Teachtaí Dála pl.)

Volunteers: *see* Irish Volunteers.

WPDL (*Women's Prisoners' Defence League*).

WSPU (*Women's Social and Political Union*).

NOTES ON SOURCES

PREFACE

11   Sean O'Faolain: *Constance Markievicz*, Jonathan Cape, 1934.

11   Ulick O'Connor: *A Terrible Beauty is Born*, Hamish Hamilton, 1975.

12   Male establishment setting standards: Dale Spender, *Women of Ideas*, Routledge and Kegan Paul, 1982.

12   *Women on the Warpath:* by David Mitchell, Jonathan Cape, 1966.

12   Sean O'Casey: *Drums Under the Window*, Macmillan, 1963.

13   Gill's *Irish Lives: Eamon de Valera*, T. Ryle Dwyer, Gill and Macmillan, 1980.

13   Robert Kee: *The Green Flag* (vol. 2), Weidenfeld and Nicolson, 1972.

13   Dale Spender: *op. cit.*

CHAPTER ONE

15   Liberty Hall encounter: recounted by William O'Brien in his introduction to James Connolly's *Labour and Easter Week*, Dublin, 1949.

15   Nora Connolly: *The Unbroken Tradition*, New York, 1918.

17   Elizabethan attitudes to the Irish: Edmund Spenser, *View of the State of Ireland*, 1595.

19   A. J. P. Taylor: *Essays in English History*, Penguin, 1976.

21   Lissadell stud groom's son's memories: cited by Jacqueline Van Voris in *Constance de Markievicz*, University of Massachusetts Press, 1967.

22   Mr E. Rowlette: quoted by Sean O'Faolain, *op. cit.*

22   W. B. Yeats in Lissadell: 'On a Political Prisoner', *Collected Poems of W. B. Yeats*, Macmillan, 1933.

25   Con dressing up as a beggar: cited by Anne Marreco in *The Rebel Countess*, Weidenfeld and Nicolson, 1967.

25   Young officer of the Royal Dublin Fusiliers: General Sir Alexander Godley, *Life of an Irish Soldier*, London, 1939.

25   Con reciting Schiller, Heine and Goethe: cited by Anne Marreco, *op. cit.*

26   Con's diaries: cited by Anne Marreco, *op. cit.*

27   'When one old woman complained . . .': Jacqueline Van Voris, *op. cit.*

27   Lady Fingall on Con's London season: Elizabeth, Countess of Fingall, *Seventy Years Young*, London, 1937.

27   Con's Dublin season: *ibid.*

28   'Eva seems heaps better . . .': Con's diary.

28   'If I could only cut the family tie . . .': *ibid.*

30   'She dressed beautifully . . .': Katharine Tynan, *Twenty-five Years: Reminiscences*, London, 1913.

30   Elizabeth Coxhead: *Daughters of Erin*, Colin Smythe, 1979.

31   County Sligo branch of the Irish Women's Suffrage and Local Government Association: see Rosemary Cullen Owens, *Smashing Times*, Attic Press, 1984.

31   Drumcliffe public meeting: Jacqueline Van Voris, *op. cit.*

32   Yeats at Lissadell: *Letters of W. B. Yeats*, ed. Allan Wade, Rupert Hart-Davis, 1954; and *Collected Poems* of W. B. Yeats, *op. cit.*.

CHAPTER TWO

36 Sean O'Faolain: *op. cit.*
36 Rumours about the relationship between Con and Casi: see Esther Roper, Introduction to *Prison Letters of Constance Markievicz*, Longmans, Green and Co, 1934. In her Introduction Esther gives a short biography of Constance and many revealing insights into her character.
36 'He fills me with the desire to do things': quoted by Anne Marreco, *op. cit.*
38 Maeve's reaction to Constance: Elizabeth Coxhead, *op. cit.*
39 Maud Gonne to Stanislas: quoted by Anne Marreco, *op. cit.*

CHAPTER THREE

44 'Did that play of mine . . .': 'The Man and the Echo', *Collected Poems, op. cit.*
44 Being prepared 'to go out to shoot and be shot': sentiment quoted by F. S. L. Lyons, in *Ireland Since the Famine*, Weidenfeld and Nicolson, 1971.
44 William Rooney: *Prose Writings*, Dublin, 1909.
44 Smoking and drinking according to Griffith: cited by P. S. O'Hegarty, *A History of Ireland Under the Union*, London, 1952.
45 Padraic Colum: *The Irish Rebellion of 1916 and its Martyrs*, Devin-Adair, New York, 1916.
47 Page Dickinson: *The Dublin of Yesterday*, London, 1929.
47 Sean O'Faolain: *op. cit.*
48 Padraic Colum: *op. cit.*
48 Con to Arthur Griffith: *Éire*, August 18, 1923.
49 Maud Gonne and Inghínidhe na hÉireann: Maud Gonne MacBride, *A Servant of the Queen*, 1938; reissued by Boydell Press, 1983.
49 Priest on the fate of Irish girls: Father Guinan, quoted by J. J. Lee in an essay, 'Women and the Church since the Famine' in *Women in Irish Society*, ed. Margaret MacCurtain, Arlen House, Dublin, 1978.
50 Irish marriage statistics: Report on the Commission on Emigration and other Population Problems, 1948–54, Dublin, 1954.
50 Ulster linen manufacture earnings: from F. S. L. Lyons, *op. cit.*
51 Arthur Griffith: in *The United Irishman*, October 10, 1903.
53 Sidney Gifford: Sidney Gifford Czira ('John Brennan'), *The Years Flew By*, Gifford and Craven, 1974.
53 Helena Moloney: quoted by Elizabeth Coxhead, *op. cit.*

CHAPTER FOUR

54 Dr Mary Gordon: Preface to *Letters of Constance Lytton*, ed. Betty Balfour, Heinemann, 1925.
56 Lancashire machinist on Eva Gore-Booth: quoted by Jill Liddington and Jill Norris in *One Hand Tied Behind Us*, Virago, 1978.
56 Sylvia Pankhurst on Christabel and Eva: Sylvia Pankhurst, *The Suffragette Movement*, Virago, 1977.
58 Frank Skeffington arguing about pacifism: incident cited by Conor Cruise O'Brien in *States of Ireland*, Hutchinson, 1972.
58 Hanna Sheehy Skeffington: *Reminiscences of an Irish Suffragette*, Dublin, 1975.
59 John Dillon against women's suffrage: quoted by Hanna Sheehy Skeffington, *ibid.*

CHAPTER FIVE

64   Fianna Éireann as model for Zionist youth organisation: Robert Briscoe, *For the Life of Me*, London, 1958.

64   Baden-Powell Scout movement in Ireland: Padraic Colum, *op. cit.*

65   Bulmer Hobson and Con: Bulmer Hobson, *Ireland Yesterday and Tomorrow*, Anvil Books, 1968.

67   The Fianna commune in Raheny and Casi's homecoming: Sean O'Faolain, *op. cit.*

69   'English' scouts and Fianna: Padraic Colum, *op. cit.*

69   *Fianna Handbook*: Dublin, 1914.

70   Dr Brighid Lyons Thornton: quoted in *Curious Journey*, by Kenneth Griffith and Timothy E. O'Grady, Hutchinson, 1982.

70   Margaret Skinnider: *Doing My Bit for Ireland*, New York, 1917.

71   Organising the Fianna: recounted by Desmond Fitzgerald to Anne Marreco, *op. cit.*

72   Dr Patrick McCartan to John Devoy: quote in *The IRA* by Tim Pat Coogan, Pall Mall Press, 1970.

73   The IRB and the Fianna: Bulmer Hobson, *op. cit.*

73   Women members of the IRB: Diarmuid Lynch, *The IRB and the 1916 Insurrection*, Cork, 1957.

CHAPTER SIX

75   Desmond Ryan: *Remembering Sion*, London, 1934.

76   Sinn Féin meeting and the royal visit: recorded in a memorandum by Dr McCartan, now in the National Library of Ireland.

76   Griffith, The O'Rahilly and the royal visit: this and other recollections of the royal visit were recorded by Con for *Éire* in different 1923 editions.

78   The Beresford Street demonstration: Esther Roper, *op. cit.*

79   Dublin housing conditions: Terence Brown, *Ireland, a Social and Cultural History, 1922–79*. Fontana, 1981.

79   Ash Street housing conditions: Margaret Skinnider, *op. cit.*

79   James Connolly: Desmond Ryan, *James Connolly: his Life, Work and Writing*, Talbot, Dublin, 1924.

80   Con giving away the shirt on her back: recounted by Anne Marreco, *op. cit.*

80   'The ladies' paper that all young men read': its own description of itself.

81   An enabling bill for Ireland: Maud Gonne, *Irish Review*, December 1911.

82   School canteens and help from 'notorious women': Margaret Ward, *Unmanageable Revolutionaries*, Pluto Press, 1983.

82   Hanna Sheehy Skeffington at Belfast demonstration: R. M. Fox, *Rebel Irishwomen*, Talbot Press, 1935.

82   Churchill's use of troops for strike-breaking: Professor R. K. Webb, *Modern England*, Allen and Unwin, 1969.

83–4   Con and Jim Larkin: quoted in *Éire*, June 16, 1923.

85   'Whips on the shoulders of those unsexed viragoes . . .': *Belfast Evening Telegraph*, July 8, 1912.

85   'Women were hunted like rats . . .': Katharine Tynan, *op. cit.*

86   Payment of agricultural workers in 1913: F. S. L. Lyons, *op. cit.*

86   William Murphy's employment methods: Anne Marreco, *op. cit.*

87   Keir Hardie: quoted in *Freeman's Journal*, September 4, 1913.

87   Casi's homecoming: Padraic Colum, *op. cit.*

87–8   The scene at O'Connell Street: Sean O'Casey, *op. cit.*

89   Con on the events at O'Connell Street: Esther Roper, *op. cit.*

89   Lenin and the Irish troubles: *Marx, Engels, Lenin on the Irish Revolution*, 1932.

90   '. . . she continued until the struggle was over': Padraic Colum, *op. cit.*

90   Harry Gosling's memories of Con: Anne Marreco, *op. cit.*

91   Sean O'Casey and the 'myth' of Countess Markievicz: Sean O'Casey, *op. cit.*

91–2 'O'Casey seemed to stumble into movements . . .': James Simmons, *Sean O'Casey*, Macmillan Modern Dramatists Series, 1983.

93   Dr Walsh's letter to the *Freeman's Journal*: quoted by Emmet Larkin in *James Larkin*, Routledge and Kegan Paul, 1965.

93   Little boy in soup kitchen: Hanna Sheehy Skeffington, *An Phoblacht*, April 14, 1928.

93   Written undertaking by transport workers: *Irish Times*, February 3, 1914.

93–4 James Connolly: *Forward*, February 7, 1914.

94   '. . . never seen her fondling a book . . .': Sean O'Casey, *op. cit.*

95   Con over-borrowing on her securities and being barred from the Dublin Repertory Theatre: Anne Marreco, *op. cit.*

CHAPTER SEVEN

96   '. . . a member of a dominant race': Lecky, *History of Ireland in the Eighteenth Century*, Longman, 1892.

96   'The pigment proved soluble in the religious wash': Emmet Larkin, *op. cit.*

100 Jim Larkin and the formation of the Irish Citizen Army: *The Story of the Irish Citizen Army*, Ó Cathasaigh (Sean O'Casey), 1919.

100 Sir Roger Casement's telegram: R. M. Fox, *James Connolly*, *op. cit.*

102 Eoin MacNeill to O'Casey: *The Story of the Irish Citizen Army*, *op. cit.*

102 O'Casey and Con's attitude to Volunteers: *ibid.*

102 Captain White's life saved by Con: Sean O'Faolain, *op. cit.*

104 Irish MP to party member: J. J. Horgan, *Parnell to Pearse*, Dublin, 1948.

104 '. . . warmest appreciation of Labour was a sneer': *The Story of the Irish Citizen Army, op cit.*

105 'A young boy with a new toy': *Drums Under the Window, op cit.*

105 '. . . Labour Hercules leaning on his club' and O'Casey's motion to Citizen Army Council: *Drums Under the Window. op cit.*

106 '. . . O'Casey versus Larkin': Frank Robbins, quoted by Jacqueline Van Voris, *op. cit.*

106 'A disgruntled fellow called O'Casey': Tom Clarke in a letter to John Devoy, leader of the extreme nationalist group, Clan na Gael, in the United States.

CHAPTER EIGHT

108 Unloading Volunteer arms at Howth: Nora Connolly, *Portrait of a Rebel Father*, Dublin, 1935.

110 Connolly girls and the Howth guns: Nora Connolly, *The Unbroken Tradition*, *op. cit.*

110 Guns from the British Army: *The Making of 1916*, ed. Kevin B. Nowlan, Stationery Office, Dublin, 1969.

111 Ina Connolly and the Howth guns: from 'James Connolly – A Biography' by Ina Connolly Heron, in *Liberty*, the journal of the ITGWU, August 1966.

112 Con on women in national movements: *The Irish Citizen*, October 23, 1915.

112–3 John Redmond's speech at Volunteer parade: S. L. Gwynn, *John Redmond's Last Years*, Edward Arnold, 1919.

115 Carson and help from 'a powerful continental monarch': *The Irish Churchman*, November 14, 1913.

116   Con's debate with Francis Sheehy Skeffington: R. M. Fox, *Louie Bennett: Her Life and Times*, Talbot Press, Dublin, 1958.

116–7   'He was pro-peace, she for a longer war . . .': Hanna Sheehy Skeffington, *op. cit.*

117   The incident with the remembrance poppy: Sean O'Faolain, *op. cit.*

CHAPTER NINE

118   'The tenement houses of Dublin . . .': *Patrick Pearse: Political Writings and Speeches*, Dublin, 1962.

119   '. . . the power that an intrepid failure has to rouse Ireland': Esther Roper, *op. cit.*

120   'Mother could only light a fire at night time': Nora Connolly, quoted in *Survivors*, ed. Uinseann Mac Eoin, Argenta, 1980.

120   Connolly and indifference of workers and union officials: *The Story of the Irish Citizen Army, op. cit.*

122   Con's salon: Padraic Colum, *op. cit.*, Hanna Sheehy Skeffington, *op. cit.*, Sean O'Faolain, *op. cit.*

123   '. . . I'd go through twice as much to pull it down': Jacqueline Van Voris, *op. cit.*

123   'We rejoined the police outside': *ibid.*

123   Connolly's disappearance: Desmond Ryan, *The Rising. The Complete Story of Easter Week*, Dublin, 1949.

124   Drawing plans of army barracks: Margaret Skinnider, *op. cit.*

125   Nora Connolly and the barracks plans: *Portrait of a Rebel Father, op. cit.*

125   'There never was an Irish rising . . .': Margaret Skinnider, *op. cit.*

125   Con wearing a skirt over uniform breeches: Anne Marreco, *op. cit.*

125   'She was lovely in uniform . . .': Jacqueline Van Voris, *op. cit.*

126–7   Nora Connolly overheard the conversation: *Portrait of a Rebel Father, op. cit.*

127   Con's overdraft: Jacqueline Van Voris, *op. cit.*

127   Connolly's speech on guerrilla warfare: Nora Connolly, quoted in *Survivors, op. cit.*

128   'Only one questioned it': quoted by R. M. Fox in *Rebel Irishwomen, op. cit.*

128   Hanna Sheehy Skeffington as part of proposed civil provisional government: Margaret Ward, *op. cit.*

128   Con as 'ghost' for Connolly: Esther Roper, *op. cit.*

129   Making the flag: recorded by Maura O'Neill Mackey in MS 18,463 National Library of Ireland.

131   Raiding Sinn Féin arsenals and rounding up leaders: 1916 Royal Commission on the Rebellion in Ireland. Minutes of Evidence.

131   Con in Liberty Hall with Connolly and MacDermott: Constance Markievicz, 'A Memory', *Éire*, May 26, 1923.

132   Con said goodbye to Tom Clarke: *ibid.*

132   Connolly's conversation with O'Brien: quoted by Desmond Ryan in his Introduction to Connolly's *Labour in Easter Week*, op. cit.

CHAPTER TEN

134   Elizabeth Bowen: *The Shelbourne*, Harrap, 1951.

135   One observer: Stephen McKenna, quoted by Desmond Ryan in *The Rising, op. cit.*

136   'Poor lad . . .': Volunteer quoted by Desmond Ryan, *ibid.*

136 British military presence in Dublin, Easter 1916: figures from The Royal Commission on the Rebellion in Ireland, *op. cit.*

136 '. . . large force of rebels intended to attack Portobello Barracks . . .': Captain Bowen-Colthurst to the Simon Report during the enquiry into the murder of Francis Sheehy Skeffington.

136 Desmond Ryan at the GPO: *The Rising, op. cit.*

137 Eoin MacNeill: Desmond Ryan, *op. cit.*

138 'There were no soldiers in sight . . .': Margaret Skinnider, *op. cit.*

140 . . . Yelling encouragement: Máire Nic Shiubhlaigh, *The Splendid Years*, Duffy, Dublin, 1955.

141 Confirmation of the Rising to Wexford Volunteers: Robert Brennan, *Allegiance*, Dublin, 1950.

142 De Valera's admission to Hanna Sheehy Skeffington: Margaret Ward, *op. cit.*

142 Sheila Humphries: quoted in *Survivors, op. cit.*

142 'With frightening accuracy': Jacqueline Van Voris, *op. cit.*

142 'Not until a bullet entered . . .': Elizabeth Bowen, *op. cit.*

143 Threatened to court martial the man who shot him: Sean O'Faolain, *op. cit.*

144 'Look at them running . . .': Elizabeth Bowen, *op. cit.*

144 College of Surgeons rebels restricting passage of reinforcements from England: Kevin B. Nowlan, *op. cit.*

144 Connolly and use of artillery as portent of victory: quoted by Bob de Coeur in *Cuimhní Cinn* (Recollections) by Professor Liam Ó Briain, Sáirséal agus Dill, Dublin, 1951. Translated for me by Martin Sheridan.

145 Hanna Sheehy Skeffington and Commission of Enquiry into the death of her husband: Dorothy Macardle, *The Irish Republic*, Gollancz, 1937.

145 Queen Victoria's portrait and raid on house by Russell Hotel: Margaret Skinnider, *op. cit.*

146 The nightdress for Margaret Skinnider: Liam Ó Briain, *op. cit.*

146 The scene at the College of Surgeons: *ibid.*

146 Nora Connolly and reports of father's death: Anne Marreco, *op. cit.*

147 The Cumann na mBan's role at the GPO: Desmond Ryan, *The Rising*, 1949.

147 'To save the men from slaughter . . .': Desmond Ryan, *The Rising, op. cit.*

147–8 Elizabeth O'Farrell's surrender negotiations: Margaret Ward, *op. cit.*

148 Dr Kathleen Lynn's surrender negotiations: *ibid.*

148 Brigadier-General Lowe asking for Con: Anne Marreco, *op. cit.*

148 Con's last night at the College: Esther Roper, *op. cit.*

149 'Almost all the women started crying . . .': Liam Ó Briain, *op. cit.*

150 Easter Rising casualty figures: from Breandán MacGiolla Choille's 'Intelligence Notes', Dublin, 1966.

CHAPTER ELEVEN

151 Bulmer Hobson and Patrick Pearse: Bulmer Hobson *op. cit.*

151 James Stephens: *The Insurrection in Dublin*, Dublin, 1916.

153 The 'evil influence of Countess Markievicz': *Belfast Evening Telegraph*, May 8, 1916.

153 The priest attending his execution: *Capuchin Annual*, 1942.

154 One Irishwoman: Elizabeth, Countess of Fingall, *op. cit.*

154 Dillon's speech: Hansard, 5th series, vol. 82, cols. 935–51.

155 F. S. L. Lyons: *op. cit.*

155 James Connolly's farewell to his wife: Nora Connolly, *The Unbroken Tradition, op. cit.*

155 Seán MacDermott's letter: *Capuchin Annual*, 1966.
155 Lord Powerscourt . . . was begging the authorities to shoot her: Anne Marreco, *op. cit.*
155–6 Evidence of the University Club page boy: in the Schedule of the Court Martial.
156 The accusations against her: Schedule of the Court Martial of Constance Georgina Markievicz, signed by J. G. Maxwell, Convening Officer, and C. J. Blackrader, Brig.-General, President, 4th Day of May, 1916. MS 10,580, National Library of Ireland.
156 'I went out to fight for Ireland's freedom . . .': in the Schedule of the Court Martial.
157 The visit of Eva and Esther Roper: Esther Roper, *op. cit.* All letters written by Con from prison are quoted from *Prison Letters of Constance Markievicz* by Esther Roper.
159 'A beautiful leather dressing-case . . .': *ibid.*
159 'For hours we tramped . . .': *ibid.*
160 Grace Plunkett: R. M. Fox, *Rebel Irishwomen*, *op. cit.*
162 Speculation as to whether Connolly and Con had been lovers: Anne Marreco, *op. cit.* Anne Marreco concludes that they were not.
163–4 'The dinners were served . . .': *New Ireland*, April 15, 1822.
164 May Sharpe's memoirs: *Chicago May, Her Story*, 1930.
164–5 Con and Mrs Wheldon: Esther Roper, *op. cit.*
166 The interview between Con and the Duchess of St Albans: Sean O'Faolain, *op. cit.*
166–7 Prison Governor's report of Eva's visit to Con : Anne Marreco, *op. cit.*
167 Father McMahon's instructions to Con: Hanna Sheehy Skeffington, 'Constance Markievicz in 1916', *An Phoblacht*, April 14, 1928.
168 'On a Political Prisoner': W. B. Yeats, *Collected Poems*, *op. cit.*
169 'A foreign parliament . . .': *Irish Independent*, February 3, 1917.
170 Arthur Griffith and the Rising: *Leaders and Men of the Easter Rising*, Dublin, 1916, ed. F. X. Martin, London, 1967.
170 Michael Collins and Arthur Griffith having 'fierce rows': Seán Ó Lúing, *I Die in a Good Cause*, Dublin, 1970.

CHAPTER TWELVE
172 Con's return to Dublin: Esther Roper, *op. cit.*
174 Michael Collins: Rex Taylor, *Michael Collins*, Hutchinson, 1958.
174 Cumann na mBan policy statement: Margaret Ward, *op. cit.*
175 Connolly on the transfer of British capitalism to Irish capitalism: 'Workshop Talks', *Workers' Republic*, 1899.
175 Helena Moloney on the Liberty Hall roof: Margaret Ward, *op. cit.*
176 Lynch defending half the murderers in Clare and being related to the other half: David Fitzpatrick, 'The Undoing of the Easter Rising' in *De Valera and His Times*, ed. J. P. O'Carroll and J. A. Murphy, Cork University Press, 1983.
176 'To that government . . . I offered my allegiance . . .': Earl of Longford and T. P. O'Neill, *Eamon de Valera*, Hutchinson, 1970.
177 'No one is preaching rebellion': Esther Roper, *op. cit.*
177 Volunteers 'the best protection . . .': Eamon de Valera, *Irish Independent*, July 16, 1917.
177 Con's conversation with Liddy and Brown: letter dated September 26, 1917, Esther Roper, *op. cit.*

178   'Dr K.L. . . . thinks . . .': *ibid.*
178   Film of Volunteers firing over Ashe's grave: Robert Kee, *op. cit.*
179   Punctuated 'by deafening roars of applause': private letter from Stanislas Markievicz, quoted by Anne Marreco, *op. cit.*
179   Hanna Sheehy Skeffington on Con's unworldliness: Esther Roper, *op. cit.*
179   ITGWU giving Con funds: Anne Marreco, *op. cit.*
181   'Collins thinks he's a big fellow': Frank O'Connor, *The Big Fellow*, Poolbeg Press, 1979.
181   The meeting between Griffith and de Valera: Lord Longford and T. P. O'Neill, *op. cit.*
182   Cathal Brugha's appointment to Chief-of-Staff of Volunteers: *Irish Independent*, October 26, 1917.
182   'It was regrettable to notice so few women delegates': *Irish Citizen*, November 1917.
182–3   Jim Larkin's writings: quoted by Emmet Larkin, *op. cit.*
183   A committee of Irish bishops: Dorothy Macardle, *op. cit.*
184   The women's slogan and prior right to work: Margaret Ward, *op. cit.*
184   A 'German conspiracy' would be sufficient for America: Sheila Lawlor, *Britain and Ireland, 1914–23*, Gill and Macmillan, 1983.
185   Darrell Figgis: *Recollections of the Irish War*, Doubleday, New York.
185   Con to Eva: Esther Roper, *op. cit.*
185   Eva and Esther Roper: *ibid.*
186   Maud Gonne's arrest: Anne Marreco, *op. cit.*
186   Kathleen Clarke and Con: Elizabeth Coxhead, *op. cit.*
186   Con's letters from internment in Holloway: Esther Roper, *op. cit.*
187   Hanna Sheehy Skeffington in America: *Hanna Sheehy Skeffington, Impressions of Sinn Féin in America*, Dublin, 1919.
188   Sinn Féin and women parliamentary candidates: *The Founding of Dáil Éireann*, Brian Farrell, Gill and Macmillan, 1971.
188   Sinn Féin election pamphlet: 'An appeal to the women in Ireland', Dublin, 1918.
188   *Irish Citizen*: December 1918.
189   Irish Labour movement in the general election: Dorothy Macardle, *op. cit.*
190   Men . . . had to make their way and support their families: Elizabeth Vallance, *Women in the House*, Athlone Press, 1979.
190   Not 'a fit and proper place for any respectable woman . . .': remark by the Conservative Member for Portsmouth, Sir Hedworth Meux.

CHAPTER THIRTEEN
191   The announcement of Sinn Féin victories in the general election: David Hogan (Frank Gallagher), *Four Glorious Years*, Irish Press, 1953.
191   'Under the new dispensation . . .': *Irish Citizen*, April 1919.
192   Elizabeth Vallance: *op. cit.*
194   P. S. O'Hegarty: *op. cit.*
195   Ambush on the cart of explosives: Dan Breen, *My Fight for Irish Freedom*, Talbot Press, 1924.
195   Seán Treacy: Desmond Ryan, *Seán Treacy and the Third Tipperary Brigade*, Tralee, 1945.
196   Collins to Stack: National Library of Ireland, MS 5848.
197   Con's reception in Dublin: Esther Roper, *op. cit.*
197   Authorities' preparation for Easter Week, 1919: H. W. Nevinson, *Last Changes, Last Chances*, London, 1928.

198 'To make good this rightful claim . . .': Dorothy Macardle, *op. cit.*
198 '. . . no clash between his interests . . .': *Watchword of Labour*, September 27, 1919.
198 Con's explanation of her Cabinet appointment: Elizabeth Coxhead, *op. cit.*

CHAPTER FOURTEEN
200 Robert Kee: *op. cit.*
201-2 De Valera 'was highly intelligent . . .': Raymond James Raymond, 'De Valera, Lemass and Irish Economic Development, 1933–48' in *De Valera and His Times*, *op. cit.*
202 Report of the American Commission on Irish Independence: Treaty of Peace with Germany. Hearing before the Committee on Foreign Relations, United States Senate, Sixty-sixth Congress, Washington, 1919.
203 Con's letter to colleague: Cabinet Papers, Dáil Éireann, State Paper Office, Dublin.
204 The rosary-bead factory arbitration: R. M. Fox, *Louie Bennett*, *op. cit.*, and Sean O'Faolain, *op. cit.*
204 De Valera's speech to the Dáil: Dáil Éireann, Minutes of Proceedings, April 10, 1919.
205 Con in court: Jacqueline Van Voris, *op. cit.*
205 Con's letters to Eva from Cork Prison: Esther Roper, *op. cit.*
206 '. . . all that turnout for one lone woman': quoted by Nora Connolly in 'In Jail with Madame de Markievicz', *Irish Citizen*, September 1919.
207 'We're fighting for the working class . . .': Jacqueline Van Voris, *op. cit.*
208 Ellen Wilkinson: Dr Edith Summerskill recalls Ellen Wilkinson's remark in her book, *A Woman's World*, London, 1967.
208 Sean O'Faolain: *op. cit.*
208-9 Con and William Norman Ewer: Desmond Ryan, *Remembering Sion*, *op. cit.*
209 'I spoke five times . . .': Esther Roper, *op. cit.*
209 The Chief Commissioner's directive: quoted by Anne Marreco, *op. cit.*
210 'When civilians are seen approaching . . .': Jeremiah Mee interviewed by Anne Marreco, *op. cit.*
210 'Dignified bearing and direct . . . manner': *ibid.*
210-11 Con escaping raids on her office: *ibid.*
211 Constables in khaki trousers: *Freeman's Journal*, April 16, 1920.
211 The Black and Tans: F. S. L. Lyons, *op. cit.*
212 'I have just received . . . a Death notice . . .': Esther Roper, *op. cit.*
212 Eva's audience with the Pope: Anne Marreco, *op. cit.*
212-13 Frank Robbins on Con's disguise: *ibid.*
213 Nora Connolly: *The Unbroken Tradition. op. cit.*
213 'Dragon-ridden' days: W. B. Yeats, 'Nineteen Hundred and Nineteen'. *Collected Poems*, *op. cit.*
215 'Night after night they wake people up . . .': Esther Roper, *op. cit.*
215 Jeremiah Mee: quoted in Anne Marreco, *op. cit.*
215 Maurice Bourgeois: Robert Brennan, *op. cit.*
216 It would be better not to govern it at all: H. A. L. Fisher, President of the Board of Education, to Lloyd George, November 16, 1920, quoted by Sheila Lawlor, *op. cit.*
217 Avoiding bringing in 260,000 Roman Catholics: *Hansard*, May 18, 1920.
217 The death of Terence MacSwiney: Ulick O'Connor, *op. cit.*
217 Shooting innocent officer in Gresham Hotel: Rex Taylor, *op. cit.*

217 '. . I got in first' (Collins): quoted by F. S. L. Lyons, *op. cit.*

218 Collins found evidence that his men had been beaten up: Frank O'Connor, *op. cit.*

218 'Disastrous to the government's whole policy in Ireland': Sheila Lawlor, *Britain and Ireland, 1914–23*, Gill and Macmillan, 1983.

219 Cathal Brugha had a gun in his pocket: Lord Longford and T. P. O'Neill, *op. cit.*

219 'If England can show any right . . .': Easter Message to the Irish People, April 1921.

220 'De Valera and Michael Collins have quarrelled . . .': Lord Riddell, *Intimate Diary of the Peace Conference and After, 1918–1923*, London, 1933.

220 '. . . eggs in one basket': quoted by Piaras Béaslaí, *Michael Collins*, Harrap, 1926.

221 Eithne Coyle's trial: Margaret Ward, *op. cit.*

221 The unforgettable summer of 1921: Elizabeth, Countess of Fingall, *op. cit.*

222 Mary MacSwiney warned of the precedent: Margaret Ward, *op. cit.*

CHAPTER FIFTEEN

224 Modern history lessons in Ireland: Maria McGuire, *To Take Arms*, Macmillan, 1973. Maria McGuire was a one-time member of the Provisional IRA, who later denounced its policies for their violence.

224 'The shock of success': Margaret O'Callaghan, *Irish Historical Studies*, April 10, 1985.

225 De Valera's belief that he was 'born to be king': Lord Longford and T. P. O'Neill, *op. cit.*

225 Lloyd George's negotiations with de Valera: T. Ryle Dwyer, *De Valera's Darkest Hour*, Mercier Press, Dublin, 1982.

226 'Either way, it will be wrong' (Collins): Lord Longford and T. P. O'Neill, *op. cit.*

226 Attitude 'of Griffith and Collins to women in politics:' *ibid.*

226 Collins' interpretation of de Valera's decision not to partake in the talks: Frank O'Connor, *op. cit.*

226 De Valera's reasons for not partaking in the talks: Lord Longford and T. P. O'Neill, *op. cit.*

227 'The complete text . . . will be submitted to Dublin . . .': *ibid.*

227 Eithne Coyle in Mountjoy: Anne Marreco, *op. cit.*

227 Con lending Eithne £5: Margaret Ward, *op. cit.*

228 'Woman the consumer . . .': *ibid.*

228 Con's letter on discrimination: *Irish Bulletin*, November 29, 1921.

228 Cumann na mBan Convention: Margaret Ward, *op. cit.*

228–9 Con to Eva: Esther Roper, *op. cit.*

229 Con to Casi: MS Letter, National Library of Ireland.

230 'Will anyone be satisfied at the bargain? . . .': Michael Collins writing to a friend, cited by Rex Taylor, *Michael Collins*, Hutchinson, 1958.

231 The Catholics of Northern Ireland 'thrown to the wolves': Dorothy Macardle, *op. cit.*

231–3 The Dáil debate on the Treaty: 'Official Report Debate on the Treaty between Great Britain and Ireland signed in London on December 6, 1921', Dublin Stationery Office, *ibid.*

233 Frank Gallagher: *The Anglo-Irish Treaty*, Hutchinson, 1965.

234 P. S. O'Hegarty: *op. cit.*

235 'Good enough to fight, good enough to vote': Esther Roper, *op. cit.*
237 Con describing US tour: *ibid.*
238 Con to Eva: *ibid.*
238–9   Con to Stanislas: Anne Marreco, *op. cit.*

CHAPTER SIXTEEN
240 Con to Eva: Esther Roper, *op. cit.*
240 Orangemen firing on Catholic Hospital and Lloyd George's reply in the Commons: Hansard, June 2, 1922; May 1, 1922.
240 Sir Henry Wilson: Sheila Lawlor, *op. cit.*
243 Collins' speech: reported by Dorothy Macardle, *op. cit.*
244 Arthur Griffith and Maud Gonne: Margaret Ward, *op. cit.*
244 De Valera and the Four Courts garrison: *Poblacht na hÉireann*, War News, No. 2, June 29, 1922.
245 Con and the Henry Street snipers' post: *The Sunday Press* (Manchester), October 30, 1960.
245 The death of Cathal Brugha: Dorothy Macardle, *op. cit.*
246 Máire Comerford: related to Uinseann MacEoin, *Survivors, op. cit.*
246 Cumann na mBan organising funerals: Margaret Ward, *op. cit.*
246 Michael Collins and Cathal Brugha: Rex Taylor, *op. cit.*
246 The death of Harry Boland: *ibid.*
246 News of Collins' death at Kilmainham Jail: *ibid.*
247 Kevin O'Higgins: Irish Free State, Dáil Debates. Vol X.
248 Eithne Coyle and the bishops: Margaret Ward, *op. cit.*
248 De Valera and the death of Childers: Lord Longford and T. P. O'Neill, *op. cit.*
248 De Valera and 'official' reprisals: *ibid.*
249 Erskine Childers forgiving his enemies: John N. Young, *Erskine H. Childers*, Colin Smythe, 1985.
249 Jeremiah Mee: told to Anne Marreco, *op. cit.*
249 De Valera's vision of Ireland: St Patrick's Day broadcast, quoted in *Irish Press*, March 18, 1943.
250 'Life for the poor is a calvary . . .': Constance de Markievicz, *James Connolly's Policy and Catholic Doctrine*, 1924. National Library of Ireland.
250 'The majority has no right to do wrong': Lord Longford and T. P. O'Neill, *op. cit.*
250–1   Jim Larkin's speeches and writings: Emmet Larkin, *op. cit.*
253 Con to Eva: Esther Roper, *op. cit.*
254 The wounding of Máire Comerford Margaret Ward, *op. cit.*
254 'God pity you, girls . . .': Margaret Ward, *op. cit.*
255 Con to Eva: Esther Roper, *op. cit.*
256 Tom Derring and the hunger strike: Dorothy Macardle, *op. cit.*
256 Con and Baby Bohan: Anne Marreco, *op. cit.*
256 Sheila Humphries: quoted in Margaret Ward, *op. cit.*

CHAPTER SEVENTEEN
259 'I do not care what women's organisations there are . . .': de Valera, quoted by Margaret Ward, *op. cit.*
259 The number of women in elective politics in 1952: Maurice Manning, 'Women in Irish National and Local Politics, 1922–77' in *Women in Irish Society*, ed. Margaret MacCurtain, *op. cit.*

260 P. S. O'Hegarty: *The Victory of Sinn Féin*, Talbot Press, 1924.

260 John O'Dowd: quoted by Sheila Lawlor, *op. cit.*

260 Frank O'Connor: 'The Future of Irish Literature', *Horizon*, January 1942.

261 Yeats and Con's image: Bonnie Kime Scott, *Joyce and Feminism*, Indiana University Press and Harvester Press, 1984.

261 'Have I not seen the loveliest woman born . . .': W. B. Yeats, 'Prayer for My Daughter', *Collected Poems*, *op. cit.*

261 'Helen of social welfare dream . . .': W. B. Yeats, 'Why Should Not Old Men Be Mad?', *ibid.*

262 Elizabeth Coxhead: *op. cit.*

263 Con's speech to Cumann na mBan: Margaret Ward, *op. cit.*

263 Declaration of allegiance to Free State Constitution: Conor Cruise O'Brien, *op. cit.*

263 Subsidising workshops for women: Margaret Ward, *op. cit.*

263 Con to Stanislas: letter in the Markievicz collection, National Library of Ireland.

264 AE told Sean O'Faolain: Sean O'Faolain, *op. cit.*

265 Con at AE's At Home: Mary Colum, *Life and the Dream*, New York, 1947.

265 Con's car repairs: Sean O'Faolain, *op. cit.*

267 The trial of the Fianna boys: Jacqueline Van Voris, *op. cit.*

268 Robert Kee: *op. cit.*

268 The protest of the Republican deputies: Longford and O'Neill, *op. cit.*

269 Con to Eva: Esther Roper, *op. cit.*

270 The *Irish Times*: June 16, 1934, on the publication of *Prison Letters*.

271 'God guard me from those thoughts men think . . .': W. B. Yeats, 'A Prayer for Old Age', *Collected Poems*, *op. cit.*

271 Eithne Coyle: quoted by Margaret Ward, *op. cit.*

272 Sheila Humphries: *ibid.*

272 Con and Maeve: Esther Roper, *op. cit.*

273 Getting in touch through telepathy: *ibid.*

275 Con to Baby Bohan: quoted by Anne Marreco, *op. cit.*

275 De Valera and the oath of allegiance: Lord Longford and T. P. O'Neill, *op. cit.*

276–7 Esther with Con in hospital; Esther Roper, *op. cit.*

BIBLIOGRAPHY

Books and Pamphlets
Balfour, Betty, ed., *Letters of Constance Lytton*, Heinemann, 1925
Béaslaí, Piaras, *Michael Collins and the Making of a New Ireland*, Harrap, 1926
Bell, J. Bowyer, *The Secret Army*, Anthony Blond, 1970
Bowen, Elizabeth, *The Shelbourne*, Harrap, 1951
Breen, Dan, *My Fight for Irish Freedom*, Talbot Press, 1924; Anvil Books, 1981
'Brennan, John', *see* Gifford Czira, Sidney
Brennan, Robert, *Allegiance*, Browne and Nolan, 1950
Briscoe, Robert, *For the Life of Me*, London, 1958
Brown, Terence, *Ireland, a Social and Cultural History*, Fontana, 1981
Caulfield, Max, *The Easter Rebellion*, Muller, 1965
Churchill, W. S., *The World Crisis: The Aftermath*, Butterworth, 1929
Colum, Mary, *Life and the Dream*, New York, 1947
Colum, Padraic, *The Irish Rebellion of 1916 and its Martyrs*, Devin-Adair, New York, 1916
Connolly, James, *Labour in Ireland*, Dublin and London, 1917
—*Labour and Easter Week*, Dublin, 1949
Connolly, Nora, *The Unbroken Tradition*, New York, 1918
—*Portrait of a Rebel Father*, Dublin, 1935
Coogan, Tim Pat, *Ireland Since the Rising*, Pall Mall Press, 1966
—*The IRA*, Pall Mall Press, 1970
Coxhead, Elizabeth, *The Daughters of Erin*, Colin Smythe, 1979
Currell, Melville, *Political Women*, Croome Helm, 1974
Delaney, Frank, *James Joyce's Odyssey*, Hodder and Stoughton, 1981
Dickinson, Page, *The Dublin of Yesterday*, London, 1929
Dwyer, T. Ryle, *Eamon de Valera*, Gill and Macmillan, 1980
—*Michael Collins and the Treaty*, Mercier Press, 1980
—*De Valera's Darkest Hour*, Mercier Press, 1982
Edwards, O. Dudley and Pyle, Edward, *1916: The Easter Rising*, Macgibbon and Kee, 1968
Edwards, Ruth Dudley, *James Connolly*, Gill and Macmillan, 1981
Ellis, Peter Beresford, *A History of the Irish Working Class*, Gollancz, 1972
Farrell, Brian, *The Founding of Dáil Éireann*, Gill and Macmillan, 1971
Fianna Handbook, Dublin, 1914
Figgis, Darrell, *Recollections of the Irish War*, Doubleday, New York, n.d.
Fingall, Elizabeth, Countess of, *Seventy Years Young*, London, 1937

Fox, R. M., *Rebel Irishwomen*, Talbot Press, 1935
—*James Connolly*, Dublin, 1946
—*Louie Bennett: Her Life and Times*, Talbot Press, 1958
Gallagher, Frank, *Four Glorious Years*, Irish Press, 1953
—*The Anglo-Irish Treaty*, Hutchinson, 1965
Garvin, Tom, *The Evolution of Irish Nationalist Politics*, Gill and Macmillan, 1981
Gifford Czira, Sidney, *The Years Flew By*, Gifford and Craven, 1974
Godley, General Sir Alexander, *Life of an Irish Soldier*, London, 1939
Gonne, Maud, *see* MacBride, Maud Gonne
Griffith, Kenneth and O'Grady, Timothy E., *Curious Journey*, Hutchinson, 1982
Gwynn, *John Redmond's Last Years*, Edward Arnold, 1919
Hobson, Bulmer, *Ireland Yesterday and Tomorrow*, Anvil Books, 1968
Horgan, J. J., *Parnell to Pearse*, Dublin, 1948
Hyde, Douglas, *The Revival of Irish Literature*, London, 1894
Keatinge, Patrick, *A Place Among the Nations*, Institute of Public Administration, Dublin, 1978
Kee, Robert, *The Green Flag* (3 vols.), Weidenfeld and Nicolson, 1972
Krzywoszewski, Stefan, *A Long Life*
Larkin, Emmet, *James Larkin*, Routledge and Kegan Paul, 1965
Lawlor, Sheila, *Britain and Ireland, 1914–23*, Gill and Macmillan, 1983
Lecky, *History of Ireland in the Eighteenth Century*, Longman, 1892
Liddington, Jill and Norris, Jill, *One Hand Tied Behind Us*, Virago, 1978
Longford, Earl of, *Peace by Ordeal*, Sidgwick and Jackson, 1972
Longford, Earl of, and O'Neill, T. P., *Eamon de Valera*, Hutchinson, 1970
Lynch, Diarmuid, *The IRB and the 1916 Insurrection*, Cork, 1957
Lyons, F. S. L., *Ireland Since the Famine*, Weidenfeld and Nicolson, 1971
Macardle, Dorothy, *The Irish Republic*, Gollancz, 1937
MacBride, Maud Gonne, *A Servant of the Queen*, Boydell Press, 1983
MacCurtain, Margaret, ed., *Women in Irish Society*, Arlen House, 1978
MacEoin, Uinseann, ed., *Survivors*, Argenta, 1980
Markievicz, Constance, *What Irish Republicans Stand For*, 1923 (Pamphlet)
—*James Connolly's Policy and Catholic Doctrine*, 1924 (Pamphlet)
Marreco, Anne, *The Rebel Countess*, Weidenfeld and Nicolson, 1967
Martin, F. X., ed., *Leaders and Men of the Easter Rising*, Dublin 1916; Methuen, 1967
McGuire, Maria, *To Take Arms*, Macmillan, 1973
Missing Pieces, Irish Feminist Information Publications Ltd., with Women's Community Press, 1983
Mitchell, David, *Women on the Warpath*, Jonathan Cape, 1966
Nevinson, H. W., *Last Changes, Last Chances*, London, 1928
Nic Shiubhlaigh, Máire, *The Splendid Years*, Duffy, Dublin, 1955
Nowlan, Kevin B., *The Making of 1916*, Stationery Office, Dublin, 1969
Ó Briain, Liam, *Cuimhní Cinn*, Sáirséal agus Dill, Dublin, 1951

O'Brien, Conor Cruise, *States of Ireland*, Hutchinson, 1972
O'Brien, Nora Connolly, *see* Connolly, Nora
O'Carroll, J. P., and Murphy, J. A., eds., *De Valera and His Times*, Cork University Press, 1983
O'Casey, Sean (S. Ó Cathasaigh), *The History of the Irish Citizen Army*, 1919, Journeyman Press, 1980
—*Drums Under the Window (Autobiographies)*, Macmillan, 1963
O'Connor, Frank, *The Big Fellow*, USA, 1937; Poolbeg Press, 1979
O'Connor, Ulick, *A Terrible Beauty is Born*, Hamish Hamilton, 1975
O'Faolain, Eileen, *Irish Sagas and Folk Tales*, Oxford University Press, 1954
O'Faolain, Sean, *Constance Markievicz*, Jonathan Cape, 1934
O'Hegarty, P. S., *The Victory of Sinn Féin*, Talbot Press, 1924
—*A History of Ireland Under the Union*, Methuen, 1952
Ó Luing, Seán, *I Die in a Good Cause*, Dublin, 1970
O'Malley, Ernie, *On Another Man's Wound*, Anvil Books, 1979
Owens, Rosemary Cullen, *Smashing Times*, Attic Press, 1984
Pankhurst, Sylvia, *The Suffragette Movement*, Virago, 1977
Patrick Pearse: Political Writings and Speeches, Dublin, 1962
Riddell, Lord, *Intimate Diary of the Peace Conference and After, 1918–1923*, London, 1933
Rooney, William, *Prose Writings*, Dublin, 1909
Roper, Esther, *Prison Letters of Constance Markievicz*, Longmans, Green and Co, 1934
Ryan, Desmond, *Remembering Sion*, London 1934
—*Seán Treacy and the Third Tipperary Brigade*, Tralee, 1945
—*The Rising. The Complete Story of Easter Week*, Dublin, 1949
—*James Connolly: his Life, Work and Writing*, Talbot, Dublin, 1924
Schleiger, Ronald, ed., *The Genres of the Irish Literary Revival*, Wolfhound Press, 1980
Scott, Bonnie Kime, *Joyce and Feminism*, Indiana University Press and Harvester Press, 1984
Sharpe, May, *Chicago May, Her Story*, Sampson Low, London, 1929
Sheehy, Michael, *Is Ireland Dying?*, Hollis and Carter, 1968
Simmons, James, *Sean O'Casey*, Macmillan Modern Dramatists Series, 1983
Skeffington, Hanna Sheehy, *Impressions of Sinn Féin in America*, Dublin, 1919
—*Reminiscences of an Irish Suffragette*, Dublin, 1975
Skinnider, Margaret, *Doing My Bit for Ireland*, New York, 1917
Spender, Dale, *Women of Ideas*, Routledge and Kegan Paul, 1982
Spenser, Edmund, *View of the State of Ireland*, 1595
Stephens, James, *The Insurrection in Dublin*, Dublin, 1916
Summerskill, Dr Edith, *A Woman's World*, London, 1967
Taylor, A. J. P., *Essays in English History*, Penguin, 1976
Taylor, Rex, *Michael Collins*, Hutchinson, 1958
Tynan, Katharine, *Twenty-five Years: Reminiscences*, London, 1913
Vallance, Elizabeth, *Women in the House*, Athlone Press, 1979
Van Voris, Jacqueline, *Constance de Markievicz*, University of Massachusetts Press, 1967

Ward, Margaret, *Unmanageable Revolutionaries*, Pluto Press, 1983
Webb, R. K., *Modern England*, Allen and Unwin, 1969
White, Terence de Vere, *Kevin O'Higgins*, Tralee, 1966
Yeats, W. B., *Collected Poems*, Macmillan, 1933
Yeats, W. B., *Letters of W. B. Yeats*, ed. Allan Wade, Rupert Hart-Davis,
    1954
Young, John N., *Erskine H. Childers*, Colin Smythe, 1985
Younger, Carlton, *Arthur Griffith*, Gill and Macmillan, 1981

Newspapers and Journals

An Phoblacht   *Irish Independent*
Belfast Evening Telegraph   *Irish Press*
Bean na hÉireann   *Irish Review*
Éire   *Irish Times*
Evening Telegraph   *Liberty*, the journal of the ITGWU
Forward   *New Ireland*
Freeman's Journal   *Poblacht na hÉireann*
Horizon   *Sligo Champion*
Irish Bulletin   *Sunday Press* (Manchester)
Irish Churchman   *United Irishman*
Irish Citizen   *Watchword of Labour*
Irish Historical Studies   *Workers' Republic*

Other Documents

Constance Markievicz papers, National Library of Ireland, Dublin
Cabinet Papers, Dáil Éireann, State Papers Office, Dublin
Dáil Éireann, Minutes of Proceedings
Irish Free State, Dáil Debates
Hansard
MacGiolla Choille, Breandán, 'Intelligence Notes', Dublin, 1966
Report on the Commission on Emigration and Other Population Problems,
    1948–54, Dublin, 1954
Royal Commission on the Rebellion on Ireland. Minutes of Evidence, 1916
Simon Report on the enquiry into the death of Francis Sheehy Skeffington
Sinn Féin Rebellion Handbook

INDEX

the Four Courts siege, 244–5
grief over death of colleagues, 249
and social issues, 250–3
*James Connolly's Policy and Catholic
Doctrine*, 251–2, 263
What Irish Republicans Stand For, 252,
  262–3
  re-elected (1923), 255
  arrest and hunger strike of, 255,
  256
  released, 256–7
  rebuilding of republican morale,
  262–3
  life in Dublin, 263–7
  a visit from Casi, 264
joins Fianna Fáil, 271–2
death of Eva, 273
last years of, 273–4
re-elected to Dáil, 274–5
illness, death and funeral of, 276–8
as artist, 25, 28, 40, 56
as mother, 38–40, 61, 163, 239, 272
principles of, 269–72
  and suffragette movement, 31–2,
  49, 57, 59, 62, 84, 112, 121, 191,
  235
  and Irish nationalism, 41, 252
  and Home Rule, 75
  and socialism, 41
  and Boer War, 35, 41
  and First World War, 115, 116–7
appearance of, 30–1, 35, 165, 265,
  274
image through history and biography,
  11–14, 261–2, 269
biographers' and historians'
  assessment of, 94–5, 138–40, 173,
  191, 197, 261, 271
and Eva Gore-Booth, 23–4, 272–3
and Maeve Markievicz, 38–9, 163,
  239, 272, 276
and O'Casey, 12–13, 90–2, 102,
  104–6
and Yeats, 22, 32–3, 161, 168, 187–8,
  261
extracts from articles, letters and speeches:
  on women's role, 26; on family ties,
  28; on family politics, 31; first
  political speech of, 31–2; article for
  Bean na hÉireann, 59; lecture to
  Students' National Literary
  Society, 59; on Arthur Griffith, 63;
  on Fianna Éireann, 64, 64–5;
  article for *Fianna Handbook*, 69; on

royal visit protest, 76, 77, 78; on
being arrested, 78; on Jim Larkin,
83, 84; on Ladies' Auxiliaries, 112;
poem on eve of Rising, 127; on
preparations for Rising, 132; poem
to William Partridge, 148–9; first
letter from Mountjoy, 157–9; poem
to Connolly, 162; letter on transfer
to Aylesbury, 163; on conditions at
Aylesbury, 163–4, 165, 166; on a
fellow prisoner, 164–5; on her
appearance, 165; on prison visits,
166; speech in Sligo, 177; on
hunger strikes, 177, 178; on
publicity value of imprisonment,
185, 206; letters from Holloway,
186–7, 196; election address, 189;
on leaders, 190, 270; on her
election, 192; on welcome to
Dublin, 197; on Cabinet
appointment, 198, 199; letter from
Cork Prison, 205, 206; anxiety
about Casi and Stanislas, 206–7; in
hiding from police, 207–8, 208,
215; on women in local elections,
209; on receiving a death notice,
212; on being rearrested, 215; on
learning Gaelic, 216; on her court
martial, 218; on religious
discrimination, 228; speech to
Cumann na mBan, 228; on
freedom, 228–9; to Casi, 229;
speech on Treaty, 233; on America,
238; to Stanislas, 238–9, 263, 272;
on poverty, 250; on criminal assault
cases, 252; on organisations, 253;
on hunger-striking, 256; on social
issues, 263; on Free State
Parliament, 269; on her family, 273;
on Eva's death, 273
Markievicz, Count Casimir
  Dunin-(Casi), 78, 187, 279
  character of, 34, 35, 36
  courtship and engagement of, 35, 37
  relationship with Con, 36, 61, 62
  marriage and family life, 38–9
    in Dublin, 42, 45, 46–8
    and playwriting, 60–1, 95
    and Fianna, 64, 67–8
    and Larkin, 87, 88
    and Bloody Sunday, 89
  leaves Dublin, 95
  sends for Stanislas, 122
  Con seeks news of, 206–7